Cases and Exercises in Human Resource Management

Cases and Exercises in Human Resource Management

Fifth Edition

George E. Stevens
University of Central Florida

IRWIN

Homewood, IL 60430
Boston, MA 02116

Sponsoring editor: Karen L. Johnson
Project editor: Jane Lightell
Production manager: Carma W. Fazio
Cover designer: Mark Swimmer Design
Compositor: Weimer Typesetting Co., Inc.
Typeface 10/12 Times Roman
Printer: R. R. Donnelley & Sons Company

Library of Congress Cataloging-in-Publication Data

Stevens, George E.
    Cases and exercises in human resource management / George E. Stevens. — 5th ed.
      p.   cm.
    Rev. ed of: Cases and exercises in personnel/human resources management. 4th ed. 1986.
    ISBN 0-256-06672-8
    1. Personnel management—Problems, exercises, etc. 2. Personnel management—Case studies. I. Stevens, George E., Cases and exercises in personnel/human resources management. II. Title.
HF5549.S845   1990
658.3—dc20   90–4530
                                  CIP

Printed in the United States of America
1 2 3 4 5 6 7 8 9 0 DO 7 6 5 4 3 2 1 0

Preface

The purpose of this edition is consistent with each of the previous editions: to provide current and realistic materials that apply the theories and research findings in personnel. This edition, more than any of the previous ones, attempts to integrate the most recently evolving case law into the fiber of this learning experience.

Cases. The student is once again exposed to numerous cases that occur in a variety of settings. They are of varying lengths. The cases describe conditions that are sometimes good, sometimes bad, and frequently a mixture of both. All of the cases done by the author are based on real situations. However, most of the situations are disguised, and names of people and organizations are changed. In the previous edition, 57 cases were included. This edition contains 65 cases. Twenty-five (25) of the cases were included in the previous edition. The other forty (40) are new to the book.

Incident Cases. These "minicases" are designed to determine if the user can ask the right questions from preliminary data to adequately analyze the problem situation. Also, these brief cases draw the students' attention to an aspect of HRM/personnel that is especially timely and relevant without having to devote numerous pages to the topic. Eight new incident cases are provided in this edition.

Role-Playing Exercises. Role-playing exercises allow participants to experience a different kind of learning by placing themselves in the focal persons' positions. Five role-playing exercises are provided; of these, three are new.

Cost-Benefit Exercises. These exercises that focus on assessing the value of a HRM/personnel activity are included in this edition. Two new ones have been added to this edition.

Field-Experience Exercises. These exercises require the student to do field research to understand a problem or to analyze a HRM/personnel activity.

Experiences in HRM/Personnel. These exercises involve the student in solving a personnel problem or responding to a survey instrument on a topical issue. Two of the retained exercises have been rewritten and updated.

In-Basket Exercises.   Five new in-basket exercises are included in this edition. The in-baskets are a bit briefer than those used in previous editions. This should allow exposure to additional personnel issues. Various job levels are involved. Numerous personnel issues and problems are imbedded among items in each in-basket exercise.

Glossary.   The glossary represents a major new feature of the book. A number of HRM/personnel terms are listed in the glossary for quick reference.

Index.   The last item in the book is an alphabetical listing of the cases.

A very thorough, relevant, and current *Instructor's Manual* (IM) has been prepared for this edition. Each contributor was asked to develop a useful instructor's note for each case user's guidance. The IM contains new sections on how to maximize the benefits of the case method, how to use in-baskets, and how to grade in-baskets.

A number of people have graciously granted permission to reprint their items for this book. These individuals and organizations are listed in the section called *Contributing Authors*. A special thanks goes to Assessment Designs, Inc. and Executive Enterprises, Inc.

I wish to thank former Dean Cliff Eubanks; Halsey R. Jones, chairman, department of management; Christine Kaisler, Linda Fowlkes, Susan Devor, the college's administrative services department; my colleagues in the department of management and all Office of the Dean staff members at the University of Central Florida for their help and encouragement.

I also wish to thank Judy Ryder for her help. She did an outstanding job of preparing major portions of the manuscript. Her work was excellent even in the face of my incomplete instructions, pressing deadlines, and my all-or-nothing approach to writing.

A debt of gratitude is owed to Craig Beytien and the Irwin staff for their patience, understanding, support, and guidance as I worked on this project.

Finally, I want to thank my wife and son, Pam and Charlie, for allowing me to devote so much time to the role of Dean and to this endeavor. Without their sacrifices and support this book could not have become a reality. In addition, Pam participated in the writing of a case and in the preparation of the manuscript. The completion of this manuscript is a positive reflection of a most special person's love—my mother. She has been the No. 1 member of my fan club in all that I do.

George E. Stevens

Contributing Authors

Walter A. Bogumil, Jr., PhD (University of Georgia), is an associate professor of management at the University of Central Florida specializing in human resources and labor relations. In addition to his teaching, research, and writing activities, Dr. Bogumil is president of the Accent Consulting Group, a consortium of university professors engaged in management consulting since 1973.

George W. Bohlander, PhD (University of California, Los Angeles), is professor of management at Arizona State University and specializes in teaching labor relations and human resource management. Dr. Bohlander serves as a labor arbitrator with the American Arbitration Association and is a member of the Academy of Management. He is coauthor of *Managing Human Resources*.

Alan Cabelly, PhD (University of Washington), has taught for many years in the fields of management and human resource management. He has been actively consulting in both public and private sectors, and is a member of the American Society for Personnel Administration and the Industrial Relations Research Association. His current research and consulting interests focus on the areas of pay equity and performance appraisal.

Ronald W. Clement, PhD (Michigan State University), is professor of management and Director of the Waterfield Center for Business and Governmental Research as well as editor of Business & Public Affairs at Murray State University. Clement, a former personnel manager at Ford Motor Co, is author of over 30 articles and formerly taught at Arizona State University.

Kathryn H. Dansky, MBA (Ohio University), is a doctoral student at Ohio State University in the department of management and human resources. Her work history includes 10 years of management experience in health care, and 4 years of teaching. Her research is in the areas of organizational behavior and health care administration. She is a member of the Academy of Management and the American Nurses Association.

Joseph P. Grunenwald, DBA (Kent State University), currently serves as Dean of the College of Business Administration at Clarion University of Pennsylvania. Dr. Grunenwald had previously taught in the department of marketing and served as departmental chairperson at Clarion. Dr. Grunenwald's research interest lies in the area of small business management, nonprofit marketing, and entrepreneurial development. His writings have appeared in *Personnel Journal*, the *Journal of Marketing Education*, the *Law Library Journal*, and the *Business Education Forum*, among others.

Cliff Harrison, PhD (Fairleigh Dickinson University), is an assistant professor of management at the University of Wisconsin, Oshkosh. He teaches courses in human resource management and organizational behavior. Prior to joining the University of Wisconsin, he held numerous field and corporate positions in human resource management, including personnel manager of a 1,500-employee plant and director of corporate training and development for a $3 billion company. Dr. Harrison has done consulting, management development, labor relations, and executive outplacement for many organizations.

Theodore T. Herbert, DBA (Georgia State University), is professor of management in the Crummer Graduate School of Business at Rollins College, Winter Park, Florida. Dr. Herbert has written a reference book and four textbooks which have been published in several editions, and over 50 articles and research monographs. His research has been presented in almost 100 papers to professional and academic groups in the United States, Canada, Mexico, Australia, and Europe. He has held many leadership positions in academic and professional societies. He is a Fellow of the Academy of Management.

James C. Hodgetts, PhD (University of North Dakota), is a professor of management at Memphis State University where he teaches human resources, compensation, and labor relations courses. He has published many case studies in human resources administration and articles in church management. He has also been employed in various human resources capacities in the business community.

Shirley A. Hopkins, DBA (University of Colorado, Boulder), is an assistant professor of statistics and operations research at the University of Denver. She has extensive managerial experience in banking and other financial institutions, has published several articles, and consults with companies on implementing operations technology.

Willie E. Hopkins, DBA (University of Colorado, Boulder), is an associate professor of management at Colorado State University. He is the author of several journal articles and is a member of both the Academy of Management and Academy of International Business. His current research interests include impacts of managerial characteristics on company performance.

Henry F. Houser, PhD (St. Louis University), is currently associate professor in the management department of the school of business of Auburn University at Montgomery. He has 30 years experience in industry, including 12 years as manager, training and development, for Monsanto Company's corporate engineering department. Dr. Houser has been a member of the faculty at Auburn University at Montgomery since 1978.

Vandra L. Huber, DBA (Indiana University), is an associate professor of personnel and human resource management at the University of Utah. Her research interests span performance appraisal practices, technological innovation, and compensation theory. She is the author of numerous cases in human resource management and is coauthor of *Personnel and Human Resource Management* (4th edition).

Vicki Kaman, PhD (Colorado State University), is an associate professor of management at Colorado State University. Previously she worked in the employee development department for the city of Fort Collins. She is involved with research on training and the behavioral aspects of computerization.

Margaret Foegen Karsten, MBA (University of Wisconsin, Madison), is an assistant professor in the department of business administration at the University of Wisconsin, Platteville, where she teaches courses in human resource management, management principles, and women in management. Her research interests include career paths of executive women, sexual harassment, and corporate downsizing. She has published articles dealing with the impact of participation in extracurricular activities in future business success. She is a member of the Academy of Management.

Pamela S. Lewis, PhD (University of Tennessee), is an assistant professor of management at the University of Central Florida in Orlando, Florida. She joined UCF in 1986 from the University of Tennessee where she received her PhD in strategic planning. She presently teaches courses and conducts research in the areas of general management theory, strategic planning, and international management. She has published articles in the *Journal of Applied Business Research*, the *SAM Advanced Management Journal*, and the *International Journal of Management*.

R. Penny Marquette, DBA (Kent State University), is a professor of accounting at The University of Akron. Her previous positions include an assistant professorship at Cleveland State University and several years as a systems analyst at the University of Florida Medical School.

She is the author of numerous articles and cases. In addition, she holds leadership positions and is a member of many professional organizations.

Jack L. Mendleson, DBA (Michigan State University), is professor of management at University of the Redlands. He is the author of many articles and has coauthored two books on management by objectives. He has served as president of a local chapter of the Society for Advancement of Management and is a member of the Academy of Management and of ABSEL.

Marcia Parmalee Miceli, DBA (Indiana University), is associate professor of management and human resources at The Ohio State University. She has experience in the employee benefits area and has published numerous articles on human resource management topics. She has conducted many workshops on pay equity and related subjects.

Thomas R. Miller, PhD (The Ohio State University), is professor of management and associate dean at Memphis State University. He previously served as chairman of the department of management at Memphis State. His professional activities include authorship of numerous articles, papers, and cases in management and business administration. Dr. Miller is an active member of the Academy of Management, Southern Management Association, Southeast AIDS, and the Case Research Association. He is presently director of graduate studies at Memphis State.

Ed Mueller, MBA (Memphis State University), is an executive with a national consumer electronics corporation, having previously held various sales management positions with the firm. He served as instructor of management at Memphis State University from 1975 to 1979.

John E. Oliver, PhD (Georgia State University), is professor of management at Valdosta State University. He has managerial and consulting experience in financial institutions, manufacturing plants, professional firms, and government organizations. His articles on organization and job design, leadership, and personnel management have appeared in several management journals including the *Academy of Management Journal*, *Manage*, *Akron Business and Economic Review*, and *Psychological Reports*.

Chimezie A. B. Osigweh, Yg. (The Ohio State University), is a professor of management at Norfolk State University. He is the recipient of many awards, is founder and has served as editor-in-chief of the *Employee Responsibilities and Rights Journal*, and is president of the Council on Employee Responsibilities and Rights. His prodigious publication efforts include seven books and over 50 articles. He was the recipient of the 1989 Outstanding Virginian Faculty Award.

James G. Pesek, PhD (University of Pittsburgh), is a professor of management and chairperson of the department of administrative science at Clarion University of Pennsylvania. His articles have been published in the *Journal of Small Business Management*, *Journal of Applied Business Research*, *American Business Review*, *Business and Public Affairs*, and the *Public Library Quarterly*. His current research interests lie in the areas of employee leasing and recruitment source effectiveness.

Lawrence H. Peters, PhD (Purdue University), is an associate professor of management in the department of administrative sciences at Southern Illinois. Dr. Peters has consulted with or conducted research projects in organizations on topics such as turnover, motivation, situational performance constraints, and job satisfaction. He has contributed research and theoretical papers from his work to a variety of academic and professional journals in the behavioral science field.

Donald P. Rogers, PhD (The Ohio State University), is professor of business administration at Rollins College. He teaches courses in human resource management, career management, marketing communication, consumer behavior, and organizational theory. His current research focuses on employee communication, organizational commitment, and market segmentation. He is a member of the Academy of Management, the American Marketing Association, the Association for Business Communication, and the Society for Human Resource Management (formerly ASPA).

Allen J. Schuh, PhD (The Ohio State University), is a professor of management and finance at California State University, Hayward. He is active in community, professional, and university activities and consults with public and private organizations on individual, group, and organizational practices. He has published over 30 articles. Professor Schuh's major areas of expertise are effectiveness evaluation and training of individuals, groups, and organizations.

Larry E. Short, DBA (University of Colorado), is a professor of management and director of graduate programs in business at Drake University. In addition to serving as a consultant to business, he formerly served in various federal agencies in such positions as personnel director, employment and employee relations supervisor, and training and development specialist. Dr. Short has published articles in *Management Review*, *Resource*, *MSU Business Topics*, *Personnel Journal*, *Public Administration Review*, and *Training and Development Journal*.

William P. Smith, DBA (Arizona State University), is an assistant professor of management at Hofstra University. He is a member of the Academy of Management and local chapters of the American Society of Personnel Administration and American Society of Training and Development. His professional interests focus on temporary employment and employee turnover and absenteeism.

James M. Todd, PhD (University of Texas), is professor of management at the Fogelman College of Business and Economics, Memphis State University. He is the author of several cases. In addition, he served as president of the Southern Management Association.

Jerry L. Wall, PhD, SPHR (University of Missouri, Columbia), is director of the Center for Business and Economic Research and professor of management at Northeast Louisiana University. He holds senior-level accreditations in both personnel research and training and development from the Personnel Accreditation Institute. He has consulted extensively in both the public and private sector, is the author of numerous articles, papers and books, and served as president of the Midwest Society for Human Resources and Industrial Relations.

Elizabeth C. Wesman, PhD (Cornell University), is an assistant professor of personnel and industrial relations at the School of Management, Syracuse University. Her research interests are in the area of employment discrimination and international labor relations. She has published articles on sexual harassment, comparable worth, and the study of unions as organizations.

OTHER CONTRIBUTORS

James Ball
Robert S. Burns
Curtis Campbell
Paul J. Champagne
Karen Baretta Chandler
Kendra Clausen
Toni A. Denton
Linda Dudgeon
Felicia A. Finston
Cliff Hodge
Penny Richards

Pamela A. Stevens
John C. Sulzer
Mike Struth
Janet Taynor
James R. Terborg
Robert L. Williams
Assessment Designs, Inc.
Executive Enterprises, Inc.
West Publishing Company
John Wiley & Sons, Inc.

Contents

PART 3
Other Exercises and Experiences in
Human Resource Management

Introduction

This book provides a series of experiences designed to help you understand better the management of people at work. The media used include cases, incident cases, role-playing exercises, cost-benefit, field, and in-basket exercises. The section of the book that introduces each medium will explain what it is, why it was chosen, and how to use it. A variety of experiences is provided to involve you in real-world problems and thus help you gain an understanding of people at work. Some of you will be introduced to personnel work through these media. Most will already have been exposed to the literature and research of personnel. Many of you have had experiences at work that will help you deal with the exercises.

Most of the topics that are usually considered as part of personnel or managing people at work are treated herein. Cases or exercises are included about such topics as employment (manpower), planning, recruiting people, and selecting applicants. Experiences also are given about orienting and assigning people to jobs, developing careers, and evaluating employees' performance. Some cases or exercises deal with developing managers, compensating people for their work, training, providing safe working conditions, and coping with unions. Other cases and exercises deal with difficult employees, minority employment, leadership and supervision, and evaluation of the effectiveness of the personnel program.

People work for many different kinds of organizations; therefore, many different kinds of examples are given. The settings include small, medium, and large organizations from many places in the United States and abroad. The settings are in business, government, hospitals, universities, and symphony orchestras. Some cases depict good personnel practices; others depict poor personnel practices. Rarely is there just one factor to be considered. Most often there are one or more major factors and some secondary factors.

In doing these exercises, which stimulate real life, you may often feel you don't have all the information you'd like to have before making a decision. Actually, there are many real-life situations where there isn't sufficient time or money to acquire enough information. Sometimes the information isn't available. You may often wish to state what additional information you would *like* to have; however, based on what you know now and what you can reasonably infer, you can make your decisions accordingly.

Most of the situations presented here are disguised; nevertheless, they are all based on real situations. Few organizations like to reveal real situations. Cases are not designed to illustrate optimum conditions but to serve as learning mechanisms that will allow you to distill your experience, the theories you have learned, and the research you have carried out and to apply them to a given situation.

Part 1

Cases in Human Resource Management

A case is a description of an administrative situation and usually includes information about the setting of the situation. This information includes such things as geographic location, organization size, and business or sector. Often, the case describes the background of the key factors involved in the experience. Finally, the case describes the happenings in the administrative situation.

PURPOSES OF CASES

The purposes of objectives of analyzing cases in personnel include the following:

1. To improve the decision-making ability of managers or potential managers. Decision making is a skill which can be improved with practice. This is especially true when the individual first analyzes a case on his or her own and then discusses it in a group. Each member of the group benefits from the insights and solutions offered by others in the group. Many management experts believe that decision making is at the core of effective management. The cases treated herein are centered on the person at work. The role to be played by the analyst can be that of a supervisor of persons or a personnel specialist.

2. In addition to developing managerial abilities, such as more effective decision making, the case method is designed to expose management students to the environment of managerial decision making and to develop facilitative attitudes useful for effective decision making. Thus, cases present to the analysts situations which require them to make decisions and take risks under time pressure and with uncertainty surrounding the decision. The student must make a choice by discussion time. He or she often may feel that there is inadequate information provided in a case for making an optimal decision. This is also true in much managerial decision making. There is information the decision maker would like to have, but it is not available, or there is no time to get it, or it would be too costly to acquire. The decision maker must make a decision based on the limited information available. Because cases are necessarily short and lack some information, they help to provide students with the situations for developing facilitative attitudes.

3. Another major purpose in using cases is to provide the opportunity to apply research findings and theoretical explanations to real situations and test their applicability. Frequently, one may have learned cognitively what a research study found or have understood what a theorist said about why people behave the way they do. But the ultimate purpose of managerial training is to improve managerial behavior and thus, it is hoped, improve the satisfaction and development of the employees, the organization's performance, and the manager's satisfaction and success. If management students cannot apply these findings to real situations, they may have been taught a body of knowledge which is interesting and intellectually challenging, such as a study of optics might be to a clergyman or chemistry to a social worker; but this knowledge is not likely to contribute significantly to the students' successful careers. Unless students can apply the research and theory accurately and insightfully to simulations of reality, such as cases and exercises, it is not likely they will be able to do so in the real problem situation.

STRUCTURING CASE ANALYSES

There are many ways of analyzing cases and discussing them. To be most effective, all members of the class or discussion group must contribute something. This moves the learning situation away from the one-way communication method, or lecture. Lectures, no matter how brilliantly done, involve only a few human faculties. If care is not taken, the lecturing process degenerates into the sounds being emitted from the lecturer's mouth, traveling through the air, and scarcely pausing in the receiver's brain, before passing into the pencil-taking notes. In case discussions, each discussant delivers his or her thoughts, reacts to others' thoughts, and defends his or her own. The discussant, thus, is using brain, mouth, eyes, ears, and probably hands to convey the message. This is how learning is accelerated or enriched, or both.

One useful technique is to structure the discussion, at least to some extent. If the discussion jumps from point to point, it may be difficult for many discussants to follow. One model for structuring these cases is the following:

Step one: Clearly define the major and secondary problems involved in the case. These problems can be classified by such topics as personnel activity—for example, selection, evaluation, and compensation. Stating and agreeing upon the topics and rank ordering of them sets the agenda of the discussion. This is not always easy to do. Because of differences in the discussants' backgrounds, there will be varying interpretations of the data. Moreover, not all the information in the case is essential or even useful in understanding the situation. In a real-work situation, the supervisor (manager, administrator, etc.) is flooded with clues and information. The effective supervisor must separate the relevant from the irrelevant and focus on the former.

Step two: Develop a model of the cause of the problem (or success). There are many possible relations that influence the results. These factors include:

A. Individual factors: The cause might be in the perception, motivation, abilities, or attitudes of the persons in the case.

B. Dyadic factors: The significant factor can be the relationship between two crucial actors in the case, such as superior-subordinate.

C. Small group factors: The work-group interrelationships might be the paramount factor influencing such problems as restriction of output or success of the football team.

D. Intergroup relations: The cause of the problem can be systematic differences in several groups who must interact: salespersons and production managers, doctors and nurses, unions and managements.

E. Environmental factors: There may be factors in the work environment which are crucial—time pressures, economic factors, governmental pressures, and so forth—that lead to the results described. So, too, in a case, you must arrange the data, the variables, and so forth into a model of the situation. In some cases, the ages of the people may be vital information, for example, when evaluating future pension costs or management succession. In other situations, it may be interesting, but not crucial, to know ages. The race of an applicant may be important information in a firm under affirmative action pressure. On the other hand, it may be totally irrelevant to the analysis of a health and safety case.

Step three: Consider alternative solutions to the problem or explain the successful experience: Once you have defined your problem and modeled the relationships, the next step is to consider a reasonable number of solutions—the more the better. However, one usually cannot consider a large number because of time pressures and the limited ability of most people to compare a large number of alternatives. Most of us eliminate from serious consideration those solutions which seem least likely to solve the problem quickly and expeditiously. Three or four alternatives are systematically compared factor by factor.

Step four: Choose and implement a solution: The analyst chooses a solution and is prepared to defend that choice. The analyst also plans how she or he would make it work. Thus, if the solution is to fire a person, several things must be considered to make sure the choice was the right one and one which is workable. For example, when the firing should be done, how it should be done, and by whom it should be done must be considered, as well as clearing the matter with superiors.

There are many analytical structures to which cases can be fitted. The structure just described has proved to be a useful one.

STUDENT PREPARATION FOR CASES

A few hints may help you prepare good case analyses. First, read the case, underlining important points and making some rough notes of what you think are the key problems and their causes. Do some preliminary thinking about solutions. If you have the opportunity, discuss your ideas with others in the class. Then lay the case aside for a while.

Second, return to the case later and reread it. Make added notes. Where there is not enough information, make reasonable assumptions and state them. Remember, in your proposed solution, that what you suggest being done might affect others. Make sure you don't solve a problem in one department and cause one in another. Write up your first draft report now. Put the case down again.

Third, return to the case later and make sure it says all you want to say and the way you want to say it.

This approach will help you begin to develop your analytical abilities. First, you will learn to separate the important information from the less important. Next, you will begin to apply the research and theories you have learned to the problems. Then, you will begin to increase your repertoire of solutions and analyze them rationally and logically, computing the trade-offs. Finally, you will remember to anticipate the implementation problems.

CATEGORIZING CASES

The cases are given in the next section of this book. It has been customary to classify cases by topics, and this has been done here. If a case is classified under Orientation, you can be sure that this is a major focus of the case. However, it may not be the only focus of the case. The cases are realistic; rarely are they single problems or singly caused problems. Look for all the personnel and human aspects that seem relevant.

Section A

Introduction to Human Resource Management

1 Choosing a Professor

"Professor Marks, you're always asking us to answer questions; could you answer one for the class?"

"What do you want to know, Paul?"

"I know that some professors don't like the idea that the students have an opportunity to evaluate their performance but we do get to do so. Why don't we get a chance to help the college choose new professors? We're the ones most affected by them! Many of us have wondered aloud about the uneven teaching we receive. That is, each professor is so different. Some are very entertaining and most make the subject relevant. Others practically put us to sleep. Most seem receptive to questions and are more than willing to provide multiple examples to illustrate a concept or help us understand an idea. On occasion, however, we encounter a professor who acts offended that we ask a question or do not understand something. In fact, a couple of our professors are notorious for insulting us and telling us how dumb we are so we no longer ask those professors any questions. It just seems that some are much better teachers than others and some appear to really enjoy what they do."

Jerry chimed in: "I think it's worse than that. One professor told our class that if it wasn't for students this would be a great place to work!" Now, that really made us mad! How can people work here, a public university, and have such a negative attitude?"

Professor Marks responded, "Hold on, hold on a minute. You have not asked one question—you've asked several. What you have done is raised a number of issues surrounding the selection of professors for this and other colleges of business. First, let's think about the hiring of a professor. What recruitment methods and sources should we use? What is available? For example, can we hire one through our personnel office in the form of a "walk-in"? By walk-in I mean a person who applies for a position on his/her own without any prior knowledge that an actual opening exists," explained Professor Marks. The professor, after a lengthy discussion, mentioned several options, including advertising in the *Chronicle of Higher Education.*

"Let's assume that you have received résumés or what we call *curriculum vitae* from several prospective professors. What should be your next step?" Professor Marks asked. "Let's assume the teaching interest and expertise of these individuals match openings within your college of business. Do you invite them to campus? Do you have the department chair fly out to each candidate's home city? Do you give them a test?" What became obvious very quickly is that not only have students not been involved in the selection process but they had no idea as to how teachers were selected and what criteria were used. Also, they had no information about the decision maker(s) or criteria used. Professor Marks seemed particularly vague about how the selection process worked at the college. The only information he offered was that university performance appraisals considered three very broad areas: (1) teaching, (2) research, and (3) service. He shed no light on the type of activities that count or how such performance is measured.

As the class period drew to a close, Dr. Marks added one little zinger. He said that the market for business professors is quite firm. He said that for business disciplines (e.g., accounting, finance, computer science, quantitative methods), the demand for professors far outpaces supply. The result, he claims, is that new and more recent graduates are asking for nine-month contracts with a salary over $50,000 and they are demanding that they teach two sections of the same class each quarter or semester. He likened the salary demands of these potential new hires to the suffering of "sticker shock" when someone goes to buy a car. Professor Marks explained that getting the money to pay the new hires is just half of the problem. "A greater difficulty is salary compression."

As the bell rang announcing the end of the class period, Dr. Marks gave them the assignment of addressing the issues and questions raised. Some of the students were really excited about the chance to do something truly relevant for a change. Others walked away wondering just what they'd gotten themselves into.

Discussion Questions

1. What training or preparation does a professor need to qualify him/herself to become an effective and successful teacher?
2. How does your college or university go about filling its professor vacancies?
3. What factors or criteria should your university or college consider in deciding who to hire from a pool of qualified applicants?

4. What factors or criteria does your college or university use in selecting those individuals it wishes to hire?
5. What is salary compression? How does this apply to faculty? What can a school do to overcome the problem?

2 *Phoenix Department of Human Services*

"Man, I am really scared! I couldn't believe my ears when Ronnie told me that Jack died of AIDS. Rumor has it that he caught it from his old lady. She supposedly hooked up with a dude that was heavy into drugs. . . ."

It was quite a shock for everyone to learn of Jack's death. Two months have gone by since his passing yet his co-workers were still trying to come to grips with Jack's death and the cause of his demise. Employees were particularly fearful because of the nature of their jobs at the department. The department provides a community-based program that offers residential, vocational, counseling, and other specialized services for the mentally disabled. A major component of the program is to allow clients to retain their dignity. One means of accomplishing this objective is to permit them as much autonomy as possible. One step in that direction is to permit clients to live in a community setting.

The staff members face many diverse situations. Employees receive training in "passive defense skills to enable them (the staff members) to deal with violent and/or aggressive clients in a nonabusive manner." Evidence of violence was shown, including "numerous incidents involving biting, scratching, throwing of objects, hitting, violent outbursts, and pinching by the clients."

As publicity regarding AIDS increased, and when more employees became aware that Jack died of AIDS, the agency, effective January 20, 1989, required its staff members to complete an AIDS antibody screening test.

Requirement

In this situation is mandatory AIDS testing legally defensible? Why or why not? Explain.

3 *What Do You Do with a Blocker?*

J.T. Bingham, vice president for personnel for CLW Industries, turned to Frank Wilkins, president of the company, and fumed, "What are we going to do with Jim Walters? He's constantly in the way of our developing new managers. We simply can't give new people that kind of training anywhere else. Without those new people with fresh ideas, we're not going to remain at the top of our industry for long."

Frank, after contemplation, replied, "Yes, but Jim has been with this company for almost 20 years. He helped make it what it is today and, with his health, he's got at least another 15 or so good years of service left. It doesn't seem fair that his reward should be forced retirement or a demotion."

To this J.T. replied, "Do we really have any other choice—and besides, hasn't he forced us to it? And he would get a generous pension."

Jim Walters really was the best plant manager that the company ever had. He knew the precision forging business inside and out, having come up through the ranks. He had started out with a degree from a technical institute and had gone on to get a bachelor's and master's degree in business at a nearby college. In the meantime, he had moved from worker to foreman to supervisor, then through several other supervisory and staff positions to his present job. CLW Industries was a two-plant operation, with a separate national headquarters and a total employment of about 2,000 employees. Jim's plant was the larger of the two and the more important. The precision forging industry, in which this plant of CLW Industries was operated, was quite competitive and necessitated managers who were technically knowledgeable and cost conscious. These same attributes were necessary in those who were promoted to corporate headquarters. Jim Walters was a manager with those talents and, over the last few years, had been offered several chances to move from his present position to a company vice presidency. There is little doubt that he also would have been a prime candidate for president. The midwestern town in which Jim's plant was located had a population of about 30,000; it also was located on an interstate, making access to a neighboring town of over 100,000 quite easy. However, the corporate headquarters was located in metropolitan Chicago.

When Jim had been offered his first opportunity for a promotion and raise, he had some anxiety concerning his ability to do the new job but had rushed home with the good news. The reception of the news by his

This case was prepared by Professor Jerry L. Wall, Northeast Louisiana University.

family was anything but positive, as follows: "Well, it's nice that *you're* going to Chicago. Have fun, but *we're* staying here." This deflating experience was followed by a detailing of all that the family collectively and individually would lose by the move (e.g., school and business activities, friends, social position, country club membership, church ties, and so on). Jim's wife was very active in the real estate business and in social and community affairs, and his children were leaders in many athletic and school events in the community.

Subsequent offers for promotion had met with the same family response, and Jim decided that it was in his own best interest to stay in his present job. In fact, he now had serious personal reservations about his ability to do a higher-level job. When J.T. had brought Jim the latest offer for promotion, their conversation was as follows: "No, J.T., I just don't think I could accept that offer. The kids and wife are doing so well lately and enjoying life here so much. In fact, I've recently been reading that book called *The Peter Principle*—you know, how 'cream rises to the top then sours'? Well, I don't want to go sour and don't think I will in this job since I enjoy it so much. I'm not sure what would happen if I tried to do my thing in the corporate jungle."

To this J.T. replied, "Yes, but Jim, you'll never know until you've tried, and all of us at headquarters know you're the man for the job. And we've really made an offer to make it worth your while." However, Jim had the courage of his conviction and still refused the job.

Discussion Questions

1. What should J.T. do, now that this latest offer has been refused?
2. What are the available alternatives?
3. Would it make any difference if Jim were an incompetent or obsolete manager?
4. Would a company be within its rights to take action against Jim?
5. Is this the wave of the future, with the increasing incidence of two-career families?

4 The Challenge

Delaware Agricultural and Technical is a small state-supported school situated in a quiet, rural area just south of the state capital. Chartered in 1911, it has become an integral part of the community, with programs aimed primarily at preparing students to enter four-year colleges and universities, although a few are two-year paraprofessional programs. Like most schools, Delaware uses a traditional A, B, C, D, F grading system. Karen Miller, an instructor at Delaware A&T, was soon to find herself seriously questioning this time-honored tradition.

Miller took her teaching seriously, working hard to balance the demands of her doctoral studies at Temple University with her teaching duties at the college. In the classroom, she was "relationship-oriented," trying to involve the students in active discussions of the material. The students seemed to respond well to her participative style of teaching.

Today she had taught her Introduction to Management class. The class became energetic, and she got caught up in their enthusiasm. The cause of the excitement was a case study about grading and the problems it caused at a particular university. The case was complicated because the class had been subjected to three different teachers during a term. Predictably, these teachers had different styles and different expectations.

The class discussion quickly became a discussion of grading at Delaware A&T. Here, too, many teachers at the college had different styles. Some lectured exclusively; others, like Miller, lectured and led class debate; others relied almost entirely upon class participation. Professors used different testing methods—objective tests, essay tests, or both. Nevertheless, despite these varied inputs, practically all teachers used the traditional grading system and, in the opinion of the class members, it left a lot to be desired.

"Grades, grades, grades, why do we need them anyway?" Leroy Lark asked.

"You don't like them because you can't get good ones—that's why you complain," Pamela Johnson said.

"It's not that at all; they just aren't fair. They don't measure what I've learned. You mean to tell me that when I can answer questions well in class, but not on some test, I should only get graded for my test answers? That's not fair!" Leroy retorted.

Prepared by George E. Stevens, University of Central Florida, and R. Penny Marquette, University of Akron.

"That's true, Leroy's got a point. Plus, we know teachers use the old A, B, C scale. Somebody's got to get Ds and Fs. But what happens if the whole class is pretty smart?"

"Well, why don't they give all As and Bs, then nobody's hurt," Richard Green suggested.

Peggy Vandero chimed, "Now that idea I like!"

And so the discussion raged, back and forth, back and forth. Alternatives were suggested and rejected. Even when the bell rang, the discussion went on; no one in the class moved! Finally, Miller stopped them. But now, reflecting on what she'd suggested, she was beginning to wonder if she'd let things go too far.

"I hate to interrupt this lively discussion, but the bell's rung, and there's another class coming in," Miller said. "To summarize, I hear you saying that there are a number of grading systems being used, including our traditional A, B, C, D, F system. Furthermore, you believe the traditional system is unfair and does not always reflect the quality of your work. Here today you've discussed some alternatives including pass-fail and blanket grades, yet these appear to have faults as well. Let me make a proposition. I challenge you to put your money where your mouth is. We're only in the second week of class and if you can come up with a grading system that meets the dual criteria of being fair and reflecting the quality of work done, I'll implement it. You have from now until Friday to prepare your proposals, either individually or in groups. During Friday's class, the proposals can be presented and voted on, and the one deemed most acceptable will be instituted."

Discussion Questions

1. Grading, of course, is a form of performance appraisal with which all students can readily identify. What are some of the more common types of grading systems?
2. What factors influence the grade a student may be assigned?
3. How might the grades and grading systems used affect people after graduation?
4. Does the problem go beyond just grading? What are the social implications of coping with varying grading systems? How does it affect equity in the university environment?
5. Would or should students who intend to apply for admission to graduate or professional schools care about which grading system is used by their school? Explain.
6. If a university changes its grading system from an A, B, C, D, F scale to pass-fail, what might be some of the behavioral implications?

5 *Eastern Seaboard Bus Lines*

The year 1976 was the year of the bicentennial. Many patriotic Americans celebrated their country's 200th anniversary. Numerous celebrations, parades, and historical enactments took place. Many organizations permitted their male employees to sport full beards in honor of the first settlers. The new year brought a much less permissive attitude. For most males, this change of heart was not a problem because at the end of the bicentennial year they had shaved off their beards. All were not so lucky, however.

The bus company felt that beards were not appropriate. In fact, all of its employees who dealt with the public were expected to conform to a dress code. These employees were to be appropriately attired and properly groomed. Good grooming meant that no one who had contact with the public could wear a beard. After reading research on customers' likes and dislikes, buying habits, and reactions to other people's attire, a top executive believed that people distrust those who have goatees or beards. He, and other top executives, reasoned that people tend to trust clean-shaven men more than bearded men. Not long after these top executives reached an agreement on this issue, a rule forbidding beards was communicated to all employees.

THE MEETING

One week after the memorandum was posted on the bulletin board at the busy Harrisburg, Pennsylvania, bus terminal, Leroy Walker, returning from New York City, found a short memo from his supervisor. The supervisor asked Leroy to see him before Leroy made his run to Cleveland. Leroy and his supervisor, Bill Barrett, had worked together for the past five years. They had gotten along quite well and typically dispensed with the formalities of playing superior-subordinate games. Leroy was surprised to get such a formal memo from Bill. After meeting with Bill, he knew why the memo was written. Leroy was surprised and disappointed. At various times since joining Eastern, people had given him a hard time about his full beard. Bill was no exception. Bill kidded him a lot but never seemed too upset about the beard. Now Bill had given Leroy an ultimatum—get rid of the beard or else!

Leroy thought about the ultimatum throughout his drive to Cleveland. At each stop—Breezewood, Pittsburgh, and Youngstown—he steamed and stewed. By the end of the trip, he was firm in his resolve. He would not cut off his beard. Leroy believed that he had done his best to explain to Bill why he needed to keep his beard. He was not being difficult, obstinate, or any of the other big words his supervisor had used to describe him.

True to his word, Bill fired Leroy for "just cause." Leroy had just returned from a trip to Ocean City, Maryland. The weather had been lousy—cold and wet all the way. No sooner had he pulled his bus into the terminal and unloaded than Bill appeared, thrust a letter in his hand, and walked off, mumbling something about insubordination. The discharge came as quite a surprise to the bus driver. He just didn't believe Bill would do it.

Leroy had quite a surprise for the company. He wasted little time running to the Philadelphia office of the Equal Employment Opportunity Commission (EEOC). What did Leroy complain about? He charged the company with discrimination. He believed that, although all employees who had contact with the public were obligated to obey the rule, the rule discriminated against blacks. Leroy said he had asked his supervisor if he noticed anything different about Gary Maddox, the center fielder of the Philadelphia Phillies. He had been the only bearded member of the former clean-cut, closely shaven team. Leroy explained that he and Gary shared a medical problem that was very common to blacks. Leroy suffered from a skin condition known as pseudofolli-culitis barbae (PFB). PFB, a condition that affects a high percentage of black males, occurs when shaved hair curls back and pierces the skin. The result is skin inflammation, which sometimes leads to abscesses. The solution to the problem, according to Leroy, is not to shave.

Because the condition is especially prevalent among blacks, Leroy claimed that a rule calling for the dismissal of those who grow a beard has a disparate impact on blacks. The EEOC, after listening to the employee's side of the argument, chose to take the bus company to court for an alleged violation of the Civil Rights Act.

In court, the bus company argued that the rule was lawful because (1) it was applied equally to all employees who had contact with the public and (2) it was a business necessity. Customers, the company claimed, are distrustful of employees who have beards or goatees. Because of the competitive nature of their business, a company must respond to the needs and wants of the customer. The good-grooming policy is evidence (to the customer) of courteous, motivated, and disciplined employees. Finally, the company's lawyer cited examples from case law to justify its "no beard" rule. In at least one instance, a federal court recognized a similar rule to be a legitimate business necessity.

The EEOC disagreed with the company on the appropriateness and legality of the no beard rule. EEOC showed that Leroy's doctors had instructed him to grow a beard as a means of curing the PFB problem.

EEOC medical researchers claimed that various studies indicated that PFB affects between 45 percent and 85 percent of all black males who shave.

Discussion Questions

1. Can a rule which is enforced uniformly in regard to employees be deemed illegal? If yes, why? If no, why not?
2. Does the company have the right to impose a grooming policy, one that includes a no beard rule, on its employees?
3. If you were the judge in this case, would the bus company's business necessity defense succeed or fail? Why?

6 *Paradise Valley Hospital*

Karen Vogel, 41, is a registered nurse (RN) who works full-time as operating room supervisor at St. Vincent's Hospital. In the short time (one year) that she has been at the 104-bed hospital, she has come to really enjoy her work. St. Vincent's Hospital holds American Hospital Association (AHA) membership and has Joint Commission of Accreditation of Hospitals (JCAH) approval. It is a general medical and surgical institution that employs 362 people (excluding medical and dental interns as well as residents or other trainees). During the previous 12 months, the hospital admitted 4,040 patients. The occupancy rate is 72.1 percent, and most patients come for a short-term stay of less than 30 days.

Karen still gets angry when she thinks about her unceremonious dumping at Paradise Valley Hospital. On practically a daily basis she had thought about suing her former employer for firing her unjustly. In the Paradise Valley employee handbook, Karen noticed a list of three categories of employees. Paradise Valley's book listed her as a "permanent employee."

At Paradise Valley, Karen had risen to the position of director of nursing. Getting to the top job in nursing was not a simple process. Her 16 years of hard work and dedication at Paradise Valley had paid off. Along the way she had worked each shift, worked many double shifts, and served in a number of wards. In addition, Karen had worked her way up through the various supervisory levels. She had served as shift supervisor, operating room supervisor, and head nurse.

Mrs. Vogel was viewed as an exceptional nurse. She seemed to possess just the right amount of interpersonal skills to go along with her technical competence. Over the years she had observed the many mistakes made by her predecessor, Joyce Kinicki. The knowledge gained from this vicarious learning experience had served her well. Despite her good performance evaluations and apparent success in the job, Karen found the director of nursing job to be too demanding. After 18 months in the job, she understood why Joyce often drank her lunch.

Karen's position on the Paradise Valley Hospital staff required a great deal of adjustment. Although the job seemed overwhelming at times, Paradise Valley was similar to St. Vincent's Hospital but (from Karen's perspective) with two important differences: (1) The former was larger and (2) unlike St. Vincent's, was managed by an incompetent administrator. While the second point is subjective and open to question, there can be no doubt about the first point. Paradise Valley Hospital is a 611-bed, not-for-profit hospital that admits an average of 24,686 people annually. It is an AHA member and has JCAH accreditation. This general medical and surgical hospital has an occupancy rate of 81.6 percent, employs 2,147 people (excluding certain interns, residents, and other trainees), and over half its patients are hospitalized for less than 30 days.

Paradise Valley Hospital is a large, bustling institution that caters to the needs of a rapidly growing population. The hospital serves a large Phoenix suburb of over 100,000 people. Nearly three years ago, the hospital received permission to undertake an expansion program. The result, after approval by the zoning board, was a badly needed, new 100-bed wing and additional office space for hospital staff. Unfortunately for Karen, the completion of the new wing occurred nearly one year after she was fired. Exhibit 1 offers a partial organizational chart.

Limited space was one of many problems the former director of nursing faced. Her most difficult problem, however, was her boss, Julian Anderson. Anderson had come to Paradise Valley Hospital 25 years ago. Now he serves as the hospital's chief executive officer. Over the years he had developed a systematic approach to handling any administrative problem that arose. He firmly believed that if you let a problem alone long enough it would go away. Julian believed in his philosophy and practiced it. The result: problems became larger, not smaller. Paradise Valley Hospital's bigger facility and larger census no longer functioned well under the direction of a laissez-faire manager who had become obsolete.

Anderson's problems often became problems to be handled by the director of nursing. Karen learned how good Julian was at throwing problems and issues back in the laps of those who made him aware of the problem. As relates to the nursing staff, Karen had to solve major problems: (1) state and nationwide surveys as well as informal discussions indicate that job satisfaction is low among nurses; (2) the demand for nurses' services are such that nurses are highly mobile; (3) despite

EXHIBIT 1   Paradise Valley Hospital Partial Chart

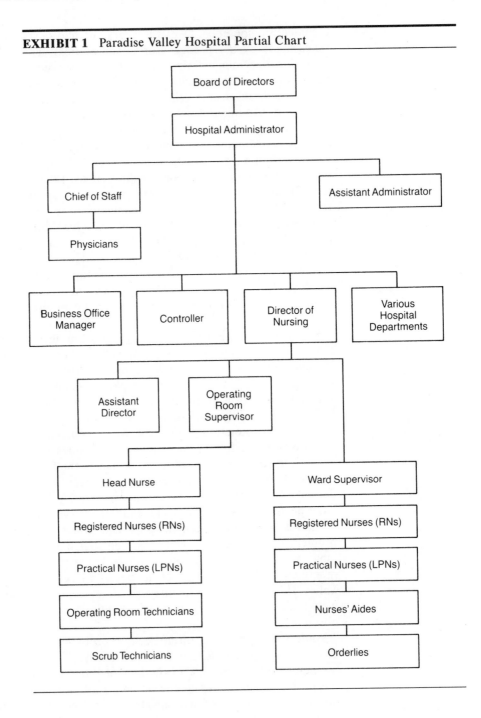

the fact that continuing education is so essential, the hospital does not support or encourage nurses who seek educational opportunities while working; (4) understaffing and outdated hospital policies lead to large amounts of overtime, reduced professional efficiency, burdensome paperwork, and an inefficient use of nursing skills, as well as scheduling inflexibility; (5) a very limited fringe benefit package for nurses exists; (6) nurses' salaries are not competitive with those offered by Phoenix, Scottsdale, Glendale, and Mesa hospitals; and (7) all of the previous problems lead to low effectiveness of patient service, low morale of the nursing personnel, as well as high turnover. Although Anderson was told about these problems, nothing was done.

About two weeks before her dismissal, Karen and Julian met in his office.

Karen

Mr. Anderson, I have received your appraisal of my work.

Julian

In a little over 18 months you seem to have mastered a very difficult job. I could not expect anyone to do better.

Karen

If my performance is so great, why don't you listen to me when I tell you about staffing and other problems?

Julian

I *do* listen to you!

Karen

You're right, you listen, but you never seem willing or able to take my advice, or follow my suggestions, or help solve problems we discuss. I need support—not resistance.

Julian

Are you telling me how to do my job! As director of nursing, it is your job to solve nursing problems, not mine.

Karen

It's a little late for that. Realistically, I know you have a lot of pressure on you, but so do I. For the past six months I have tried to do my job realizing that things would not change.

Julian

You can think what you want. The hospital's paying you well to do your job. Do your job or let somebody else do it!

Karen

I am going to do just that. Let me go back to my old job as operating room supervisor and I will gladly let someone else have the headaches.

Julian

No problem. By next week we'll have your replacement. I have just the person for the job.

In less than two weeks Karen was replaced. Julian selected someone who would do everything he asked without questioning his decisions. Karen did not get what she expected. Instead of a demotion to the job she requested, she received a "pink slip." According to Julian, "no suitable positions were available." Prior to leaving the hospital, Karen was given an exit interview by Cyprian Devine, the hospital's vice president of personnel. Although the vice president was cordial and took care to record Karen's answers to each question, the interview went well as long as Cyprian was able to stick to her list of questions. When Karen asked about the *real* reason for her dismissal and the availability of the job she had requested, Cyprian was quite evasive. A frustrated and disappointed Karen Vogel left the vice president's office. She was convinced that Julian Anderson had had her fired for no good reason.

Discussion Questions

1. What are the major problems?
2. How would you describe Julian Anderson?
3. How effective do you feel Karen was as director of nursing?
4. Did Paradise Valley Hospital have the right to discharge Karen Vogel?
5. What legal action might Karen take? Would you recommend that she take legal action? Why or why not?

7 *Dynamic Airlines, Inc.*

Dynamic Airlines, Inc., is a small, regional airline company that has served the small towns of Arizona for years. The airline, based at Sky Harbor Airport in Phoenix, flies from there to places such as Winslow, Flagstaff, Yuma, Gila Bend, Bullhead City, and the Grand Canyon. Some of its planes are small, propeller-driven planes that are 15 years old, others are newer small jet-propelled aircraft.

The company has maintained a good reputation for reliable, courteous service at reasonable prices. In recent years, the most difficult problem has been the battle to keep prices down. Although the airline has virtually maintained a monopoly in the areas it serves, keeping prices down has been a difficult task. The cost of fuel, air fleet, and labor costs have all risen sharply.

Arizona is a state with many geographical contrasts. The diversity can be seen in the red rock beauty of Sedona, the big city atmosphere of Phoenix, and the picturesque desert landscape of Casa Grande. Flagstaff, for example, is located at an elevation of nearly 7,000 feet above sea level while Phoenix is only 1,100 feet above sea level. Many of the winter trips to places such as Flagstaff, home of Northern Arizona University, contained a measure of excitement. Temperatures there were often much, much colder than those in the desert towns such as Phoenix. Often, there was snow and plenty of wind. Pilots really had to know how to handle the company's small planes in rugged weather.

Recently a Dynamic Airlines employee was overheard telling another employee at the ticket counter in Sky Harbor:

"I can't believe it! Not Captain Jody Foster! Are you putting me on? He's the best at flying in the tricky wind currents and bad weather. You know that Jody has been flying for us for 27 years. Now they want him to retire at age 60. I tell you, after reading about the Age Discrimination in Employment Act, I know that our management is in trouble. No one, under that law, can be forced to retire at some mandatory age. I have looked into this issue for years. We should not forget that recent court decisions suggest that people who are willing and able to work cannot be discriminated against. That law says that no one can be forced to retire because of age."

Pilots are a critical resource at the airline. Often they get the pilot who wants to get his/her flying experience in so that he/she can qualify to fly planes for the major airlines. So, Dynamic is a good starting place. Lately though, a number of more experienced pilots, all 60 or over, have been looking for a commercial airline that would hire them. They contend that in areas such as Winslow or Flagstaff during the winter, their experience makes them uniquely qualified to cope with unforeseen circumstances and to handle crises effectively.

Discussion Questions

1. What do you think about the experienced pilots' contention that they are uniquely qualified?
2. To what extent do laws such as the Age Discrimination in Employment Act (as amended in 1986) protect these pilots?

Human Resource Planning

1 Who Reports to Whom?

The Oscar Metz Tool Company is a closely held manufacturer of bottling and canning equipment located in a large midwestern city. It was organized in the early 1920s and in recent years has experienced rapid growth. The company hopes to double in size in the next 10 years. At present Metz employs approximately 300 persons. It manufactures bottling and canning equipment to order. The entire management group takes great pride in the quality of their products and in the company in general.

The casewriter was requested by the executive vice president to investigate the organizational structure of the manufacturing division of the company. A preliminary investigation revealed the following problems: (1) a tendency on the part of lower echelon managers to try to shift all possible decisions up to higher management, (2) confusion on the part of most frontline supervisors regarding the functions and authority of the management levels above them, and (3) a tendency to bypass intermediate levels and to take problems and complaints to the vice president of manufacturing and even to the president.

Permission was granted the casewriter to make a more complete investigation of the situation. This investigation resulted in the discovery of the following organizational problems:

The Organizational Problem in the Shop. The management group in manufacturing consisted of a vice president of manufacturing, a shop superintendent, a night general supervisor, nine day supervisors, and four night supervisors. Although the manufacturing functions of the various supervisors are clearly defined and do not appear to offer a major problem, there are few clear-cut lines of authority. The shop superin-

---

This case was prepared by Professor James C. Hodgetts of Memphis State University as a basis for class discussion. Cases are not designed to present illustrations of correct or incorrect handling of administrative situations.

tendent believes that he reports to the president, but the vice president of manufacturing believes that the shop superintendent reports to him. The shop superintendent believes that the nine day departmental supervisors report to him, but his opinion is not shared by many of the supervisors. They made the following comments:

1. The supervisor of the miscellaneous machining department says that he reports to the vice president of manufacturing.
2. The supervisor of the lathe department also says that he reports to the vice president of manufacturing.
3. The supervisor of the grinding department says he reports to the vice president of manufacturing and to the miscellaneous machining supervisor.
4. The supervisor of the milling machine department says he reports to the production control manager and to the vice president of manufacturing.
5. The supervisor of maintenance says that he reports to the shop superintendent and to the vice president of manufacturing.
6. The supervisor of the drilling department says he reports to the shop superintendent and to the vice president of manufacturing.
7. The supervisor of the tool and die room says he reports to the vice president of manufacturing and to a minor degree to the chief engineer.
8. The supervisor of assembly says he reports to the president, vice president of manufacturing, and to the shop superintendent.

In summary it appears that only one of the nine day supervisors reports entirely to the shop superintendent. Only three acknowledged a partial responsibility to him, and five did not even mention his name when asked who was their immediate boss. About the only undisputed authority the shop superintendent appears to have is in connection with the heat treat department, but he believes that he is in charge of the entire shop.

The Organizational Problem in Production Control. The production control manager says that he supervises the work of the shipping supervisor, the final inspection supervisor, and six clerks. Both the final inspection supervisor and the shipping supervisor say they report to both the production control manager and the vice president of manufacturing. The milling machine department supervisor says that he reports to the production control manager as well as to the vice president of manufacturing. Other comments from the various production supervisors also indicate that the production control manager has some authority over them. The production control manager reports to the vice president of manufacturing.

The Organization Problem on the Night Shift.   Discussions with the four night supervisors, the night general supervisor, the vice president of manufacturing, and the shop superintendent indicate differences of opinion relative to lines of authority on the night shift. The vice president of manufacturing believes that the night general supervisor reports to him. So does the shop superintendent. The shop superintendent believes that the night general supervisor also reports to the president; but the night general supervisor says this is definitely not correct and that he reports to the vice president of manufacturing. The vice president of manufacturing believes that the night lathe supervisor reports to the day lathe supervisor but the night general supervisor does not believe a night lathe supervisor has been appointed but believes this should happen and that he should report to him.

The person who believes that he is the night lathe supervisor says he reports to the night general supervisor. The vice president of manufacturing believes the night supervisor of assembly reports to the day supervisors of both assembly and milling. However, the night supervisor of assembly says that he reports both to the day supervisor of assembly and to the night general supervisor. The night general supervisor says he reports to him. Both the night shipping supervisor and the night milling machine supervisor say they report to the vice president of manufacturing, but the night general supervisor says that he is their immediate supervisor.

Discussion Questions

1. What are the problems in this case?
2. What can be done to overcome them? (Be specific.)

---

2 *Monongahela Mittens Manufacturing*

Monongahela Mittens Manufacturing (MMM) is a medium-sized manufacturing facility that produces high-quality gloves and mittens. Its product line consists of three basic models: a driving glove (Model 101), a dress glove (Model 102), and a ski mitten (Model 103). There is a strong seasonal demand for this product; 70 percent of all sales occur in the four-month period from November through February. The marketing

This case was prepared by Professor Marian M. Extejt, John Carroll University.

and manufacturing departments have arrived at the following production schedule (Table 1) for the next fiscal year, and have asked for your comments. This schedule minimizes inventory costs, a major consideration of the firm.

As a human resources manager, one of your tasks is manpower planning. This involves calculating how many people will be necessary for the firm to meet its production plans, and instituting plans and programs to ensure that they will be available. There are certain assumptions you must make, based on information gathered from the industrial engineering department and your own department's records. The following pieces of information concern things that cannot be changed in the short run.

1. Standard labor hours. The total standard labor hours needed to produce each unit (pair) are:

Model	Hours
101	0.33
102	0.33
103	0.40

2. Standard workday. The union contract defines a standard workday as eight hours. Any overtime is paid at 150 percent of standard wages.

3. Time loss. Absenteeism varies by quarter.

Quarter	Percent of Actual Hours Lost
1	2.5%
2	1.0
3	1.5
4	2.0

TABLE 1 Production Schedule for FY 1985 (one unit = one pair)

Model	Quarter 1 (July–Sept.)	Quarter 2 (Oct.–Dec.)	Quarter 3 (Jan.–Mar.)	Quarter 4 (April–June)	Total
101	5,551	3,629	4,296	9,180	22,656
102	5,551	3,629	4,296	9,180	22,656
103	16,653	13,131	8,400	29,784	67,968
Total	27,755	20,389	16,992	48,144	113,280

4. Wage rate. The current average wage rate is $6.50/hour. Fringe benefits costs equal 15 percent of salary costs. All employees receive fringe benefits.

5. Production schedule. The total annual demand for products is:

Model	Number of Units
101	22,656
102	22,656
103	67,968

The maximum number of units that can be produced in any one quarter is:

Model	Number of Units
101	9,200
102	9,200
103	30,000

The following pieces of information concern things that can be changed in the short run. You can manipulate these items, but consider the costs as well as the benefits of doing so.

1. *Productivity.* People do not or cannot produce at 100 percent efficiency. The standard hour figures given for production assume that a person is working continually and, therefore, do not reflect what is really going on. At this point, your department has measured productivity at 82 percent. Without the introduction of new technology or machinery, it is your best guess that productivity could be improved a maximum of 4 percent.

2. *Staffing levels.* Currently 21 people are engaged in the production process. The skills and abilities of all labor are interchangeable. Additional persons are not difficult to obtain, but hiring, training, and layoff costs do exist.

Discussion Questions

1. If current staffing levels are maintained, are there enough employees available to allow MMM to achieve its production schedule? If not, how many additional personnel are required? What alternatives does MMM have to secure these personnel?

2. If there are too many persons during any one production quarter, what alternatives does MMM have to deal with the surplus? Be sure to consider both the costs and benefits associated with each of these alternatives.
3. What effect will improving productivity have on staffing levels?
4. Can you suggest any shifts in production from one quarter to another that would help smooth out staffing requirements?

---

3 Worldwide Manufacturing Corporation

Worldwide is a corporation manufacturing a large assortment of products in several different divisions. The particular division discussed in this case consists of four manufacturing sites. Two sites are located in New York and two are located in Tennessee. There is also a headquarters located in Houston, Texas. The central headquarters was a concept developed by the corporation in the late 1950s and completed in the early 1970s. The manufacturing sites had been in operation for over 65 years in New York and for 15 years in Tennessee. Before the inception of the headquarters, each site in this division was highly decentralized. Many of the jobs overlapped greatly from one site to another. Half the division was managed from one New York location, and the remainder of the corporate leaders were located in another part of the state, 600 miles away.

In 1976, projections indicated that business would decline over the next 10 years. The corporate powers decided that this would be a good time to centralize authority and key functions over the entire operations. Plans were then made to find a suitable site for the central headquarters. The corporation decided that a site should be chosen that would get the headquarters function away from the influence of the manufacturing operations. It also wanted to get away from the old ways of doing things, to a "Dawn of a New Age."

"Dawn of a New Age" was to become the motto for the corporation over the five-year period required to make the move. After much deliberation and several false starts, it was decided to locate the central headquarters in Houston, Texas. Management felt that the move would be the perfect time to change the way things had been done at the old sites. Management's first strategy was to ask only the best and most

This case was prepared by Richard Sledz, University of Central Florida, under the supervision of Professor George E. Stevens.

capable people to transfer to the new headquarters. This also would be the perfect time to consolidate many overlapping functions. Many departments, up north, could be eliminated once their functions were taken over by a central organization.

Once all the logistics were completed, the plan to move the 600 people was formulated. The move was to be made in three phases, covering a two-year period. Phases one and two were to move to the Houston area and into temporary headquarters. Phase three would involve moving directly into the new site, when complete.

Of the 600 people to be moved, 400 would be engineers and the rest would be white-collar workers. Most of the engineers would be moved in phase three. Since the northern plants were unionized, a massive campaign was started by the unions against the move. The unions felt that one of the main reasons for the move was to get away from the unions.

As soon as the unions started their campaign, the company countered with its own campaign. It began to sing the praises of the new locations and of how different everything would be in Houston. "Dawn of a New Age" would be the rallying cry used to kick off the company's campaign. One of the first and most prominent problems was how to convince the people who would be chosen for the move to leave the area. Over 65 percent of the people chosen were over 45 years old. Over 10 percent were five to eight years from retirement. Most of the people would be chosen from the northern sites and had lived in that area all their lives. (The people chosen would be from the northern sites, because that is where headquarters and engineering functions had been located.)

One of the missions of the human relations department was to create an attractive package of incentives to entice people to move. The package consisted of:

1. Payment of all moving expenses.
2. Two weeks with pay to view the Houston area and to house-hunt.
3. Company-paid trips with spouse to explore new area and house-hunt.
4. A monthly interest discount (MID) program was devised, in which the company paid the difference between the mortgage the employee had up north and the new one he or she would get in Houston. The MID refunds would last five years. (Mortgage rates at the time of the move were as high as 16 percent and many of the employees had rates of between 8 and 10 percent.)
5. If the employee's house was not sold by the time of the move, the company would buy the house.

As word began to spread about the move, the Houston headquarters was touted as being in the land of opportunity. There would be a new merit plan for raises. Only the best employees were to be chosen. There would be many chances for advancement. Houston was a beautiful city, where it never snowed . . . and on and on the praise for the new headquarters was sung. Over the two-year period while the headquarters was located at their temporary site, all went well. Phases one and two moved down south with very few problems. Most of what the company had promised was coming true. The building program was on schedule.

While at the temporary site, many new programs were instituted. One such program was a merit appraisal system (MAS). This system entailed peer evaluation in such areas as communication, organization and planning, leadership, resourcefulness, and any other skills that were appropriate to a job. These skill areas were chosen by the employee. After a consensus was reached by the employees, the human relations department then chose the specific skills that would be used for the evaluation. The employee then chose four to six of his or her peers to do the evaluation. The MAS evaluations were computerized. The employee was to evaluate one person's skills against another. An example: John N. is (more/less/equal) to Mary B.; Mary B. was (less than/equal to/higher than) average, and so on. After the evaluation had been given, two types of rankings were given. First was an overall rank for the whole division. The second was a rating of 1, 2, 3, 4; 1 representing low, 2 for average, 3 for high, 4 for very high. The evaluation was to be given once a year. Each year the entire process of picking raters and criteria for rating would be repeated. The evaluation was given for the first time four months before the move into the new building. Only one person scored a "1" out of the 350 people given the evaluation. The rest of the scores were average to high, with about 10 percent very high. Keep in mind that, since only the "best" people were chosen to move to Houston, and the support people hired in the Houston area were of the highest caliber, the company did not expect to have many people in the lowest category.

At the same time the move was taking place, many people were being laid off in the northern plants. Soon it became very easy to recruit people to move to Houston—it became a choice between the move and being laid off. Although not a week went by that Houston did not hear of layoffs in the north, Houston felt that there would be no chance of layoffs at the new site. People never dreamed that two months before the move into the new building there would be a layoff of 20 percent of the Houston personnel.

Word of the pending layoffs came in the form of rumors one month before the official word. At first no one wanted to believe it ("No way would the company spend all that time and money to bring us here just to lay us off"). No member of management at the Houston site would confirm or deny the rumors. Within two weeks people were beginning to really worry. It became so bad that management finally released a statement that "in one week there would be an announcement concerning layoffs." At the same time, booklets were issued explaining employees' rights and privileges, should a layoff occur. This announcement brought productivity to a standstill.

For the next week, the 350 people at the Houston site were numb with disbelief. Some people were at the point of panic, while others worked twice as hard to keep busy. As management promised, the announcement confirmed the rumors of the pending layoffs in Houston. The reason was because business had declined below the anticipated level. There was no way that the company, at the present sales level, could support the number of people now employed. One of the first questions asked was, How would the company decide who was to be laid off? They were told that the following procedures would be followed: (1) people who were close to retirement (one to three years) would be offered incentive to take early retirement; (2) volunteers; (3) if the desired number of people could not be found by the implementation of procedures (1) and (2), people would be chosen by a combination of MAS standings, management, and the human relations department's guidelines.

Management then told the employees that it would take one week to see if enough volunteers could be found. At the same time, a list would be made of those who would be laid off. One week later, 10 percent of the people needed to be laid off had volunteered. After a final tabulation, 50 people from the Houston headquarters were laid off.

Discussion Questions

1. What options, other than layoffs, could the company have tried to reduce overhead?
2. Was the merit appraisal system a valid criterion to help choose who would be laid off?
3. Design a package of benefits for those people who were to be laid off.
4. What issues are involved when companies consider laying people off who have been transferred from another location?

4 Downsizing the Organization

Alpha Gamma Company is a multidivision company serving worldwide consumer and technical markets. Annual sales are in excess of $1 billion. Its history dates back well over 100 years, during which time it has had a centralized authority structure and paternalism in terms of its culture.

The company has been quite successful and profitable over the years. However, sales dropped 8 percent in 1980 from the previous year. While sales and net profits both rose somewhat in 1981, 1982 showed a reduction in total sales, with the company operating at a significant loss, due primarily to the severe impact of the 1981–82 recession.

The year 1982 was troublesome in other ways, with the company becoming the target for an unfriendly takeover by another corporation. As a defense strategy, the company was forced to sell off one of its most profitable businesses, since that business was what the unfriendly suitor was after. This action effectively warded off the takeover bid.

While successfully blocking the 1982 takeover attempt, the company was facing new challenges. The newly appointed chairman and chief executive officer was moving to a philosophy of decentralization, which led to a corporate restructuring of the organization. This, coupled with the divestiture of a major division and the state of the economy, was producing a surplus of employees at the headquarters level. With one less business to service (the divested division), and fewer corporate services needed by the decentralized divisions, the company was faced with the need to reduce its staff of headquarters, managers, professionals, and other support personnel.

The decision was made to reduce overhead costs significantly, including payroll expenses. With corporate overhead now too high for operating divisions to absorb, the chairman decided that significant cost reductions would be required, although no specific dollar or headcount objectives were mandated.

Each department head was charged with the task of determining where personnel, programs, or other costs could be cut. Lists of employees who could be "surplused" were drawn up, along with the plan for other cost reductions. These plans were discussed with the CEO and, in cases where the plans were not rigorous enough, further negoti-

This case was prepared by Professor Cliff Harrison, University of Wisconsin, Oshkosh.

ations and pressures were applied to increase them to a level satisfactory to the chairman.

The initial program called for reduction of the corporate headquarters staffs by 150 employees, including clerical. The initial list of 150 employees to be terminated was carefully reviewed. The employee files and performance data were scrutinized by the human resources chief and internal law department to reduce, as much as possible, the risks of discrimination complaints and litigation.

Following considerable debate among the senior managers about the use of external outplacement services, it was decided that outplacement services would be provided by using internal human resources professionals, rather than engaging an external outplacement consulting firm. Consistent with its historical paternalistic culture, there was considerable concern for the surplus employees, especially those with long service and being more senior in age. It was anticipated that these employees would experience severe termination trauma and would need carefully planned and orchestrated assistance.

When the staff reduction plans were complete and the reduction date established, group meetings were held with key managers by human resources professionals to train them in how to handle the termination interviews. Each manager was given a script to follow in conducting the interviews so that inappropriate statements would be avoided as much as possible. A packet of materials for each employee to be terminated was provided during these briefings.

Final selection of employees to be terminated was done by department heads, with careful oversight by the CEO and human resources director. It was the department head who later conducted the terminations, rather than the immediate supervisors. Final decisions on which employees would go were made by the department heads. Selection was made principally by selecting those who were incumbents of positions being eliminated and by the selective judgments of department managers. Performance was a lesser factor, due to the lack of objective performance data. Seniority was indicated as a factor when it related to newer employees.

There was heated debate over how much notice employees should be given prior to termination day. Due to the concern that there could be disruption, rebellion, and possible destruction, especially in data processing areas, it was decided that the day of notice would also be the last day worked. The best the human resources chief could do was to get agreement to move the termination date to midweek, rather than Friday. This meant that terminated employees could begin work with the human resources counselors immediately, rather than having to agonize over a weekend without any constructive work being initiated.

While the human resources executive believed that the employees were mature and loyal enough to handle advance notice in an appropriate manner, he was not able to convince top management of that. This appears to be in conflict with the indicated paternalistic nature of the organization.

The severance formula was 3 percent of annual salary multiplied by years of service (a $40,000-a-year employee with 20 years of service would have received $24,000, paid out as salary continuation). Minimum amount of severance was four weeks' pay. Benefits—health, dental, and life insurance—were kept in force for the duration of the severance payment period. The period of payment was also counted as time worked for pension calculation purposes.

By the time the termination date arrived, a career counseling center and placement center had been established (in the headquarters facility, but with a separate entrance). Internal counseling, desk space, telephone usage, word processing, and printing of résumés was provided for those who wished to take advantage of the centers' services. About 70 percent of those discharged did use the centers. In addition, the company wrote to 500 employers in the area, advising them of the staff reduction and of the types of employees who were available for other positions. Considerable response was received, which resulted in many employees being hired from this activity. The company also paid for résumés to be put on a regional computerized job bank utilized by subscribing organizations.

Following the staff reduction, the chairman held a series of group meetings with remaining headquarters employees to discuss what was done and to provide the reasons for the action. No other formal efforts were made to assess the impact of the staff reduction on the remaining organization or on steps taken to overcome the negative consequences. The managers interviewed during this study stated that the impact was very negative on morale, employee loyalty and commitment, and productivity. This condition continued for a number of months, employees being obsessed by the fear that the "other shoe" would drop and that they might be next to be terminated. Their concerns turned out to be accurate; about nine months later, the second reduction was decided upon. Fifty more headquarters employees were to be dismissed.

Discussion Questions

1. Assess the conditions that led to the retrenchment decision. What alternative strategies could have been employed to reduce or eliminate the staff reduction?
2. What effect would you expect the reduction to have on those being terminated?
3. Discuss how the employees to be terminated were selected. What would you have done differently? What potential risks do you see?

4. What are the advantages of an in-company outplacement program versus using an external consulting firm?
5. What are the positive and negative consequences of the firm's strategy of giving no advance notice to the selected employees?
6. What impact do you believe the staff reduction will have on the remaining organization? What actions could the company take to minimize negative impact of such a reduction?
7. How adequate and appropriate was the company's severance package and other assistance provided?
8. What steps would you take to plan and implement the second staff reduction? What specific things would you do differently from the first cutback?

5 Job Descriptions at HITEK

INTRODUCTION

Jennifer Hill was excited about joining HITEK Information Services after receiving her MBA. Her job involved examining compensation practice and her first assignment was to review HITEK's job descriptions. She was to document her work and to make recommended changes, which would include the reduction of the more than 600 job descriptions.

BACKGROUND

To its stockholders and the rest of the outside world, HITEK is a highly profitable, highly aggressive company in the computer business. In addition to its numerous government contracts, it provides software and hardware to businesses and individuals. From its inception in the late 1960s, it maintained its position on the leading edge by remaining flexible and adaptable to the turbulent environment in which it operated. It is a people-intensive organization that relies enormously on its human resources; therefore, it is in HITEK's best interests to establish policies and procedures that nurture productivity and enhance the satisfaction of its employees. A memo from the president to HITEK employees that exemplifies this approach appears as Exhibit 1.

Because the computer industry is growing at an incredible pace, opportunities for placement are abundant and the competition for high-quality human resources is tremendous. HITEK had grown about 30 percent in the last three years, and its management knows that just as easily as it attracted new employees, it could lose them. Its turnover rate is about average for its industry.

HITEK remains relatively small at 1,000 employees and it prides itself on its "small company culture." This culture is maintained partly by the use of a computer memo system that can put any employee in touch with anyone at HITEK and by the utilization of open office spaces—with no doors, in many cases. The relatively flat organizational structure (see Exhibit 2) and the easy accessibility of all corporate levels also promotes an open-door policy. All-in-all, employees enjoy working for HITEK, and management is in touch with the organization's "pulse."

With the notable exception of the human resources department (HRD), there are few rules at HITEK. Work in a department is often shared by all levels of employees, and positions are redefined in order to match the specific skills, abilities, and interests of the incumbent. Overqualified and overachieving individuals are often hired, but then are promoted rapidly. Nothing is written down, and if newcomers want to

---

EXHIBIT 1   O'Hara's Computer Memo to Employees

Subject: Share a Thought Luncheons
To: All Employees
From: Billy O'Hara
Date: July 31

HITEK has always been a company whose employees contribute innovative and creative ideas. For this to continue, our environment needs to be one where employees are comfortable expressing their ideas.

The Share a Thought Luncheon that I introduced in the recent issue of our newsletter is one avenue for you to informally share an idea or a concept. This time is intended to be an informal session with Andy Simms, Joe Feldon, and me.

Our first luncheon is scheduled for August 13. To join us, just drop me a brief summary of your idea. You will receive additional details as the luncheon date approaches.

I welcome your ideas and look forward to some interesting "brainstorming" sessions.

EXHIBIT 2   HITEK's Organizational Chart

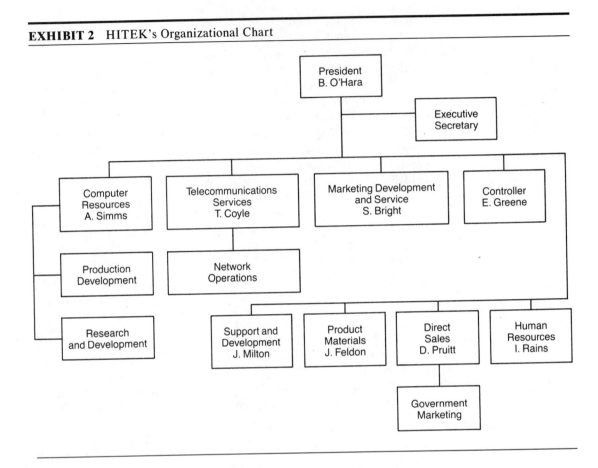

know why something is done a certain way, they must ask the person(s) who created the procedure. There is extensive horizontal linkage between departments, perpetuating the blurring of distinction between departments.

THE HUMAN RESOURCES DEPARTMENT

The HRD stands in stark contrast to the rest of HITEK. About 30 people are employed in HRD, including the support staff members or about one human resource employee per 33 HITEK employees. As can be seen in Exhibit 3, in addition to the vice president for human resources, there are managers of: (1) compensation and benefits, (2) human relations, (3) employment, (4) training and development, and (5) the fitness center. On average, four people report to each of these managers, including one person, such as the compensation analyst, who is expected to hold a professional degree.

The vice president for human resources, Isabel Rains, rules the department with an *iron fist*. HRD employees are careful to mold their ideas to match Rains's perspective. When newcomers suggest changes, they are told that "this is the way things have always been done," because "it's our culture." Most of the HRD functions are bound by written rules and standard operating procedures. HRD employees know their job descriptions well and there is little overlap in duties.

With the exception of one recruiter, all 12 of the incumbents whose positions are represented in Exhibit 3 are women. Only half of them have degrees in industrial relations or human resources management, and only a fourth have related experience with another company. Most of them have been promoted from clerical positions. In fact, some employees view the vice presidency (of HRD) as a "gift" given to Isabel, a former executive secretary, the day after she received her bachelor's degree at a local college, rather than a position of authority and expertise. Connie Yarro's background is in library work, and although the other four managers have HRM degrees, their only experience is in college internships—with HITEK. Their subordinates found their way to human resources through various channels, from fashion merchandising to secretarial work.

In other departments, it is widely believed that professional degrees and related experiences lead to expertise. Mentoring, whereby a senior employee helps socialize a newcomer into the company and arranges

EXHIBIT 3   The Structure of the Human Resources Department

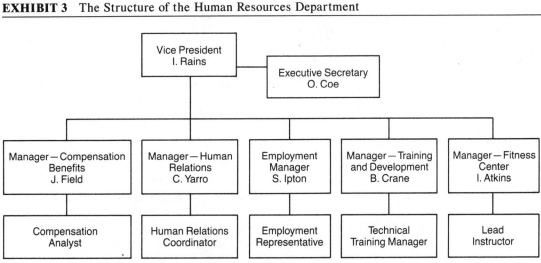

experiences to increase the newcomer's skills and competencies—and hence his or her confidence—is common. But because none of the HRD employees can be considered a senior employee, mentoring is minimal. Consequently, HRD employees tend to be defensive and secretive in dealings with employees in other departments, perhaps as a result of their insecurity.

The major reward systems of the company are not linked to the human resources department. Even the company's annual employee recognition dinner is perceived as a reward from Billy O'Hara, not from HRD. Thus, the HRD is perceived as an ineffectual group of clerical employees.

One incident that conveyed the HRD's image to Jennifer Hill occurred during her second week on the job. While preparing a job description with Dave Pruitt, Jennifer explained that she would submit the job description to Janet Voris for final approval. Dave became confused and asked, "but Janet is only a clerical person; why would she be involved?"

JENNIFER HILL'S DUTIES

At HITEK, the pool of job descriptions had grown almost daily as newcomers were hired, but many of the old job descriptions were not discarded even when obsolete. Other job descriptions needed updating. Because the job descriptions, particularly those representing benchmark positions, were going to be important in HITEK's hiring and revised compensation program, Jennifer knew she would have to do a careful

---

EXHIBIT 4   An "Old" Job Description

ASSOCIATE PROGRAMMER

Basic objective	Perform coding, testing, and documentation of programs, under the supervision of a project leader.
Specific tasks	Perform coding, debugging, and testing of a program when given general program specifications.
	Develop documentation of the program.
	Assist in the implementation and training of the users in the usage of the system.
	Report to the manager, management information services, as requested.
Job qualifications	Minimum: (*a*) BA/BS degree in relevant field or equivalent experience/knowledge; (*b*) programming knowledge in FORTRAN; (*c*) good working knowledge of business and financial applications.
	Desirable: (*a*) computer programming experience in a time-sharing environment; (*b*) some training or education in COBOL, PL1, or assembler languages.

EXHIBIT 5 A "New" Job Description

ASSOCIATE PROGRAMMER

General statement of duties	Perform coding, debugging, testing, and documentation of software under the supervision of a technical superior. Involves some use of independent judgment.
Supervision received	Works under close supervision of a technical superior or department manager.
Supervision exercised	No supervisory duties required.
Examples of duties	(Any one position may not include all the duties listed, nor do listed examples include all duties that may be found in positions of this class.)
	Confers with analysts, supervisors, and/or representatives of the departments to clarify software intent and programming requirements.
	Performs coding, debugging, and testing of software when given program specifications for a particular task or problem.
	Writes documentation of the program.
	Seeks advice and assistance from supervisor when problems outside of realm of understanding arise. Communicates any program specification deficiencies back to supervisor.
	Reports ideas concerning design and development back to supervisor.
	Assists in the implementation of the system and training of end users.
	Provides some support and assistance to users.
	Develops product knowledge and personal expertise and proficiency in system usage.
	Assumes progressively complex and independent duties as experience permits.
	Performs all duties in accordance with corporate and departmental standards.
Minimum qualifications	Education: BA/BS degree in relevant field or equivalent experience/knowledge in computer science, math, or other closely related field.
	Experience: No prior computer programming work experience necessary.
	Knowledge, skills, and abilities: Ability to exercise initiative and sound judgment. Knowledge of a structured language. Working knowledge in operating systems. Ability to maintain open working relationship with supervisor. Logic and problem-solving skills. Develop system flowcharting skills.
Desirable qualifications	Exposure to BASIC, FORTRAN, or PASCAL. Some training in general accounting practices and controls; effective written and oral communication skills.

job of determining what changes were needed. She also felt that it would be beneficial to HITEK and to the HRD if she could help managers understand other ways in which the job descriptions could be used.

Jennifer spent some time thinking about how to proceed. She considered the uses of the job descriptions and what steps she would need to take to accomplish all that was expected of her. Support from within the HRD was scarce, because other employees were busy gathering materials for the annual review of HITEK's hiring, promotion, and development practices conducted by the Equal Employment Opportunity Commission.

After six harried months on the job and much frustration, Jennifer had revised all of the descriptions that were still needed (an example of "old" and "new" job descriptions appear as Exhibits 4 and 5). She also was beginning to develop some strong opinions about how the HRD functioned at HITEK and what needed to be done to improve its effectiveness and its image. She decided to arrange a confidential lunch with Billy O'Hara.

Discussion Questions

1. What are the goals of HITEK? What are the goals of the human resources department? Why does the conflict create problems for HITEK?
2. Organization members can draw from several bases of power, such as referent power or reward power. Is the human resources department powerful? Why is it important for HITEK to maintain a professional competent human resources function?
3. Jobs change frequently at HITEK. Shouldn't the HRD simply discontinue the practice of job analysis and stop writing job descriptions?
4. What steps should Jennifer Hill take in performing the tasks assigned to her? How do your answers to the earlier questions affect your answer?
5. Is the new job description (Exhibit 5) better than the old one (Exhibit 4)? Why or why not?
6. What should Jennifer suggest to the president concerning the image and operation of the HRD?

Staffing, Entry, Orientation, and Placement

1 Who Has the Authority to Recruit Applicants?

Seaside College is a small church-related liberal arts college. The human resources department is having a very difficult time securing secretarial personnel. Although Seaside is considered an excellent place to work, secretarial salaries were considerably below average in the area. Also, most departmental secretaries had to work for more than one department head.

On June 1 the Science Division notified the human resources office that the secretary for the chemistry and biology departments was leaving at the end of the month. When asked for details regarding the replacement, Dr. Overmeyer, chairman of the chemistry department, said that he would like to have someone who was a good typist and who could take shorthand but that the shorthand was not absolutely necessary. He also stated that, if possible, he would prefer an older person who was likely to stay in the position longer than the usual year or two. This had been the pattern in this department. The replacement was requested by June 23 in order that she could learn the job prior to the departure of the present secretary. Dr. Overmeyer was assured that a replacement could be secured.

On June 23 Dr. Overmeyer called the personnel office regarding the replacement. He was informed that no one had been found. At about 10 A.M. on June 24, Miss Greystone visited Dr. Overmeyer in his office and said that she was interested in the secretarial position. Miss Greystone had just graduated from Acme Business College and was seeking a position at Seaside. She knew of the Overmeyer position through a close friend who was secretary to two other department heads in an-

---

This case was prepared by Professor James C. Hodgetts of Memphis State University and is intended to be used as a teaching device rather than to show correct or incorrect methods of operations.

other division of the college. Dr. Overmeyer suggested that she see Mrs. Hansen in the personnel office as she was responsible for interviewing applicants for the position. Miss Greystone stated that she had already talked to Mrs. Hansen and was told that she was not qualified for the position. Further conversation revealed that Miss Greystone had been an excellent student, had all As in typing and shorthand and was held in high regard by all the faculty and staff at Acme. However, her attendance record was very bad. Miss Greystone stated that she missed a lot of school because she worked with her father who operated an all-night truck stop and was frequently too tired to go to class. She also stated that she had quit the night job and that attendance would be no problem. Her school records showed that her health was good and was not a factor in her attendance.

He was informed by Mrs. Hansen that she didn't like Miss Greystone's attitude and that she did not think that Miss Greystone should have taken it upon herself to visit Dr. Overmeyer after human resources had rejected her application, but that she would not let this stand in the way of her getting the position. Dr. Overmeyer next visited Professor August, the chairman of the biology department, to discuss the hiring of Miss Greystone. Professor August had not been available prior to this time. Professor August said that he would prefer not to hire someone who did not want to take dictation but that he would think about it. Miss Greystone was asked to wait a few days for an answer. She said that she could only wait until the next day because she had another job offer. Further conversation revealed that the other job paid a considerably higher salary but that she really wanted to work at the university with her friend. Dr. Overmeyer again talked with Professor August and they decided to try to obtain someone who would take dictation.

At 8:00 A.M. the next morning, Dr. Overmeyer called Miss Greystone and told her that Professor August preferred someone who could take dictation. She informed him that she had talked with Professor August and that he was interested in hiring her. A telephone call confirmed this information. Dr. Overmeyer called Mrs. Hansen in human resources and told her that both he and Professor August wanted to give Miss Greystone a try. He was asked to bring or send her to personnel. Dr. Overmeyer decided to talk with Mrs. Hansen about Miss Greystone prior to the final hiring. He was told that Miss Greystone would have to start at $25 a month less than the budgeted salary. Dr. Overmeyer stated that the budgeted salary was already $80 a month less than Miss Greystone's other offer but that he would go to the waiting room and ask her. While he was talking with Miss Greystone, Mrs. Hansen went into the next office to talk with her superior, the director of human resources. Miss Greystone agreed to accept the $25 lower salary but when Dr. Overmeyer returned to Mrs. Hansen's office she said that Miss Greystone would have to talk with the director of human resources at one o'clock.

At 2:30 P.M. Dr. Overmeyer received a call from the Dean of the Faculty who stated that the director of human resources had called him and stated that he, Dr. Overmeyer, was not following university policy and was interfering in the hiring of personnel. Dr. Overmeyer made a few choice remarks and explained the situation to the Dean. He then called the director of human resources to discuss the matter. The director informed Dr. Overmeyer that he had not hired Miss Greystone and that people like Dr. Overmeyer should keep their noses out of his business. Dr. Overmeyer told the director he didn't know his business. Dr. Overmeyer is still wondering why Miss Greystone wanted to work at the university.

Discussion Questions

1. What are the problems in this case?
2. How can these problems be avoided in the future? (Carefully explain.)

2 *Who Should Do the Hiring?*

Joe Unseld recently obtained his MBA from a large midwestern university and immediately went to work as assistant to the vice president of industrial relations of Hackney Paper Box Company. The Hackney Paper Box Company operates 46 corrugated box factories from California to Maine.

On June 18, Hackney started hiring personnel for a new plant in Cincinnati, Ohio. The plant was to hire approximately 130 persons with all higher management and other key personnel to be transferred from other plants. Twelve potential frontline supervisors were to be hired locally and sent to other Hackney plants for four to six months' training. The projected management structure at the new plant is show in Exhibit 1. Hackney was a highly centralized company, except for production, sales, and local employment. All other functions were performed by personnel from the Chicago corporate office.

This case was prepared by Professor James C. Hodgetts of Memphis State University and is intended to be used as a teaching device rather than to show correct or incorrect methods of operations.

EXHIBIT 1 Cincinnati Plant—Hackney Box Company

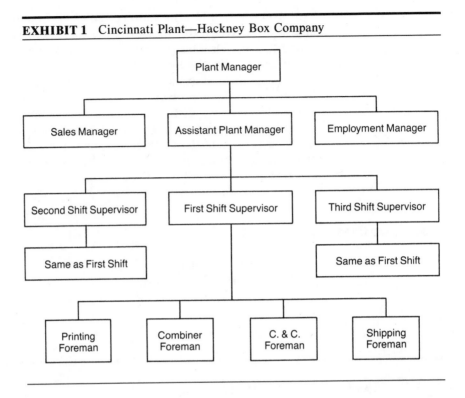

Mr. James Gulfstead, corporate employment manager, arrived in Cincinnati on June 16 and went through the mechanics of setting up an employment office in the yet to be completed Hackney plant. On June 18 he hired a secretary to help him in his work and to be the secretary to the plant manager when he arrived on the scene. On June 19 he started recruiting the 12 potential supervisors to be sent to other plants to be trained for Hackney's Cincinnati plant. This task was completed by July 22 with all 12 potential supervisors scheduled to report to work between July 20 and September 1.

Mr. Gulfstead returned to Chicago on July 22 and scheduled a July 27 meeting with the corporate director of manpower planning and the assistant vice president of manufacturing—Midwest. At this meeting, they reviewed possible promotions and transfers for the jobs of sales manager, assistant plant manager, and employment manager. During the two months that followed, various prospects were contacted and selections were made. The assistant plant manager at the Buffalo, N.Y., plant was promoted to plant manager at the new Cincinnati plant.

Although the plant was scheduled to have started production as of February 7, it was April before the first quality box was shipped and a year later the plant was only producing at 62 percent capacity. At this point in time, Mr. Jack Overan, plant manager, was asked by his boss, the assistant vice president—Midwest, to justify this low production rate.

Mr. Overan had been waiting for this opportunity for a long time. He felt that the company policy of permitting the personnel department to do the hiring was wrong and that one of the major production problems in the plant stemmed from the way people had been acquired. He had had to fire the secretary hired by Mr. Gulfstead soon after he arrived. She was quite popular with the office staff but just not willing to put forth the effort necessary to hold down the top secretarial job in the plant. This had caused considerable dissatisfaction and insecurity in the office. Also, the assistant plant manager and Mr. Overan had worked together before and never had gotten along. The assistant plant manager said he would never have accepted the job if he knew Mr. Overan was going to be plant manager. Also, he felt that he should have been in on the hiring of the frontline supervisors. Mr. Overan also believed that the frontline supervisors should have had some say in who was to work for them and also, that they could have been valuable in hiring high-level hourly paid employees such as conigator operators and printers.

When Mr. Overan's report was read by the company president, he decided that company hiring policy needed investigating and assigned Joe Unseld to the task.

Discussion Questions

1. What are the problems in this case?
2. Assume you are Joe Unseld. What should you recommend to the company president?

3 Professional Leasing Services, Inc. (A)

Professional Leasing Services, Inc. (PLS), was incorporated in 1979 in Wilmington, Delaware. The firm is located in Tempe, Arizona, but Delaware's incorporation laws are deemed by many to be the best in the country for the business owner. Over the past 10 years the firm has achieved many of the original objectives established by its first owners. The company's profit picture looks great. Everything in the company's plans points to a bright future in a booming business. In fact, plans were being made to negotiate contracts with several key professional people so as to repudiate the stereotype of temporary agencies and to better serve companies who could not afford regular high-level employees in certain job classifications. This recent strategy has meant marketing of the idea that PLS can reduce labor costs by having companies pay a higher direct compensation cost but no indirect compensation cost for leased employees. Specifically, as much as 40 percent of the total compensation dollar consists of so-called fringe benefits. Theoretically, the hiring companies, as leasing clients, would not have to pay benefit costs.

In recent years, PLS has moved far beyond its initial business of offering to companies only secretarial and clerical workers. Former and current chief financial officers, hospital administrators, computer software experts, accountants, personnel directors, and other professionals and managers have been added to the company over the past three years. Profit picture aside, however, there may be a "fly in the ointment." The company has been so profit driven that it has failed to acknowledge one important employee-related problem. While the clients that utilize the services of Professional Leasing Service, Inc.'s employees seem happy with the arrangement, the PLS employees have difficulty with the leasing concept. Traditionally, employees have some stability and, when they perform well for an employer, have an opportunity for upward mobility. Clients appear less likely to hire the PLS employees so such immediate reward is not evident. Second, the PLS employees appear less driven to act on the basis of company loyalty since they feel that their very existence is so tenuous. PLS compensates its people well but pay doesn't seem to affect the loyalty/retention issue.

Requirement

Identify the advantages and disadvantages to clients, the leasing company and those employed of participating in a leasing arrangement.

Professional Leasing Services, Inc. (B)

The owner and principal stockholder of PLS, Byron Scott, has owned and sold a number of businesses. One business that is near and dear to Mr. Scott's heart is the Arizona Light Manufacturing Company of Scottsdale, Arizona. The business, as the name implies, does light manufacturing work. Most recently, ALMC has provided Motorola Company with needed parts for their Government Products Division. Byron has held onto Arizona Light Manufacturing because it was the first company

TABLE 1 Equal Opportunity Report—Company Data

Job Categories	Male	Female	White	Hispanic	American Indian, Alaskan Native	Asian/ Pacific Islander	Black/ Non-Hispanic	Underutilization or Concentration?
Officials and manager	158	42	140	16	9	1	0	
Professionals	237	241	432	29	17	0	0	
Technicians	47	50	27	54	9	1	8	
Sales workers	35	7	40	1	0	0	1	
Office and clerical	8	43	22	23	3	0	7	
Craft workers	28	12	22	8	5	2	3	
Operatives	472	502	275	543	99	1	56	
Laborers	657	343	762	219	10	0	9	
Service workers	33	16	13	16	8	1	11	
All categories	1,675	1,256	1,733	909	160	6	95	

TABLE 2 Relevant Labor Pool Data

Male	Female	White	Hispanic	American Indian	Asian	Black
51%	49%	63%	18%	13%	4%	2%

he bought and operated. It has a sentimental value to him. He has nursed it along. The company's legal counsel has been informed of a pending lawsuit that concerns the upward mobility and representation of members of protected classes as covered by Title VII of the 1964 Civil Rights Act. Arizona Light Manufacturing and Professional Leasing have both maintained the required EEO-1 Report as required by law. This report contains work-force composition data for each of nine job categories (as specified by the Equal Employment Opportunity Commission). The job categories range from that of officials and managers to service workers.

Arizona Light Manufacturing and Professional Leasing merged two years ago. Work-force composition data are presented in Table 1.

Note: These data represent an analysis of selected EEO-1 data. An analysis of relevant labor pool data is provided in Table 2.

Discussion Questions

1. Identify those job classes (if any) that exhibit underutilization.
2. Identify those job classes (if any) that exhibit concentration.

4 Buena Vista Plant (A)

Forest Park Corporation's management has benefited greatly from its decision to acquire the Buena Vista textile plant in Macon, Georgia. The decision to rescue the unprofitable plant was a good one. After the acquisition in 1976, the plant was modernized; new, capable managers were attracted to the plant, and the labor force expanded. By 1981, despite the extensive capital outlays, the plant was operating well into the black.

All names are disguised.

BACKGROUND

The Buena Vista plant had fallen upon hard times before it became a subsidiary of Forest Park Corporation. The plant, which opened in 1955, was a major employer for 20 years. Unfortunately, things turned sour in the late 1970s, when the area suffered a mild recession at a time when foreign competition began to undercut domestic textile manufacturers. These events had a dramatic impact on the Buena Vista plant because it had aging equipment, used outdated production methods, and had no investment capital.

The town of Macon suffered along with the textile plant. The plant's decline and other area company layoffs led to a dramatically higher unemployment rate. The city fathers were happy to learn of Forest Park's interest in the plant. The Chamber of Commerce, city officials, and local business leaders did everything possible to make the acquisition look attractive. And, they were rewarded for their efforts. Since the revitalization of the Buena Vista plant, the city's unemployment rate has fallen from a high of 12 percent to its present low of 4.5 percent. In addition, new industry has been attracted to the area. Over the past three years, there has been a housing boom as people flock to the area in search of better job opportunities.

THE PERSONNEL DEPARTMENT

Al Logan came to the plant in 1957 when he was fresh out of college. When Al joined Buena Vista, there was no personnel department. As the plant's personnel director, he virtually created the department from scratch. Before Forest Park took over, he had a department consisting of one other person, Cheryl Giffhorn, his secretary. He now has a new assistant, John Turner. John has been a willing pupil. His previous experience was as a textile worker. He has no college degree or specialized training in personnel. In the three years that he has worked in personnel, he has lived up to all of Al's expectations. Cheryl has been with Al for 14 years. As a secretary, friend, and confidante, she is absolutely indispensable. In fact, she is more of a personnel paraprofessional than a secretary.

During Al's years as a personnel director, he had made good use of his intelligence, willingness to work long hours, and his interest in personnel. He often regretted that he had majored in marketing, rather than in personnel. He knew that he needed to keep up with these new laws and regulations on health and safety, labor relations, equal employment opportunity, pensions, age discrimination, and sexual harassment, but he had more or less relied on directives from headquarters and help from employee relations specialists. Al had always feared that his failure would come back to haunt him.

Back in 1979, Al discovered that he had a staffing problem. Specifically, a large number of textile workers and textile supervisors were needed to meet human resources requirements for the plant's expansion. With assistance from headquarters, he was able to recruit the necessary personnel. Specialists from headquarters personnel set up a special assessment center program for textile supervisors. The program took a great deal of his people's time at first, but once assessor training was completed, everything ran smoothly. The assessment center included a personal interview, an analysis of a management case, a group exercise, and an in-basket simulation. These tests were decided upon after the behavioral traits and skills needed for the jobs were ascertained. Workers in the plant seemed to really like the assessment center idea. Some claimed it was a more objective way of selecting supervisors than the good-old-boy method based on who fished, hunted, or played tennis together. (People who participated in the centers, however, could only be chosen by their supervisors.) The employee relations people from headquarters claimed the assessment center program would meet Equal Employment Opportunity Commission (EEOC) requirements. According to them, validity studies of assessment ratings at IBM, Sohio, Caterpiller Tractor, and AT&T all support the use of the assessment centers. Although Al knew little about such programs, if this one didn't meet all legal requirements, he felt it wouldn't be his fault.

The textile worker jobs were not filled on the basis of an assessment center. Such a procedure was judged to be too expensive. Instead, Al decided to use a psychomotor aptitude test. At first, he tried a finger dexterity test, but the preliminary validation results were not good. He had failed to find a strong relationship between scores on the test and each employee's job performance. A testing expert reviewed the data and confirmed Al's findings. The correlation between performance and test scores was only $+0.48$. The testing expert offered his own explanation for the modest correlation. He believed the finger dexterity test to be better suited for machinists, radio repairers, plumbers, and business machine operators. As a result of this discussion and job analysis of selected jobs, Al decided to try a manual dexterity test. Manual dexterity usually involves coordination with arm and eye and more gross movements than those involved in finger dexterity. Over the past two years, the personnel department has administered the Minnesota Rate of Manipulation Test.

THE TESTING PROGRAM

One evening after everyone in the department had left, Al thought about a recent discussion with John. John had told him that a Professor Sanchez had led a discussion about the Uniform Guidelines on Employee Selection Procedures. According to this professor, the guidelines re-

---

TABLE 1

Employee	Sex	Race*	Age	Test Score	Performance Rating
1	M	S	35	36	90
2	M	W	32	44	95
3	F	S	44	50	95
4	M	B	42	49	93
5	F	B	36	46	89
6	M	W	33	52	94
7	M	W	45	50	92
8	M	S	48	50	93
9	F	B	34	42	83
10	F	B	46	44	89
11	F	S	30	40	87
12	F	S	39	48	95
13	F	B	31	47	90
14	M	W	49	39	80
15	F	S	47	48	92
16	F	W	40	38	79
17	M	S	44	38	80
18	M	W	33	36	72
19	F	S	43	46	89
20	M	S	36	48	92
21	F	W	22	46	89
22	M	B	28	32	70
23	F	B	19	48	94
24	M	B	23	48	94
25	M	B	27	36	74
26	F	W	18	46	85
27	F	W	26	44	79
28	M	S	21	50	95
29	M	B	23	34	70
30	F	W	28	44	83

Sex: M = Male; F = Female.   Race: S = Spanish surnamed; W = White; B = Black.
Age: Age at time of employment.
*No native Americans applied.

quired organizations with more than 100 employees to make adverse impact determinations at least once a year.

Al realized that he planned on using the manual dexterity test for selection purposes. Although two years have gone by, no validation study has been undertaken. The last validation study was for the old finger dexterity test. Since John volunteered to do the adverse impact determination and validation study, Al didn't oppose the idea. He wasn't convinced, however, that this was necessary.

John gathered data for all those textile workers who took the test. These workers were hired regardless of their test scores. After examining the personnel files, John identified 217 cases for analysis. (The data found in Table 1 are a representative subsample of those data.) John used the Pearson product-moment correlation coefficient[1] to validate the manual dexterity text. He wanted to use the predictive validity approach described in his personnel textbook. He hoped to examine the relationship between test scores and employee performance rating.

Discussion Questions

1. Are there possible negative outcomes for individuals and organizations when assessment centers are used?
2. Do you agree or disagree with John that an adverse impact determination should have been made sooner? Why?
3. What kind of relationship did John find between scores on the test and the performance rating?
4. Was there evidence of differential validity?
5. Assuming that a cutoff score for hiring of 41 was established, would use of this test have led to evidence of adverse impact?
6. Given the validity results you found, would you recommend use of this test as a selection device? If so, how would you use it?

---

[1]This method is discussed in a number of statistical textbooks. See, for example, J. P. Guilford and Benjamin Fruchter, *Fundamental Statistics in Psychology and Education,* 5th ed. (New York: McGraw-Hill, 1973), pp. 79–98.

Buena Vista Plant (B)*

The plant personnel department at Buena Vista is extremely small. Although the work force it serves has increased dramatically, only three people handle all personnel matters. The last person to join the department, John Turner, did so in 1978. As the newest member of the department, John was the most knowledgeable about government regulations, laws, and court cases that impact personnel activities. Because John was relatively new to the department, he had little influence on Al Logan. Al also seemed a bit threatened by the fact that John was completing requirements for a degree in business administration. Much of what John knew about personnel administration he learned in classes at Emory University. He transferred into the personnel office from an assembly line job in the plant.

Cheryl Giffhorn is, in Al's eyes, the most valuable person in the personnel department. She has been his eyes, ears, and right-hand "man." As a friend and confidante, she has been absolutely indispensable. Cheryl has responsibility for prescreening nonexempt and hourly applicants, testing, and record-keeping related to staffing and employee health. At present, she is deeply involved in preparing a report of the incidence of brown lung disease (byssinosis), chronic bronchitis, and emphysema—diseases all attributable to exposure to cotton dust. (These diseases are not now a problem at the plant, but the reports are required by OSHA.)

Al likes the personnel director. He likes working with people, and, in the early years, his job as personnel director was easy. Al saw his job as one of keeping things running smoothly, helping with morale, and solving employee problems. He enjoys getting out on the shop floor where the people are. Al is proud of being chairman of the United Fund Drive, a Rotarian, and member of the Chamber of Commerce.

Recently, he has found little time for the civic activities that he likes. Each year, like clockwork, he has found himself beating back attempts by the Amalgamated Clothing and Textile Workers and other unions to organize the workers. This task is getting harder and more time consuming each year. Last week, Al talked to a consultant who wanted to be paid for telling *him* how to keep unions out. According to Al, his biggest problem is government interference. Every personnel activity seemed to involve some law or government regulation. He knew that he needed to keep up with these new laws on health and safety, equal employment

---

*All names are disguised.

opportunity, pensions, compensation, and labor relations. His duties as personnel director of a larger work force seem to leave him little time to keep up with recent amendments and court decisions.

One duty that has bugged him the most is his role in the grievance procedure. Employees complained about not having any assurance that they would be treated fairly, so the grievance procedure was developed by a committee representing employees at all company levels. The procedure seemed like a good idea at first, because it eliminated a complaint workers had, and it took away one union bargaining advantage. The problem was that more grievances were being filed and more grievances were going beyond the first and second steps. Grievances at the higher levels required Al's involvement, and he resented having to waste his time listening to petty complaints about wage discrimination, subjective performance evaluations, and being passed over for promotions. Now, a couple of these people had filed complaints with the EEOC and the Department of Labor.

THE NEW ADDITIONS

In January of 1981, two new lines were opened in the personnel department. Al now had authorization to add two new members to the department—one as an assistant personnel director and a second as a personnel assistant. Both jobs were for college-educated, trained professionals. Shortly after receipt of the job requisitions, a list of internal candidates arrived from headquarters. After examining the list (which included the name of John Turner), Al agreed to examine the records of five candidates for each job. By February, he had interviewed the top three candidates. Al selected Kathy Morris as the new assistant personnel director and Bill Benjamin became the new personnel assistant. (See Exhibit 1.) John, the heir apparent to the job, was not too pleased with Al's selection of Kathy as assistant personnel director.

Kathy had impressive credentials—she had a bachelor's degree from Delaware State College and an MBA from Golden Gate University. She had held a number of personnel positions during her six years with the company. Among her experiences were assignments as assistant personnel director at Spring Garden Research Facility, work in training, recruiting, and the EEOC office at its headquarters, as well as assignments at the Bristol, Tennessee, and Lexington, Kentucky, plants. Her performance, in all cases, was rated excellent. Bill Benjamin, the new personnel assistant, had only been with the company two years. He had majored in personnel administration at the University of Georgia. He spent his first year in the labor relations department assisting others with collective bargaining. In his second year, he worked in the wage and salary department and took on special assignments for the director of employee relations. This is his first plant assignment.

EXHIBIT 1   Organization Chart for Buena Vista's Personnel Department

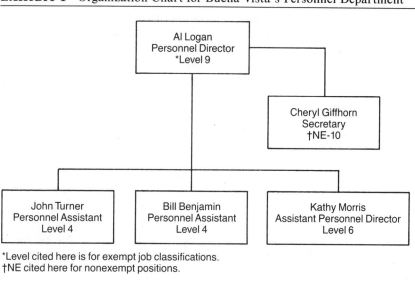

*Level cited here is for exempt job classifications.
†NE cited here for nonexempt positions.

THE TROUBLE WITH KATHY

It didn't take long for Al to realize that Kathy would be a problem. After only three months on the job, she started causing problems. She was a know-it-all. Every personnel policy was illegal. Or she disagreed with it. Al had to stop her from trying to change everything he'd ever written. Kathy fought him about the need to validate the assessment center. She claimed there was adverse impact on blacks. Kathy fought about company policy concerning pregnant women taking a leave without pay at the end of their second trimester. And she demanded that the disability policy be so written that pregnancy could be treated the same as any other disability. Well, Al had had enough. They were going to meet and have it out.

THE MEETING

"Mr. Logan, you wanted to talk to me?"

"Yes, Kathy, come in and sit down. This conversation is just between us. What I have on my mind needs being said."

"That sounds ominous; what is this all about?"

"Kathy, you have challenged our policies, disagreed with me on the handling of certain grievances, and, in general, have made a nuisance of yourself. What you are doing borders on insubordination, and I called you in to verbally reprimand you for your action."

"I am sorry you feel that way, Mr. Logan. My intent was to help you and to help the department. Some of our policies were written 10 or more years ago. As John suggested to you, some may not be consistent with current regulations, court decisions, and agency guidelines. For example, the plant policy on disability treats pregnancy differently than it treats other disabilities. In addition, policy here requires pregnant women, regardless of their health or nature of their jobs, to accept a leave of absence at the end of their second trimester. I don't believe that this policy treats women fairly."

"Kathy, do you know whether the policy is *legal*? If you know about anything that makes the policy illegal, then I will make a change; otherwise, back off."

"The legality of the policy is questionable at best, although I can't cite a specific regulation or law. But let me mention another problem area. I applaud your development of the textile supervisor assessment center, but my data on selection rates indicate a problem. While 70 percent of the whites participating in the assessment center are picked for promotion, only 52 percent of the black assessees are chosen. I think the EEOC and other agencies would question this difference. Plus, we have not done a validation study."

"You have the answer for everything, Kathy. Actually, I hear you challenging a lot of things, but I don't see anything supporting your position. As for the EEOC, when its representatives schedule a compliance review, then I'll do what they want—within reason. Now, since you have an answer for everything else, what do you think of our decision to fire Jeffrey Clement for moonlighting?"

"To be honest, Mr. Logan, I think you are making a big mistake. I believe there is precedent for firing an employee for holding two full-time jobs. Typically, the employee must make a choice. After reading the supervisor's report, however, I am concerned that the supervisor *thinks* Jeffrey is working two jobs. The supervisor has no proof, and the subordinate refuses to incriminate himself. I don't think we can force the guy, even under the threat of discharge, to admit this rule violation."

"Kathy, I think we have a difference of opinion over these policies. Maybe I am too close to them since I had to create them, but I want you to bring me something definitive—court cases, regulations, laws, and so on—rather than disagree openly with me. I have not kept up, and I know it. If you show me why change is needed, we'll make the change."

"Okay. Right or wrong, I have charged full speed without documentation or evidence to support my position. All through school and most of my previous jobs, I have been pretty independent. I'll work harder at being a better team player."

"Well, Kathy, it's just about time for a shift change. Let's see if we can get to the Coke machine before the mad rush makes that impossible. Treats on the big spender. And, by the way, please call me Al."

Discussion Questions

1. How would you describe Al?
2. What problems do you see in the personnel department?
3. Should John, the heir apparent, have been promoted? Why or why not?
4. What is the cause of the problems between Al and Kathy?
5. Examine each of the policy issues Kathy raises. Is she correct?
6. How would you describe Kathy?

5 *Delaware University (A)*

Delaware University is a medium-sized public coeducational university in Delaware, Ohio. The state school is located near the cities of Marion and Columbus, Ohio. Its enrollment is approximately 18,000 students; most are drawn primarily from Ohio, Kentucky, Pennsylvania, and Indiana. The decade of the 1970s found the university in a period of stabilized enrollment. Now, after entering the second year of the 1980s, the school has been experiencing enrollment declines.

THE ORGANIZATION

Delaware University was founded in 1891 as a normal school and was operated and supported by the state of Ohio. The school consisted of three buildings set on hundreds of acres of land. In the first years of its existence, enrollment was quite small, averaging only 35 students a year. During the early 1900s, the enrollment began to grow significantly. The school's graduates were a real credit to the institution, and their efforts and contributions enhanced the school's reputation. In 1919, the state of Ohio incorporated the institution as a land grant school and officially changed its name from Delaware Normal School to Delaware College of Ohio.

During the next 40 years, the school enrollment increased at a steady but not spectacular pace. Under the leadership of Dr. Peter Rose, the school's 11th president, the college built a quality program committed to academic excellence. The liberal arts, education, and agriculture programs were carefully developed and nurtured. For the school's efforts, these programs achieved national recognition and attracted merit scholars from all over the country. When Dr. Rose retired in 1959, he saw his dream come true. The school was granted university status. On his last day, he could look out over the 78 buildings nestled among the gently sloping Ohio hills. There was the new humanities building and spacious, elaborately equipped John Glenn Library. The education building and the health and physical education complex were both less than two years old. When Rose arrived in 1945, the depression and World War II had caused enrollment to stabilize at 6,300 full-time students. Enrollment on his last day in office stood at 12,600 students. The university now had 22 separate departments (see Exhibit 1).

The decade of the 1960s ushered in a period of dramatic growth. Dr. Bob Bryan, who succeeded Rose as president, rode in on this wave of prosperous times, few financial problems, and the student enrollment explosion that seemed to be occurring all around the country. Bryan's early years as president were not without their problems. Due primarily to student pressure, the university's old role of acting in a parental mode gradually changed to one in which students were required to control their own actions. Students also demanded a voice in any decisions that directly influenced them. Those in power—administrators and faculty—were quite resistant at first. After a couple of tumultuous years of student protests, sit-ins in the administration buildings and library, disrup-

---

EXHIBIT 1   Delaware University Academic Units

Humanities	*Education*
English	Elementary and secondary education
History	Art education
Foreign languages	Music education
Philosophy	Physical education
Speech	Educational psychology

Social Science	*Science*
Psychology	Biology
Sociology, urban affairs, and	Chemistry
social work	Engineering
Economics and business	Nursing
administration	Mathematics
Home economics	Computer science
	Physics and astronomy
	Agriculture and natural resources

tion of board of trustee meetings, and protest marches, the university leadership acquiesced. (Some hardliners called it caving in to ridiculous student demands.) It was Bryan who weathered these emotional storms and who seemed to visibly age with each new crisis.

Bryan gained little satisfaction from the knowledge that Delaware University is one of many institutions of higher education to experience disruptive student demonstrations, sit-ins, and takeovers. He did feel fortunate that, unlike a sister institution and a couple of other schools, South Carolina State College and Jackson State University, no shooting incidents had taken place.

As the 1970s approached, Bryan thought his biggest problems would relate to what he believed was a dramatic shift in students' attitudes, perceptions, and values. He often reflected upon the not-so-subtle changes around campus. Policies were so much more permissive. Students fought for and won noncredit courses and pass-fail grading for some programs. Foreign language requirements were dropped. Alcoholic beverages were not permitted on campus. Legal services existed for students and the officer of the tenants association; student government and other student-oriented organizations were housed in the student union building. The student government association had a budget of over $100,000 and allocated money to student organizations on the basis of its own established procedures. Students now had alternating male-female floors in dormitories, and whole dormitories that were coeducational. Finally, students were more vocal and less tolerant of mediocre teaching. A number of the tenured professors were surprised and dismayed by these students who challenged or disputed their words of wisdom. Nothing was sacred: test questions, grades, reading assignments, and so forth. At least one professor chose retirement over trying to cope with this new brand of student. It was not surprising, therefore, that President Bryan expected his toughest future problem to be related to the students of the 1970s. Unfortunately, he was wrong.

The real problem of the 1970s for Bryan and other administrators was one of numbers. By the early 1970s, many of the representatives of the so-called baby boom of the 1940s had passed through the colleges of their choice. In addition, the upsurge of interest in getting a college education in scientific and technical areas had subsided. People had long since switched their attention from the National Aeronautics and Space Administration (NASA) space shots to events in Vietnam. In short, the problem of the 1960s was one of constructing buildings quickly enough to have them available for a large college-bound population or developing strategies (such as raising admission standards) that would dampen demand. College administrators worried about how to get the faculty they needed to cover the classes. The next decade ushered in a change in those conditions. With a decreasing population of traditional students

(18 to 24 year olds), colleges across the nation had to adapt to the changing environment or suffer drastic consequences. Delaware University also suffered enrollment declines.

Bryan was quite successful during the expansionist economic period of the 1960s, but he had no idea how to cope with declining enrollment, budget cuts, and reduced alumni support. According to Dr. Principle, vice president for academic affairs, Bryan was too nice a guy. He didn't want to have to fire people or slice department budgets. He just didn't seem to be the type of leader needed in lean times. Ultimately, the declining enrollment at Delaware University caused financial hardship and forced the president to make some very difficult decisions. Bryan took a crisis-oriented approach to decision making that unnerved those around him. He would agonize for months over the least important of decisions. By the time a decision was made, the president had his back against the wall. Belatedly, Bryan realized that the conditions of the 1970s called into question the goals and objectives of the university. He had a Ph.D. in history, and it saddened him to see practically all liberal arts and education programs suffer financially, while engineering and business administration programs were virtually exploding. (The board of trustees established and implemented a policy of committing resources to programs having the largest enrollments.)

As a result of Bryan's inability to deal with change and unwillingness to play the role of bad guy, Delaware entered a period of rapid decline. The more competent faculty members were being hired away by other institutions. Various administrators decided to bail out in search of greener pastures. It is rumored that some potential students, including a number of national merit scholars, were counseled to go elsewhere. A state auditor's report revealed a dormitory occupancy rate of approximately 62 percent for Delaware University's 23 residence halls. In the fall of 1978, Bryan submitted his letter of resignation to become effective the following summer.

After a lengthy nationwide search for a new president, Morris Brown was selected as Bryan's successor. Dr. Brown, a relatively young man at 44, had been praised by students, alumni, and faculty alike for the job he had done as president at the University of Maryland in Baltimore. Brown wasted little time getting deeply involved in his new job. By June of 1979, one month before he officially became president, Brown had reviewed all financial and personnel data. He toured *all* the buildings, and he met with representatives of key groups on campus. In the fall, Brown systematically interviewed all middle- and upper-level administrators. These actions, particularly the interviews, really seemed to unnerve people. Many of the faculty, administration, students, and staff feared him and they feared change. Drastic change did not come immediately.

In January 1980, Brown gave the annual State of the University address. There were a number of changes detailed in the speech. He felt that the administration was too fat and the school's organizational design incapable of meeting the demands of today's environment. The top administrators and their titles are given in Exhibit 2.

Brown believed that many existing policies and practices would have to change. And, finally, he announced, much belt tightening would be needed if Delaware University was to survive into the 21st century. Brown identified three key problems: declining enrollment, shift in student demand from general education to job-oriented education, and reduced financial support from the Ohio legislature. (This latter problem was caused by the fall in state revenues. Specifically, key industries—

EXHIBIT 2   Delaware University

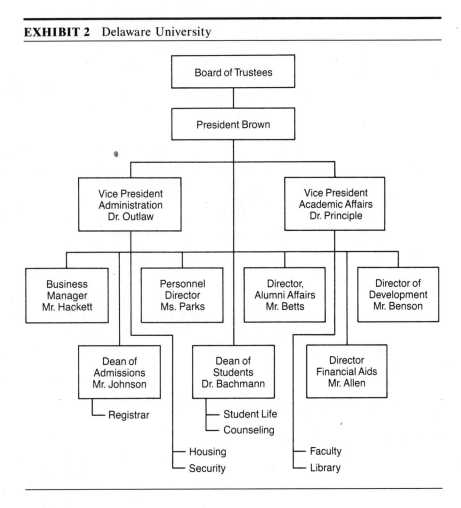

rubber, steel, and automotive—were suffering the effects of high unemployment, antiquated facilities, and foreign competition.) To overcome these and other problems, Brown told his audience that he was considering the following proposals:

1. Evening classes to attract working students.
2. Strict control over the hiring of university employees.
3. Development of training programs for business executives.
4. Alumni participation in recruitment efforts.
5. Utilization of the campus during the summer months for:
    a. Summer school.
    b. Professional football camp.
    c. Conferences.
    d. Corporate onsite training.
6. Designation of two dormitories for travelers seeking short-term, low-cost housing.
7. Use of athletic facilities for nonfootball events, including concerts and high school sports events.
8. Increased mandatory teaching load from 9 to 12 hours per semester.
9. Drop most expensive athletic programs.
10. Close selected dormitories.
11. Increase tuition and other fees.

As the faculty and administrators filed out of the auditorium after Brown's speech, much grumbling was heard. The faculty were particularly upset about the prospect of an increase in their teaching load. They were most upset, however, that they would have nothing to say about the matter. Some threatened to campaign to form a union. The administrators, meanwhile, feared for their jobs now more than ever.

Discussion Question

1. How would you describe Delaware University's work environment? Does Delaware University have a future?

Delaware University (B)

It is November 1982, and Brown has had an opportunity to observe the effects of the changes he had made back in 1980. He had done a great deal of speechmaking to student groups, administrators, teachers, and alumni. The speeches were designed to convince the university community of the need for change. Although he gained some converts, he also made some enemies. It took a strong stomach to read some of his "fan mail." If enrollment figures and financial data were accurate indicators, however, he was on the right track. The annual enrollment figures are shown in Table 1.

Brown leaned back in his large plush swivel chair and smiled. He was quite confident that the school's enrollment would continue its upward trend. In fact, he almost knew that the actual enrollment for 1983 through 1988 would exceed the projections given to him by the admissions people. It looked as though they had done a simple trend analysis. As he considered the enrollment report, the buzzer on his phone began to sound.

Brown

[answering the intercom]: Yes, Mrs. Gimble?

Gimble

[on the intercom]: Dr. Principle is on the phone. He sounds really upset. He says he needs to talk to you about Professor Johnson's contract.

Brown

[to Principle]: Peter, Morris here. What's on your mind?

Principle

Well, we have a mess, and I'm not sure how to handle it. In 15 years of administrative work, I have not previously encountered this situation . . .

TABLE 1   Enrollment at Delaware University

Year	Enrollment	Year	Enrollment	Year	Enrollment
1950	9,502	1963	17,051	1976	17,802
1951	9,881	1964	18,400	1977	16,090
1952	10,004	1965	18,862	1978	15,206
1953	9,410	1966	19,010	1979	15,917
1954	10,873	1967	20,540	1980	15,780
1955	11,998	1968	22,324	1981	17,503
1956	12,007	1969	24,970	1982	18,271
1957	11,406	1970	25,267	1983*	19,000
1958	12,961	1971	25,008	1984*	19,758
1959	12,980	1972	25,110	1985*	20,546
1960	13,100	1973	23,429	1986*	21,366
1961	14,080	1974	22,066	1987*	22,218
1962	15,905	1975	20,200	1988*	23,105

Note: These are fall semester figures.
*Projected.

Brown still couldn't believe the story. Long after he'd replaced the receiver in the phone cradle, he sat mumbling in the chair and looked off into space. The large glass windows revealed a beautiful view of the campus, but he didn't see a thing. He went over the details again in his mind.

Harry Johnson was a long-time member of the Delaware University faculty. He joined DU in 1968 as an instructor in the department of educational psychology. Johnson joined the faculty after completing a master's degree and doing advanced graduate work at the University of Southeast Pennsylvania. He has been a mediocre teacher. Yet, he cannot be found when not actually teaching a class. Typically, Johnson received only average performance ratings. In addition, after 13 years with the university, he has only attained the rank of assistant professor.

Johnson and the department chairman, Paul Simpson, had had a number of talks about Johnson's performance. For years, Dr. Simpson had been after Johnson to complete work on his doctorate. Also, Johnson seemed to have absolutely no interest in doing any research or publishing. Simpson assigned Johnson a 15-hour teaching load, after repeated warnings of the seriousness of his disinterest in research, his failure to complete requirements for the doctorate, and unwillingness to interact with students and colleagues. (Most professors had 12-hour loads, and a handful of productive researchers had three classes or a 9-hour teaching requirement.) One reflection of Johnson's perceived value to the department is his salary relative to his colleagues at the same rank. These figures are shown in Table 2.

TABLE 2   Department of Educational Psychology 1981–1982 Assistant Professors' Salaries*

Name	Years at DU	Degree	Last Evaluation†	Salary
Schoen, S. R.	4	PhD	A	$50,528
Sauldsberry, W. A.	5	EdD	B	48,310
Jackson, L. C.	3	EdD	A	48,310
Rogers, G.	5	PhD	B	48,218
George, J.	4	PhD	B	48,119
Chamberlain, W. F.	7	MA	B	47,804
Greer, H. E.	3	EdD	B	47,500
Arizin, P. C.	9	MA	B	47,320
Gola, T.	4	MA	A	46,568
Johnson, H. P.	13	PhD	C	46,304
Walker, C. B.	1	PhD	n.a.	46,110

*Does not include fall 1982 raises.
†Grading: A = Excellent; B = Good; C = Fair; n.a. = Not available (new).

According to Simpson, Johnson had threatened to quit at various times but never did so. One day around the end of the summer, Johnson arranged a meeting with Simpson. At the meeting, Johnson demanded that he be promoted and be given a substantial raise—effective immediately. A stunned Simpson was the first to learn that Johnson now had a doctorate in educational psychology. The degree had been conferred upon him during the summer of 1981. His new degree hung in his office. Within three months, Delaware University had received all confirming documentation. (And Johnson's car had on its windshield two parking decals from the school that had granted him his degree; he had, as well, a copy of his transcript and a neatly bound dissertation.) Simpson was suspicious of Johnson's new degree but processed the paperwork for a promotion and raise. Johnson's 1982–83 contract contained a hefty $5,000 raise, and he was now an associate professor.

Things began to fall apart in early October. An anonymous writer sent letters to Dean Principle and the president intimating that Johnson bought his degree.[1] Further, the letters said he had neither enrolled in a course nor visited the campus of the university in question. Principle decided to investigate the matter to determine if the allegation was true. After a few phone calls to the director of the California Department of Education, accrediting agencies, and to the school, the facts surfaced. The degree-granting institution, California Central University,[2] was unaccredited. The school was little more than a mail drop. There was one office, and the school accepted dissertations some of which were below the quality of a high school book report.

The final straw was the article in the *Los Angeles Times*. The article was headlined "Nation's Teachers, School Bosses Get Fake Degrees" and told how people bought their degrees at a local degree mill. Twenty-three recent doctoral degree recipients were identified. On October 14, a similar but broader story headlined, "To Boost Pay, More Teachers 'Buy' Degrees," appeared in *The Wall Street Journal*. This article specifically cited California Central University. It discussed the motivations for those who sought bogus degrees. *The Wall Street Journal* article quoted the head of the National Council for Accreditation of Teacher Education as saying, "Unaccredited institutions conferred 1,390 doctorates in education in 1981, or about 20 percent of all the education doctorates awarded."

---

[1]Schools assume that faculty have *earned* doctorates from accredited universities, but few schools check to confirm this.

[2]This is a pseudonym.

Discussion Question

You are Dr. Brown, president of Delaware University. Dean Principle has asked you to tell him what to do. What should be done about Johnson? What specific options might be considered?

Delaware University (C)

The department of economics and business administration had a problem that many of the other departments would like to have had: how to recruit enough professors to meet the students' demand for business courses. One got the impression of being caught up in a New York City traffic jam when a class period ended at the business building. In the judgment of the department chairperson, Dr. Bill Bass, the building was used at 100 percent capacity for day classes.

Nearly 5,000 students were majoring in a business-related major. Approximately 50 percent of these students were general business administration majors. The remainder were majors in accounting, finance, computer science, distributive education, secretarial science, business education, marketing, economics, and management. In addition, students from other parts of the university, after meeting prerequisites, could take business courses. Some majored in areas outside the business curriculum but had a business minor. In order to provide sufficient coverage for the classes, Bass had relied on adjunct professors from the business community, voluntary paid overloads by full-time tenure-track faculty, and the use of large class sizes. Occasionally, professors looking for a teaching opportunity in the area applied through Principle's office. In recent years, these methods proved increasingly inadequate. Last-minute cancellations of classes had become routine.

After years of fighting with the administration over permission to actively recruit for faculty, Bass received the okay. He submitted small advertisements of faculty positions in the *Chronicle of Higher Education* and the placement rosters of the Academy of Management and the Decision Sciences Institute.[1] In addition, Bass attends two or three regional or national meetings a year. The results of his efforts, however, have been disappointing.

---

[1]The Academy of Management and the Decision Sciences Institute are professional organizations which include large numbers of business teachers.

The following is part of a discussion between the chairman and other members of the economics and business administration faculty that took place at the December department meeting.

Bass: Folks, I want to report the results of our recruiting efforts to date. As you know, we received *curriculum vitae* from 10 applicants. Of this group, three lacked the required educational requirements or experience. After the screening process, the top three candidates were invited to the campus . . .

Greer: Excuse me, Bill. Have you received any other vitae? What happened on the offer letters we sent out?

Bass: The answer to the first question is yes, Hal. We have other vitae but, given the cost of inviting people and the low offer acceptance rate, we have to be selective about who we invite.

Gola: What do you mean "low offer acceptance"?

Bass: Tom, we decided against offering a position to Angelo Karuzi, since he was nowhere near completing his degree. As for Sally Moulton and Chico Fernandez, both were offered, but both turned us down. They spoke positively about their visit with us. They were not specific enough about why they accepted other offers. Sally took a position at Kent State where she will teach courses in the administrative sciences department. I know Buddy Myers offered her $46,100. This offer is in line with ours of $45,900. Chico went to Cincinnati. George Grean signed him on at $46,850, about $200 less than we offered.

Sauldsberry: Bill, what you are saying suggests money is not the real problem. If money is not the problem, what is?

Bass: Actually, Woody, I'm not dismissing the possibility that money is a factor. These are only two cases. We do know that some problems along those lines have developed in the past. Unfortunately, I learned, after the fact, that my counterparts have been less than candid when discussing salary offers. We chairpersons in this region meet periodically to discuss common problems, but some are offering more money to faculty applicants than they are telling me. Let me pass out a copy of the letter from Chico Fernandez. Please drop me a note giving me your thoughts as to why we are getting so many turndowns.

After the meeting, Bill Bass spotted J. R. Grimes, a department member, standing by the door. Bass asked Grimes to stop in to see him because he had something to discuss.

The following is an excerpt from the conversation that took place between Grimes and Bass in the department chairman's office shortly after the department meeting:

Bass: I'll get right to the point, J.R. During your four, almost five, years here, you have done a fine job for me. I'd bet lots of money that you'll be promoted to associate professor without any problems. Sally Moulton, as you know,

EXHIBIT 1   Letter from Sally Moulton

Dear Dr. Bass:

I want to thank you for allowing me the opportunity to be considered for a position at Delaware University. It was a pleasure to see the campus and meet with students, administrators, and faculty members. After much deliberation, I have decided not to accept your offer. My decision, however, does not reflect negatively on your department or the university. In fact, were it not for the actions and comments of one person, I might have agreed to come there despite your salary offer being substantially below most other offers. I have accepted a position at Kent State University where I will teach production and operations management courses.

As for the one person I alluded to earlier, Dr. James Grimes was a real irritant. He came across as being very sexist. He did not ask me anything about my academic credentials, made derogatory remarks about my "status-of-women type dissertation," and he repeated throughout the interview many of the stereotypes about women in management. This part of our interview I tolerated because this has happened before. What happened next was new. He bombarded me with questions about my marital status, plans for children, level of commitment to a career, location of my parents, and so forth. He wanted to know what responsibility the school should have in the event a pregnancy occurred, and he wondered aloud if I can handle today's students. Dr. Grimes stated his belief that women should not take men's jobs; and, if they do, the women should be paid less, since they are not primary breadwinners.

I tell you, I strongly resented his remarks. On a number of grounds, his comments were inappropriate. First, men would not be asked questions about children, pregnancy, and ability to handle a class. Career commitment would not be challenged nor would the other myths be stated as fact. For example, many women *are* primary breadwinners. I want to be paid on the basis of the market. Next to accounting and computer science, teachers of production and operations management courses are in highest demand.

This letter was not sent to threaten you. I plan no sex discrimination suit. I merely want you to be aware of a problem. Hopefully, this situation will be avoided in the future.

Sincerely,

Sally P. Moulton

Sally P. Moulton
Teaching Assistant

turned us down. She also called me recently to explain why. According to her, you are the major reason for her decision . . .

Grimes: What! Wait a minute. I didn't do or say anything to her. What did she claim, sexual harassment?

Bass: Hold on, J.R. No such claims were made. She did not claim you made any advances at all. She did claim that you are a sexist, however, and that you asked her personal questions that you would not have asked male candidates. Do you recall doing this?

Grimes: No, I don't. I tried to be nice to her, and this is the thanks I get. If anything, I may have been a little protective. I just kind of treated her like I would want my wife treated. Heck, I opened every door in the place for her!

Bass: Some of your comments worry me, J.R. You should treat all candidates—black or white, male or female, exactly the same—as professional colleagues. Here is a copy of the letter she sent me. (See Exhibit 1.)

After concluding his meeting with Grimes, Bass spent the next two hours talking to other faculty and staff. A great deal of what he found out seemed consistent with Sally Moulton's comments. A discussion with Gwen Miller, a senior and recipient of the Outstanding Student in Business Award, only reinforced what he suspected. Miller said she sought out J.R. for advice about résumé preparation and the job market. Among other things, she was told to put her résumé on pink paper to "show her femininity" and the bulk of the time was spent inquiring about family plans and telling her of the mismatch (for women) between demands of a career and home.

Discussion questions:

1. You are Bass. You have received virtually no feedback from department members about how to attract more faculty to the school. You are to meet with the dean tomorrow to discuss this problem. What might be done to overcome the recruiting problem? (Be specific about the actions you'd like to take.)
2. What should be done about Moulton's allegations concerning Grimes?

---

6 *Marcus A. Foster Medical Center (A)*

The Marcus A. Foster Medical Center is located on Mt. Airy Avenue in the Germantown section of Philadelphia, not far from the original "stomping grounds" of the now famous Dr. Bill Cosby. The center, one of three such centers located strategically around the city, is named after another important black Philadelphian, the late Dr. Marcus A. Foster. Foster served as superintendent of schools in Philadelphia and later in Oakland, California. The center is nationally known for the treatment of and research on childrens' illnesses, including sudden infant mortality syndrome (crib death).

One early morning in June 1988, Margie Stoker got a "wake up call" from her supervisor, Paul Adams. Hearing from Paul at 6:30 A.M. was *not* a good sign. Margie is an assistant administrator at Marcus A. Foster Medical Center. She has worked with Paul for four years. Paul, since taking over as administrator, has worked hard to place the medical center on a sound financial basis. That task was not an easy one since most of the medical center's patients came from the surrounding community. This section of Philadelphia consists of working-class people who, out of necessity, live on a week-to-week basis. Large families are the rule and jobs are often hard to find. Many of the jobs found require limited skills, pay little, and offer little security. Benefits for employees are sparse.

An hour and a half after Margie's call from Paul, she sat in a staff meeting. Stella Harvey and Bob Bryan, both assistant administrators, were there. Paul wanted some answers. He made it clear that the center had a pressing problem that had to be resolved now! He explained how frustrated he had become. Robert Grayson, the center's controller and chief financial officer, told him about the large number of uncollectible hospital bills. The post office was returning bills addressed to former patients. These individuals had received treatment in the hospital's emergency room. The bills came back stamped "Return to sender—incorrect address." On average, the post office returned 48 such bills each week. These bills represented 11 percent of those mailed. Grayson speculated that the cause of the problem was either incomplete or inaccurate histories on the emergency room registration forms. He believed these problems led to incorrect mailing addresses. Sometimes, the name which appeared on the report was correct, but the street address was incorrect; sometimes numbers were not transcribed carefully. Grayson set the hospital losses at $3,744 per week or $194,688 per year. As Grayson explained, these figures assume an average charge of about $78 a visit. He mentioned that there are wide variations in per-patient costs. The cause: treatments vary from treating a cut finger, bee stings, to overcoming broken bones, bad falls, or acute appendicitis. Severe injuries and sickness become inpatient visits rather than emergency room (e.g., a gunshot wound, stroke, or heart attack). It is not uncommon to write off two thirds of the emergency room treatment costs but Grayson was concerned that poor record-keeping may be costing the center a great deal more.

Paul and John were considering several options. One idea was to conduct a traditional training program. This program would emphasize the importance of the report to the medical center and teach the clerks how to fill out the report completely and accurately. A second thought was to replace the clerks. The clerks earn about $208 per week and have been at the medical center an average of three years. A third option considered is to conduct a systems analysis that would show why the clerks' performance was below standard.

There had to be an economical solution that would guarantee improved on-the-job performance and reduce the number of uncollectibles. Robert Grayson suggested two other alternatives. The center should only treat those who can show proof of their ability to pay (unless the situation is "life-threatening"). As a last resort, if all other bottom-line solutions fail, Robert says close the emergency room. Stella commented that the clerks may not be the problem. Bob said he hoped the medical center would never close the emergency room. After the meeting, Paul told them that he wanted solutions to the problem "yesterday." They all wondered what the center should do.

Discussion Questions

1. What are the problems in this case?
2. What action(s) should the medical center staff take?

Marcus A. Foster Medical Center (B)

As John put down the phone, he recalled the actions taken to overcome the collections problem. He thought that he finally had the emergency room out of his hair. The phone call suggested otherwise. He had just finished talking to Stella Harvey, the medical center's director of nursing and the center's risk management officer, Marjorie Murphy. Stella informed John that she had just fired Mrs. Betty Frink. Betty has worked as a nurse at the medical center since 1987.

Mrs. Frink is an active 63-year-old widow, who by all accounts is in excellent health. Her co-workers described her as "sharp as a tack, good with patients, and a hard worker." However, Stella says Betty has one small problem. In taking medical histories from patients she simply doesn't always listen or she fails to list information regarding allergies to certain medications on the registration form. She had been fortunate in the past. Doctors and other nurses prevented at least three previous near disasters where she obtained the medical history. These patients might have died or become seriously ill if given certain medications not noted on the chart. In a recent scare, a staff nurse gave a sulfa drug to a distressed patient who had a bladder infection. The patient returned to the hospital three hours later looking bloated and suffering from respiratory problems. The patient claimed he had told Betty that he was allergic to sulfa drugs. This fact was not listed on the chart. After each near miss Betty received counseling. John remembered that about seven months ago Stella had mentioned "a problem with Betty" but Stella did not elaborate at that time. He gave Stella's comment little thought and did not explore with her the nature of Betty's problem. Now John wishes that he had probed more deeply into the situation.

Margie Stoker, the assistant administrator, met with Betty for her exit interview before Betty left the center. Margie asked Betty the usual questions about her experiences with the center. Margie explained the medical center's policies and told Betty that the medical center would quickly issue a check to her. The check would cover pay for regular hours, severance, and earned vacation. Betty did not know that Margie and Stella had reached an important agreement. Since Betty was a senior citizen, the hospital would not challenge her claim for unemployment compensation if she applied. In fact, Stella wished that Betty had had the opportunity to resign. Rather than make that offer she decided to end the termination interview without adding a new complication.

Discussion Questions

1. Was the decision to fire Betty an appropriate one?
2. How should this situation have been handled? Explain your answer carefully.

Marcus A. Foster Medical Center (C)

Paul Adams stared blankly out the window. He and the top administrators had just concluded a stormy staff meeting. The staff disagreed loudly when he came to the "Cynthia Hamilton problem." Bob and Stella believe Paul made the wrong decision. Robert sided with Paul in his decision regarding Hamilton. Ms. Hamilton applied recently for the position of switchboard operator. Over the years, Paul had handled a number of unusual personnel situations but this one required all the resources at his command.

About a week ago, Cynthia Hamilton showed up at the medical center's personnel office. Normally, a walk-in candidate attracts little attention from anyone on the hospital staff but this was not so for Cynthia. Cynthia and her dog came in together. Upon reporting to the personnel office, she stated her desire to apply for the position of switchboard operator. The position, she learned from a friend, was advertised in the *Philadelphia Daily News*. Cynthia informed the personnel receptionist, Ms. Helen Porter, that she was fully qualified for the position. The skeptical receptionist called Paul on the phone to explain the situation. Paul, after meeting with Cynthia briefly, confirmed that Cynthia was legally blind. He refused to have her tested for the job and he saw no need to interview her. He took personal responsibility for the rejection of her application. He felt bad about going over Margie Stoker's head on this one. As personnel director, the decision was Margie's to make. However, Paul felt certain that only a sighted person could operate the switchboard and hospital emergency signals.

Cynthia did not say a word. She immediately left the premises. Now, Cynthia's quick, silent departure is causing Paul some anxiety. Was this a test case of some kind? He acted swiftly and decisively. He can't imagine that anyone with significant vision loss could do the job. Also, he felt that if she could do the job, the medical center would have to pay for some tremendously expensive accommodations. Rather than be saddled with that cost, he'd rather not hire her. Margie later gave him a piece of her mind about making "personnel decisions." Although he thinks he can smooth Margie's ruffled feathers, something about this one continues to gnaw at him.

Discussion Questions

1. What are the problems in this case?
2. Tell what actions you would take in solving these problems and avoiding the problems in the future.

---

7 *John Young Enterprises*

John Young is owner and chief executive officer of John Young Enterprises, Cleveland, Ohio. John Young Enterprises (JYE) is a small firm that provides security guards and other protective services. It has been in business for 23 years.

JYE has grown rapidly from a 5-man, rather loose-knit informal group into today's 486-employee company. JYE's major thrust is in the area of providing security guards for department stores, shopping malls, and a number of businesses in downtown Cleveland. In addition to this work, JYE furnishes security guard assistance for special events, such as athletic events, rock concerts, and musical programs. The most glamorous aspect of the business is its role as bodyguards to certain celebrities. In recent months, the firm provided protection for Bill Cosby, Barbra Streisand, Rod Stewart, Dollie Parton, Muhammad Ali, and former President Jimmy Carter.

John Young has thoroughly enjoyed watching his firm grow and prosper. He and his brother James (both former police officers) thought that they could carve out a niche for themselves by starting a security service. John and James had diligently saved money from their pay. John conceived the idea while attending a basketball game in Fort Wayne, Indiana. The old Fort Wayne Pistons played at the Coliseum there. He had traveled to Defiance, Ohio, to see his younger brother, Leroy. It was Leroy's idea to go to Fort Wayne. Leroy's only disappointment is his own son's disinterest in the business. Arthur is in medical school. Paul worked for the firm for five years and then quit. James's boys—Ted, Mathew, and Charles—tried the firm but have long since left it. Ted joined an architectural firm, Mathew is a stockbroker, and Charles is a drifter, living off the land. The family nicknamed him "Odd Job." At last report, he was living in Portland.

THE PROBLEM

When John hung up the phone, the words that he had heard fully registered. He was being sued, but he did not know whether to first call a personnel specialist or an attorney. No one had ever sued him over the use of lie detectors for preemployment purposes. During his 10 years as a police officer he had never heard of anyone filing a complaint against the department over its requirement that police recruit applicants pass a lie detector test. He remembered that written tests caused several problems, so he did not rely on them. John believes military or police experience, good character, the absence of a criminal record, and being at least 21 years of age are the significant factors to consider.

James Hamilton, the attorney, had spoken on behalf of his client, David Raskin. David had been rejected for the position of armed prison guard. The basic reason for the decision was the polygraphist's judgment that Raskin had given a number of deceptive responses to the questions asked. The questions asked on the examination are shown in Exhibit 1.

EXHIBIT 1   Security Officer Polygraph Examination

Arrangements

At your request, *David W. Raskin* (applicant) was administered a polygraph examination on *August 6, 1984* (date), for the purpose of verifying the applicant's employment application data and background information.

Procedure

Standard polygraph procedure was employed throughout the entire examination.

Questions Reviewed During Examination

Relevant issues pertaining to this examination were reviewed with the applicant as indicated by below test questions and responses.

1. Have you ever represented yourself to be anyone other than

   _____ .
2. Did you knowingly omit requested information from your questionnaire?
3. Did you submit information on your questionnaire which you know to be false?
4. Did you deliberately lie to your oral board?
5. Have you listed all of your regular employment?
6. Have you deliberately concealed any of your past employment?
7. Have you been asked to resign from any place of employment?
8. Have you ever been dismissed from any place of employment?
9. Have you ever quit a job because you thought you were going to be fired?
10. Have you deliberately concealed the true reason for leaving previous jobs?
11. Have you stolen any property from previous employers?
12. Have you stolen any money from previous employers?

1. Have you ever had any property repossessed?
2. Have you ever had any bills turned over to a collection agency?
3. Have you ever intentionally written a bad check?
4. Have you ever deliberately falsified any credit application?
5. Have you ever had any gambling debts?
6. Have you ever concealed any financial obligations you presently have?
7. Are you presently delinquent in payments on any financial obligations you have?

EXHIBIT 1 *Continued*

8. Have you ever had a court action taken against you in financial matters?

---

1. Have you ever used any form of narcotics without a legally signed doctor's prescription?
2. Have you ever smoked marijuana?
3. Have you ever illegally purchased any form of narcotics?
4. Have you ever illegally sold any form of narcotics?
5. Have you transported, or had in your possession, any form of illegal narcotics?
6. To your knowledge, do any of your relatives use narcotics illegally?
7. To your knowledge, do any of your friends or associates use narcotics illegally?
8. Have you ever experimented with any narcotics (heroin, cocaine, morphine, opium)?
9. Have you ever experimented with any dangerous drugs (barbiturates, amphetamines, speed)?
10. Have you ever experimented with hallucinogens (LSD, peyote, mescaline)?
11. Have you ever smoked hashish?

---

1. Have you ever completed a homosexual act with a male/female?
2. Have you ever solicited a homosexual act with a male/female?
3. Do you feel you have homosexual tendencies?
4. Have you ever accepted pay for the commission of any sex act?
5. Have you ever knowingly had sex relations with a minor female?
6. Have you ever sexually molested a child?
7. Have you ever sexually exhibited yourself in public?
8. Have you ever been a party to an illegal abortion?

---

1. Other than you have listed, have you ever been hospitalized?
2. Have you deliberately given false information about your physical or mental condition?
3. Have you ever had a nervous breakdown?
4. Have you ever had a mental breakdown?
5. Do you feel you have a drinking problem?
6. Have you ever been treated for alcoholism?
7. Have you ever been a patient in a mental institution?
8. Have you ever received psychiatric care or treatment?
9. Have you ever attempted to commit suicide?
10. Do you wear contact lenses?
11. Do you need contact lenses to correct your vision?
12. Did you wear contact lenses when you took your physical examination?

EXHIBIT 1   *Concluded*

---

1. Have you ever been a member of the Communist party?
2. Have you ever been a member of any militant organization?
3. Have you ever participated in any demonstration or riot?
4. Have you made application for the _____ at the order or request of any militant organization?
5. Have you ever engaged in any serious criminal act?
6. Have you ever committed any serious undetected crime?
7. Have you ever accompanied other people while they engaged in any serious criminal act?
8. Other than you have listed, have you ever been arrested?
9. Would the police solve any crimes if you told them all you know about a certain incident?

Conclusion

After careful analysis of the applicant's polygraphs and based on the physiological reactions indicated, it is the opinion of this examiner that:

_____ a. This applicant has told substantially the complete truth during the examination.

_____ b. Applicant has not told the complete truth and declined to give any information which may resolve deceptive responses.

_____ c. Applicant did not tell the complete truth but did give the following information regarding:

_____ d. Examination was inconclusive due to emotional, physiological inadequacies and is not rescheduled for testing.

_____ e. Results on this examination are inconclusive. Subject is scheduled to be retested on _____ .

Respectfully submitted,

_____
Polygraphist

Hamilton raised a number of objections. First, he claimed that lie detector tests are misnomers. That is, they don't measure whether someone lies. At best they measure physiological reactions. Such reactions, he believed, could be caused by nerves as well as by various medical conditions. According to some research studies, the accuracy rate is only 50 percent—with a built-in bias against the truthful or honest person. In fact, Hamilton cited a report by the American Civil Liberties

Union (ACLU) that termed lie detector tests "a form of 20th-century witchcraft." He also questioned the ability of unqualified polygraphists to interpret the results. His final comment to Young was a quote Hamilton attributed to former President Nixon: "Listen, I don't know anything about polygraphs, and I don't know how accurate they are. But I do know that they'll scare the hell out of people." Young turned these ideas over in his mind. He was concerned about adverse publicity and a lost lawsuit. He did know that he never coerced applicants or employees into taking the polygraph. All polygraph takers complete the same form. (See Exhibit 2.)

As Young thought about the polygraph problem, something else connected in his mind. This was the second personnel headache he had confronted this month. Bobby Scofield had complained bitterly about his inability to review his personnel file. Bobby left the office screaming about his right to privacy and access to employment records. Young had asked Cheryl Miller, his assistant, to look into the matter. When she reported back to him she cited four federal laws: the Privacy Act of 1974, the Family Education Rights and Privacy Act, Fair Credit and Reporting Act, and the Freedom of Information Act. He wasn't convinced that these federal laws hindered him in any way. He could not believe that the federal government would meddle with a company's personnel file policies and procedures.

When Cheryl reported to John about the federal statutes, she also mentioned something that she felt was most important concerning the Bobby Scofield incident. Bobby had applied for a supervisory position at a firm near his home in Akron. (Although he liked working for John Young Enterprises, he had grown tired of the bumper-to-bumper commute to Cleveland each day.) Everything was going fine until the Akron company called JYE to verify his employment. Bobby assumed the firm would state dates of employment and last position held. To Bobby's chagrin, other information was provided. Salary history, promotional recommendations, performance appraisal data, and information on disciplinary matters was shared with the prospective employer. The release of these sensitive data without his permission and his inability to clarify or challenge the accuracy of information on disciplinary matters is what angered Bobby. According to Cheryl, Bobby claimed that other companies, such as IBM, allow employees to see their records and to change their records when inaccuracies are discovered.

John leaned back in his chair and wondered about these problems. He pondered his next move but he also wondered what he might do to avoid these types of problems in the future.

EXHIBIT 2   Polygraph Consent Form

John Young Enterprises

I do hereby give my consent to a pre-employment polygraph examination (more commonly known as lie detector) to be administered by Joseph W. Spelman, certified polygrapher, on (date) _August 6, 1984_. I have been made aware that polygraph attachments must be made to my body and do give my consent to having the necessary attachments made. I understand that the examination is to be concerned with (subject of exam) _the validity of my work history statements, conduct in previous positions and certain disqualifying personal behavior._ and the only questions that will be asked me during any portion of the examination will be discussed with me and approved by me prior to the test. I understand that an audio tape-recording is being made of the entire test, including my discussions with the examiner before and after the actual testing, and that I may obtain a copy of that recording, at my own expense, at any time within three months from the present date. I hereby authorize the examiner to communicate the results of the examination to the requestor:

John Young Enterprises.

_____
(Witness)

David W. Raskin
(Signature of Respondent)

_____
(Witness)

Discussion Questions

1. Evaluate John Young Enterprises' use of the polygraph. What are the legal implications of utilizing polygraph examinations as a selection device?
2. Which state or federal laws provide guidance as to the legal use of the polygraph?
3. Do employees have a right to read and copy the contents of their personnel file? Explain and support your answer.
4. Do employees have the right to deny third parties access to information related to their present or previous employment? Explain.

Section D

Career Management, Evaluation, and Training

1 Forest Park Corporation (A)

During the past 10 years, Forest Park Corporation has grown from a small, relatively obscure chemical company into a diversified multinational corporation, with net sales topping the $2 billion mark. Net earnings and stockholders' equity have improved markedly during the period. Over the 10-year time span, the number of employees has increased from 13,000 to 27,000. The company has diversified into leather goods, medical instruments, pharmaceuticals, plastics, textiles, and various chemical products. Furthermore, as dramatic as this growth has been, Forest Park expects the trend to continue for at least five more years.

To a large extent, the success of Forest Park can be attributed to Don Rogers, Forest Park's director of employee relations. A neatly dressed, athletic-looking man of 46, Don had come to Forest Park 21 years ago and began with the company immediately after earning his MBA at Washington University. He was considered an outstanding problem solver; his biggest asset, his talent at solving complex problems, had won him recognition, increased responsibility, and rapid promotion. Everyone knew that it was his staffing, development, and training programs that had enabled the company to survive and flourish during 10 years of rapid growing pains. Since becoming director, however, staffing and development were no longer his major responsibility. He now was responsible for the big picture. This morning's employee relations managers meeting made it pretty clear that he'd better get involved in staffing and development again—and fast.

Don sat gazing thoughtfully out the window of his office on the 20th floor. A tugboat churned up the Mississippi River, passing within shout-

---

This case was prepared by Professor George E. Stevens, of the University of Central Florida, and R. Penny Marquette of the University of Akron.

ing distance of Saint Louis's Gateway Arch. In his hand was Cathie Stango's file, thrust there a minute ago by Bob Pelzer, manager of employee planning. The file had been the central exhibit at the morning's weekly meeting with the professional employee relations staff.

Don had initiated the weekly meetings, and, in the past, they'd been extremely productive. Those who attended the meetings are listed in the partial organization chart (see Exhibit 1). New ideas were frequently generated, enabling the employee relations group to serve the needs of the organization better. This morning's meeting had *not* been productive. Bob had blown his stack right there in front of everyone. Don had always thought of Bob as a level-headed professional. Either he'd been wrong, or the situation was really serious.

A knock at the door quickly brought Don back to the present.

"Come in. . . . Yes, Karen?"

"Don, Bob stopped by just now and left this envelope for you."

"Thanks, Karen; that's all for now." Don opened the envelope and found a long handwritten note. He hoped it would explain this morning's outburst. He began reading.

Don, I'm sorry I blew up at this morning's meeting, but we have a *serious* problem. We pride ourselves on recruiting the best people we can, and, over the past few years, we've had lots of employees involved in our tuition aid program. The program has permitted many of them to earn bachelor's and master's degrees going to school at night.

EXHIBIT 1   Partial Organization Chart for Forest Park Corporation

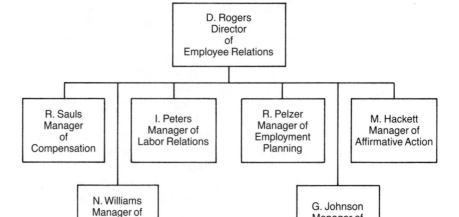

Only dedicated, highly motivated people are successful in earning degrees while working full time. It's a tremendous strain on the employee, his manager, and his family. It isn't exactly cheap for the company, either. Last year we spent *$200,000* on tuition aid. In most regards, the money has been well spent, but in too many cases, there's no payoff for the company and it's our own fault.

Cathie Stango quit the company today. As far as I'm concerned, it was the straw that broke the camel's back. She's been a member of the general bookkeeping department for nine years, working as a clerk. Her goal was to become an accountant in one of the accounting or finance departments. She's earned straight As at the University of Missouri, and it's been a whole year since she got her bachelor's in accounting, yet no one has promoted her!

I'm supposed to be responsible for the manpower planning system, and *I* didn't know about her. The system simply doesn't contain a method for identifying all the people in the organization who are promotable. Right now we're relying on four sources to identify potential talent: (1) We are conducting interviews with the recruiting department staff, initiated by employees. These interviews are exploratory in nature, designed to find out about the employees' interests and qualifications. (2) The computer system theoretically provides us the name, location, present job, and educational background of each employee. Unfortunately, lots of people are missed because the data are often incomplete or out of date. (3) Departments that have openings may suggest the names of people they know about who are promotable. Obviously, this is a narrow and usually inequitable source of information. (4) We often have had contact with good candidates through our own activities. The problem here is that most of these contacts are at headquarters, excluding people located at our other 16 domestic locations.

The point I'm trying to make is that we know about the jobs, but we don't know where the candidates are. This problem is especially infuriating where tuition aid participants are concerned because of our investment in their education. If we can't find a solution quickly, we should just discontinue the program. It's been in operation for 10 years now and it simply hasn't paid off.

Rogers reread the memo. The story seemed even more difficult to believe when he examined Cathie's file. Her performance was consistently rated superior to outstanding, her attendance record was excellent, her potential for promotion was rated high. It had taken her eight years of night school and summer school to acquire her accounting degree, and the company had paid for every penny of it. Now she was gone, doubtless bitter toward the company for not promoting her, and the company had lost a large dollar investment in her education. Where, he asked himself, had the company failed?

He reached for the phone and dialed Bob. "Bob, this is Don. I've read your memo and you're right. This is serious. How many more cases are there like this one? . . . 22 *this year!* You'd better bring me the details on all the employees who've left. I'd like to have them and any other

EXHIBIT 2

PERIODIC EMPLOYEE EVALUATION FORM

Name _Catherine Stango_

Position _Bookkeeping Clerk III_

Department _General Bookkeeping_

	Poor						Outstanding
Attendance	1	2	3	4	5	6	(7)
Attitude	1	2	3	4	5	6	(7)
Productivity	1	2	3	4	5	(6)	7
Promotability	1	2	3	4	5	6	(7)
Leadership Quality	1	2	3	4	(5)	6	7
Ability to Learn New Jobs and Tasks	1	2	3	4	5	(6)	7

Comments:

Cathie has just completed her bachelor's degree in accounting. As much as I hate to lose her, I can't recommend her too highly for promotion.

Employee's Signature _Catherine Stango_ Date _1/4/82_

Supervisor's Signature _James Truman_ Date _1/2/82_

ROUTING: Original - Employee's File Personnel Department
          Pink - Departmental File
          Yellow - Employee

EXHIBIT 3   Participants Who Left

Name	Minority Classification	Job Classification and Department where Employed	Degree Earned	Our Equivalent for the New Job Taken outside Forest Park (If Known)
1. Selma White	Female	Administration/secretary III	BS, management	Management trainee
2. George Sayer	n.a.*	Data processing/programmer I	MS, data processing	Programmer IV
3. Sondra Dreft	Female	Marketing research/clerk typist III	BS, statistics	Market analyst I
4. Manuel Diaz	Spanish American	Maintenance/janitor III	BS, data processing	Programmer I
5. Roger Ernst	Black	Payroll/bookkeeping clerk II	BS, chemical engineering	Chemist
6. Rita Little	Black/female	Data processing/receptionist	Proficiency certificate—keypunch operator I	Keypunch operator I
7. Linda Arthur	Female	Marketing research/secretary II	BS, Mathematics	Unknown
8. Samuel Brown	n.a.*	Data processing/programmer IV	MBA	Systems analyst II
9. John Smiley	n.a.*	Retail marketing/commission salesman	MBA	Assistant to the director of marketing—division level
10. Lee Arrowsmith	Native American	Transportation/vehicle maintenance worker III	BS	Unknown
11. Livingston Cooper	Black	Data processing/keypunch operator I	Proficiency certificate—computer operator	Computer operator II

EXHIBIT 3 *Concluded*

Name	Minority Classification	Job Classification and Department where Employed	Degree Earned	Our Equivalent for the New Job Taken outside Forest Park (If Known)
12. Sarah Elims	Female	Steno pool/clerk typist II	Proficiency certificate—typing and shorthand	Secretary II
13. Roberta Dicks	Female	Marketing research/secretary II	BS, marketing	Unknown
14. Jose Rodriguez	Spanish American	Generic drugs research/lab technician II	BS, accounting	Staff accountant
15. Lloyd Sanders	Black	Receiving/shipping clerk I	BS, management	Unknown
16. Gloria Atlas	Black/female	Data processing/clerk typist I	BS, data processing	Programmer I
17. Arlene Dailey	Female	Cafeteria/food service clerk II	Proficiency certificate—typing and shorthand	Secretary III
18. Carol Singleton	Female	Marketing research/market analyst I	MS, statistics	Market analyst III
19. Jack Grinlin	n.a.*	Mail room/general clerk III	BS, management	Mail room supervisor
20. Ada Winston	Female	Accounts payable/bookkeeping clerk II	BS, accounting	Staff accountant
21. Sally Donner	Black/female	Legal/general clerk III	BS, home economics	Dietician
22. Lester Ridgeway	n.a.*	Advertising/general clerk II	Proficiency certificate—laboratory technology	Unknown
23. Catherine Stango	Female	General bookkeeping/bookkeeping clerk IV	BS, accounting	Staff accountant

*n.a. = Not applicable.

supporting information you can provide. I'll be meeting with the vice presidents at 4 P.M. today and I'd like to present them with a strategy to overcome this problem." (Exhibit 2 is a copy of Cathie Stango's Employee Evaluation form; Exhibit 3 gives information on employees who had received tuition aid but had left the company because they had not been promoted.)

Discussion Questions

1. What are the key problems?
2. How would you rate Bob's performance?
3. Should the tuition aid program be discontinued?
4. Devise a plan to identify promotable people and ensure that promotions are filled, from within, in an equitable fashion, whenever possible.
5. Do the data in the appendix indicate any special problems needing attention? What can be done about them?

2 *Performance Appraisal: The Case of the Second Evaluation*

Marcus Singh is an economist in the city of Rock Falls Department of Human Resources and Economic Development. He is 40 years old and has worked for the city of Rock Falls for the past 10 years. During that time, Marcus has been perceived by his supervisors as being an above average performer, although no formal evaluations have ever been done in his department. About 10 months ago he was transferred from the department's industrial development unit to the newly formed Office of Research and Evaluation. Other employees also were transferred as part of an overall reorganization in the department. The organizational chart for the department is depicted in Exhibit 1.

Out of concern for equal employment opportunity, the department director, Victor Popelmill, recently issued a directive to all of the unit heads to formally evaluate the performance of their subordinates. Attached to his memorandum was a copy of a new performance appraisal form to be used in conducting the evaluations. Garth Fryer, head of the

Prepared by Professor James G. Pesek, and Dean Joseph P. Grunenwald, both of Clarion University of Pennsylvania.

EXHIBIT 1   City of Rock Falls
Department of Human Resources and Economic Development—Organizational Chart

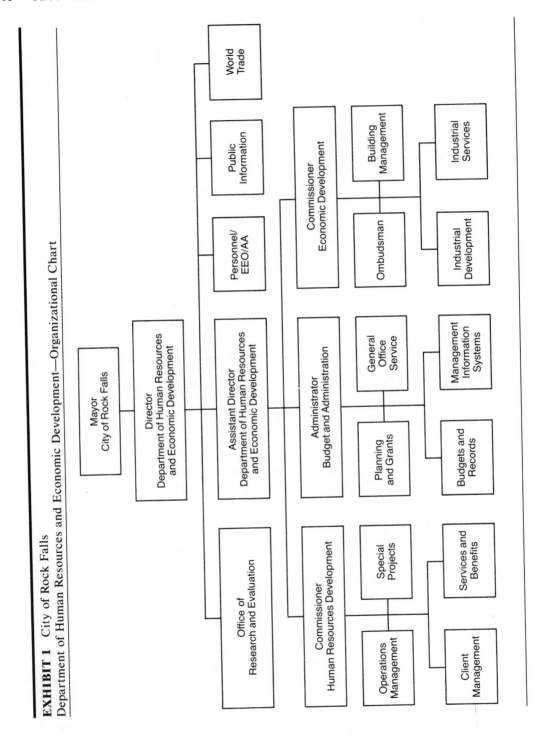

Office of Research and Evaluation, decided to allow his subordinates to have some input in the evaluation process. (In addition to Garth Fryer, the Office of Research and Evaluation was comprised of two researchers, Marcus Singh and Jason Taft, and one secretary, Connie Millar.) He told both of his researchers to complete a self-appraisal and a peer appraisal for the other researcher. After reviewing both the peer and self-appraisals, Garth completed the final and official appraisal of each researcher. Before sending the appraisal forms to Mr. Popelmill's office, Mr. Fryer met with each employee individually for the purpose of reviewing and explaining his ratings to the employee. Each employee signed his evaluation and indicated that he agreed with the ratings.

About one week after submitting the evaluations to the department director, Mr. Fryer received a memorandum from Mr. Popelmill stating that his evaluations of subordinates were unacceptable. Mr. Fryer was not the only unit head to receive this memorandum. In fact, all unit heads received the same note. Upon close examination of the completed appraisal forms from the various departments, the director noticed that not one employee was given a "fair" or "satisfactory" mark in any category. In fact, the vast majority of the employees were rated as outstanding in every category. Mr. Popelmill felt that his unit heads were too lenient and his purpose was to have the department heads redo the evaluations in a more objective and critical manner.

Garth Fryer explained the director's request to his subordinates and proceeded to ask them to redo their self- and peer appraisals with the idea of being more objective this time. Once again, after reviewing his subordinate's appraisals, Garth formulated his ratings and discussed them individually with each employee.

Mr. Singh was not pleased at all when he found out that his supervisor had rated him one level lower on each category. (Compare Exhibit 2 and Exhibit 3.) Although Marcus signed the second evaluation form, he clearly indicated on the form that he did not agree with the evaluation. Jason Taft, the other researcher in the Office of Research and Evaluation, received all outstanding ratings on his second evaluation. Like Mr. Singh, Jason has a master's degree in economics, but has been working for the city of Rock Falls for less than two years and is only 24 years old. Mr. Taft also worked closely with Garth Fryer before being transferred to his new assignment 10 months ago. Recently, the mayor of the city received a letter from the regional director of a major government agency praising Mr. Taft's and Mr. Fryer's outstanding research.

Although Jason and Garth are white and Marcus is a naturalized U.S. citizen from India, Marcus' working relationship with them and others in the department was good. On some occasions, though, he found himself in awkward disagreements with his co-workers in areas where he held strong opinions.

EXHIBIT 2 Employee Evaluation Form

Employee Name: Marcus Singh _____   Date: October 4, 1985

Job Title: ___Economist/Researcher_____

Please indicate your evaluation of the employee in each category by placing a check mark ( ) in the appropriate block.

	Outstanding	Good	Satisfactory	Fair	Unsatisfactory
KNOWLEDGE OF JOB Assess overall knowledge of duties and responsibilities of current job.	☑	☐	☐	☐	☐
QUANTITY OF WORK Assess the volume of work under normal conditions.	☐	☑	☐	☐	☐
QUALITY OF WORK Assess the neatness, accuracy, & effectiveness of work.	☐	☑	☐	☐	☐
COOPERATION Assess ability & willingness to work with peers, superiors, & subordinates.	☐	☑	☐	☐	☐
INITIATIVE Assess willingness to seek greater responsibilities & knowledge. Self-starting.	☐	☑	☐	☐	☐
ATTENDANCE Assess reliability with respect to attendance habits.	☑	☐	☐	☐	☐
ATTITUDE Assess disposition & level of enthusiasm. Desire to excel.	☑	☐	☐	☐	☐
JUDGMENT Assess ability to make logical decisions.	☐	☑	☐	☐	☐

Comments on Ratings: Valuable employee! _____
_____
_____
_____

Supervisor's Signature: _Garth Fryer_____   Date: _Oct. 4, 1985_

Department: Office of Research and Evaluation _____

Employee's Signature: _Marcus Singh_____

Does the employee agree with this evaluation? _X_ Yes ____ No

EXHIBIT 3   Employee Evaluation Form

Employee Name: __Marcus Singh__   Date: __October 18, 1985__

Job Title: __Economist/Researcher__

Please indicate your evaluation of the employee in each category by placing a check mark ( ) in the appropriate block.

	Outstanding	Good	Satisfactory	Fair	Unsatisfactory
KNOWLEDGE OF JOB Assess overall knowledge of duties and responsibilities of current job.	☐	☑	☐	☐	☐
QUANTITY OF WORK Assess the volume of work under normal conditions.	☐	☐	☑	☐	☐
QUALITY OF WORK Assess the neatness, accuracy, & effectiveness of work.	☐	☐	☑	☐	☐
COOPERATION Assess ability & willingness to work with peers, superiors, & subordinates.	☐	☐	☑	☐	☐
INITIATIVE Assess willingness to seek greater responsibilities & knowledge. Self-starting.	☐	☐	☑	☐	☐
ATTENDANCE Assess reliability with respect to attendance habits.	☐	☑	☐	☐	☐
ATTITUDE Assess disposition & level of enthusiasm. Desire to excel.	☐	☑	☐	☐	☐
JUDGMENT Assess ability to make logical decisions.	☐	☐	☑	☐	☐

Comments on Ratings: __Marcus needs to increase the quantity of his work to__
__receive higher ratings. Also, he should take a greater initiative in his job.__

Supervisor's Signature: _Garth Fryer_   Date: _Oct. 18, 1985_

Department: __Office of Research and Evaluation__

Employee's Signature: _Marcus Singh_

Does the employee agree with this evaluation? ____ Yes   X No

After Mr. Singh and Mr. Taft had signed the evaluations, Garth forwarded them to Mr. Popelmill's office where they were eventually added to the employee's permanent file. When pay raises were awarded in the department three weeks later, Marcus Singh did not receive a merit raise for the next year. He was told that it was due to his less than outstanding evaluation. He did, however, receive a general increase of $500 which all employees received regardless of their performance evaluation.

Mr. Singh has refused to speak one word to Mr. Fryer since they discussed the evaluation, corresponding only through Ms. Millar or in writing. Marcus has become demotivated and has complained bitterly to his colleagues about his unfair ratings. While Marcus reports to work at 8:00 A.M. sharply and does not leave until 5:00 P.M. each day, he has been observed to spend a lot of time reading newspapers and books while at work.

Discussion Questions

1. What is the problem in this case? Who is to blame?
2. How would you have reacted if you were Marcus Singh?
3. How could this problem been avoided?
4. Critically evaluate the rating form used in this case.
5. What can be done to motivate Mr. Singh?

3 *Performance Evaluation at Western Savings*

Charlene Brown has been a senior teller in the commercial loan department, at the main office of Western Savings and Loan Bank, for the past three years. Charlene and Darla Johnson, supervisor of the department, are both black and very good friends. Darla has recently learned that she is soon to be promoted to loan officer, and has indicated to Charlene that she may be selected to replace her as supervisor of the department.

Terri Burke, who is white, has been a senior teller at one of Western Saving's branch offices for the past five years. Because she had a college degree, longer experience as a commercial loan teller, excellent rapport

Prepared by Willie E. Hopkins and Shirley A. Hopkins, Colorado State University. This case is based on a supervisor's actual experiences; therefore, all names in this case are fictitious.

with co-workers, supervisory and managerial personnel, and customers, and because she exhibited desirable leadership qualities, she was selected to replace Darla as supervisor of the commercial loan department at the main office.

When Terri arrived at the main office she was introduced by Darla to her staff, which consisted of four senior tellers and one unfilled position. Darla began to show Terri all of the duties she was expected to fulfill as the new department supervisor. Terri immediately realized that many of the procedures she was familiar with at her branch office were handled differently at the main office, so she proceeded to learn the new procedures.

After a few days in her new position, Terri noticed that Charlene was not very friendly nor cooperative when she (Terri) asked questions concerning procedures. Terri talked to Darla about Charlene's attitude and was informed that Charlene had been hoping to be promoted to department supervisor, and was angry that someone from one of the branch offices had been promoted over her. Terri was concerned about how well Charlene would accept her as a supervisor.

Over the next few weeks Terri noticed that at times Charlene would be joking with the other senior tellers, until she came around. Charlene would then stalk off with a scowl on her face, and the other tellers would look like children caught stealing cookies from the cookie jar. Terri was convinced that Charlene was trying to stir up resentment against her. Terri also learned that Charlene felt that she (Terri) wasn't qualified to be supervisor, because she was always asking questions about how certain things were done in the department. (Terri had been forced to ask questions about transactions, because the procedures at the main office were different from her experience at the branch office. Charlene interpreted Terri's inquiries as lack of knowledge and incompetence instead of adapting to new procedures.) Charlene had been pointing this out to the other tellers, causing them to challenge Terri's authority. Terri felt that Charlene was determined to make her look incompetent so that she would be demoted and Charlene would be promoted to the position "she deserved," that of departmental supervisor.

Terri began to note that Charlene had several unacceptable habits. Charlene was consistently late for work, she had difficulties balancing her teller drawer, and she consistently made errors in figuring interest due on the commercial loans. Terri felt it was important that she talk with Charlene about these problems. Since Terri was inexperienced in these supervisory responsibilities, she talked to the operations manager, Mr. Tunston, about how she should proceed in this matter. Mr. Tunston told Terri that Charlene was a difficult employee, and several supervisors had had problems with her. He recommended that Terri document in Charlene's personnel file the content of their conversation, and what the result was.

After her talk with Mr. Tunston, Terri took Charlene's personnel file with her to study. She was amazed! Mr. Tunston had told her that Charlene was a problem employee, yet all of her performance evaluations were quite high. She had received above average raises, there were no problems documented in her file, and she had been promoted after short periods in her new assignments. Terri didn't understand the large discrepancy between what Mr. Tunston had told her about Charlene and the information she read in Charlene's personnel file. Nevertheless, she proceeded with plans to talk with Charlene.

Terri called Charlene into the conference room the next day. Terri was very nervous; she wanted to handle this well. She didn't have a problem with Charlene being black, Terri's husband was black; she just wanted to understand Charlene and hopefully diffuse the tension between them. Terri began to explain to Charlene that her consistent tardiness and teller errors were not an acceptable performance. She asked Charlene whether there were problems that she could help her with. Charlene was visibly angry but she refused to open up to Terri, she just said that she would do better. Terri tried to show Charlene that she was concerned and wanted to help, but Charlene was intent on not showing any signs of vulnerability. Terri ended the meeting and documented the event as Mr. Tunston had advised her.

A few more weeks passed and Charlene's performance had not improved at all. It was nearing the date for Charlene's performance evaluation. Terri was troubled. She did not want to be unfair to Charlene. She knew that Charlene's personnel file depicted her as a model employee, with the exception of her documented meeting of a few weeks ago. Terri decided that she could not give Charlene an extremely poor evaluation with such little supporting documentation, so she gave her an average evaluation. She mentioned Charlene's poor performance in the comment section, and recommended a small raise. Mr. Tunston supported Terri's evaluation and the raise. Terri was then faced with presenting the performance evaluation to Charlene; she was nervous again.

A one-word description of Charlene's response to the evaluation would be indifference. Terri was concerned because the other senior tellers were showing signs of sympathy with Charlene and greater signs of uncooperativeness toward her. Terri knew that something had to be done about the situation. She talked with a friend, Tina, in personnel and asked for her advice. Tina was well versed in equal employment opportunity laws. She warned Terri to carefully document all conferences and problems with Charlene to protect herself and the bank against any possible discrimination suit. Tina told Terri that a possible problem existed because incidences of poor performance had not been documented in Charlene's personnel file. Tina advised Terri to continue to document any problems she had with Charlene, and if she could convince the operations manager to allow her to place Charlene on probation, to find out from him how it would need to be handled.

Terri began to carefully document all of Charlene's errors. She still wondered why prior performance evaluations indicated that Charlene had been such a model employee until she became her supervisor, and she began to research Charlene's history at the bank in hopes of finding out just what was going on. She researched Charlene's progress from her beginnings as a new loan clerk through operations, to new accounts, and finally a promotion to her present position. Terri found out that Charlene had been a problem employee from day one. It became obvious that her previous supervisors were intimidated by the fact that Charlene was black and they were worried about being accused of racial discrimination; so they gave Charlene good reviews and promoted her to get her "out of their hair," until finally Charlene was moved on to senior teller under Darla. The consensus was that since Darla was also black, Charlene would finally quit causing them problems. This was true until Darla was promoted and Terri, unsuspecting, walked into the problem. Now Terri was forced to handle the problem no one wanted to face: Charlene was incompetent, and there was no documented evidence of this fact.

Several months passed, with the status quo in commercial loans, until Mr. Ring, the assistant operations manager, received a phone call from a preferred customer. Charlene had sent the customer a bill for his loan interest due, and he was calling to tell Mr. Ring that the bill was $620.00 short. Mr. Ring hung up the phone and immediately called Terri to his office. Terri was not surprised, and reminded Mr. Ring of the times she had told him about Charlene's errors. Mr. Ring had always told Terri that Charlene was so nice, that she must just be having a bad day. Mr. Ring rubbed his chin and admitted that perhaps he had been wrong. Terri asked whether he would be willing to support her in placing Charlene on probation. He thought for a few seconds and said yes.

Terri carefully documented the terms of the probation. Charlene was to work in foreign exchange for two months and she was not to be late nor have excessive transaction errors. If she violated her probation she was to be terminated. Charlene was called into the conference room and Terri presented the probation terms. Terri told Charlene that she had tried everything else, and since Charlene persisted in her behavior, drastic measures were required. Charlene seemed a little more concerned than usual, but still refused to talk openly with Terri. The next day Charlene moved over to the foreign exchange position and a new teller, Rachel, took over Charlene's responsibilities.

The days passed, and in spite of Charlene's efforts to meet her probation terms, she continued to make errors. However, Charlene seemed more willing to communicate with Terri, and actually asked for her assistance a time or two, but it was obvious that she was in a job that she was just not able to perform well. Two weeks before Charlene's probation was over, Mr. Tunston retired and an operations manager was brought to the main office from one of the branches. The new operations manager, Jean, had been the operations supervisor who was responsible for hiring Charlene three years earlier.

Jean walked into the main office early Monday morning. Charlene walked in shortly after Jean's arrival and as Charlene saw Jean, a smile flashed across her face; she ran up to Jean and gave her a hug. Later that morning Terri went over to talk to Jean. Terri was apprehensive because she had witnessed the reunion of Jean and Charlene earlier that morning. Terri proceeded to fill Jean in on her department's current status. As she started to leave, Terri sat back down and began to tell Jean about the problems with Charlene. Jean's expression changed, she listened intently to the events of the last year unfolding. When Terri told Jean that Charlene had already violated her probation and would be terminated at the end of the next two weeks, Jean showed signs of concern. Jean told Terri that she didn't want Charlene to be terminated, that she could handle Charlene. Jean said she was going to take Charlene off of probation and talk to her. Terri protested, but Jean was determined to have her way.

Terri was totally disheartened. She had worked for over a year to manage this difficult problem and Jean destroyed everything in one day. Terri also knew that it would be even more difficult to interact with her staff, especially Charlene, now that Jean had undermined her authority. Terri dreaded coming to work the next day. When she arrived, Charlene was back at work in commercial loans and she was even in early. Charlene gave Terri a sneering smile and forced out a "good morning" when she walked into the department. Terri hoped things would not be as bad as she expected, but within a week Charlene was back to her old ways. Terri talked to Jean about Charlene's work, even Mr. Ring talked to Jean about the interest error, but Jean was confident that Charlene could be turned around by her efforts.

Jean continued to talk to Charlene, but her work performance and attitude deteriorated further. After two months of this situation, Jean finally admitted to Terri that perhaps she had been wrong about Charlene. During this time Mr. Ring had been promoted to vice president and moved to an office upstairs. Several more months passed and Charlene continued to make more and more errors. Jean was finally exasperated; she called Terri over to her desk. Jean told Terri that the only way to handle the problem was to get Charlene out of the main office. Jean said she knew of a promotion that would be available on the floater staff. The floater staff was composed of senior tellers who were supposed to be self-motivated, and could be sent to branch offices to cover vacations and leaves of branch personnel.

Jean said that she was going to recommend Charlene for this position. Terri protested and said she didn't think that was the way to handle the problem. Jean said it was the only way. Terri refused to sign the recommendation. So Jean decided to sign it herself. Charlene was delighted. She was sure she would be a supervisor in no time at all. Charlene was finally gone. Terri found that her staff began to work together better. It was even easier to come to work. However, word got back to the main office that Charlene was a disaster at the branches. Mr. Ring heard of the problems and asked Terri why she had recommended Charlene for the promotion. Terri told Mr. Ring that she hadn't recommended Charlene, and she told him about her discussion with Jean. He was very serious and walked away with a strange look on his face. A week later Jean was fired. According to the grapevine, Charlene is still raising havoc at the branches. Terri later left the bank to move to a different state, and has since began a new career. But she has never forgotten the years of trials with Charlene.

Discussion Questions

1. What mistakes did management make in this case?
2. How could these problems have been avoided?
3. What can be done to avoid these problems in the future?

---

4 A Training and Development Problem at Sumerson Manufacturing

George Lewis began working for the Sumerson Manufacturing Company as a human resources department trainee a few days after he received his MBA degree in Management from a large midwestern university. After a one-year training program he served two years as assistant director of training and development in one of Sumerson's large machining and assembly plants. He was promoted to plant director of training and development in which capacity he served for approximately four years. When this assignment ended George was transferred to corporate headquarters as staff assistant to the corporate director of training and development. The corporate director was scheduled for retirement in 25

This case was prepared by Professor James C. Hodgetts of the Fogelman College of Business and Economics at Memphis State University as a basis for class discussion.

months. George hoped to become the next corporate director of training and development but knew this was very much dependent on how well he handled his first major assignment.

Sumerson was planning to open a new plant in 16 months. The new plant was to hire approximately 4,000 employees within three years. However, only one of eight production lines was to go into operation when the plant opened. The other seven would be phased in during the following three years. Construction of the new plant had just started in a small town of 10,000 persons 18 miles south of Memphis, Tennessee. The plant would be very similar to the plant in which George had been director of training and development. George was asked to submit a plan for training the personnel for the new plant. He was given four months to do the job.

Top management had made the decision that personnel from its other 21 plants would be transferred to fill all second-level and higher management positions. For most of these employees this would be a promotion. Also, most nonmanagement employees in the company would be offered jobs in the new plant but few were expected to accept. All frontline management must be trained by Sumerson, not hired "off-the-street."

George had 16 months, including his planning time, to decide how to train a work force of approximately 450 new employees. About 55 to 60 management employees would be transferred to the new plant when it opened. He also had to make plans for training personnel for the expansion of the plant to 4,000 employees by the project's full operations date.

He was not sure what he should do, as this was the first time the company had ever built and staffed a new plant. There was no past experience on which way to go. He decided his first task was to identify his major problems.

Discussion Questions

1. In general, what training must take place prior to the opening of the new plant in 16 months?
2. What training must take place between the time the plant opens and all eight production lines are in operation?
3. How many frontline supervisors had to be trained?
4. How were they to be trained?
5. How many nonmanagement employees had to be trained?
6. In what skill areas must they be trained?
7. How were they to be trained?

5 *The Northeast Health Center*

Angelo Kinicki, the person responsible for all personnel matters at the center, leaned back in his comfortable chair and gazed out the window. His thoughts turned to his stormy meeting with Mrs. Cecilia Gambiccini, the Health Center's best medical records clerk. What could he do?

Until today, his job seemed simple enough. All he had to do was keep the Health Center running smoothly. As administrative services officer of Northeast Health Center, he had responsibility for all administrative matters. After 15 years as a civil servant in Saint Louis's city government, including 10 years at Northeast, he had grown accustomed to handling any kind of problem. He liked the staff here, and he wanted them to like him. Angelo had a special knack for getting the doctors, nurses, specialists, clerical people, and maintenance staff to work as a team. The job, in general, became especially easy when Barb Fisher, his secretary, arrived two years ago. Barb was a super organizer and planner. Performance evaluations were properly scheduled, files were up to date, people were paid on time. There hadn't been a single snafu of this type since she came. Kinicki had thought that the toughest part of his job was the friction caused by just these kinds of snafus. Given this problem with Cecilia, he wasn't so sure.

THE HEALTH CENTER

The Northeast Health Center is one of 12 such centers in metropolitan Saint Louis. The centers were built for the express purpose of serving the health needs of Saint Louisians, particularly those who do not have their own personal physicians. A wide range of services, from inoculations for preschoolers to testing for tuberculosis or venereal disease, are offered at no charge to the people who go to the centers. The Northeast Health Center is quite typical of the other centers. It is located in one of the more densely populated areas of the city. The center serves a large geographical area. People in the area are basically working-class people who have little money with which to meet medical crises.

Dr. Hal Lear, the Health Center director, directs the activities of a 45-member staff. The staff consists of 8 physicians, 15 nurses, 6 medical paraprofessionals, 9 clerical workers, a 6-man maintenance crew, and an administrative services officer. Despite the diversity of this large staff,

All names are disguised.

the center is noted for its warm and friendly environment. Over the years, staff members have worked well together and many employees participate in various activities together after work. Unlike many medical settings, employees have avoided forming cliques on the basis of professional or status differences. One reason for this is the lengthy associations that exist among employees. Most have been at the Health Center for at least five years. Employees know their jobs and go about their duties with little or no direct supervision. Although the daily patient load has steadily risen to a peak of 350 people, each clinic within the center dispatches its patients with uncanny efficiency. When these clinics are opened for business, each unit springs into action. It is usually impossible to tell which of the workers is the supervisor because of the strong team orientation present among staff members. (Exhibit 1 shows the organizational chart of the Northeast Health Center.)

THE CLERICAL STAFF

It takes a lot of people, people of various skills and abilities, to make a health center function smoothly. One such group of people is the clerical workers. Although their task seems rather simple—have the medical records of patients where they are needed when they are needed—accomplishing this objective is often made difficult by doctors who misplace or misfile cases, absentminded technicians, and the boss, Hal Lear, who is known as the case hoarder.

As recently as three months ago, everything ran quite smoothly. Few people had anything negative to say about the clerical unit. Over the years, this group had become the closest, most efficient team of any at the center. Everyone worked to get the job done. There was some play, however. The workers arrived at 8 A.M. each morning, but it was not uncommon to see them on long coffee breaks which concluded at 8:30 A.M. Such long breaks tended to occur on the average of twice a day. People could set their watches by the afternoon coffee break. At exactly 3 P.M., people seemed to gravitate toward the vending machine and employees' lounge area. Around 3:20 P.M., people would begin to quietly excuse themselves. Although an outsider would deem the 50 minutes of time spent on such breaks a total waste, such was not the case. Break time was used to unwind. Except for these two long breaks, people worked hard right through the day. Often workers would pass up lunch to get a patient finished so the patient would miss only a half-day's work. Despite the breaks, the center staff seemed productive. Their motto seemed to be "Work when you are scheduled to work and relax when you are supposed to relax." Also, the mingling of people and their interactions contributed much to the feeling of one big team. Doctors, nurses, and similar high-status people came to respect the opinions and

EXHIBIT 1   The Northeast Health Center

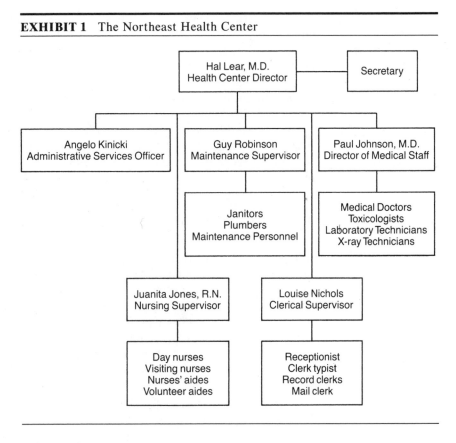

abilities of the "peons" of the center. Such respect carried over into the staff's daily work activities. This situation was often illustrated by the interactions between doctors and clerical workers. Doctors who held on to needed medical records longer than necessary were actually apologetic when their "crime" was discovered. When a search was under way for a particular patient's records, all the center staff members participated. A lot of this effort involved a form of medical detective work, and the clerical staff, based on their knowledge of record-keeping and particular routines the center followed, seldom failed.

On July 3, the entire staff celebrated the good news. Liz Sinclair, one of the best-liked people in the center, was being promoted from her clerical supervisor job to that of administrative services officer of another health center. This was quite an important occasion. Few people in the history of the city had accomplished such a feat. Liz began her career with the city's health department over 16 years ago as a mail clerk. She moved through the clerk, clerk-typist, and secretarial ranks rather quickly. Nine years ago, she passed the test to become a clerical supervisor. Not long after she began her job as clerical supervisor of the Northeast Health Center, she decided to earn a college degree. After eight years of night classes and summer sessions, she triumphantly reached her goal. Shortly after earning her degree, Liz took and passed the administrative services officer (ASO) I test. (The ASO performs the duties of a personnel director.)

Liz was liked for a lot of reasons. One of the reasons was the manner in which she related to other people. She had the respect of all because of her knowledge of the center's operations, skill in relating to others, and a special skill for getting things done through others. She seemed to know just the right technique to use on each person. The clerks loved her. She demanded a lot from them, but she never asked anything that she would not demand of herself. During the past few years, she directed her staff with a light touch. The staff knew the work and the routine. And, having been well trained by Liz, the workers needed little direct supervision. Liz could not remember the last time she had had to discipline anybody. She knew the two daily breaks were long, but her girls really made up for it during the other eight hours of the day. Liz also knew that her superior performance ratings as a supervisor were a true reflection of the kind of quality staff she had. Now, she would be leaving. Her last words to her staff were to enlist their full support for the new supervisor. Liz left feeling confident that the staff would help the new supervisor in every way.

On July 6, Louise Nichols, the new clerical supervisor, reported to Angelo Kinicki, the center's ASO, for her first day of duty. Angelo welcomed Louise warmly and, with little in the way of orientation, proceeded to take her to the clerical staff's work area. Afterward, he returned to his office where he decided to look over her personnel file. In reading through the file, he discovered that she had worked six years in city government. Louise had quickly risen through the ranks in a minimum amount of time. Her test score on the supervisor's examination was a 99, the highest score he had ever seen. Her work as a clerk and clerk-typist was consistently superior. According to her supervisors, Louise was viewed as meticulous, dedicated, hardworking, and intelligent but a perfectionist to an extreme.

THE MEETING

Five months had passed since Louise first arrived at Northeast. Although Angelo had not formally met with her to conduct her probationary performance review, he assumed that all was well. He had planned to talk with other staff members before conducting the formal performance review. This review, he realized, would be extremely important because passing grades would mean she now had permanent status as a clerical supervisor. As Angelo contemplated this decision, he heard a commotion outside his office door. The intercom crackled.

"Angelo, Angelo!" It was Barb. There was the sound of urgency in her voice.

"Yes, Barb, what's the matter?"

"Angelo, Cecilia, I mean Mrs. Gambiccini, is here to see you and she's practically in tears."

"Well, send her on in so I can find out what in the world is going on all of a sudden."

Cecilia complained about her new supervisor. Louise was driving everyone crazy. First, Louise wanted everyone to explain to her what their duties were, and she made everyone write new job descriptions. The new ones were out of date. She was brown-nosing the doctors but treating everyone else like dirt. People could not go to the bathroom without her timing them. The clerical staff was not allowed to talk at the desk or fraternize with patients. The final straw was her "law" that coffee breaks were limited to two 15-minute breaks. According to Cecilia, Louise had a way of making life miserable for everyone.

After Cecilia left, Angelo began to check out her allegations. One by one, each was proven to be true. He could not believe it! The more he asked about her, the less he liked what he heard. Why hadn't anyone talked to him? Suddenly something occurred to him. Four of his clerks had transferred out in the last four months. He had assumed that they just wanted a change of scenery. He had not conducted exit interviews before, but maybe now he should. As he sat back, he tried to determine what he should do.

Discussion Questions

1. How would you describe the Northeast Health Center?
2. Could anything have been done to prevent the friction caused by Louise Nichols?
3. Describe the management styles of the two clerical supervisors (Louise Nichols and Liz Sinclair). How did they differ?
4. If you were Angelo Kinicki, what would you do? Why?

Management and Development

1 How Do You Evaluate Your Employee Appraisal Program?

The Hackney Paper Box Company is having trouble deciding what should be done about its employee evaluation program. Hackney operates 46 corrugated box factories located from Maine to California and has a highly centralized corporate personnel department in New York City. Each plant employs about 125 persons.

The company policy in the Hackney Company allows a junior employee to be promoted over a senior employee if the junior employee has "noticeably" better qualifications for the job. In the South Bend plant a junior employee was promoted to a combiner operator job over an employee, Bob Peller, with more experience as a combiner 1st helper and two more years of seniority. They went to court. The company correctly contended that the senior employee was not responsible, was lazy, not cooperative, not very bright, and had a horrible attendance record. During the court hearing the attorney for Bob Peller produced copies of all the past employee evaluation forms for his client. These forms were prepared by Bob's immediate supervisors over the past 10 years, the time Peller had been an employee. On a scale of one to five he was rated (4) above average or (5) excellent in all categories on every evaluation instrument. Bob Peller won the court case, was promoted with back pay, and now the company has to have a qualified operator stay with Peller at all times in order to get the job done.

The above-mentioned situation caused Mr. Green, corporate vice president of personnel, to call a meeting of selected plant personnel managers, the corporate compensation manager, and the corporate

---

This case was prepared by Professor James C. Hodgetts of Memphis State University and is intended to be used as a teaching device rather than to show correct or incorrect methods of operations.

training and development manager. The purpose of the meeting was to decide what was to be done about the existing employee evaluation program.

This meeting produced four suggestions that Mr. Green is considering. They are as follows:

1. Junk the employee evaluation program.
2. Substitute Management by Objectives (MBO) for the present evaluation program.
3. Have the personnel manager at each plant do the evaluation and conduct the evaluation interview that follows evaluation.
4. Leave the program as it is but give every supervisor adequate training in employee evaluation and evaluation interviewing.

The idea to junk the program was advanced by the personnel manager at the South Bend plant. He contended that supervisory personnel were not qualified to evaluate or counsel. He also contended that they would only rate a subordinate high, as it was much easier to discuss this kind of rating with the subordinate. In addition to this, if an employee was rated low, the supervisor had to determine and explain to the employee how he could improve. This took effort.

The MBO suggestion was made by a new plant personnel manager who had been transferred to the position from outside the personnel field. He admitted that he didn't know much about MBO but he had heard lots of good things about it.

The suggestion to have the personnel manager do the evaluation and counseling came from a plant personnel manager who had a master's degree in psychology as well as considerable plant experience both as a production supervisor and hourly paid employee. He thought this would work at Hackney as all the plants were small, having approximately 125 employees each.

The suggestion to keep the present evaluation system and train the supervisors in evaluation and evaluation counseling was made by the corporate director of training and development.

Mr. Green is currently trying to decide which suggestion is best or if there is a still better solution.

Discussion Questions

1. What are the personnel problems in this case?
2. What should Mr. Green do? Explain.

2 *The Delta Electronics Corporation*

BACKGROUND

The Delta Electronics Corporation is a large national organization with a chain of company-owned retail stores specializing in the sale of small electrical home appliances. The company has enjoyed tremendous growth over the last decade, penetrating new market areas with store openings at a rapid pace. Corporate sales increases have averaged 17 percent for each of the last six years. Store locations range from large metropolitan areas to small cities in rural settings.

Delta's growth has provided many advancement opportunities for young, aggressive managers who are strongly sales oriented. Promotion is fairly typical of a large retail organization. When an individual is hired as a managerial candidate, he or she enters a training program, which consists of learning store operations, gaining product knowledge, and becoming familiar with company policies and procedures. Most of one's time in the program is spent in personal selling. Promotion to the position of store manager is contingent on mastery of unit operations and achievement of a strong sales record.

Once one has become a store manager, advancement to a larger store is based on effectiveness in increasing sales and profits. After successful performance as a store manager and several years' experience, one may be considered for the position of district manager. Further advancement to the regional or divisional level follows a similar process. Delta's organizational structure is shown in Exhibit 1.

Promotion from within is rigidly observed at Delta Electronics. Upper-level management adheres to the "old school," where employees start at the bottom and work their way up "through the ranks." One's formal education is secondary; performance is what counts.

A NEW EMPLOYEE

As Bob Allan was completing his last semester in the MBA program at Ivy State University, he became seriously interested in taking a job with Delta Electronics. From his research on the firm and his discussions with company officials, Bob learned of the fast growth of the organiza-

---

This case was prepared by Thomas R. Miller, James M. Todd, and Edward A. Mueller of Memphis State University.

EXHIBIT 1   Partial Organization Chart for the Delta Electronics Corporation

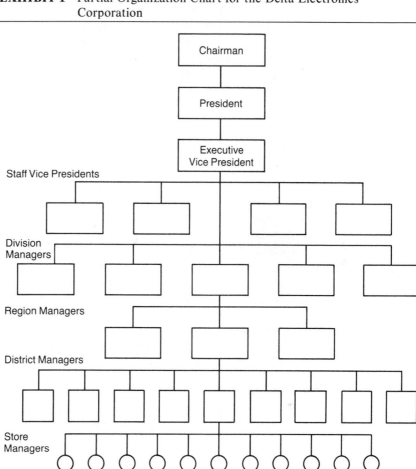

tion and saw an unusual opportunity to rapidly advance his managerial career. Although he was aware of Delta's policy of employees starting at the bottom and working up, he was not discouraged by it. In fact, Bob felt that his educational background would help him progress quickly since most of his direct competition did not have college degrees. After much deliberation, Bob joined Delta. Within only one month a manager's position became available in a small store in Eagleton, a nearby city, and Bob was selected for the position. Although he had had little experience with the firm, his ability and accomplishments were quickly recognized by Delta's management.

Bob's exceptional performance as a store manager was soon apparent to both his superiors and peers. Often other store managers would call to ask for advice or help. Thus, it surprised no one when Bob was promoted to district manager after only two years with the corporation. Rather than be faced with the customary transfer, Bob persuaded his regional manager, John Frederick, to assign him the open district manager position in the same district where Bob was a store manager.

CHANGES IN MANAGEMENT

Soon after Bob's promotion, several major shifts occurred in management personnel. The major change affecting Bob was John Frederick's promotion to division manager from his regional manager position. John had been a friend as well as a boss, and Bob regretted his leaving but was happy that John had moved up. Bob's new regional manager was George Stewart, who had been transferred from the West Coast division and was relatively unknown in his new area.

After a few months working with George, Bob realized that John and George were very different kinds of managers. However, corporate management apparently thought their differences would complement each other. John had been successful as a manager by playing "by the book" adhering closely to corporate policies and procedures. In contrast, George's approach was looser and less straightforward. He was not opposed to bending a rule here and there or even breaking it if he thought it would be to his advantage. Whereas John had always been open and direct in his dealings, George was less vocal with his opinions and appraisals. Initially, Bob felt that the skepticism shown by store managers toward George was normal. After all, isn't any change of management viewed with caution or suspicion? However, even months later, he still heard comments from the other managers, such as "George is hard to get to know" or "I just don't know where I stand with him."

DEVELOPING PROBLEMS

During the same period that these changes occurred in corporate management, another important development took place. Over the past decade, Delta had grown so rapidly that companywide sales increases of 20 percent per year had become common. Sales growth had always been strong, because general economic conditions had never before been a major limiting factor for Delta. Now, for the first time, sales in existing stores were on the decline, and new markets for outlets were increasingly harder to find. Bob, along with the other district managers in his region, was deeply concerned. The major emphasis at Delta had always been on sales. Now, instead of reporting healthy revenue increases, most of the district managers had sales that were either the same or worse than the previous year. The bad news was no secret, for every week a sales report was sent to each district manager from the home office. The report showed sales for the current week and month compared to the same figures for the previous year. The decline was widespread throughout the company and put considerable pressure on the sales organization.

Although sales were down in his district, Bob felt they would compare favorably with sales in other districts. In fact, when Bob became a district manager, his district was dead last out of nine in percentage of sales increase. One year later, with overall sales declining, Bob's district had risen to third out of nine in sales increase. Nevertheless, it was at this time that Bob was removed as a district manager and, reluctantly, became a store manager in the district again. Bob was surprised when John and George confronted him with the news, but he was even more surprised at the vague reasons he was given. He was told that under his leadership "the district was not working as a team" and that "new managers had not developed quickly enough." George even expressed skepticism that Bob may have been "too smart" for the job. However, no reasons pertaining to measurable performance were given.

The new district manager, Butch Lawson, came from the same area of Delta as had George. Indeed, it was well known that, before his promotion and transfer, George had hired and worked with Butch. George made it clear to the store managers that Butch was "strict and tough and would expect at least 110 percent." Soon after Butch took over the district, the store managers knew he did things differently. He was in favor of working around rules, not by them, and he had stated to the managers that they were "too straight for their own good."

Butch had some ingenious, but indiscreet, methods of improving his district's performance. His favorite piece of advice involved "slightly falsifying" insurance claims. For example, he would advise any store manager who might have a leaky roof to make sure that some merchandise was damaged even if by only one drop of water. Then the store could have a big "water damage sale," sell the merchandise at half price or less to move it quickly, and file an insurance claim for the entire value of the items. Thus, a store manager could increase both sales and profits at the same time. If a store front window should be broken in the middle of the night, that provided an additional opportunity for the "enterprising" manager. Usually, only a few hundred dollars of merchandise was displayed in such a window. However, after one such break-in, the store manager filed an insurance claim for over $8,000 at retail! This incident was known throughout the district. Butch personally assisted in preparation of the insurance claim for the store manager just to make certain it was done "right."

Store employees were uncertain, to say the least, about participating in some of these activities. Butch would try to get them actively involved in the misdeeds to ensure that they would remain "discreet." After a break-in at one store, he asked the employees if they needed a stereo system. He explained that now would be the time to get it and to go ahead and pick one out. No one took up his offer.

With the low level of sales in general over recent months, store managers were discouraged and morale had been suffering. Now, some were even more disturbed to see not only unethical but sometimes criminal actions being tolerated and even encouraged.

After Butch had been district manager for six months, his performance was not better than Bob's in many areas, and in some cases it was worse. Butch was under increasing pressure from above to show an improvement over Bob's performance of the previous year. George, the regional manager, visited the area to talk with Bob, his former district manager, about the situation. During their meeting George stated his belief that one of Butch's main problems was the store managers' continued loyalty to Bob. George felt that these relationships made Butch's job more difficult, and the implication was strong that Bob was turning the store managers against Butch. George suggested that Butch probably could achieve a higher level of performance in the district if Bob were not around. Bob was shocked and indignant at this indictment by George, and he remarked that any problems that Butch experienced were of his own making.

BOB'S DILEMMA

Within a few weeks after Bob's meeting with George, Bob was offered an assignment to manage the largest store in George's region at Lincoln City, which is in another district. George explained that everyone's interests would be served by Bob's taking a new assignment. The store was in a regional shopping mall in a prime location, and the sales and profit potentials were great. Success in this store could mean another district manager's job for Bob. Bob's new boss would be Al Barnhart, a newly promoted district manager who had worked with George for several years. Al had extended his welcome to Bob to join the district.

Several thoughts flashed through Bob's head. The sales commissions and bonus at the Lincoln City store could be fantastic. The prospect of the district manager position was even more attractive. But what would it be like working in another district under George's control? Would Al Barnhart "operate" like Butch? What if he didn't accept this assignment? Could he reasonably stay put under the present conditions? Or should he get out now and give up his comfortable income and three and a half years with the company? What should he do? What can he do? What will his wife, Barbara, think?

George said he must have Bob's answer by the end of the day.

Discussion Questions

1. What problems does the Delta Electronics Corporation face?
2. What course of action should Bob choose?

3 *State Insurance Company*

State Insurance Company has its headquarters located in the Ohio Valley. The organization consists of a main office and 60 branch offices. The insurance company does most of its business in the automobile sector, with a marginal amount of life insurance being sold.

The organization was formed in the mid-1940s, with a rapid growth throughout the area. Branch offices were located in major cities that were growing rapidly in the mid-60s through the mid-70s. Each branch office is headed by a manager with supporting personnel below him (see Exhibit 1). The claims manager is responsible for all claims that are handled by his adjusters. If there are any serious customer problems that an adjuster cannot handle, it is up to the manager to resolve them. Each office has at least 5 to 7 adjusters, with a maximum of 11 adjusters, depending on the size of the territory assigned. The peak of the claims for each office is experienced in the winter months. The level of claims drops significantly during the summer months.

The normal routine of an adjuster is to spend the first half of the day in the office processing claims and contacting clients who will be called on in the afternoons. Adjusters usually leave the office around noon to go out on the road to settle claims. The sales manager has between 20 and 25 full-time salesmen and a handful of part-time salesmen. It is a practice to promote within the company to a sales position. Each salesman is paid on a straight commission basis. Depending on the skill of the salesmen, they enjoy substantial rewards for their work. The com-

---

This case was prepared by Robert S. Burns, University of Central Florida, under the supervision of Professor George E. Stevens.

EXHIBIT 1

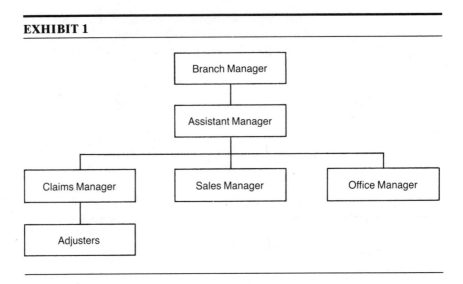

pany has strict codes of ethics and rules that each salesman has to follow to keep his job.

The office manager is responsible for the secretarial staff, office clerks, and tour agents. All hiring was done through the main office. Whenever any help was needed, a request would be sent to the branch manager and then to the main office. The bulk of all training and development was done at the main office with little, if any, at the branch. The office manager would only adjust hours to be worked by the staff at each branch.

The company has an extensive benefit package for its employees. The package includes school tuition and dental and health insurance, as well as a generous pension program. The productivity of its employees is quite high, with compensation serving as a prime motivator.

Rich Watson was hired by the company in 1975. Prior to working at the insurance company, he had attended various trade schools studying automobile repair. After completing school, he served in the military for three years. After the service, he worked as a master mechanic at various dealerships in the area.

When Rich was interviewed by the company, his interviewers were impressed by his mechanical knowledge, which is a key asset for any claims adjuster. When he was hired, he went through an extensive training program that lasted for six months. Each adjuster had to attend a certain number of hours in auto class. Rich, however, was exempt from the classes. After the six-month training program was over, each person was given a review to determine if he was going to be retained and if he was judged to determine merit pay. The pay was determined by the performance of the trainee. Rich received the largest increase in the company's history.

After the training period, Rich was assigned to a branch for a six-month field training program. The branch where he was assigned was close to home, which helped reduce his driving expenses. The main branch was an hour away from his home. The branch manager, Bill Foster, was the one who talked Rich into interviewing with the company. Rich and Bill knew each other through family connections, and they played cards together on Friday nights.

Bill assigned Rich to a senior adjuster position under the claims manager, Jim Moore. Jim knew of Rich's impressive record and decided to be his coach for the six months. Jim was a good coach and an efficient claims manager who had no desire to progress further in the company. Jim was able to give Rich an extensive field training program, exposing him to many different situations.

Rich was at Bill's branch for five years. During that time he encountered very few problems there. As time went by, he began to notice that very few people were being promoted to claims manager. The offices were expanding but the managerial staff remained the same size. Rich and Bill attended many social functions together, and their wives belonged to the same social clubs. Rich did not want to damage his relationship with his boss, so he did not discuss the matter with him.

In 1981, Rich was interviewed for a claims adjuster position at another branch 60 miles north of Bill's branch. Rich decided to apply for the open position at the smaller branch with hopes of moving into a claims manager position. The interview was conducted at the main office with the personnel director and Harry Hanna, branch manager. After an extensive interview, Rich was given the job.

That following Monday, Rich reported to the Port Huron branch, which was 120 miles from the main office. Harry and Rich spent most of the morning discussing how things were done at the branch. At the Port Huron branch, because of distance, little contact was made with the main office. Harry managed the branch in such a manner that few problems would occur. Only when there was a case that could not be solved would the main branch be informed. Harry had been with the company for many years. That seniority gave him a great deal of autonomy in operating his branch. Although Harry was considering retirement, he was reluctant to give up the office.

During Rich's two-year stay at the office, he seldom talked with Harry. Rich was performing his duties with extreme professionalism and received high ratings on his evaluations from the claims manager, who sent the evaluations to the personnel department in the main office. Salary increases were given semiannually. He was rewarded generously. Rich considered himself to be doing quite well for his stay with the company.

The company posted a listing of jobs that had opened up in the company. State Insurance Company made it a policy to promote from within. To be considered for a position, a recommendation had to be given from the branch managers. Rich decided to apply for a claims manager position. He went to his claims supervisor for a recommendation, who would, in turn, get a letter from the branch manager.

When Rich returned to his office the next day, he learned that Harry Hanna would not write him a letter of recommendation. After discussing the matter with his claims manager, he learned that Harry did not want to lose Rich. After many attempts to secure a position as claims manager, Rich became quite concerned about his possibilities of being promoted. He was making a good salary and had use of a company car. Rich decided he would call his former boss to see if he could give him any insight. That afternoon, Rich returned to the office after having been on the road so he could talk to his former boss, Bill Foster. Rich decided he would talk to Harry before he consulted Bill. Rich went to his office to see Harry, but to his surprise he was not there. Rich then decided he would talk to Harry's secretary to find out when he would return.

Rich could not believe what he had just been told. He was quite upset with the news that he learned from Ruth. The conversation went as follows:

Rich

Ruth, have you seen Mr. Hanna this afternoon?

Ruth

No. Don't you know what he does in the afternoon hours?

Rich

No. I am on the road in the afternoons trying to get my work done so it does not pile up too high. It seems I am getting the worst claims of all the other adjusters. I have to do my work, as well as help the other adjusters because they lack the knowledge and experience.

Ruth

Rich, I think it is time someone lets you know what he does in the afternoons. Mr. Hanna likes to golf in the afternoons and usually leaves the office about a half hour after all the adjusters go on the road. Tom has to do all of Mr. Hanna's work, as well as his own duties of assistant manager. The reason he doesn't want to lose you through a promotion or transfer is due to your expertise. If he lets one of his people out of the branch, the main office might find out what is happening up here. He did promote two other people because, I think, they played golf with him.

Rich

When I first came here I was wondering why Hanna talked so much about his golf game. He asked me if I played golf. I laughed and said I didn't care for the sport. Now it is clear to me why I haven't been promoted. This branch is so far away from the main office that no word gets back about what is really happening up here. I am going to call Jim and talk to him to see what I should do.

Ruth

Rich, don't rock the boat. It has been this way for a long time.

Rich went back to his office, sat down, and looked at his phone, contemplating his next move.

Discussion Questions

1. You are Rich Watson. What would you do now?
2. Should the main office continue the practice of a branch manager recommendation to be promoted?
3. If you are manager from another branch, would you help to change the Port Huron branch manager?
4. What changes should be made in terms of the evaluation program of the personnel department?

Compensation and Benefits

1 Jergins Department Store (A)

Jergins is a well-recognized retail department store operating nearly 50 stores in various cities throughout the Southeast. By decentralizing its operations, Jergins focuses its attention on customer service. Management at the store level is responsible for supplying merchandise and services which reflect the tastes and needs of its local community. Each local store's management team consists of a general store manager, several department buyers, and department managers. (Job descriptions for these positions are shown in Exhibit 1.)

Mr. Harvey Hampton is the general store manager of Jergins' Coral Gables store. Harvey has been with the company for 14 years, all spent in the Miami area Jergins' stores. He began as a salesclerk in the shoe department of the downtown Miami store. Later, Harvey became the men's department manager there. He rapidly rose through the ranks. Harvey was promoted to department buyer and then quickly to the general store manager at the Coral Gables store.

Mr. Hampton believes that in order to best serve the customer, you must begin with good salesclerks. He attempts to maintain a "one big happy family" atmosphere. This is attempted despite the fact that there are some 70 employees at the Coral Gables store. As is the case in most retail stores, many of the store's employees are part-timers. This fills the company's needs for flexible schedules and is usually well suited to local students seeking employment. Fortunately, the store never lacks for employees because of the close proximity of the University of Miami. One such student, Bruce Stillwell, was hired four years ago by Mr. Bill Johnson, the men's department buyer. Over the past nine months some things have changed. Both Bruce and Mr. Johnson have

This case was prepared by Professor George E. Stevens and Mark E. Nugent, University of Central Florida.

EXHIBIT 1   Selected Job Descriptions

Store Positions

General store manager.   Responsible for effective and efficient operation of the local store. Reviews departmental performance and staff support positions. Interfaces with the community and acts as figurehead in representing the company.

Department buyer.   Responsible for locating, acquiring, and selling goods desired by the community. Directly responsible for staffing and operations within assigned department. Frequently travels to buying shows and must deal directly with various vendors. Must also coordinate advertising with other local stores and make arrangements with local media. May be responsible for opening and closing store on a rotating basis.

Department manager.   Responsible for day-to-day operation of department including weekly scheduling of salesclerks. Must maintain sufficient salesclerk coverage on the sales floor at all times. May be responsible for opening and closing store on a rotating basis. Must maintain accurate inventory counts. Keep records of all merchandise sold at prices other than that at which it was originally marked (markdowns). Must effectively display currently advertised merchandise in high traffic areas. May also be required to maintain some level of selling record.

Sales clerk.   Responsible for meeting the customer and providing selection assistance where possible. Must effectively use the cash register and be able to correctly handle money.

---

noticed a shift in attitudes. The family atmosphere, which Mr. Hampton now is trying to develop storewide, no longer prevails in the men's department.

For Bruce, the part-time job he had had now expanded well beyond the responsibilities of a part-time salesclerk. As a current student at the local university, he had hoped to maintain a balance between his schoolwork and a job that was not too demanding. Unfortunately, the store was doing extremely well and there was a need for hardworking, dedicated employees who would not only work during the regular Monday–Friday schedule but would also be available for Saturday assignments. The burden of additional hours and increased responsibility threatened his ability to maintain an acceptable grade point average *and* perform well at work.

In January of 1990 Bruce felt really tired. He sat down and figured out just how many hours he had devoted to the store. Over the period of August 1989 until December 1989, he discovered, he had been working an average of 50 to 55 hours a week. No wonder he had to drop those two finance classes during the fall semester! Bruce knew that the problem was directly attributable to the fact that the men's department had been without a replacement for the manager. During the period cited above, the manager's duties were performed almost entirely by Bruce and another salesclerk. He went to Mr. Hampton asking for either a promotion to department manager or reduction in hours but Mr. Hampton refused. Mr. Hampton told Bruce that they needed him badly but a replacement manager would be assigned. Mr. Hampton conceded that he could get all the student help they wanted but they could not always get *reliable* workers. When Bruce continued to badger him, Mr. Hampton told the department's buyer to make Bruce understand that the store could require Bruce to work as many hours as it wished. When Bruce continued to complain, the buyer gave him a big surprise. He terminated Bruce right in mid-complaint one day. Bruce wanted to file a complaint with someone or some agency—he did not care whom. No one should be required to work excessive hours, even with pay! Bruce believed that overtime should be voluntary.

Discussion Questions

1. Who's correct regarding overtime?
2. What recourse does an employee have if he/she feels that he/she is being required to work too many hours?

2 Karl Ranston's Problem (A)

Karl Ranston was supervisor of respiratory therapy at Silvertown Municipal Hospital, located in a community of 11,000. Though he worked at the local hospital, Ranston was paid and actually employed by Breathing Care Services, Inc., a contract company providing respiratory therapy personnel and equipment to hospitals nationwide. Breathing Care Services' headquarters was in Boston, Massachusetts.

Ranston reported to Russ Bilderford, area manager. Bilderford was in charge of overseeing Breathing Care's contracts with hospitals in the northern part of the state.

When Ranston began working in Silvertown on December 28, 1988, two full-time certified respiratory therapy technicians reported to him.

Prepared by Professor Margaret F. Karsten, University of Wisconsin—Platteville. Copyright © 1989, Professor Karsten.

Karl was a working supervisor. Besides performing administrative duties, he gave patients various types of breathing treatments, obtained blood gas samples, set up respirators as needed, and performed many other tasks that a registered respiratory therapist would do. Karl estimated that he spent 75 to 80 percent of his time on nonsupervisory activities.

Ranston had an undergraduate chemistry degree from a state university in Minnesota. Having worked as an orderly and a respiratory therapy aide while going through school, he decided to pursue a career in health care. He was accepted in a two-year respiratory therapy program affiliated with the Mayo Clinic in Rochester, Minnesota. Shortly after finishing this program, he passed an exam to become a registered respiratory therapist.

Karl liked his job at Silvertown Municipal Hospital. Things went well until March 1989 when Gloria Bowman, a respiratory therapy technician, resigned. Russ Bilderford said that he could not authorize Karl to hire a replacement. This meant that Karl probably would have to work more overtime hours, for which he was not compensated. Being an amiable sort and dedicated to his job as well, Karl didn't mind working overtime occasionally. Whenever a patient had to be put on a respirator, which was about once a month, Karl could expect to work around 70 hours a week. He thought that was somewhat excessive, given his salary that averaged slightly more than $9.00 an hour. At that rate, with no overtime pay, the technician reporting to him could easily take home more money than he did. When Karl talked to his boss about these concerns, Russ just shrugged his shoulders and said, "You're a salaried employee. That means we don't have to pay you for overtime hours. You're expected to work overtime."

In June 1989, Karl Ranston received a promotion of sorts. Silvertown Municipal Hospital recently had affiliated with Leadville Municipal Hospital. Ranston now was in charge of respiratory care in both hospitals. The new organization chart for the combined respiratory care department is shown in Exhibit 1.

Ranston continued to perform nonsupervisory duties 75 to 80 percent of the time. He did not receive a raise and still worked many overtime hours, because his department now had to serve two separate facilities.

Karl again tried to discuss his compensation concerns with Russ. It soon became obvious that Bilderford didn't want to hear about the problem.

Since no help from his boss was forthcoming, Karl decided to call his friend, Fran Magan, who taught personnel courses at Silvertown State University. He thought she might be able to give him some advice. She suggested that he become familiar with a law called the Fair Labor Standards Act and lent him a book explaining that law.

EXHIBIT 1 Organization Chart

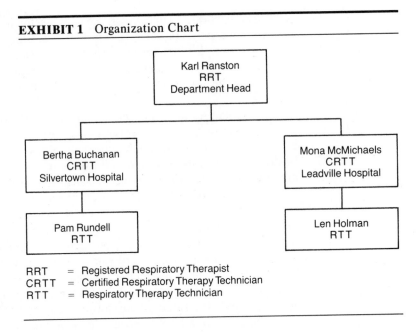

RRT = Registered Respiratory Therapist
CRTT = Certified Respiratory Therapy Technician
RTT = Respiratory Therapy Technician

Discussion Questions

1. What are the issues in this case?
2. Explain, in detail, the parts of the Fair Labor Standards Act with which Karl must become familiar. (What does Karl need to know?)
3. Critique Russ Bilderford's statement, "You're a salaried employee. That means we don't have to pay you overtime."
4. What should Karl do now?

Karl Ranston's Problem (B)

After studying the Fair Labor Standards Act, Karl still was unsure about whether or not he was legally entitled to overtime. Some of the examples in the book Fran lent him just didn't seem to apply in his situation. One helpful item he did find was the address of the nearest office of the Wage and Hour Division of the U.S. Department of Labor. He wrote a letter to that office, and was asked to complete an *Employ*

Prepared by Professor Margaret F. Karsten, University of Wisconsin—Platteville. Copyright © 1989, Professor Karsten.

EXHIBIT 1

U.S. DEPARTMENT OF LABOR   Employment Standards Administration
Wage and Hours Division

Date: May 23, 1990
Reply to Attn of: Dolores A. Bern
                  (212) 264-5221
Subject: Visit by Wage and Hour Compliance Officer

To: Breathing Care Services, Inc.   Scheduled visit to begin:
      c/o Silvertown Municipal Hospital   Date: June 14, 1990
      1000 11th Street   Tuesday
      Silvertown, CA 96435   Time: 8:30 a.m.

The Wage and Hour Division is responsible for the administration and enforcement of a number of Federal laws involving labor standards as outlined
in the enclosed pamphlet "The Wage and Hour Representative Is Here."

   This is to advise you that I will call at your establishment on the date and
at the time shown above to determine compliance with the labor standards
laws which may apply to your business. Every effort will be made to conduct
this assignment expeditiously and with a minimum of inconvenience to you
and your employees. Please note that I will initially need to meet with someone regarding the background of your business (including annual dollar volume of your business and pay practices). Subsequently I will need to review
payrolls and time records for all your employees for the previous two years
from the date of my visit.

   If you or your designated representative or the records mentioned above
will not be available on the date and at the time and place indicated above,
please let me know as soon as possible so that we can work out some other
arrangement. Likewise, since it may be necessary for me to return on subsequent days in that week and/or the next few weeks to finish my check, it is
essential that you notify me at 264-5221 should you have potential time conflicts. Please prepare a list of your current employees showing the following
information:

Name   Address   Phone No.   Birthdate   Starting Date   Job Function
Pay Rate

Sincerely,

Compliance Officer

---

ment Information Form (Exhibit 2, pp. 124–25). As a result of his action,
Compliance Officer Dolores A. Bern was sent to investigate Breathing
Care Services, Inc.'s operations at Silvertown and Leadville Municipal
Hospitals. (See Exhibit 1.) After the investigation, Karl was asked to
provide Dolores with a copy of his job description and a list of hours

EXHIBIT 2   Employment Information Form

U.S. DEPARTMENT OF LABOR EMPLOYMENT STANDARDS ADMINISTRATION WAGE AND HOUR DIVISION	EMPLOYMENT INFORMATION FORM

This report is authorized by Section 11 of the Fair Labor Standards Act. While you are not required to respond, submission of this information is necessary for the Division to schedule any compliance action. Your identity will be kept confidential to the maximum extent possible under existing law.

1.   PERSON SUBMITTING INFORMATION

A. Name (Print first name, middle initial, and last name)

Mr.   Karl Ranston
Miss
Mrs.

B. Date   May 31, 1983

C. Telephone number
(Or no. where you
can be reached)   (214) 843-9435

D. Address (Number, Street, Apt. No.)

338 Pleasant Hill Drive

(City, County, State, ZIP Code)

Silvertown, CA 96435

E. Check one of these boxes

[X] Present employee
of establishment

[ ] Former employee
of establishment

[ ] Job Applicant

[ ] Other _____
(Specify: relative, union, etc.)

2. ESTABLISHMENT INFORMATION

A. Name of Establishment

Breathing Care Services, Inc.

B. Telephone Number

1-800-256-5031

C. Address of establishment: (Number, Street)

9 Militia Drive

(City, County, State, ZIP Code)

Boston, Massachusetts 02173

D. Estimate number of employees

about 500

E. Does the firm have branches?   [X] Yes   [ ] No   [ ] Don't know

If "Yes," name one or two locations: Central Region, Arlington

Heights, IL

F. Nature of establishment's business: (For example; school, farm, hospital, hotel, restaurant, shoe store, wholesale drugs, manufactures stoves, coal mine, construction, trucking, etc.)

contracting service for hospitals

G. If the establishment has a Federal Government or federally assisted contract, check the appropriate box(es).

[ ] Furnishes goods   [ ] Furnishes services   [ ] Performs construction

H. Does establishment ship goods to or receive goods from other States?

[X] Yes   [ ] No   [ ] Don't know

3. EMPLOYMENT INFORMATION
(Complete A, B, C, D, E, & F if present or former employee of establishment; otherwise complete F only)

A. Period employed (month, year)

From: 12-28-81

To: present
(If still live there, state present)

B. Date of birth if under 19 or if information concerns age discrimination

Month _____ Day _____ Year _____

C. Give your job title and describe briefly the kind of work you do

Department Head of Respiratory Therapy

(See attached sheet)

EXHIBIT 2 Employment Information Form *(concluded)*

D. Method of payment

D. Method of payment

$ _____ per __year__
  (Rate)   (Hour, week, month, etc.)

E. Enter in the boxes below the hours you usually work each day and each week (less time off for meals)

M	T	W	T	F	S	S	TOTAL
2	12	10	12	0	9.5	10	55.5

F. CHECK THE APPROPRIATE BOX(ES) AND EXPLAIN BRIEFLY IN THE SPACE BELOW the employment practices which you believe violate the Wage and Hour laws. (If you need more space use an additional sheet of paper and attach it to this form.)

☐ Does not pay the minimum wage

☒ Does not pay proper overtime

☐ Men and women perform equal work but do not get equal pay

☐ Discrimination against employee or applicant (40-65 years of age) because of age

Approximate date of alleged discrimination

_____

☐ Does not pay prevailing wage determination for Federal Government or federally assisted contract

☐ Discharged employee because of wage garnishment (explain below)

☐ Excessive deduction from wages because of wage garnishment (explain below)

☐ Employs minors under minimum age for job

☐ Other (explain below)

Though I am a salaried employee and have had professional

training, I only devote about 20 - 25% of my work time to super-

visory activities. I directly supervise two employees and in-

directly supervise two other full time employees

G. Describe briefly the kind of work you do.

I perform the following types of respiratory therapy treatments: chest physiotherapy, hand held nebulizer, incentive spirometry, ultrasonic nebulizer. I perform and analyze arterial blood gas tests, pulmonary function tests, and electroencephalograms. In addition, I set up holter monitors, cold steamers, croup tents, and oxygen. I also set up home oxygen equipment.

My supervisory duties include scheduling employee hours, ordering respiratory therapy equipment, and preparing weekly and monthly reports of numbers of treatments given and types of equipment used. I also attend infection control meetings, department head meetings, and respiratory therapy committee meetings.

(NOTE: If you think it would be difficult for us to locate the establishment or where you live, give directions or attach map.)

COMPLAINT TAKEN BY:

D.A.B.

worked from the week of January 2, 1989, through the week of June 30, 1990 (Exhibit 3 and 4, respectively). Dolores told Karl he would be notified of the outcome of the investigation.

EXHIBIT 3   Job Description

Title:
   Supervisor/respiratory therapy

Definition:
   A supervisor/respiratory therapy is defined as an individual providing supervision, direction, and control to the management function of the cardiorespiratory department assigned to and employed at contracted health care facilities.

Education requirements:
   Individual must be a high school graduate and a registered respiratory therapist (RRT), or be a certified respiratory therapy technician (CRTT), or have advanced training in cardiopulmonary care.

General duties:
   In addition to being able to provide all levels of technical skills required of a respiratory therapy technician/therapist (attached) the supervisor/respiratory therapy provides the following:

1. Determines equipment and staffing needs for the shifts or services being supervised. Plans, schedules, and makes determinations of priorities of aspects of therapy and administrative duties.
2. Organizes work load in logical sequences using personal experience and management tools to rate, rank, and modify tasks.
3. Directs the specific tasks by determining the most efficient use of personnel, equipment, and work load.
4. Controls the service by evaluating results of procedures performed. Makes the necessary modifications in the methods used for distribution of services.

Description of Specific Tasks Performed

1. In addition to general supervisory duties, this person specifically performs the following:
   a. Ensures the quality and efficiency of the diagnostic and therapeutic procedures performed by evaluating results of tests in accordance with quality control standards.
   b. Confers with various department directors in need of respiratory therapy services with regard to type, quantity, time, etc.
   c. Participates in the review of care, with the medical director, and shares in studies and data gathering.
   d. Participates in JCAH and medicare audits.
2. Plans and organizes the activities of the respiratory therapy department.

EXHIBIT 3 *(continued)*

  a. Assists in planning additions to or changes of type of equipment including evaluation of new devices.

  b. Assists in planning the manpower requirements and appropriate wage factors to ensure the maintenance of an efficient and dependable work force.

  c. Plans and implements continuing education programs. Makes presentations on current concepts of cardiopulmonary care to technicians, physicians, nurses, and other paramedical personnel.

  d. Establishes inventory control of department equipment and supplies.

  e. Maintains department files and records. Provides monthly and weekly summaries of department activities. Keeps statistical data for medicare and JCAH audits.

  f. Confers regularly with Medical Director concerning the clinical practices and procedures performed by the department. Participates in clinical experimentation and evaluations.

 3. Supervises the respiratory therapy department personnel.

  a. Is responsible for hiring, orientation, evaluating, training, assigning, and ensuring the efficiency of the technical staff.

  b. Provides counseling to subordinates as requested or required. Uses performance appraisal for review.

  c. May terminate subordinates as per hospital and department policies.

  d. Oversees facilities to ensure that safety precautions are observed.

Title:

Registered respiratory therapist

Definition:

A registered respiratory therapist is defined as an individual providing therapeutic and diagnostic respiratory care for inpatients and outpatients at contracted health care facilities and who has been accredited by the National Board for Respiratory Therapy (NBRT) as registered.

Education requirements:

Individual must have successfully completed formal training in respiratory therapy through a program approved by the Joint Review Committee for Respiratory Therapy Education (JRCRTE).

Description of duties:

The registered respiratory therapist possesses sufficient training and experience to perform respiratory care procedures, as prescribed, with supervision in accordance with department policies and approved procedures. The registered respiratory therapist may also be called upon for expert advice in matters of cardiopulmonary care. The respiratory therapist will share in the clinical evaluation of care, including the establishment of therapeutic objectives and the review of care.

EXHIBIT 3   *(concluded)*

---

1. Therapeutic Cases
   a. Administer therapeutic gases, such as oxygen, as prescribed, in accordance with accepted procedures.
   b. Monitor bulk oxygen systems.
2. Treatments
   a. Administer positive pressure breathing treatments (IPPB) as prescribed.
   b. Administer prescribed medications, including bronchodilators, via inhalation.
   c. Administer humidified therapeutic gases, including high-humidity therapy as prescribed.
   d. Induce from the patient a sputum specimen for cytological or bacterial examination.
   e. Perform incentive spirometry treatments as prescribed.
   f. Perform bronchial drainage and chest physiotherapy as outlined in department procedures and policies.
3. Critical Care
   a. Establishes, maintains, monitors, and evaluates continuous ventilatory support. The respiratory therapist may share in decisions affecting continuous ventilatory support based on clinical findings.
   b. Participates in cardiopulmonary resuscitation.
   c. Performs airway care, including trachea bronchial aspiration, and other procedures aimed at establishing and/or maintaining natural and artificial airways as outlined in the department procedures and policies.
   d. Assists in transport of critical patients as required.
4. Diagnostics
   a. Performs sampling and analysis of arterial blood as described in the department procedures and policies.
   b. Performs pulmonary function tests in accordance with department procedures and policies.
   c. Performs and/or assists in special diagnostic procedures as required by the department.
5. General Duties
   a. Performs regular equipment maintenance, preparation, cleaning, and sterilization.
   b. Is responsible for documenting procedures in the medical record and department files. Assists in the quality assurance program within the department and the hospital as described by department procedures and policies.

EXHIBIT 4 Hours of Work while Employed by Breathing Care
Services, Inc.

Week Starting	Regular Hours	Overtime Hours	Call Hours
01/02/89	40	10.50	24
01/09/89	40	4.25	36
01/16/89	40	3.00	48
01/23/89	40	3.00	36
01/30/89	40	16.50	48
02/06/89	40	3.25	36
02/13/89	40	6.00	48.50
02/20/89	40	9.50	67.50
02/27/89	40	21.75	58.00
03/06/89	40	27.50	60.00
03/13/89	40	9.00	61.00
03/20/89	40	13.50	78.75
03/27/89	40	21.00	75.50
04/03/89	40	26.50	72.50
04/10/89	40	10.00	64.00
04/17/89	40	4.25	62.75
04/24/89	40	0.00	60.00
05/01/89	40	8.50	48.00
05/08/89	40	0.25	50.00
05/15/89	40	17.75	37.00
05/22/89	40	28.50	73.25
05/29/89	38.50	0.00	38.00
06/05/89	30.00 + 10.00 (holiday)	0.00	0.00
06/12/89	40	4.50	60.00
06/19/89	40	13.00	51.50
06/26/89	40	7.00	51.00
07/03/89	40	7.00	39.00
07/10/89	37.00 + 10.00 (holiday)	0.00	41.75
07/17/89	40	29.00	38.50
07/24/89	40	25.50	12.00
07/31/89	40	4.50	12.00
08/07/89	40	7.75	23.50
08/14/89	40	3.50	0.00
08/21/89	40	4.25	14.00
08/28/89	40	3.00	14.00
09/04/89	40	4.00	0.00
09/11/89	34.50 + 8.00 (holiday)	0.00	0.00
09/18/89	40	2.00	0.00
09/25/89	40	9.50	28.00
10/02/89	22	0.00	0.00
10/09/89	29	0.00	0.00

EXHIBIT 4   *(concluded)*

Week Starting	Regular Hours	Overtime Hours	Call Hours
10/16/89	40	13.00	65.50
10/23/89	40	8.50	13.50
10/30/89	40	12.00	21.00
11/06/89	40	6.25	13.50
11/13/89	40	19.50	28.00
11/20/89	40	17.50	27.00
11/27/89	40.2 + 8.0 (holiday unpaid)	0.25	73.25
12/04/89	40	6.50	27.50
12/11/89	40	16.50	56.50
12/18/89	40	10.00	43.50
12/25/89	28.5 + 8.0	0.00	0.00
01/01/90	24 + 16 (holiday)	0.00	0.00
01/08/90	40	2.50	0.00
01/15/90	40	4.25	28.00
01/22/90	40	7.50	22.00
01/29/90	40	23.50	70.00
02/05/90	40	19.50	55.00
02/12/90	40	15.00	72.00
02/19/90	40	26.00	83.00
02/26/90	40	17.00	71.50
03/05/90	40	8.00	49.00
03/12/90	40	7.50	58.50
03/19/90	40	17.50	59.00
03/26/90	40	15.50	71.50
04/02/90	40	33.50	14.50
04/09/90	40	1.00	28.50
04/16/90	40	1.50	60.00
04/23/90	40	6.50	73.00
04/30/90	40	23.50	84.50
05/07/90	40	10.50	43.00
05/14/90	37 + 8.0 (holiday)	0.00	42.00
05/21/90	18.5 + 21.5 (vacation)	0.00	45.50
05/28/90	40	2.50	43.00
06/04/90	37.50	0.00	66.50
06/11/90	40	9.50	42.00
06/18/90	40	0.50	0.00
06/25/90	8 + 32.0 (vacation)	0.00	0.00
06/30/90	33.50	0.00	6.50

Discussion Question

1. Do you think Karl is legally entitled to overtime pay or not? Justify your answer.

---

3 *The Aria: A Family Restaurant*

The Aria is an 80-seat, elegant Italian restaurant located off Arapaho Drive in a suburb of Boulder, Colorado. The owner, Tony Contos, was originally from southern Italy. As a young man, Tony emigrated to Chicago in the early 1950s, where he tried his hand in the entertainment industry. After an unsuccessful bout in the theater, he began a career in the restaurant business.

Having started at the bottom and worked his way up, Tony became a very well-known and financially successful maître d' and restaurant manager. Tony worked in only the finest restaurants in Chicago, made a reputable name for himself, and decided to move on to greater and greener pastures.

In 1979, Tony brought his wife, Gena, and their 20-year-old son, Ricardo, to the Boulder area, where, with the money he had saved, he bought The Aria.

The first order of business was to staff the restaurant with the proper personnel. Tony wanted to bring to Boulder fine, authentic, New York–Italian cuisine and decided to call upon some of the many cooks and chefs he had worked with or known in Chicago. After a number of unsuccessful tries at recruiting those he considered the best, Tony finally found a second cook named Paulo, who accepted Tony's offer to relocate and take the position of chef at The Aria. Tony had known Paulo and his wife and two daughters for several years prior to the move they all made to the Boulder area.

Tony then hired three or four other men, already from the Boulder area, to supplement the kitchen staff and work with Tony in food preparation and cleanup. Although Tony did a great deal of the early morning preparation, including buying fresh food each day, and cooked most of the specialty dishes, Paulo was responsible for the line and the final preparation and presentation of all the food leaving the kitchen and being served to customers.

This case was prepared by Matthew David Popkin, under the supervision of Professor George Stevens. All case names are disguised. Copyright © 1984 by M. D. Popkin.

The next group hired was the service staff. Since there was to be quite a bit of tableside cooking done, Tony required that applicants possess a minimum of two years' experience in fine Continental dining room service.

Tony was most fortunate in finding qualified waiters and captains in the immediate area. Most of the men hired were young, in their early 20s to late 30s. All had a reasonable amount of experience in fine dining service and tableside cooking. Of the eight men hired to be captain-and-waiter teams, most held either full-time professional positions or were in the process of completing their educations at local colleges and universities.

As in many restaurants, there exists a fair amount of rivalry or even open hostility between the kitchen crew and service personnel. The back of the "house"—the kitchen—and the front—the dining area—can become battlegrounds for the most heated debates in any fine restaurant. The Aria was no exception and, within a relatively short period of time, the battle raged nightly.

The kitchen personnel felt that the waiters made much more money than they deserved, for, if it were not for the kitchen, they would be serving frozen dinners. It irritated the cooks working in the hot, stuffy, smelly kitchen to hear the captains and waiters discuss how much money they made in tips each night. It seemed very unfair to them that, although they worked the hardest and longest and with much more expertise, the waiters made considerably more income than they.

The waiters' rebuttal to the kitchen crew's outrage was that anyone could chop an onion and wash a glass. They felt themselves far superior, both personally and professionally,

The fact that all but two of the eight waiters and captains were part-timers in the restaurant business greatly affected the way they perceived their current positions. Many had aspirations of greater things for themselves, considering their jobs as waiters as transitory in nature.

The effects of this blatant rivalry often culminated in sharp words and loud-voiced objections to the most mundane suggestions from either side. Tricks and pranks were played, with the opposing teams going into their neutral corners only long enough to regain momentum and mount a counterattack. Tony, who in his long restaurant career had witnessed this rivalry countless numbers of times, seemed to feel that it was all in a day's work. The business flourished despite the pettiness and childishness, and Tony felt it better to leave well enough alone.

Tony insisted that all dissension and discussion be brought to him as arbitrator so he could have the final word. It seemed to the kitchen crew that all too often, especially on extremely busy nights, Tony sided with the front of the house. It seemed to the service personnel that Tony always sided with the back, and his role as arbitrator was often ignored.

The dissension and discussion carried on into the next day, in the form of employee meals, of which Paulo was in charge. Tony demanded that his waiters arrive at The Aria between one and two hours prior to opening to prepare the tables and side specialties and to share the evening meal with The Aria staff like a family.

These meals were often more raucous than those at a summer camp for hyperactive children. If the kitchen staff was angry with the waiters and captains, the evening meal was often barely edible. If the service personnel wanted to get back at the kitchen crew, they would bring their own dinner and segregate themselves from the rest of the restaurant's staff.

Although the teams that worked together every evening, and sometimes during the lunch hour shift, got along tremendously well and enjoyed a pleasant working relationship, there was sometimes an inordinate amount of strife between the members of the teams themselves. Tony, as maître d', owner, and general manager of all The Aria's operations, was always at the door to greet customers and seat them. As if the problems with the kitchen crew weren't bad enough, Tony would aggravate the situation by seating the larger and better parties with the older waiters and with the family men. He justified his actions with the fact that men with families had greater expenses and, therefore, needed to make as much money as possible.

This was the cause of more agitation and aggravation from the younger men, with no other dependents than themselves, who felt that the job should be done by the man who is most capable. More than once, one or two teams would be extremely busy while the others had little work of their own. Upon seeing the swamped teams in dire need of assistance, Tony would direct those with little work to help out. This caused a greater amount of ill feelings, because the busy teams never shared their tips with those who assisted them in their hour of need.

Though all of these personnel problems had persisted through the four years The Aria had been open for business, the rate of turnover at the small restaurant was practically nil. Most of the crew that had started with Tony remained. The probable reason for the low turnover rate, in spite of the problems encountered almost daily by the staff, was that many of these situations were considered normal by all parties involved. The crew believed that many restaurants, large and small, suffered from many of the same ailments that plagued The Aria daily.

Another major cause of aggravation for the staff of The Aria was the fact that the restaurant was a family-owned and -operated business, with Tony's wife, Gena, their son, Ricardo, and his wife, Buffy, all involved in the day-to-day operation of the business.

Ricardo, who before his father opened The Aria had little experience (practically none in the restaurant business), has been the greatest cause of strife for the dining room staff.

Within three years of opening the restaurant for business, Tony placed Ricardo in charge of the waiters and busmen, in the position of restaurant manager. Ricardo was put in charge of all scheduling, and the hiring and training of all personnel for the dining room.

Ricardo's wife, Buffy, took care of the daily accounting along with Tony's wife, Gena. Gena was also responsible for assisting Tony in the preparation of specialty dishes and desserts, something they did quite well together. At times, when Tony and Gena were not there, Ricardo and Buffy were in complete authority at The Aria.

The waiters and captains were often offended at the orders given by Ricardo, a person whom they considered to be uneducated in the business, and showed him and his wife the greatest amount of disrespect possible—short of risking their livelihood. The lack of respect was brought on not only by Ricardo's total inexperience but was compounded by his flippant manner in the delegation of his responsibilities. Both Ricardo and Buffy were arrogant toward the dining room staff, probably because they considered themselves totally superior to the patriarch's employees.

Ricardo's parents, especially Tony, worked from daybreak until closing, while Ricardo came to work at the last possible minute and retreated at his earliest possible convenience. While the Contos usually ate a quick sandwich before shutting off The Aria's lights for the night, Ricardo and Buffy would often be seated and served by a team whose evening was over, making the kitchen crew and dining room staff work for them.

Ricardo's parents saw the disgruntled looks and overheard the comments made by many of the staff, but never took their son and daughter-in-law aside to explain the unfairness of other actions. This greatly disturbed the staff.

The staff was also bothered by personal matters in the Contos family. While his father drove a very beat-up old car, Ricardo raced around town in a brand-new foreign sports car. Ricardo was often insolent to his father in front of the staff, and sometimes even in front of The Aria's patrons.

Another problem and the cause of much grief among the staff was the religious beliefs of the Contos family. Tony, Gena, Ricardo, and Buffy were very, very religious—in fact, they called themselves "Born-Again Christians." They were always talking about how they were saved and were always, or so it seemed to the staff, trying to save and convert all "wayward souls" who came their way. It was not unusual for Gena to call members of the staff, either kitchen crew or dining room personnel, into her small office and read them scriptures from the family Bible. It was always very uncomfortable for the persons she called, for, no matter what their own personal beliefs were, they could not leave without fear of offending her. An intelligent or rewarding discussion was always out of the question, due to their adamant beliefs.

It always seemed to the waiters and cooks that the Contos family's religious beliefs and business ethics were quite contradictory. Tony would often add extra bottles of wine to large parties to boost the bill. In dishes that called for veal, as described on the menu, the kitchen often substituted less expensive pork. Ricardo, who often preached the morals of being a Born-Again Christian, carried a pistol in his coat and constantly reminded the staff of its presence. The men found this especially agitating and uncomfortable.

As in many small family-owned and -operated businesses, the owners always told the staff that they thought of them as family. The Contos would gather the staff and their families for traditional Thanksgiving and Christmas dinners and would often preach gospel during grace. The families of the staff would attend these functions, because they found it obligatory to assist in keeping goodwill with the Contos family. It did not raise morale to hear Buffy comment, "No, that's for the help," as she passed along items she felt were inferior.

The wives and girlfriends of the staff would often gather together in rebuttal to Buffy's feelings of superiority over them. Many times these dinners caused strife in the families of the staff whose livelihoods depended on being two-faced.

Real trouble began at The Aria almost three weeks after the fourth anniversary of the restaurant's opening. It was a very busy Thursday night. The kitchen was extremely backed up; the dining room was buzzing with activity and tempers were flaring. Jim, a very personable and competent waiter (captain) who had worked at The Aria since its inception, had a number of parties whose food was late in coming.

As was customary in situations like this, Jim went back to the kitchen to ask Paulo to speed things up, for the restaurant patrons were getting restless. Paulo, who was often surly with the waiters, especially when the kitchen was backed up, began to curse and carry on, ranting and raving at Jim.

Jim, instead of following Tony's policy of retreating and alerting Tony, returned fire with words as harsh as those of Paulo. The argument went back and forth with voices and tempers rising. Rapidly, the argument escalated from curses to threats of physical violence.

The next thing anyone knew, Jim's black tuxedo jacket was stained red. Jim had been stabbed with a small kitchen knife in his lower left side, under the rib cage. Tony appeared and ordered one of the waiters to take Jim to the hospital and everyone, including Paulo, returned to work.

Jim's wound took 11 stitches and he was told by the attending physician that he was fortunate the knife did not enter an inch higher than it did, for he probably would have left behind a widow. As upset and hurt as he was, Jim decided not to call the police, but instead waited to return to The Aria to speak with Tony.

The next day Jim sat down to speak with Tony about the events that had transpired the night before. At first Tony was very sympathetic toward Jim and told him that he would do everything possible to make it up to him. Jim told Tony that if Paulo was not fired, he would press charges against him. Jim and Tony, both knowing that Paulo had a family and had been in trouble with the law before, did not want to cause him any grief.

Tony told Jim that he would give Paulo two weeks' notice and place him on the day shift for the remaining time. All of this was agreeable to Jim, as long as he did not have to work with Paulo ever again.

The first week passed quietly without mention of the incident by anyone. At the end of the second week, Tony approached Jim and told him that he needed to keep Paulo another week because he had not found a replacement and the restaurant was booked almost solid. Jim and the rest of the staff were all aware that Alex, the second cook at The Aria, was more than capable and qualified to step into the allegedly vacant position.

Jim began to question the sincerity of Tony's promise to fire Paulo, and he also began to wonder if there were an underlying reason for Tony's not having fired Paulo already. There were rumors to the effect that Tony had loaned Paulo a substantial amount of money, perhaps as much as $5,000.

The following day, Jim confronted Tony and Gena, asking if the real reason Paulo had not been dismissed was an outstanding loan to the Contos. They both confirmed the fact that they had loaned Paulo $5,000 and that they could not afford to lose so great an amount of money. They then asked Jim to understand their predicament and told him that they would keep Paulo on days so they would not have to work together.

Jim, a proud man, realized he had been taken. He asked Tony and Gena what they would have done if Paulo had stabbed their son Ricardo instead of him. He could not believe their reply.

Tony and Gena told Jim that had Paulo stabbed Ricardo they would immediately have called the police, pressed charges, and fired him in one breath.

At the end of the week, Paulo was still in the kitchen—and Jim resigned. Jim pressed charges against Paulo, who was released on bail to await trial.

Several months have gone by. Paulo is still the chef of The Aria and Jim remains unemployed. Tony's once almost nonexistent rate of turnover is now quite high, 90 percent. In fact, only one of the original eight dining room staff is still at The Aria.

Patrons of The Aria who once dined there regularly do not feel comfortable with the new staff. They once enjoyed the "family atmosphere" of which the Contos were so proud, and the entire business has suffered from the high rate of turnover.

Those who are no longer employed at The Aria share Jim's feelings of betrayal, for their friend and cohort, and for themselves. They all believe that all the talk of religion and goodness was a front for the true concern of the Contos family—money.

Discussion Questions

1. What could have been done to curtail the dissension between the dining room and kitchen staff?
2. Is there any validity to the notion of treating employees of any company like members of the family?
3. How do you feel about Tony's pattern of seating larger and better parties to be served by the older waiters?
4. Would the incident between Paulo and Jim have been treated differently in a larger organization?
5. Do you think money was the only factor in Tony's decision to keep Paulo?

4 Chancellor State University

THE SETTING

Chancellor State University is a large, urban university in the Midwest. Although the university experienced rapid growth in the 1960s and 1970s, overall enrollment has now stabilized. The School of Business Administration, however, has continued to grow, drawing students away from programs in the School of Education and in the College of Arts and Sciences, as well as attracting new students concerned with future vocational opportunities. The faculty and administration of the business school are pleased to see the enrollment growth because it signals acceptance of their degree program, but the enrollment expansion has created strong pressure to expand the business faculty.

This case was prepared by Professor Thomas R. Miller, Memphis State University.

Under normal circumstances, faculty expansion would simply mean an active recruitment effort by school administrators. But the situation at Chancellor State is representative of a national phenomenon of enrollment growth in business schools, resulting in a strong demand for doctorally qualified faculty in the face of a relatively short supply. Thus, faculty recruitment at many business schools has become a priority activity, rather than merely one of the many administrative responsibilities of deans and department heads.

At Chancellor State, Fred Kennedy, chairman of the management department, has been actively seeking new faculty members for its staff, which has the heaviest course load in the school. As is often customary in academia, the faculty in the department of management participates in recruitment, spending considerable time meeting with the faculty candidates in an effort to evaluate their candidacy for a faculty position. Faculty members may then make recommendations about whether the prospect should be tendered an offer to join the staff.

THE CONFERENCE

It was now late in February, and several prospective faculty members had visited Chancellor State for campus job interviews. Early one Friday morning, Fred was in his office reviewing the job files of prospective faculty members. He looked up as he heard the voice of Larry Gordon, an assistant professor of management who was now in his third year at Chancellor State.

"Good morning, Fred," said Larry, as he walked into the department office. "Do you have a couple minutes? I want to talk with you about something."

Fred gestured to him to come into his office. "Sure, Larry, what's on your mind?"

After entering Fred's office, Larry closed the door, indicating to Fred that this was not to be just a casual and friendly conversation.

"Fred," Larry began, "I was wondering what you thought about the prospective faculty member we had in here for an interview last week. I've been talking with a couple of other faculty members about him, and they're not really all that impressed. He seems to be OK, I guess, but we may be able to do better. Are we going to make him an offer? If we do, he's sure not worth top dollar in my opinion."

"Well, I've received some of the written evaluations back from the faculty, and they seem to be fairly positive," replied Fred. "They're not as favorable as they could be, but the others on the faculty seem to think that he would be acceptable and that he could work out pretty well on our staff. His academic credentials are not bad, and he has had some good experience. Given the state of the market for business faculty in his specialty, I expect that we'll extend an offer to him. By the way, I know that he already has a couple offers in hand from our competition."

Fred could readily see that Larry was not pleased to hear all of this. From their earlier conversations, Fred could anticipate Larry's next comment.

"Yeah, OK, I can see that we could use him. But what kind of money are we offering in these new positions?" questioned Larry. "I don't mean to pry into somebody else's business, but what sort of salary is the department offering our new faculty?"

Fred winced at this question. He had in the past made no secret about general salary ranges for new faculty members. In fact, this information was generally known throughout the school. But this had become a very sensitive issue in the last few years, given the rapid increases in starting salaries for new business faculty members.

"Well, Larry, I guess you know that we're paying competitively for our new faculty. With our enrollment increase we've got to increase our teaching staff, and to do that we're probably going to have to meet the market," Fred responded.

Larry was obviously not satisfied with this response and was becoming irritated with the conversation. "Fred, I assume that by 'meeting the market' you mean that we're going to offer this guy two to three thousand dollars more than some of us who have been here for several years are now making. This new guy has not yet finished his doctorate, has very little teaching experience, has no publications, and, in my opinion, is not as good as a lot of our current faculty. How much can you justify paying for an unknown quantity? I think it's just unfair to the present faculty to offer him more money than many of us are making. When is somebody going to do something for us? Fred, I'm not unhappy here in this department, but I'm sure going to keep my eyes open for other opportunities. I feel sure that I could move to another school at a higher rank and increase my salary significantly. You may think I'm wrong and maybe I shouldn't feel this way, but this situation is just not fair!"

Fred sighed and tried to calm Larry. "Larry, I know what you're concerned about, and I'm certainly sympathetic to the problem. After all, this salary compression issue affects me in the same way it does you. I I can assure you that I have reservations about paying the kind of money we are for new faculty in light of our existing faculty salaries, but I don't believe that we can attract the kind of faculty we want by paying less than competitive rates. Although this seems to create some internal inequities, I hope that we'll have sufficient salary increase money to make some adjustments to reduce these discrepancies. Certainly I want to be able to reward and retain our productive people . . ."

Larry, feeling a little embarrassed by his earlier emotional statement, interjected: "I know you've got other problems, Fred, and I didn't mean to lash out at you. I know it's not really your fault, but a lot of the other faculty are talking about this salary issue. It surely doesn't help morale any when a new, inexperienced assistant professor is hired for more than some of the associate professors are making."

"Yes, I'm well aware of this, Larry, and I'm making the dean aware of it as well. We're certainly going to do what we can to try to resolve this salary compression problem," Fred responded.

As Larry moved toward the door, he continued to make his point: "Well, I hope you can do something soon because it's most inequitable at the present time. People are pretty upset about it, and it's likely to cause the department some turnover problems in the future. No one likes to be treated unfairly. I'll see you later, Fred. I've got to run to class. Maybe we can talk about it again later."

As Larry walked out of his office, Fred reflected on their conversation. It reminded him of other discussions he had had previously with several other faculty members. In fact, Larry had hinted at his dissatisfaction before but had not been so outspoken about it. Yes, the salary compression problem was reaching a crisis. No longer was it a matter of the "new hires" nearing the salaries of some present faculty; it was a matter of their exceeding them. Never in his experience had Fred recalled a labor market for faculty that was this chaotic.

Fred had puzzled over this dilemma before but had not been able to come up with a solution for the problem. He wondered if, in fact, there was a solution that would enable him to hire the new personnel he wanted without offending some of the present staff. Maybe it's just one of those "no win" administrative situations, he mused.

Perhaps this was something that could be discussed with the other department chairmen and the dean since some of them had basically the same problem. Maybe then he would have a better idea of how to deal with the situation. He certainly hoped so!

Discussion Questions

1. What are the problems in this case?
2. What actions should be taken to overcome the problems cited?

5 Secrid Manufacturing Company, Inc.

(The case is a technical problem provided for solution, typical of those faced by human resource professionals. The setting is Dayton, Ohio, 198X. The task is to prepare a compensation structure for nonexempt employees of a single-plant local firm, using the technical data provided in the case. The data consist of job titles, salary guidelines, position descriptions, an office salary survey, area wage survey from the Bureau of Labor Statistics, employee information, etc.)

"This system is no system, Clare, and I want you take it and make some sense of it."

Rosa McMillan, junior partner of Moss and McMillan Associates, Inc., consultants to management, addressed the newest member of the

---

EXHIBIT 1   Job Titles

Group I	
PBX operator-receptionist	A. Peler
Order-billing clerk I	L. Parnell
Data entry operator I	P. Pendleton

Group II	
Clerical—sales administrator	J. Carr
Accounts payable clerk II	W. Thorne
Data entry operator II	T. Oehler
Clerk—Accounts payable/inventory control/traffic	S. Joyner

Group III	
Sales department secretary	D. Art, L. Level
	K. White
Payroll clerk III	B. Sellers
Maintenance supply and record clerk	R. Toler

Group IV	
Executive secretary	P. Pulley, M. Tarkington
Personnel generalist	B. Welch
Purchasing department secretary	W. Kale
Traffic and credit administrative assistant	P. Arlington

Group V	
Industrial nurse	J. Jasper

Prepared by Professor Theodore T. Herbert, Rollins College, with the assistance of Ann Moss Joyner, MBA, University of North Carolina.

consulting firm. "Here's some information on the current employees and their jobs. Your task is to find relevant market information, evaluate the process Secrid has been using to determine the compensation of its nonexempt employees, and develop a new system. Everything you need is in the library, but with this new librarian in the middle of his work in there, I don't know where things are. You're on your own. Good luck. It shouldn't take more than 10 hours—at least, that's all we can bill Secrid for. Just give me a call if you run into any major snags."

With this, she handed over a stack of papers (see Exhibits 1–3) and left Clare's office. "The first job of any good consultant," Clare thought to herself, "is to come up with an analysis of the problem and a plan for attacking that problem."

EXHIBIT 2 198X–198(X + 1) Salary Administration Guide—
Nonmanagement Salaried Employees

Secrid Manufacturing Co., Inc.

The following monthly salary Guide is to be in effect from February 1, 198X, until superseded to cover nonmanagement salaried office personnel and salaried technicians in the plant and administrative offices in Dayton.

	Group I	*II*	*III*	*IV*	*V*
Start rate	750	810	925	1,055	1,200
Maximum	1,110	1,190	1,370	1,560	1,770
Target	965	1,035	1,190	1,355	1,540

The target salaries will be the expected top rate within the Group to be reached by February 1, 198(X + 1). Only employees rated "above average" may exceed the target salary.

Employment should start at the Group start rate, or will be commensurate with background experience. The first salary review will be made in no less than four or no more than seven months. Subsequent reviews will be no longer than 12 months thereafter.

It is expected that the average new employee with no experience should reach the target salary in about five years. The average new employee with experience could reach the target sooner based on previous experience.

Performance	*Time in Group to Reach Target*
Above average	3 years
Average	5 years

The salary guidelines for the five groups will be reviewed annually by comparison with the current A.M.S., or other data published for the Dayton area. Necessary adjustments will be made as required to keep Secrid salaries at approximately the average actual salaries in the Dayton area.

EXHIBIT 3 Position Descriptions (Samples)

Secrid Manufacturing Co., Inc.

POSITION DESCRIPTION

Title: Executive secretary   Location: Dayton
Organization: Secrid Manufacturing   Description No.:
Division/Department: Administration/Sales   Supersedes:

I. Position in organization
   A. Reports to: vice president—finance and vice president—sales
   B. Directly supervises: None
   C. Indirectly supervises: None
II. Major responsibility
Handle confidential tasks of a broad spectrum for the vice president—finance and the vice president—sales including payrolls' correspondence and financial records.
III. Specific responsibilities (If more space is required, please attach a separate page.)
   1. Voucher all expense reports and various other bills for payment.
   2. Maintain audit control on cash advances.
   3. Maintain audit control on publications and memberships for sales, administration, and manufacturing.
   4. Record and pay for all airline tickets and balance airline accounts.
   5. Voucher and type special checks.
   6. Sign all checks issued by the company.
   7. Prepare various monthly reports.
   8. Record all absenteeism and vacation for administrative and sales personnel.
   9. Make distribution of salaried paychecks to departments.
   10. Type management Minutes' extract Management Resolutions; prepare F–800s for salary increases and post to DO 18s.
   11. Make bank deposits for factory payroll, civic fund, pension fund, and special account.
   12. Take dictation and handle vice president—finance and vice president—sales correspondence.

Personnel Generalist

Job responsibilities:

A. Basic functions
   1. Full responsibility for administration of Service Pin Program.
     a. Maintain current employee lists.
     b. Inventory and order pins.
     c. Distribute pins to appropriate managers.
   2. Maintain all eligibility records for Secrid hourly employees' pension plan; send annual letters of information to employees.

EXHIBIT 3   *(continued)*

3. Handle all records for hourly employees' United Way contributions and Flower Fund contributions.
   a. Understand function of Civic Committee; substitute, as necessary, for personnel supervisor at meetings.
   b. Participate in organization of United Way Campaign.
4. Control weekly sale of soap to employees.
   a. Order tickets.
   b. Verify number of tickets sold with amount of money received; coordinate with accounting department.
   c. Provide supplies to person who sells soap, tickets/substitute for this person when necessary.
5. Assist with security functions.
   a. Monitor, on a scheduled basis, emergency exit alarm system.
   b. Monitor daily guard logs; take corrective action, as necessary.
   c. Relieve security guard.
   d. Participate in organization of review schedule for corporate security department.
6. Maintain current orientation materials; assist with orientation of new employees.
7. Assist in planning and implementation of Christmas gift distribution program.
8. Assume responsibility for special projects.
   a. Compilation of data for negotiations' planning.
   b. Substitute for plant manager's secretary, when needed.
   c. Assist the personnel secretary on as-needed basis.
   d. Plan for retirees' luncheon.
9. Keep records relative to employee payments for medical coverage.
10. Coordinate with department manager/payroll department hourly employees' vacation eligibility.
11. Compile and distribute all hourly employment reports.

Maintenance Supply & Record Clerk

Job responsibilities:

A. Basic functions
   1. Purchasing—locate or select supplier; initiate and/or check purchase requisitions; follow up and expedite orders; receive goods and initial receiving reports for manufacturing expense and AE items. Maintain purchasing files.
   2. Inventory—maintain manufacturing storeroom supplies; issue upon need; reorder when necessary.
   3. Fixed asset accounting—maintain fixed asset books by assigning new equipment numbers, initiating FADO's, maintaining asset file system.
   4. Clerical
      a. Typing and filing; answer phone for maintenance.

EXHIBIT 3   *(continued)*

    b. Maintain attendance records, time cards, vacation schedules for maintenance and engineering personnel.

B. Behavioral expectations and training requirements

    1. Must be able to organize and plan time in order to complete all tasks.

    2. Must be strong in communication skills to successfully interface with managers, hourly employees, and suppliers.

    3. Must be able to evaluate priorities and self-direct activities based on this evaluation.

    4. Must be able to perform well under critical pressure situations.

POSITION DESCRIPTION

Title: Receptionist
Organization: Secrid Manufacturing
Division Department: Sales/Sales Service

Location: Dayton
Description No.:
Supersedes:

  I. Position in Organization

    A. Reports to: Sales service manager.

    B. Directly supervises: None.

    C. Indirectly supervises: None.

 II. Major Responsibility

  Handles switchboard.

III. Specific Responsibilities (If more space is required, please attach a separate page.)

    1. Switchboard operator.

    2. Takes messages for Eastern salespeople.

    3. Handles excess typing.

POSITION DESCRIPTION

Title: Accounts payable clerk
Organization: Secrid Manufacturing
Division/Department: Administration

Location: Dayton
Description No.:
Supersedes:

  I. Position in Organization

    A. Reports to: Manager—traffic/inventory control.

    B. Directly supervises: None.

    C. Indirectly supervises: None.

 II. Major Responsibility

  Process for payment invoices relating to all items of expense.

III. Specific Responsibilities (If more space is required, please attach a separate page.)

    1. Verify receipts of goods and/or services for general expense items.

    2. Audit purchase orders with related invoices and prepare voucher for payment.

EXHIBIT 3   *(continued)*

---

3. Prepare bank deposit for cash receipts.
   a. Mail petty cash, expense reports.
4. Handle written and phone communications.
5. Sales—shipment audit.
6. Bank reconciliation—factory payroll checks.
7. File maintenance.
8. Purchase order audit control.

POSITION DESCRIPTION

Title: Clerk—accounts payable/inventory control/traffic

Location: Dayton

Organization: Secrid Manufacturing

Description No.:

Division/Department: Administration

Supersedes:

I. Position in Organization
   A. Reports to: Manager—traffic/inventory control.
   B. Directly supervises: None.
   C. Indirectly supervises: None.
II. Major Responsibility
   Maintains financial detail records on inventories of all raw materials and supplies. Maintains inventory control records of most materials and advises purchasing how much of a material to order.
III. Specific Responsibilities (If more space is required, please attach a separate page.)
   1. Process all receiving reports.
   2. Keypunch all inventory items into computer.
   3. Reorder for a bogey system as required.
   4. Maintain an essential oils' Hewitt compound, raw materials, additives, and foreign compounds kardex.
   5. Distribute daily production report.
   6. Request, audit, and post all monthly inventories.
   7. Prepare and maintain manufacturing head sheets for production orders.
   8. Prepare for sales account managers specific inventories of customer furnished items.
   9. Post and file completed production orders.
   10. Assist in new manufacturing specification system. All specifications are to be keypunched into the computer.
   11. Maintain and update the file retention system.
   12. Update and maintain supply master on CRT.
   13. Follow-up purchasing on all incoming materials and supplies to make sure they were ordered.
   14. Follow up all incoming materials and supplies from vendors to ensure timeliness for production and scheduling.
   15. Audit and pay invoices covering such items within area of authority and terms of the transaction.

EXHIBIT 3 *(continued)*

---

16. Record and establish inventory costs.
17. Record, price, and total all month-end inventories.
18. Typing:
    a. Freight claims.
    b. Steiner and V.T. Bills of Lading.
    c. Miscellaneous correspondence as needed.
19. Keypunch freight bills into computer.
20. Maintain customer master list
    a. New customers.
    b. Address changes, etc.

POSITION DESCRIPTION

Title: Data entry operator I
Organization: Secrid Manufacturing
Division/Department: Administration

Location: Dayton
Description No.:
Supersedes:

I. Position in Organization
   A. Reports to: Manager—data processing.
   B. Directly supervises: None.
   C. Indirectly supervises: None.
II. Major Responsibility
   Entry of data via terminal into HP3000 computer and serve as backup computer operator.
III. Specific Responsibilities (If more space is required, please attach a separate page.)
   1. Ability to enter and verify both production and technical data accurately.
   2. Achieve at least 8,000 key strokes per hour.
   3. Meet established schedules for production work.
   4. Have a thorough knowledge of all data entry jobs in the shop.
   5. Be able to use good judgment in detecting errors and determining the appropriate follow-up.
   6. Perform occasional clerical duties.

POSITION DESCRIPTION

Title: Payroll clerk
Organization: Secrid Manufacturing
Division/Department: Administration

Location: Dayton
Description No.:
Supersedes:

I. Position in Organization
   A. Reports to: Supervisor payroll/process accounting
   B. Directly supervises: None
   C. Indirectly supervises: None

EXHIBIT 3 *(continued)*

II. Major Responsibility
Prepares weekly the payroll for all hourly employees with data processing assistance.

III. Specific Responsibilities (If more space is required, please attach a separate page.)
   1. Audit Line Production Sheets for input data to data processing.
   2. Record input data relating to all status changes and deductions.
   3. Audit input controls and master file update prior to check writing.
   4. Prepare payroll distribution summary and weekly check number control count.
   5. Promptly advise supervisor or manager of current processing delay affecting completion of weekly payroll.
   6. Calculate, prepare distribution of charges, and request payment for monthly hospital care, disability, and life insurance premiums/related reports.
   7. Make necessary adjustments on payroll for previous weeks.
   8. Coding of weekly time cards.
   9. Record all special rates affecting current week.
  10. Post daily incentive hours to master worksheet.
  11. Post time card hours detail to master worksheet.
  12. Post status change items to master worksheet.
  13. Spot audit of input control and balancing hours.
  14. Run balancing tapes.
  15. Record details from weekly payroll as needed for future corporate and government reporting/analysis.
  16. Process garnishments.
  17. Process Employee Savings Bonds.
  18. Furnish detailed information as required for corporate, state, and federal reporting.
  19. Work with plant accountant auditing production tickets with line production sheets. Also assisting with information for the budget versus actual report.
  20. Plan and schedule for short workweek periods.

POSITION DESCRIPTION

Title: Data entry operator II
Organization: Secrid Manufacturing
Division/Department: Administration

Location: Dayton
Description No.:
Supersedes:

   I. Position in Organization
      A. Reports to: Manager—data processing.
      B. Directly supervises: None.
      C. Indirectly supervises: Data entry operator I—on occasion.
  II. Major Responsibility
      Input data via terminal to HP3000 computer.

EXHIBIT 3   *(continued)*

III. Specific Responsibilities (If more space is required, please attach a separate page.)
   1. Ability to enter and verify both production and technical data accurately.
   2. Achieve at least 8,000 key strokes per hour.
   3. Meet established schedules for production work.
   4. Have a thorough knowledge of all data entry jobs in the shop.
   5. Be able to use good judgment in detecting errors and determining the appropriate follow-up.
   6. Perform occasional clerical duties.
   7. Organize and coordinate the data entry work load.
   8. Collect statistics on production data entry and other related statistics as required.
   9. Coordinate work schedules of other data entry operators if applicable.
   10. Maintain data entry operating instructions.
   11. Contribute ideas and evaluate alternatives to improving data entry operations.
   12. Train and develop new data entry operators.
   13. Learn basic computer operations to be able to back up the computer operator.
   14. Aid in designing data entry forms.

POSITION DESCRIPTION

Title: Clerical—sales administrator II
Organization: Secrid Manufacturing
Division/Department: Administration

Location: Dayton
Description No.:
Supersedes:

   I. Position in Organization
      A. Reports to: Sales service manager.
      B. Directly supervises: None.
      C. Indirectly supervises: None.
  II. Major Responsibility
      Handles correspondence and reports generated by sales service manager and senior account manager.
 III. Specific Responsibilities (If more space is required, please attach a separate page.)
      1. Types dictation to customers.
      2. Takes phone messages.
      3. Handles requests by customers regarding status of contracts, stock, etc.
      4. Handles distribution of mail.
      5. Relief on switchboard.
      6. Does several reports which are sent to customers.

EXHIBIT 3   *(continued)*

POSITION DESCRIPTION

Title: Order—Billing clerk   Location: Dayton
Organization: Secrid Manufacturing   Description No.:
Division/Department: Administration   Supersedes:

I. Position in Organization
   A. Reports to: Order—billing supervisor.
   B. Directly supervises: None.
   C. Indirectly supervises: None.
II. Major Responsibility
   Prepare input for preparation of shipping papers and invoices. Verify machine-prepared ship papers and invoices.
III. Specific Responsibilities (If more space is required, please attach a separate page.)
   1. Visual checking to verify shipping order data (OSBIC) versus original customer order.
   2. Visual checking to verify shipments (yellow copy) versus invoice (OSBIC).
   3. Coding, pricing, and furnishing all pertinent data on input form (OSBIC) for each Hewitt-controlled and private brands order entry.
   4. Does daily V-T and Steiner orders.
   5. Filing orders and shipping copies.
   6. Types miscellaneous invoices (other than OSBIC).
   7. Mailing invoices and internal distribution of copies.
   8. V-T Monthly Inventory report.
   9. Auditing—making changes/adjustments on shipments (yellow shipping copy) prior to invoicing (OSBIC).
   10. Enters contracts into OSBIC on make and hold orders.
   11. Furnish financial analysis department copy of PB orders.
   12. Furnish traffic/credit departments copies of shipment when freight charges.

POSITION DESCRIPTION

Title: Purchasing department secretary   Location: Dayton
Organization: Secrid Manufacturing   Description No.:
Division/Department: Administration   Supersedes:

I. Position in Organization
   A. Reports to: Manager—purchasing department.
   B. Directly supervises: None.
   C. Indirectly supervises: None.
II. Major Responsibility
   Daily work flow in purchasing operation consisting of manager and secretary. Handles all clerical/steno functions while bringing judgment to job.

EXHIBIT 3 *(continued)*

III. Specific Responsibilities (If more space is required, please attach a separate page.)
   1. Reviews purchase requisitions and/or production request material requirements for validity before placing order.
   2. Places purchase orders via telephone or mail. Types purchase orders.
   3. Chooses suppliers on own or after consulting with purchasing manager.
   4. Takes incoming phone calls and handles matters on own or consults purchasing manager.
   5. Responsible for record files (purchase orders, Rec. reports, etc.)
   6. Arranges for appointments with vendors for purchasing manager.
   7. Secures material costs for cost estimating for financial analysis department, when required.
   8. Expedites materials needed to meet production commitments.
   9. Has a large amount of contact with vendors via phone and in person. A good working relationship is a must.
   10. Handles manager responsibilities when manager is out of the office. Makes decisions on own or consults with other managers.
   11. Annual purchases handled are $8 to $10 million.
   12. Handles purchasing manager's correspondence, typing, etc.

POSITION DESCRIPTION

Title: Traffic/credit administration assistant   Location: Dayton
Organization: Secrid Manufacturing   Description No.:
Division/Department: Administration   Supersedes:

   I. Position in Organization
      A. Reports to: Manager—Traffic/inventory control.
      B. Directly supervises: None.
      C. Indirectly supervises: None.
   II. Major Responsibility
   Perform all traffic-related functions for the company. Provide credit liaison with ASR.
   III. Specific Responsibilities (If more space is required, please attach a separate page.)
      1. Handles credit/traffic department mail.
      2. Verify freight rates.
         a. Inbound.
         b. Outbound.
      3. Tracing of freight.
         a. Inbound.
         b. Outbound.
      4. Handles and expedites the following:
         a. Air shipments.
            (1) Outbound.

EXHIBIT 3 *(concluded)*

  b. Rail shipments inbound.
   (1) Tallow.
   (2) CNO.
   (3) Miscellaneous.
  c. Glycerine shipments.
  d. Overseas shipments.
 5. Phone communication.
  a. Traffic.
  b. Credit.
   (1) Credit references.
 6. Handles freight claims.
 7. Handles outside traffic personnel in credit/traffic manager's absence.
 8. Vacation relief for credit/traffic manager.
 9. Liaison on credit matters between Secrid and ASR.

POSITION DESCRIPTION

Title: Clerical—Sales administrator III   Location: Dayton
Organization: Secrid Manufacturing   Description No.:
Division/Department: Sales/field sales   Supersedes:

 I. Position in Organization
  A. Reports to: District manager.
  B. Directly supervises: None.
  C. Indirectly supervises: None.
 II. Major Responsibility
  Handles correspondence and reports generated by district manager.
 III. Specific Responsibilities (If more space is required, please attach a
  separate page.)
  1. Types dictation to customers.
  2. Takes phone messages.
  3. Handles requests by customers regarding status of contracts,
   stock, etc.
  4. Relief on switchboard.
  5. Does several reports generated by district manager.

After looking through the material Rosa had given her, she found a relevant survey (see Exhibit 4) and drew up the following plan.

1. Call Secrid and check the currency of the information in hand. (Changes and current salaries are in Exhibit 5.)
2. Analyze the current situation by graphing the position of the incumbents within their current grades. Evaluate for inner consistency and probable effects upon employees.
3. Check adequacy of job descriptions and select key jobs.

EXHIBIT 4   Dayton Area Wage Survey

DAYTON AREA WAGE SURVEY

DECEMBER 198X

U.S. DEPARTMENT OF LABOR

BUREAU OF LABOR STATISTICS
(Bulletin 3000-64)

Secrid Manufacturing Company, Inc.

EXHIBIT 4   *(continued)*

DAYTON AREA WAGE SURVEY
DECEMBER 198X
U.S. DEPARTMENT OF LABOR
BUREAU OF LABOR STATISTICS
(Bulletin 3000-64)

Secrid Manufacturing Company, Inc.

Class A.   Work requires the application of experience and judgment in selecting procedures to be followed and in searching for, interpreting, selecting, or coding items to be entered from a variety of source documents.   On occasion may also perform routine work as described for class B.

NOTE: Excluded are operators above class A using the key entry controls to access, read, and evaluate the substance of specific records to take substantive actions, or to make entries requiring a similar level of knowledge.

Class B. Work is routine and repetitive. Under close supervision or following specific procedures or detailed instructions, works form various standardized source documents which have been coded and require little or no selecting, coding, or interpreting of data to be entered. Refers to supervisor problems arising from erroneous items, codes, or missing information.

* * * * * * * * * *

COMPUTER OPERATOR

In accordance with operating instructions, monitors and operates the control console of a digital computer to process data. Executes runs by either serial processing (processes one program at a time) or multiprocessing (processes two or more programs simultaneously). The following duties characterized the work of a computer operator:

 * Studies operating instructions to determine equipment setup needed.
 * Loads equipment with required items (tapes, cards, disks, paper, etc.).
 * Switches necessary auxiliary equipment into system.
 * Starts and operates computer.
 * Responds to operating and computer output instructions.
 * Reviews error messages and makes corrections during operation <u>or</u> refers problems.
 * Maintains operating record.

May test-run new or modified programs. May assist in modifying systems or programs. The scope of this definition includes trainees working to become fully qualified computer operators, fully qualified computer operator, and lead operators providing technical assistance to lower level operators. It excludes workers who monitor and operate remote terminals.

EXHIBIT 4   *(continued)*

Class A. In addition to work assignments described for a class B operator (see below) the work of a class A operator involves at least one of the following:

  * Deviates from standard procedure to avoid the loss of information or to conserve computer time even though the procedures applied materially alter the computer unit's production plans.
  * Tests new programs, applications, and procedures.
  * Advises programmers and subject-matter experts on setup techniques.
  * Assists in (1) maintaining, modifying, and developing operating systems or programs; (2) developing operating instructions and techniques to cover problem situations; and/or (3) switching to emergency backup procedures (such assistance requires a working knowledge of program language, computer features, and software systems).

An operator at this level typically guides lower level operators.

Class B. In addition to established production runs, work assignments include runs involving new programs, applications, and procedures (i.e., situations which require the operator to adapt to a variety of problems). At this level, the operator has the training and experience to work fairly independently in carrying out most assignments. Assignments may require the operator to select from a variety of standard setup and operating procedures. In responding to computer output instructions or error conditions, applies standard operating or corrective procedures, but may deviate from standard procedures when standard procedures fail if deviation does not materially alter the computer unit's production plans. Refers the problem or aborts the program when procedures applied do not provide a solution. May guide lower-level operators.

Class C. Work assignments are limited to established production runs (i.e., programs which present few operating problems). Assignments may consist primarily of on-the-job training (sometimes augmented by classroom instruction). When learning to run programs, the supervisor or a higher level operator provides detailed written or oral guidance to the operator before and during the run. After the operator has gained experience with a program, however, the operator works fairly independently in applying standard operating or corrective procedures in responding to computer output instructions or error conditions, but refers problems to a higher level operator or the supervisor when standard procedures fail.

SWITCHBOARD OPERATOR

Operates a telephone switchboard or console used with a private branch exchange (PBX) system to relay incoming, outgoing, and intrasystem calls. May provide information to callers, record and transmit messages, keep record of calls placed and toll charges. Besides operating a telephone switchboard or console, <u>may</u> also type or perform routine clerical work (typing or routine clerical work may occupy the major portion of the worker's time, and is usually performed while at the switchboard or console). Chief or lead operators in establishments employing more than one operator are excluded. For an operator who also acts as a receptionist, see Switchboard Operator-Receptionist.

SWITCHBOARD OPERATOR-RECEPTIONIST

At a single-position telephone switchboard or console, acts both as an operator—see Switchboard Operator—and as a receptionist. Receptionist's work involves such duties as greeting visitors; determining nature of visitor's business and providing

EXHIBIT 4   *(continued)*

appropriate information; referring visitor to appropriate person in the organization or contacting that person by telephone and arranging an appointment; keeping a log of visitors.

ORDER CLERK

Receives written or verbal customers' purchase orders for material or merchandise from customers or sales people. Work typically involves some combination of the following duties: Quoting prices; determining availability of ordered items and suggesting substitutes when necessary; advising expected delivery date and method of delivery; recording order and customer information on order sheets; checking order sheets for accuracy and adequacy of information recorded; ascertaining credit rating of customer; furnishing customer with acknowledgement of receipt of order; following up to see that order is delivered by the specified date or to let customer know of a delay in delivery; maintaining order file; checking shipping invoice against original order. Exclude workers paid on a commission basis or whose duties include any of the following: Receiving orders for services rather than for material or merchandise; providing customers with consultative advice using knowledge gained from engineering or extensive technical training; emphasizing selling skills; handling material or merchandise as an integral part of the job.

Positions are classified into levels according to the following definitions:

Class A. Handles orders that involve making judgments such as choosing which specific product or material from the establishment's product lines will satisfy the customer's needs, or determining the price to be quoted when pricing involves more than merely referring to a price list or making some simple mathematical calculations.

Class B. Handles orders involving items which have readily identified uses and applications. May refer to a catalog, manufacturer's manual, or similar document to insure that proper item is supplied or to verify price of ordered item.

ACCOUNTING CLERK

Performs one of more accounting clerical tasks such as posting to registers and ledgers; reconciling bank accounts; verifying the internal consistency, completeness, and mathematical accuracy of accounting documents; assigning prescribed accounting distribution codes; examining and verifying the clerical accuracy of various types of reports, lists, calculations, postings, etc.; preparing journal vouchers; or making entries or adjustments to accounts.

Levels C and D require a basic knowledge of routine clerical methods and office practices and procedures as they relate to the clerical processing and recording of transactions and accounting information. Levels A and B require a knowledge and understanding of the established and standardized bookkeeping and accounting procedures and techniques used in an accounting system, or a segment of an accounting system, where there are few variations in the types of transactions handled. In addition, some jobs at each level may require a basic knowledge and understanding of the terminology, codes, and processes used in an automated accounting system.

Class A. Maintains journals or subsidiary ledgers of an accounting system and balances and reconciles accounts. Typical duties include one or both of the following: Reviews invoices and statements (verifying information, ensuring sufficient funds have been obligated, and if questionable, resolving with the submitting unit, determining

EXHIBIT 4   *(continued)*

accounts involved, coding transactions, and processing material through data processing for application in the accounting system); and/or analyzes and reconciles computer printouts with operating unit reports (contacting units and researching causes of discrepancies, and taking action to ensure that accounts balance). Employee resolves problems in recurring assignments in accordance with previous training and experience. Supervisor provides suggestions for handling unusual or non-recurring transactions. Conformance with requirements and technical soundness of completed work are reviewed by the supervisor or are controlled by mechanisms built into the accounting system. NOTE: Excluded from class A are positions responsible for maintaining either a general ledger or a general ledger in combination with subsidiary accounts.

Class B. Uses a knowledge of double entry bookkeeping in performing one or more of the following: Posts actions to journals, identifying subsidiary accounts affected and debit and credit entries to be made and assigning proper codes; reviews computer printouts against manually maintained journals, detecting and correcting erroneous postings, and preparing documents to adjust accounting classifications and other data; or reviews lists of transactions rejected by an automated system, determining reasons for rejections, and preparing necessary correcting material. On routine assignments, employee selects and applies established procedures and techniques. Detailed instructions are provided for difficult or unusual assignments. Completed work and methods used are reviewed for technical accuracy.

Class C. Performs one or more routine accounting clerical operations such as: Examining, verifying, and correcting accounting transactions to ensure completeness and accuracy of data and proper identification of accounts, and checking that expenditures will not exceed obligations in specified accounts; totaling; balancing, and reconciling collection vouchers; posting data to transaction sheets where employee identifies proper accounts and items to be posted; and coding documents in accordance with a chart (listing) of accounts. Employee follows specific and detailed accounting procedures. Completed work is reviewed for accuracy and compliance with procedures.

Class D. Performs very simple and routine accounting clerical operations, for example, recognizing and comparing easily identified numbers and codes on similar and repetitive accounting documents, verifying mathematical accuracy, and identifying discrepancies and bringing them to the supervisor's attention. Supervisor gives clear and detailed instructions for specific assignments. Employee refers to supervisor all matters not covered by instructions. Work is closely controlled and reviewed in detail for accuracy, adequacy, and adherence to instructions.

* * * * * * * * * * * *

KEY ENTRY OPERATOR

Operates keyboard-controlled data entry device such as keypunch machine or key-operated magnetic tape or disk encoder to transcribe data into a form suitable for computer processing. Work requires skill in operating an alphanumeric keyboard and an understanding of transcribing procedures and relevant data entry equipment.

Positions are classified into levels on the basis of the following definitions:

LS-2

a.   Secretary to an executive or managerial person whose responsibility is not equivalent to one of the specific level situations in the definition for LS-3, but whose organizational unit normally numbers at least several dozen employees

EXHIBIT 4   *(continued)*

and is usually divided into organizational segments which are often, in turn, further subdivided. In some companies, this level includes a wide range of organizational echelons; in others, only one or two; or

b.   Secretary to the head of an individual plant, factory, etc., (or other equivalent level of official) that employs, in all, fewer than 5,000 persons.

LS-3

a.   Secretary to the chairman of the board or president of a company that employs, in all, fewer than 100 persons; or

b.   Secretary to a corporate officer (other than chairman of the board or president) of a company that employs, in all, over 100 but fewer than 5,000 persons; or

c.   Secretary to the head (immediately below the officer level) over either a major corporatewide functional activity (e.g., marketing, research, operations, industrial relations, etc.) or a major geographic or organizational segment (e.g., a regional headquarters, a major division) of a company that employs, in all, over 5,000 but fewer than 25,000 employees; or

d.   Secretary to the head of an individual plant, factory, etc., (or other equivalent level of official) that employs, in all, over 5,000 persons; or

e.   Secretary to the head of a large and important organizational segment (e.g., a middle management supervisor of an organizational segment often involving as many as several hundred persons) of a company that employs, in all, over 25,000 persons.

LS-4

a.   Secretary to the chairman of the board or president of a company that employs, in all, over 100 but fewer than 5,000 persons; or

b.   Secretary to a corporate officer (other than the chairman of the board or president) of a company that employs, in all, over 5,000 but fewer than 25,000 persons; or

c.   Secretary to the head, immediately below the corporate officer level, of a major segment or subsidiary of a company that employs, in all, over 25,000 persons.

NOTE: The term 'corporate officer' used in the above LS definition refers to those officials who have a significant corporatewide policymaking role with regard to major company activities. The title 'vice president,' though normally indicative of this role, does not in all cases identify such positions. Vice presidents whose primary responsibility is to act personally on individual cases or transactions (e.g., approve or deny individual loan or credit actions; administer individual trust accounts; directly supervise a clerical staff) are not considered to be 'corporate officers' for purposes of applying the definition.

Level of Secretary's Responsibility (LR)

This factor evaluates the nature of the work relationship between the secretary and the supervisor, and the extent to which secretary is expected to exercise initiative and judgment. Secretaries should be matched at LR-1 or LR-2 described below according to their level of responsibility.

LR-1

Performs varied secretarial duties including or comparable to most of the following:

EXHIBIT 4   *(continued)*

a.   Answers telephones, greets personal callers, and opens incoming mail.
b.   Answers telephone requests which have standard answers.   May reply to requests by sending a form letter.
c.   Reviews correspondence, memoranda, and reports prepared by others for the supervisor's signature to ensure procedural and typographical accuracy.
d.   Maintains supervisor's calendar and makes appointments as instructed.
e.   Types, takes and transcribes dictation, and files.

LR-2

Performs duties under LR-1 and, **in addition**, performs tasks requiring greater judgment, initiative, and knowledge of office functions including or comparable to most of the following:

a.   Screens telephone and personal callers, determining which can be handled by the supervisor's subordinates or other offices.
b.   Answers requests which require a detailed knowledge of office procedures or collection of information from files or other offices.   **May** sign routine correspondence in own or supervisor's name.
c.   Compiles or assists in compiling periodic reports on the basis of general instructions.
d.   Schedules tentative appointments without prior clearance.   Assembles necessary background material for scheduled meetings.   Makes arrangements for meetings and conferences.
e.   Explains supervisor's requirements to other employees in supervisor's unit. (Also types, takes dictation, and files.)

The following tabulation shows the level of the secretary for each LS and LR combination:

		LR-1	LR-2
LS-1	. . . .	Class E	Class D
LS-2	. . . .	Class D	Class C
LS-3	. . . .	Class C	Class B
LS-4	. . . .	Class B	Class A

* * * * * * * * * *

EXHIBIT 4 *(continued)*

APPENDIX B
OCCUPATIONAL DESCRIPTIONS

The primary purpose of preparing job descriptions for the Bureau's wage surveys is to assist its field representatives in classifying into appropriate occupations workers who are employed under a variety of payroll titles and different work arrangements from establishment to establishment and from area to area.   This permits grouping occupational wage rates representing comparable job content.   Because of this emphasis on interestablishment and interarea comparability of occupational content, the Bureau's job descriptions may differ significantly from those in use in individual establishments or those prepared for other purposes.   In applying these job descriptions, the Bureau's field representatives are instructed to exclude working supervisors; apprentices; and part-time, temporary, and probationary workers. Handicapped workers whose earnings are reduced because of their handicap are also excluded.   Learners, beginners, and trainees, unless specifically included in the job description, are excluded.

Listed below are several occupations for which revised descriptions or titles are being introduced in this survey:

Accounting clerk	Drafter
Key entry operator	Stationary engineer
Computer operator	Boiler tender

* * * * * * * * * *

OFFICE

SECRETARY

Assigned as a personal secretary, normally to one individual. Maintains a close and highly responsive relationship to the day-to-day activities of the supervisor. Works fairly independently receiving a minimum of detailed supervision and guidance. Performs varied clerical and secretarial duties requiring a knowledge of the office routine and understanding of the organization, programs, and procedures related to the work of the supervisor.

Exclusions.   Not all positions that are titled 'secretary' possess the above characteristics. Examples of positions which are excluded from the definition are as follows:

a.   Positions which do not meet the 'personal' secretary concept described above;

b.   Stenographers not fully trained in secretarial-type duties.

c.   Stenographers serving as office assistants to a group of professional, technical, or managerial persons;

d.   Assistant-type positions which entail more difficult or more responsible technical, administrative, or supervisory duties which are not typical of secretarial work, e.g., Administrative Assistant, or Executive Assistant;

EXHIBIT 4   *(continued)*

---

e.   Positions which do not fit any of the situations listed in the sections below titled 'Level of Supervisor,' e.g., secretary to the president of a company that employs, in all, over 5,000 persons;

f.   Trainees.

Classification by Level.   Secretary jobs which meet the required characteristics are matched at one of five levels accounting to (a) the level of the secretary's supervisor within the company's organizational structure and, (b) the level of the secretary's responsibility.   The tabulation following the explanations of these two factors indicates the level of the secretary for each combination of the factors.

Level of Secretary's Supervisor (LS)

LS-1

a.   Secretary to the supervisor or head of a small organizational unit (e.g., fewer than about 25 or 30 persons); or

b.   Secretary to a nonsupervisory staff specialist, professional employee, administrative officer, or assistant, skilled technician or expert. (NOTE: Many companies assign stenographers, rather than secretaries as described above, to this level of supervisor or nonsupervisory worker.)

EXHIBIT 4 (continued)

Table A-1. Weekly Earnings of Office Workers in Dayton, Ohio, December 198X

Occupation & industry division	Number of workers	Average weekly hours (standard)	Mean[2]	Median[2]	Middle range[4]	110 and under 120	120–130	130–140	140–150	150–160	160–170	170–180	180–200	200–220	220–240	240–260	260–280	280–300	300–320	320–340	340–380	380–420	420–460	460–500	500–540	540–580
Secretaries	1,557	39.0	257.00	237.00	202.50–288.50			16	22	42	60	58	149	237	222	175	112	145	66	46	71	29	38	36	16	17
Manufacturing	1,062	39.5	278.00	255.00	219.00–304.00			16	22	42	6	33	101	146	155	135	87	120	46	41	57	29	37	36	16	17
Nonmanufacturing	495	38.5	212.00	205.00	167.00–240.00			2		24	54	25	48	91	67	40	25	25	20	5	11		1			
Public utilities	93	39.0	226.50	191.00	155.00–288.50			2			8	7	8	4	3	8	9	6	5	5	11					
Secretaries, class A	138	39.0	339.50	309.50	255.00–361.00									6	4	24	4	21	21	8	17	4	4	4	6	17
Manufacturing	105	39.5	364.50	320.00	280.50–462.50											16	8	15	15	8	14	3	4	4	6	17
Nonmanufacturing	33	37.5	260.50	247.00	224.00–310.00						2	2	5	6	8	8	2	6	6	1	3	1				
Secretaries, class B	270	39.5	288.00	280.00	240.00–301.50						2	2	7	27	34	34	30	52	19	21	30	24	35	21		
Manufacturing	201	39.5	307.00	288.00	264.50–314.50					6	2	13	5	8	23	23	26	44	11	21	30	24	34	21		
Nonmanufacturing	69	39.0	232.50	226.00	212.00–259.00				2	6	2	8	27	19	11	11	4	8	8		1					
Secretaries, class C	571	39.5	272.50	245.00	210.50–300.50			2		30	53	23	76	109	66	31	30	11	5	5	11	2	1			
Manufacturing	425	39.5	291.00	258.00	226.50–351.50			2			47	15	64	84	52	30	1	2	1	5	11	2	1			
Nonmanufacturing	146	39.0	219.50	209.50	196.00–240.00			2	2	30		8	12	25	14	1		9	5							
Secretaries, class D	452	38.5	212.00	209.50	180.00–232.50			14	20	6	2	20	10	9	13	8	6	6								
Manufacturing	273	39.0	215.50	215.50	195.00–232.50							10	6	9	13	8	6	6								
Nonmanufacturing		38.5	206.50	182.00	162.00–225.00																					
Public utilities	67	38.5	230.50	170.00	154.00–318.00																					
Secretaries, class E	114	38.5	190.00	176.00	145.00–229.50			5	1	25	6	1	12	10	6	11	1		5	4						
Manufacturing	58	39.0	225.50	229.00	194.50–252.50			5	1	9	3	1	8	4		2	1		4	1						
Switchboard operators	75	39.5	192.00	176.00	151.00–212.00		22	9	23	43	15	22	40	43	15	11	1	4								
Manufacturing	39	39.0	213.50	198.00	161.50–229.50		18	1	14	31	6	6	13	21	15	2	1	4								
Nonmanufacturing	36	39.5	169.00	150.00	150.00–182.50		4	9	9	12	9	16	27	22		9										
Switchboard operator-receptionists	250	40.0	180.50	176.00	150.00–201.00			2	12	40	10	30	35	20	2	11	12	1				1	1			
Manufacturing	133	40.0	181.00	161.00	150.00–201.00					12		3	11	3	2	9	3	1				1	1			
Nonmanufacturing	117	40.0	180.00	179.50	155.00–208.00			2	12	40	10	30	35	13		1	12	1								
Order clerks	167	40.0	182.00	178.50	150.00–195.00			2	12	40	6	32	32	13	2	1	1	1								
Manufacturing	72	40.0	196.00	178.50	176.50–212.50				12	12	6	30	11	11	2	1	3	1								
Order clerks, class B	143	40.0	173.00	176.00	150.00–190.00			2	12	40	6	32	35	13	2	1	1	1								
Manufacturing	57	40.0	179.00	178.50	176.00–195.00					12		30	11	1	2	1	1	1								
Accounting clerks	1,506	39.5	201.50	190.50	167.00–221.00		6	42	108	137	109	191	317	203	144	95	47	22	7	12	43	8	9	6		
Manufacturing	650	40.0	222.50	207.00	186.00–242.00		7		8	7	28	74	165	120	73	72	42	15	1	6	16	8	9	6		
Nonmanufacturing	856	39.5	186.00	173.00	155.00–200.00		6	42	101	129	81	117	152	83	71	23	5	7	6	6	27					
Public utilities	83	39.5	257.50	240.00	152.00–374.00		1		16	4	4	5		1	2	2	1	1	6	6	27					
Accounting clerks, class A	240	40.0	261.50	250.00	215.50–284.00				2	6	8	10	25	25	24	54	21	14		4	37	2	2	6		
Manufacturing	125	40.0	273.50	251.00	186.00–283.00				2	6	8	9	9	7	7	38	18	8		4	10	2	2	6		
Nonmanufacturing	115	39.5	248.50	234.50	183.00–290.00							10	16	19	17	16	3	6			27		3			
Accounting clerks, class B	395	39.5	189.50	186.00	164.50–200.00		12	12	34	40	37	56	92	65	85	26	21	12	4	4		2	2	6		
Manufacturing	107	40.0	221.50	198.00	176.00–240.00						21	21	23	21	50	7	18	12	4	4		2	2	6		
Nonmanufacturing	288	39.5	178.00	178.00	155.00–199.50		12	12	34	40	26	35	69	53	35	19	3									
Accounting clerks, class C	591	39.5	197.50	193.00	170.00–216.00		6		35	47	46	76	144	93	85	28	14	2		4	5	4				
Manufacturing	313	40.0	212.00	205.00	177.00–234.00				4	21	46	36	108	69	50	21	12	1	1		5	4				
Nonmanufacturing	278	39.0	180.50	157.50	156.00–202.00		6	6	31	47	4	40	36	24	35	7	2	1	3	3						
Public utilities	28	38.5	185.00	157.50	147.00–183.00				12	2	3	4		2		2			3	3						
Accounting clerks, class D	280	39.5	176.50	172.00	150.00–189.00		6	24	37	44	18	49	56	20	9		2		6	6						
Manufacturing	105	39.5	193.00	184.00	168.50–206.00				3	18	17	17	25	18	9		2									
Nonmanufacturing	175	40.0	166.50	155.00	140.00–177.00		6	24	34	36	1	32	31	2					6	6						

162

EXHIBIT 4 (concluded)

Table A-1. Weekly Earnings of Office Workers in Dayton, Ohio, December 198X—Continued

Occupation & industry division	Number of workers	Average weekly hours (standard)	Mean²	Median²	Middle range⁴	110 and under 120	120–130	130–140	140–150	150–160	160–170	170–180	180–200	200–220	220–240	240–260	260–280	280–300	300–320	320–340	340–380	380–420	420–460	460–500	500–540	540–580
Key entry operators	603	39.5	198.50	184.00	161.00–208.50	—	—	35	22	76	49	62	167	87	36	8	3	14	14	2	5	9	14	—	—	—
Manufacturing	268	40.0	220.50	199.00	180.00–223.00	—	—	—	10	17	18	19	71	62	25	5	1	1	9	2	5	9	14	—	—	—
Nonmanufacturing	335	39.0	181.50	178.00	155.50–196.50	—	—	35	12	59	31	43	96	25	11	3	2	13	5	—	—	—	—	—	—	—
Key entry operators, class A ...	286	39.5	214.50	196.50	184.00–210.00	—	—	—	4	6	11	26	125	62	14	3	2	5	5	1	3	5	14	—	—	—
Manufacturing	159	40.0	228.50	198.00	184.00–218.50	—	—	—	—	2	8	13	59	39	12	1	1	1	—	1	3	5	14	—	—	—
Nonmanufacturing	127	39.0	198.50	196.50	186.00–201.50	—	—	—	4	4	3	13	66	23	2	2	1	4	5	—	—	—	—	—	—	—
Key entry operators, class B ...	317	39.5	184.00	169.00	154.00–199.00	—	—	35	18	70	38	36	42	25	22	5	1	9	9	1	2	4	—	—	—	—
Manufacturing	109	40.0	211.00	201.50	163.50–224.50	—	—	—	10	15	10	6	12	23	13	4	—	—	9	1	2	4	—	—	—	—
Nonmanufacturing	208	39.0	170.00	160.00	153.50–179.50	—	—	35	8	55	28	30	30	2	9	1	1	9	—	—	—	—	—	—	—	—
Computer operators	470	39.5	264.00	245.00	231.00–297.50	—	4	11	34	43	125	88	23	71	4	21	1	7	13	6	13	5	1	—	—	—
Manufacturing	170	39.5	292.00	260.00	226.00–332.00	—	—	4	10	20	23	27	17	17	3	11	1	5	6	13	6	—	1	—	—	—
Computer operators, class A ...	144	39.5	310.00	297.50	274.00–326.50	—	—	—	—	9	5	15	12	62	2	10	5	5	10	—	8	3	1	—	—	—
Manufacturing	60	39.5	335.50	301.50	272.00–370.50	—	—	—	—	1	1	10	8	10	2	8	5	5	8	—	8	3	1	—	—	—
Computer operators, class B ...	168	40.0	260.00	245.00	226.00–258.00	—	—	13	17	28	14	13	10	5	1	11	1	1	1	4	5	2	—	—	—	—
Manufacturing	79	40.0	276.50	253.00	224.50–292.00	—	—	4	4	14	9	10	8	4	1	3	1	1	1	4	5	2	—	—	—	—
Nonmanufacturing	89	40.0	245.50	245.00	245.00–245.00	—	—	—	—	3	56	56	2	1	—	8	—	—	—	—	—	—	—	—	—	—
Computer operators, class C ...	158	40.0	225.50	233.00	203.50–233.00	—	4	11	20	17	92	3	9	2	2	2	2	2	2	—	—	—	—	—	—	—
Manufacturing	31	40.0	247.00	222.00	187.50–275.50	—	4	4	5	6	4	3	4	2	1	1	1	2	2	—	—	—	—	—	—	—
Registered industrial nurses ...	59	40.0	390.00	411.00	316.00–452.00	—	—	—	—	—	1	2	2	9	2	1	7	6	17	8	8	3	—	—	—	—
Manufacturing	58	40.0	390.00	414.50	314.50–452.50	—	—	—	—	—	1	2	2	9	1	1	6	6	17	8	8	3	—	—	—	—

4. Evaluate data available on market salaries, and select sources for comparison.
5. Extract market salaries for key jobs and construct a new grade system, if necessary, independent of the current system.
6. Plot current jobs in new system and compare against market midpoints.

EXHIBIT 5 Information Obtained and/or Verified from Secrid

Secrid Manufacturing Co., Inc.

Position	Years with Company	198X Rate	Present Rate	Name	Notes
Executive secretary—sales/financial	17	1,290	1,380	Pulley	None
Data entry operations	—	845	—		Vacant as of 5/1/8(X + 1)
Maintenance supply/receiving clerk	8	1,065	1,155	Toler	None
Clerk—sales administration	2	810	925	Carr	Promoted to grade 3
Traffic/credit administration assistant	12	1,240	1,340	Arlington	None
Data processing operations	1	860	925	Oehler	None
Industrial nurse	8	1,470	1,470	Jasper	Last raise 9/8X
Executive secretary—manufacturing	4	1,185	1,300	Tarkington	None
Sales department secretary	10	1,145	1,145	Art	Last raise 7/8X
	14	1,105	1,190	White	None
	2	1,015	1,095	Level	None
Accounts payable clerk	3	880	950	Thorne	None
Order-billing clerk	1	765	820	Parnell	None
Clerk—accounts payable/inventory control/traffic	—	810	—	—	Vacant as of 5/1/8(X + 1)
Purchasing department secretary	18	1,165	1,260	Kale	None
Switchboard operator/receptionist	1	750	805	Peter	None
Personnel generalist	9	1,160	1,275	Welch	None
Payroll clerk	3	930	1,085	Sellers	None

Occupational Health and Safety

1 Breyer Meat Packing, Inc.

The Breyer Meat Packing, Inc., is one of the largest meat-packing firms in the Midwest. The firm, located in Sioux City, Iowa, employs 580 workers. The administrative staff includes plant management, clerical workers, infirmary staff, and a two-person personnel office. However, most of the employees (540) are considered line employees. Their view of the administrative staff is that that group represents overhead. In private, workers talk about how much more they themselves could make if the plant manager, Melvin Flournoy, would trim some of the "fat." These employees had come to know and like Charmaine, Mel's administrative assistant. There wasn't much that happened around the place that she didn't know about. A number of workers trusted and confided in her. Charmaine never violated anyone's confidence. So, it was no surprise that Brenda and other meat cutters told her about their hopes, dreams, and fears.

"Charmaine, my hands have been bothering me something terrible! I really think it's part arthritis and part having to do the same movements all the time at my workbench. I can't prove it but other veteran meat cutters are having trouble with their wrists and hands, too." These comments were the first indication that Charmaine had that her friend Brenda was having the same kind of trouble other employees in the firm had complained about over the past 10 years. Of course, the workers didn't want to complain too often or too loudly, since there was little support from management to solve or even investigate the problem. In fact, Brenda remembers when Willie Wooten complained to his supervisor about numbness and trouble moving his arms and hands. It wasn't long before Willie had joined the unemployment lines.

Many employees, Charmaine included, had heard the rumors about Willie and other employees who complained about hand, wrist, and arm problems. The grapevine had it that those who complained would be let go, so that the company could avoid any workers' compensation claims.

Charmaine didn't know what to believe. They had always treated her well. She had worked for BMP, Inc., for 15 years. As a secretary in the plant manager's office, she had seen a number of changes take place, and she also had watched the company grow from a small shop of less than 100 employees to a medium-sized firm of 580 employees.

During the past year, BMP, Inc. had been visited by many compliance agency representatives. Of course, on a continuous basis, U.S. Department of Agriculture meat inspectors remained on the premises examining the meats to be certain that they were graded properly. In January, the Environmental Protection Agency (EPA) visited and inspected the plant. Their concern was to see that waste and meat by-products were being disposed of properly. The EPA inspectors wanted to verify that there were no air or water pollution violations. The Occupational Safety and Health Administration (OSHA) has jurisdiction over the workplace when it comes to health and safety matters. The OSHA people came during the summer months. Their visit appeared to surprise plant management. The OSHA inspectors spent most of their time checking industrial accident and sickness records. Little time was spent observing the actual meat-packing processes. The last agency to visit was the Immigration and Naturalization Service (INS). They had never been to the plant before. Charmaine had been told by her boss, Mr. Bob Riley, that the INS had taken on the task of enforcing something called the Immigration Reform and Control Act. This fairly new act required that only people who have the right to live and work in the United States be employed by American companies. The companies are responsible for any violations of the law. Charmaine wasn't sure what the INS wanted. She did know that when their inspectors left, they seemed upset that the company had not modified certain personnel and record-keeping procedures. One inspector asked Charmaine if she was aware of any changes in personnel background checks or citizenship verification procedures. Mel had gone on a two-day tirade over the federal government and all its record-keeping demands.

As Charmaine thought about what Brenda and others told her, she wondered if anything should be done about this recurring problem. She wasn't sure what responsibility, if any, the company had to those who complained of arm, wrist, and hand troubles. Finally, she asked herself, what role would any of the government agencies mentioned play in resolving the physical problems?

Discussion Question

Tell how you would respond to Charmaine's questions.

2 The Philadelphia Bulletin (A)

The *Philadelphia Bulletin* is one of three daily newspapers in a thriving market—the metropolitan Philadelphia area. In recent weeks there has been a great deal of talk about news from within the organization, as opposed to the reporting of activities which have occurred outside of the firm. All of the employees were still in a state of shock over the discovery that many of the workers suffered from a debilitating work-related ailment.

The personnel office had to turn its attention from the daily ritual of screening application forms for replacement personnel in a rapidly changing, high-turnover environment. Instead of the immediate concern of getting the right person in the right job, the personnel office had to find ways of keeping healthy the employees the *Bulletin* has hired. The problem: RSI. RSI, or repetitive strain injury, affects the wrists, elbows, or arms, and it is caused by spending long hours writing or editing with some kinds of computers.

THE BUSINESS SECTION

Roberta Peters is an author and national financial securities writer for the *Bulletin*. She was told not to pick up a pencil. She has been forced to wear splints and stop writing for weeks at a time. "Of all the injuries I've had in my life, this is the worst. Your hands are so essential to everything you do in this business. I earn my livelihood by using my hands. Writers have no choice in the matter." Other employees in this section are affected. Fortunately, some of them simply report a little tenderness in their elbows or wrists that is relieved by exercises, better posture, or an occasional break from the video terminal.

Roberta describes the progression of the disease. "The pain progressed slowly. It began in the hands and wrists like a twinge of arthritis or numbness. Some of my athletic friends might see similarities between this condition and tennis elbow. I tried to work through it. The result was intense pain; pain so intense that I could not sleep at night. In fact, even the most routine tasks became impossible to do." Picking up a book or folding laundry caused waves of pain to shoot up along my hands, wrists, and arms."

The hard part, Roberta said, was dealing with her feelings. "I alternated between being angry that my work had led to this problem and fearful that I would never be able to return to doing the work I loved."

Requirement

1. What can the employees and the employer do to help overcome the problem of RSI?

The Philadelphia Bulletin (B)

The meeting was a somber one. Crowded into the small room that served as the office of Carter Jones, city editor, were William Hines, associate sports editor; Jonathan Randal, general counsel; Eleanor Randolph, education editor; Sandy Rovner, health editor; Don Colburn, county news; Paul Reisner, science editor, and the managing editor, Daniel Burnside. Last to enter the room was the publisher and editor, Steven Altman. The publisher addressed the group, "As you all know, Frank suffered a mild heart attack two weeks ago. He was taken to University Hospital on the Penn campus. He suffered the attack while relaxing at home. Thank goodness, the hospital is located only a few blocks from his home."

"I've asked William Hines to serve as sports editor during Frank's recovery period. It is a demanding job, but I feel certain that Bill can do what needs to be done during Frank's absence. Bill has worked with Frank over the past nine years and knows the routine and demands of the job."

"One thing I hope you all realize, and I say this for Bill as much as for anyone in this room: Frank's heart attack should help us realize the inherent stress and demanding nature of the jobs we do. The deadlines are 'tight' and the hours are long. Every day we each feel the pressure. Back in journalism school our professors tried to help us understand and appreciate this aspect of the job. Everyone who completed a journalism program was required to do an internship at a newspaper so that he/she would have a firsthand acquaintance with the hustle and bustle of our business. We were told that if we wanted a typical 'nine-to-five' existence we were in the wrong field of endeavor'."

"You might be wondering why I invited Mr. Randal to this meeting and why I made this previous comment about the demands and nature of the job. These two are connected. I thought that I would ask Jonathan to explain the connection."

Randal explained to the group that there is an increasing amount of litigation occurring in this country. "One area of rapid change involves that dealing with personal legal liability of managers under employment discrimination law. We are discovering that tort claims (e.g., assault, battery, defamation, infliction of emotional distress) are being made against employers and their agents. Closer to home—we have been informed by an attorney that Frank and his family have brought a tort action against us in state court. According to the documents we have received, the newspaper and Mr. Altman are judged directly responsible for the stress-related illnesses suffered by Frank. He charges that the nature of the job is such that we knew or should have known that the tasks and demands of the job would directly lead to stress-related outcomes. It is our intent to proceed by hiring independent legal counsel to obtain an evaluation of Mr. Altman's rights and whether there exists any conflict of interest with the corporation."

Discussion Questions

1. Discuss the nature of the job and the lawsuit now filed against the newspaper.
2. What rights and responsibilities do employees and employers have in relation to high-stress jobs?

3 *Hargrove Petrochemicals (A)*

Hargrove Petrochemicals is composed of 10 autonomous divisions and corporate headquarters, as Exhibit 1 indicates. The case focuses on the Bristol Works. Its organization is given in Exhibit 2.

Bristol Works is housed in a building erected in 1904. The building is five stories high. The top two are not used since the floors are too dangerous. The second and third floors have holes and rotted places in them.

The third floor holds the rock shop lab and the marketing departments. The second floor contains the office, some warehousing, and some buffing compound production lines. The first floor contains the warehousing for heavier materials and the rest of the manufacturing lines. The main operation is chemicals. The work is nonunion.

Jesse Fuller has been with Hargrove for 20 years, all in conjunction with the Bristol Works. He holds a BS in chemistry from City University of New York. He worked his way through college. He's done almost everything at Bristol. He started as a foreman in the manufacturing unit. He's run the rock shop, supervised the warehouse for two years, and sold the compounds. The office and lab are white-collar or technical jobs so he's not worked there. His employees like him, although they are a

EXHIBIT 1 Hargrove Petrochemicals Organization Chart

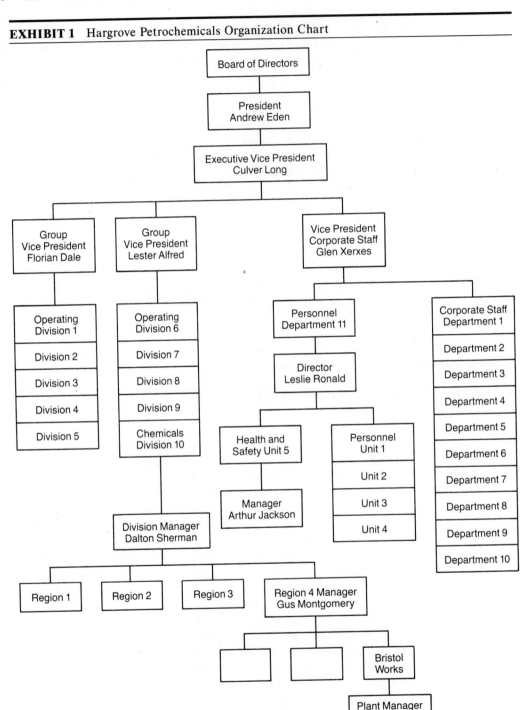

EXHIBIT 2   Organization Chart: Bristol Works

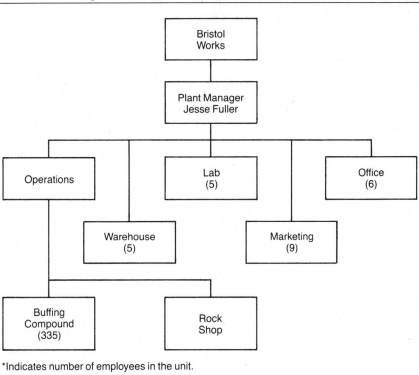

*Indicates number of employees in the unit.

bit afraid of him, too. He has a terrible temper, which he loses about once a month. When that happens, everyone tries to get out of the way.

Jesse is now 53 years old. He's happy with the Bristol Works. He likes the town and wouldn't move. Bristol is like his own firm since he's isolated geographically from Hargrove.

Since Bristol makes more money for Hargrove than his budget calls for, they let Jesse alone. He has lower turnover than expected. Absenteeism is also low. His safety and health record is above average. All in all, Hargrove and Jesse are happy with the Bristol Works.

During the past years since the effective date of the Occupational Safety and Health Act, Bristol has been subject to routine but infrequent visits by OSHA inspectors. In February 1984, James Munsey, a new inspector, was assigned to the region. In April, James came to Bristol when Jesse was at a meeting at headquarters. The OSHA inspector determined that the buffing manufacturing was producing unsafe gases.

As is his right, he shut down the plant that day. Jesse flew back and modified the gas filters. James passed the filters, and Bristol started production again. Before leaving the plant, James informed Jesse that, because various toxic substances, such as benzene, were utilized at Bristol, he thought it best to inspect the plant more frequently.

In May, James came back and shut the plant again when Jesse was at a Rotary meeting. Again, the filters were cleaned and modified. This time Jesse was really angry. After the plant was reopened and James was gone, Jesse held a meeting of all employees. At the meeting he said:

> Look, this OSHA guy is killing us. This is an old works. We can't afford to be shut down. At my recent meeting at corporate headquarters, I tried to make the case that we needed a new building here. The sharp-pencil boys pointed out that we are profitable now, but not if we have to build a new plant. The industry is overcrowded, and Hargrove will close this plant, rather than spend money on it. If we get shut down or have to buy a lot of antipollution crap, they could shut us down. That OSHA guy is the enemy—just like a traffic cop. We've got to pull together, or we could all sink together.

The employees had never seen Jesse so angry before, and they feared for their jobs now more than ever. There was a lot of unemployment in the area. Before adjourning the meeting, Jesse asked his people for ideas on how to deal with the OSHA inspector. Responses ranged from beating up James to barring him from the plant.

In July, James Munsey appeared at the Bristol Works gate. In accordance with their instructions, the guards stopped James until he could be signed in and given a badge. Once the guards received authorization, then he could be allowed on the premises. Security guard Clarence Smith phoned Jesse.

Smith [*to Fuller*]

>   The OSHA inspector is here to see you.

Fuller

>   Oh, my God! [pause] You go out there and tell him I'm too busy to see him today.

Munsey

>   Ask your boss if he's too busy tomorrow.

Smith [*on the intercom*]

>   Mr. Fuller, are you too busy tomorrow to see the inspector?

Fuller [*on the intercom*]

>   What do you want this time, Munsey?

Munsey

>   Because of previous violations, you're due for another inspection.

Fuller

>   Look, I'm busy. I am not sure when I will be able to see you. In fact, I

don't feel obligated to let you in unless you can produce a search warrant. That, and only that, will convince me that you have a legitimate purpose.

After Fuller left, the place was bedlam. Everyone was put on red alert. No work was done. The whole plant was cleaned up. The lab was put in order. Bottles that leaked were secured. Shelves were straightened. The rock shop was cleaned up. Machines without safety guards were moved and covered up, as if they were no longer used. Machines too heavy for the third floor were moved. The filters were cleaned. The water bath was cleaned. The slippery floor made of metal, which was supposed to be neutralized and scrubbed daily (though it usually got it monthly), was neutralized and scrubbed. Everyone helped. Even the secretaries and lab technicians helped with the cleaning. The lab was put in order.

The next day the inspector returned. He did not have a warrant. The guard waved him on and sent him to Fuller's office. James and Jesse toured the plant and the inspector passed the Bristol Works. But the employees wondered if the inspector didn't have to realize what had happened.

Discussion Questions

1. Under what conditions does a company have the right to refuse OSHA inspectors admission to the facilities?
2. What are the real problems and issues in this case? Explain.

Hargrove Petrochemicals (B)

On August 15, a group of federal inspectors pulled up to the Bristol Works gate. They stopped there and asked to see Jesse Fuller, the plant manager. Security guard Wesley Walker called Fuller.

Walker [to Fuller]

Federal inspectors are here to see you.

Fuller

Inspectors! Don't tell me James Munsey thinks he needs help?

Walker

No, sir. I met Mr. Munsey. He is not here. These gentlemen are from an agency called the EPA.

Fuller

> EPA! Keep them there. I will come down to the gatehouse to meet them.

Walker

> Issue badges and sign them in, sir?

Fuller

> No. Just wait until I get there.

Fuller went over to the gatehouse. When he arrived, he introduced himself. He met the five representatives of the Environmental Protection Agency. The agents were armed with a search warrant from a U.S. magistrate. The team had been sent to check compliance with the Toxic Substances Control Act. The team's makeup was interesting. Of the five people, two were agency officials, one was a state environmental worker, and two were employees of a private company, Bildisco Environmental, Inc., which was one of a number of consulting corporations hired by the EPA to conduct inspections.

Jesse looked thoughtful for awhile, then turned to the security guard. He told Walker not to issue badges or to sign in anyone. Jesse told the EPA inspectors that they would not be admitted to the plant. After a very lengthy argument, the five men left the premises waving the search warrant and vowing to return.

In a formal letter to the Environmental Protection Agency, the company explained that it did not object to an inspection but it was dissatisfied with the makeup of the EPA inspection group. Hargrove management claimed to be particularly concerned about protecting their trade secrets. If the EPA sends a team consisting of its own agents, the company said, they will have free access to the plant and be made privy to the specifics of any chemical process. Hargrove felt that they were protected by federal law, because EPA employees were restricted in terms of the information they learned. Few private consultants are subject to the same sanctions imposed by the Trade Secrets Act or other federal law. Also, the company believed that private consultants abuse their power. These outsiders like to throw their weight around.

The federal agency's response wasn't long in coming. The EPA did not accept the company's position. The EPA believed it was a smoke screen used to prevent the government from detecting noncompliance with the Toxic Substances Control Act. Further, the worry about consultants being untrustworthy was seen as unwarranted. Since the EPA began using large numbers of consultants, it has encountered no increase in complaints regarding trade secrets. The EPA also informed Hargrove that a lawsuit would be forthcoming. When Jesse Fuller received his copy of the letter, he wondered if he had gotten the company into big trouble.

Discussion Questions

1. Does a company have a right to bar EPA inspectors from the company's facilities?
2. Evaluate the company's stated reasons for barring the EPA inspection team. Are the reasons legitimate? Tell why or why not.

Hargrove Petrochemicals (C)

Arthur Jackson is manager of the health and safety division of Hargrove's personnel department. Arthur is a graduate of Case Western Reserve University, with a BS in industrial engineering. He has taken additional short courses in safety management offered by various professional associations. He had five years' experience in the safety department of Allied Chemical before coming to Hargrove a year ago. He was safety manager for several operating divisions (including this division) prior to coming to the home office staff last year. He has tried to visit each division and plant since then, although he has never been to the Bristol Works. Hargrove has many plants, and he has personally visited about one third of them since he went to the home office.

The role of corporate-level health and safety is to set policy for the corporation. The office keeps the divisions and plants informed on the latest information, trains divisional and (where appropriate) plant-level people, and is responsible to the president for safety for the whole company. It also is responsible for seeing that all operations meet all health and safety standards of the company and OSHA. Jackson has three professionals on his staff.

Arthur has received word about Bristol's recent experiences with OSHA and has decided to go down to Bristol and see what's going on. He arrives the week after the EPA visit. Jesse is sick that day. Arthur inspects the works and finds numerous OSHA violations. The works also violates a number of Hargrove's own safety and health regulations.

When Arthur returns to his office, he decides to call a meeting of his subordinates to discuss how the company might approach the problem of making Bristol Works safe and hazard-free for employees there. He decides to generate his own list of alternative actions, just in case his subordinates come up empty. In rummaging through his files he discovers a report on genetic screening for employment purposes.[1] The more

---

[1]Genetic screening in the employment context involves the identification of applicants hyper susceptible to occupational disease, thus facilitating selective placement or exclusion of candidates on the basis of the genetic information.

he reads, the more he likes the idea. A professor at the University of Maryland, Judy D. Olian, had done an extensive study on the current level of corporate involvement in genetic screening, and she identified a series of public policy issues related to the use of genetic screening devices. Arthur silently thanked her for her thoroughness. He believed that the home office would be unwilling to make major improvements at Bristol, but that minor improvements, emphasis on the use of protective clothing including respirators, and genetic screening might do the trick. So, he would propose this short-term solution. He had his secretary reproduce Professor Olian's study as well as a report by the Office of Technology and Assessment, "The Role of Genetic Testing in the Prevention of Occupational Disease." These materials, along with a couple of recent newspaper articles on the subject, were distributed to his subordinates.

Discussion Questions

1. Assume you are one of Arthur's subordinates. How effective do you believe genetic testing would be in making Bristol Works a safer and healthier workplace?
2. What kinds of issues and legal implications are raised in using genetic screening for employment purposes?

---

4 A-1 Electronics

A-1 Electronics, located in Cincinnati, Ohio, is a wholesale distributor of electrical equipment and parts. During the past few years, A-1 has enjoyed a steady sales growth, which has allowed for an expansion in the geographical territory A-1 covers and a broader product line. Six years ago A-1's sales were limited to the greater Cincinnati area. Currently there are customers in a five-state region. Over the same period, the number of inventory items has increased from 14,000 to approximately 20,000 items. Business growth and the need for greater efficiencies, particularly in A-1's record handling, are responsible for a modernization plan in the main office. This modernization plan includes

This case was prepared by Professor William P. Smith, Hofstra University.

purchasing more automated office equipment and recruiting qualified persons to operate such equipment.

The company's main office is the workplace for 3 managers and 16 clerical staff. Robert Riley, the general manager, has his own secretary, as do the purchasing manager, Steven Phillips, and the accounting manager, Elizabeth Seale. All of the managers' offices are adjacent to a large work area, where all of the office employees are located. Of the remaining 13 office staff, 5 are responsible for purchasing and accounts payable functions, another 5 oversee inventory control, outgoing shipments, and accounts receivable records, and 3 employees perform typing and filing tasks. See Exhibit 1 for a basic floor plan of the office.

The area where all office employees work is basically a large room, 1,000 square feet in area, with no subdivisions, partitions, or walls to separate the workers. There is one door at the front of the office that is used as a main entrance. A corridor at the rear of the office leads to the main warehouse. There are no windows in the main office area and the building is centrally heated and air-conditioned.

All of the 16 office employees are women. Nine have been with the company 10 years or more, 11 are 45 years or older, and 12 are married. Their pay is average for those persons with comparable skills in the local labor market. A basic benefit package includes life and health insurance, a pension plan, and paid vacations. These benefits are modest, but typical for the labor market, and accrue slowly as a function of seniority.

As part of the modernization plan for A-1's office, a word processing system was leased. None of the current employees is sufficiently skilled or particularly interested in learning to operate this new piece of equipment. Thus, the decision was made to hire someone who already possessed word processing experience. To assist with recruitment, the services of a local employment agency were retained. A-1 had had good success in the past with this agency.

By the end of the second week of recruitment, two qualified persons had been referred by the employment agency. After interviews with both applicants, Robert Riley and the office manager offered the job to Kathryn Palmer. Riley was quite satisfied with the selection and was anxious to have her begin work, because the expense of leasing word processing equipment and of the recruiting process was making this transaction a costly one.

Kathryn's first few days in the job appeared to go very well. Her past experience on an identical word processing system was a definite asset. She also seemed to get along quite well with the other people in the office. However, the afternoon of her fourth day on the job Kathryn complained of headaches and nausea and asked to go home. The following morning she reported to work in apparently fine health. After work-

EXHIBIT 1 Floor Plan of A-1's Office

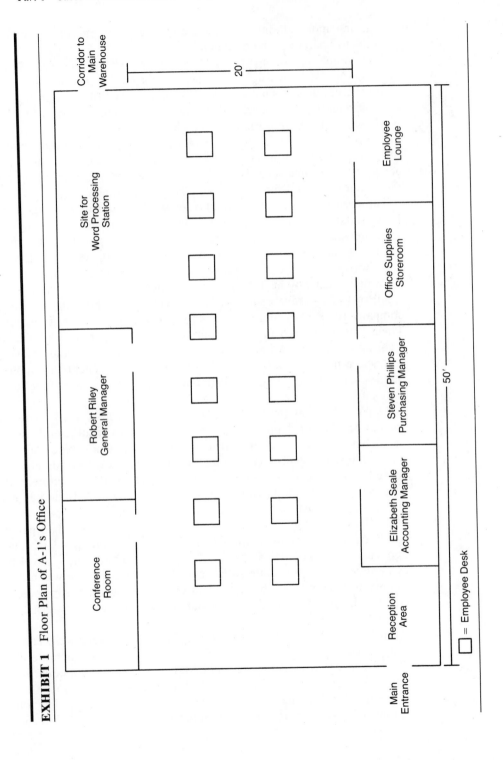

ing a couple of hours, she began suffering from the same complaints and again asked to go home. Later that day, Kathryn called Riley from her home and apologetically submitted her resignation. She said the cigarette smoke in the office created by other employees was responsible for her illness. Kathryn's resignation and her reason caught Riley totally by surprise. He sensed Kathryn must have really had another reason for wanting to quit and was looking for an excuse in the cigarette smoke. Riley knew a majority of the office employees smoked at their desks. Occasionally, jokes were made about "air pollution" in the office, but the jokes never seemed too serious or critical. No one had ever formally complained about the smoking. Riley was tempted to dismiss Kathryn as some sort of fanatic, yet he realized he now faced a rather serious problem. A-1 was back at "square one" and would have to reinitiate a search for another word processing operator.

Riley informed the employment agency of Kathryn's resignation on what he felt to be spurious grounds. The agency assured him they would not charge a fee for placing Kathryn and would commence a new search immediately. Unfortunately, they told him, the other qualified applicant was no longer available and that, at this time, the supply of experienced word processing operators was not keeping pace with demand. In the meantime, another division of the employment agency specializing in temporary employment could refer experienced persons who were available strictly for short-term assignments. Riley contracted to have a temporary employee come to work at A-1 while a search for a full-time replacement was conducted. Riley was anxious to settle on someone and get the word processing operation going, because by now there were other, what he considered more pressing, matters for his attention. It was Friday afternoon and the temporary employee was contracted to begin work on the following Monday for two full weeks.

On Monday, the temporary employee reported to work and remained all day. She also had experience on this same system and caught on quickly for her first day. Later that evening, Riley received a call at his home from a representative of the agency, saying the temporary worker had asked to be removed from the assignment and that another temporary worker would have to be assigned. The reason for the reassignment: the temporary employee could not tolerate the smoke in the office.

On Tuesday morning the second temporary employee (or third, as Riley had come to think of it) reported to A-1. Both the temporary service and Riley spoke to the new worker about smoke in the office, and the employee, although a nonsmoker, indicated smoking did not bother her. Over the course of the next several days this employee would remain with the assignment. Riley considered her performance to be adequate.

The sudden resignation of two promising workers for the same reason gave Riley cause to consider their complaint. As the search for a permanent replacement continued into its second week without success, Riley began to contemplate the "fish that got away" and if there might have been a way both resignations could have been avoided. He began to examine the situation more fully.

Of the 16 people in the office, 10 were smokers. Most of the smoking employees were among those who had been with A-1 for several years and had a demonstrated loyalty to the firm. It was true that, despite the centrally controlled cooling system, by late afternoon a hazy fog would accumulate and the temperature might increase to 80 degrees. These factors had never seemed important before, but they began to take on a new significance as Riley reflected on a recent article he had read in the newspaper citing nonsmokers' complaints about public smoking. The article referred to recent legislation in San Francisco, California, and in Suffolk County, New York, which required employers to accommodate a smoke-free work environment for nonsmoking employees who request one. Riley felt sure nothing like that would happen in Cincinnati, but it did cause him to speculate on the challenge his own firm might begin to face in the near future. Several of the younger, more promising office employees were nonsmokers and with time might become more assertive about their right to work in a smoke-free environment. At the same time, Riley sensed nothing but problems should he try to restrict what had become a well-entrenched social norm among a group of dedicated and loyal employees. He did not want a potential conflict on this issue to escalate into a situation where one group or the other would feel as if their rights were being unfairly sacrificed. At this time A-1 did not have a smoking policy, but Riley considered it a matter of time before one would have to be implemented. He wondered if he should wait until more complaints were raised or try and initiate a fair-minded policy now.

Discussion Questions

1. Should Riley institute some sort of no-smoking policy at A-1 at this time?
2. Should the failure to attract a qualified word processing employee be a significant factor in deciding how to handle this situation?
3. Since some localities (e.g., San Francisco and Suffolk County) have adopted "indoor air" laws, what guidelines would you suggest to an organization forced to implement a no-smoking policy?

5 *Andromeda Chemical, Inc. (A)*

Andromeda Chemical, Inc., had its start at the beginning of the 20th century. Today, the company operates 110 plants throughout the world. Andromeda also has 17 research laboratories across the country. It is a chemical company engaged primarily in the manufacture and sale of a diversified line of specialty chemicals. The firm's products include:

1. *Consumer products*—Personal care and grooming products, women's fragrances, and household maintenance and cleaning aids.
2. *Specialty chemicals*—Specialty chemicals for industrial water treating; mining and paper chemicals; enhanced oil-recovery products; aerospace products, process chemicals, and catalysts; dyes, plastics additives; fine, rubber, and textile chemicals; inorganic and organic pigments; industrial safety equipment; and acrylic fibers for apparel, home furnishings, and industrial applications.
3. *Medical*—Antibiotics, steroids, vitamins, and other pharmaceuticals; vaccines; fine chemicals and bulk pharmaceuticals.
4. *Formica*—Formica brand decorative laminates for residential construction, commercial construction, furniture, and adhesives.
5. *Agricultural*—Animal feed, health and veterinary products, insecticides, herbicides, fungicides, and phosphate and nitrogen fertilizer products.

In 1978, Paul Green was promoted to the position of personnel director of the Denver plant of Andromeda Chemical, Inc. When interviewed for the position, Paul was led to believe that the problem areas of the job related to recruitment of technical people, turnover, and union demands for a stronger role in decision making. Once he landed the job, however, he was to learn about a more pressing problem.

Paul was really pleased that he was chosen for the personnel director's job. In his seven years with Andromeda Chemical, he had worked in a variety of positions. After graduation from Colorado State University, he accepted a personnel assistant's job with the company. He was lucky that his first assignments were all at the corporate headquarters. He received his MBA from Rutgers University exactly two months prior to leaving to take his first plant personnel assignment. Paul believed his two-year stints as assistant personnel director in plants at Omaha, Nebraska, and Cedar Rapids, Iowa, would prove invaluable to him in his

---

This case was written by Professor George E. Stevens and by Kendra Clausen and Cliff Hodge, Arizona State University. All names in the case are disguised.

new job. The Denver plant assignment seemed to be an excellent indication of the company's confidence in his abilities. Paul considered the promotion as a reward for top performance and completion of degree requirements. The plant was one of the company's largest unionized operations. The position of personnel director is critical to the successful operation of the facility.

One day, Paul looked up to see Dr. Rick Morrison, the plant's physician, striding purposefully toward his office. Seldom did he see or hear from Rick, so Paul was surprised and puzzled by this unexpected visit. Rick must have noticed Paul's bewilderment because the following conversation ensued as they met at the door:

Rick

Paul, I hate to burden you with another problem since you've only been on the job a matter of months, but I have little choice in this instance.

Paul

What's up? Is it anything serious?

Rick

I am afraid so. For some time, corporate has been studying the problem of worker exposure to toxic substances. As plant physician, my charge was to determine the existence of any work-related health or safety problem here. A plant area which has come under close scrutiny is Building 21. This building contains our lead pigment division.

Paul

Yes it does. We have a number of lead smelter workers in there who have responsibility for manufacturing and assembling certain key products.

Rick

Our studies and those of other researchers indicate a link between lead exposure and anemia, central nervous system damage, kidney disease, and "female problems."

Paul

What does that mean? We have eight women, ages 26 to 43, working in the lead pigment division. They have done an excellent job there. Women don't leave as quickly as men, and the quality of their work is higher. Is there anything wrong about women working in Building 21?

Rick

We now know that lead exposure may lead to sterility, miscarriages, and birth defects in the employees' unborn children. These problems are particularly tragic. I focus on women because their health problems are more visible and affect their babies as well.

After the conversation, Paul sat there thumbing through the report that Rick had left with him. Clearly, there was a problem. A breakdown by production process and by building location indicated that the incidence of certain medical problems was significantly higher in Building

21. That building was the only one which involved a lead chromate pigments process. The kinds of problems found were consistent with the National Institute for Occupational Safety and Health (NIOSH) research studies concerning the potential dangers of lead. If there is a link between these workers' health problems and the production process (and there seems to be), then Paul must develop alternative courses of action.

Three days after his meeting with Rick, Paul wrote a memo to Patrick Livers, the plant manager. He reviewed the events leading up to his meeting with the plant physician and the implications of the medical data. In concluding his memo, he identified a few alternative courses of action that might be taken: (1) take no action, (2) forbid women of child-bearing age from working in Building 21, and (3) discontinue the production process. Although Paul recognized that his list was not exhaustive, he felt these alternatives were the most obvious.

Discussion Question

1. You are Patrick. The company has given you a great deal of responsibility and autonomy. What can you do about the health problem? What other alternatives might you consider? On what basis (criteria) will you choose the best alternative?

Andromeda Chemical, Inc. (B)

In 1979, less than 12 months after Paul had been promoted to personnel director of Andromeda Chemical's Denver plant, five women filed a complaint against the company. They claimed that Andromeda had forced them to be surgically sterilized in order to keep their jobs. All females who worked in the plant were made an offer. The women could accept other positions in the plant. They would be transferred from their present jobs (which paid $225 a week plus overtime) to "utility" jobs that paid $175 a week without extras or to jobs in other departments. For a 90-day period, each transferee would be kept at her old pay rate. The offer to female workers in Building 21, however, went one step further. The company believed that female workers in certain jobs in Building 21 were exposed to concentrations of lead that might cause miscarriages and serious disorders. The executives felt that it was impossible to reduce the lead concentrations to even safer levels without committing large amounts of capital to that purpose. In the interest of "fetus protection," the company excluded women from such areas unless they had proof that they were sterile. A staff report by the Occupational Safety and Health Administration (OSHA) revealed that those female workers who actually were sterilized all retained their jobs.

OSHA cited Andromeda for violations it detected during its October 1979 inspection of the Denver plant. The agency alleged that the company's sterilization policy violated OSHA's 1970 charter. By the end of the month, Andromeda received notification from OSHA that the agency had proposed total penalties of more than $40,000. These penalties were the result of a number of citations issued following the recent comprehensive safety and health inspection of the plant. OSHA issued a citation in which the agency alleged that Andromeda Chemical "adopted and implemented a policy which, as a condition of employment in certain specified areas, necessitated sterilization of female employees." This policy, in OSHA's words, "did not fulfill the general duty requirements"[1] of the Occupational Safety and Health Act of 1970. Furthermore, one OSHA medical officer condemned the company when she stated her belief that no worker must be forced to sacrifice his or her right to conceive children in order to hold a job. As the company was preparing to defend its position on the alleged policy before two federal administrative law judges, word arrived that a class action suit had been filed on behalf of five of the women who worked in Building 21. The Colorado Civil Rights Commission had notified the company of the suit and the allegations made by the plaintiffs.

A lump formed in Paul's throat as he thought about the events of the past year. The company had acted quickly once it discovered a lead-exposure problem, and the decision to offer women of child-bearing capacity other jobs was an indication of its concern and benevolence. The class action suit was a shock to management. The women had given not the slightest hint that they would sue the company. Thirteen women were party to the sex discrimination suit. The OSHA citations were another matter. The company, in general, and the Denver plant, in particular, seemed to be a favorite target of OSHA. Now the newspaper and other media coverage of the situation was making the company look like an insensitive, money-grubbing monster. The public relations department was working hard to counteract the negative publicity and to salvage the company's image.

The situation was viewed quite differently by Andromeda. Back in 1977, the company had made a statement regarding a medical policy excluding women from the lead pigment division at the plant. The women were told that no one would lose her job or sustain a loss of

---

[1]The general duty clause of the act requires employers to provide employment free from recognized hazards likely to cause death or serious physical harm.

wages as a result of the policy. According to company officials, at no time were female workers pressured. In fact, Rick Morrison said they were discouraged from seeking sterilization procedures.

In two days, Paul must attend a big meeting at the headquarters office in New Jersey. As plant personnel director, he has responsibility for all personnel matters so he has no choice but to go. Key executives, including representatives from the legal department, will have lots of questions to ask him. His answers and those of the plant manager are to be used to help the company develop a legal strategy for the upcoming hearings and determine the likelihood of a successful defense.

Discussion Questions

1. Can a company exclude female employees from hazardous work areas unless they're sterile?
2. Does a company sterilization policy as described here fulfill the general duty requirements of the Occupation Safety and Health Act of 1970?
3. Evaluate the positions of OSHA and that of Andromeda Chemical on the sterilization policy issue. As the federal administrative law judge, how would you rule? Why?

6 *Missouri Mining & Metal Works, Inc.*

". . . If you are in conformity with OSHA regulations and any of its state counterparts, if you are actively promoting a safe work place, and if you respond when unsafe conditions are called to your attention, then you are unlikely to open yourself up—as a corporation or as an individual—to criminal liability. But if you believe that ignorance is bliss, then criminal culpability is one more reason to change your ways." (James O. Castagnera, *Personnel,* September 1985, p. 12.)

Missouri Mining & Metal Works, Inc. (MMM), is a small company that prepares electrical wire for manufacturers' use. The electrical wire is fed through a production process that coats wires with liquid enamels and polyvinyl chlorides. The company has been in business in the same neighborhood for 48 years. Workers at the plant often are related to each other and learned about their jobs from friends, neighbors, and relatives who served as co-workers, subordinates, and supervisors. The company seldom employed more than 75 employees. Despite their size, however, MMM was well known among regional building trades and industrial firms. The company supplied many firms in the St. Louis area with the quantity and quality of wire each desired for the job that had to be done.

Sales of the small wiring company had continued on an upward trend since 1941, when this country was at war. The president, two vice presidents, and the plant manager had all been with the company for more than 30 years. These company officers and all other company employees knew that the company's success meant a great deal to them because of MMM's profit-sharing plan.

The economic aspect of working for MMM had become a most important issue and the major factor in understanding why so many people had long years of service with the company. One area of improvement had been largely ignored—the cleanliness of the plant floor and limited attempts to remove certain fumes from the air system. Many employees had complained over the years that the ventilation system could not handle the fumes from the polyvinyl chloride and liquid enamel coatings.

Employee complaints don't tell the whole story. Over a period of approximately one year beginning in November 1988, and ending in December 1989, 40 employees became ill. It was discovered that some of them suffered from lung and nerve disorders. According to the employees' doctors, the cause of the illnesses was overexposure to a dozen hazardous chemicals at the plant. Company officials considered taking action to overcome the ventilation problem and exposure to hazardous chemicals, but they realized that the old plant and equipment would be hard to replace economically. If protective measures were taken, it was likely that the plant would no longer be profitable. The officials weighed their options.

A letter from an attorney spurred them into action. An employee talked to the Attorney General's Office about filing *criminal* charges against the company. He believed, according to his attorney, that the company "willfully and knowingly exposed its employees to great harm. . . ." The attorney also mentioned that the state environmental agency and the Occupational Health and Safety Administration were being made aware of conditions at the plant.

Given the threat of litigation, the company retained an attorney. After weeks of review, the attorney for the company reported the following:

1. That something called *preemption* implies that federal health and safety laws preempt the enforcement of state criminal laws by local and state prosecutors when an unsafe workplace causes death or injury to a worker.
2. Other defenses protect the employer as well.
3. He identified three "tried-and-true" legal theories that allegedly protect employers from tort liability:
    a. Assumption of risk.
    b. Contributory negligence.
    c. The fellow-servant doctrine.

After hearing the company-appointed attorney's presentation, the president had a queasy feeling down in the pit of his stomach. It was all too neatly packaged, too smooth, too certain. There was a great deal at stake yet the attorney seemed all too smug. Vaguely he recalled a case about the experience of Film Recovery Systems. Now he remembered. The television show "60 Minutes" did a program on a suburban Illinois plant where a worker allegedly died from overexposure to cyanide. That case was tied up in the courts but the state attorney brought criminal charges against the top management. As he gathered up his briefcase to go home that night he wondered how greatly exposed the company was to legal liability.

Discussion Questions

1. Are companies preempted from state criminal prosecution when federal health and safety rules apply?
2. What action(s) should the Occupational Safety and Health Administration and other similar agencies play in preventing such problems as are described in this case?

EEO, Affirmative Action, Reverse Discrimination

1 EEO and AIDS: A Right to Know

Service Supervisor Ellen Leary didn't need to be a doctor to know that Jim Fleermond, a fifth-year service rep, didn't look well. She was sure it had something to do with his many recent requests for time off to see his doctor.

"You feeling all right, Jim?" she asked when she met him at the water fountain.

"Why, did I do something wrong?" he asked defensively.

"Not at all, you're doing fine," she assured him. "Just asking."

In the following weeks, Vic Marconi, service supervisor in another unit, approached her. "How's Jim Fleermond?" he inquired.

"Okay . . . well, not okay, I guess. He has to see his doctor all the time. Why do you ask?"

"I heard he hangs out with a gay crowd. One of them just died of AIDS, and another has been diagnosed positive. I thought you'd want to know."

"Oh!" Leary was stunned. "I . . . thanks for telling me, Vic."

When Fleermond asked her for time off to see his doctor again, she used the opportunity to confirm her suspicions.

"I'd like to say yes, Jim, but you're asking for a lot of time off these days," she said. "It would help me to know what this is all about."

"I don't have to tell you," he retorted.

"I've stretched the rules for you more than once," she said firmly. "If you want more time, I want to know the reason."

"You won't tell anyone," Fleermond said anxiously.

"Anything you tell me is confidential," said Leary.

Fleermond acknowledged that he had been diagnosed as having ARC—AIDS-related complex.

Leary was saddened to hear her suspicions confirmed. She consulted with the medical department to see if she needed to take any special measures for Fleermond or other employees. But they said no special steps were necessary.

At the next staff meeting, Vic Marconi asked her, "Whatever happened with Fleermond? Was there anything to those rumors?"

Leaning toward him, she said quietly, "Don't spread it around, Vic, but you were right. The poor guy has ARC."

"What a rotten break," Marconi sighed.

Within two weeks, Leary's department began to have morale problems. She no longer saw Fleermond chatting with co-workers. And he suddenly had a lot of space around him. He seemed to be isolated from other employees.

Then she heard that several employees would not use the water fountain. She explained to them that it was perfectly safe, but got nowhere. "I'm not going to take a chance of getting AIDS," one of them said.

Poor Fleermond, she reflected. He now has to cope with unfriendly co-workers in addition to his illness.

Finally, Fleermond resigned. She expressed her sympathy and well wishes—but was relieved at his departure.

To Leary, it seemed that a difficult problem had been solved for her—until she was informed by personnel that Fleermond had filed suit against the company, claiming constructive discharge (being forced to resign), discrimination because of handicap (AIDS), and invasion of privacy.

Discussion Questions

1. What, if anything, did management do wrong in this case?
2. Do you think the lawsuit against the firm will be successful? Why or why not?

2 *Affirmative Action and Whom to Hire*

Mr. Green, vice president—personnel, of the Hackney Paper Box Company has to make a decision as to whom to hire to be personnel manager for a 125-employee Hackney box plant located in Philadelphia, Pa.

The company affirmative action office has strongly advised him to hire a young black woman, June Triss, who has applied but Mr. Green believes a young white male applicant, Bob Young, to be better qualified for this specific job. Mr. Green has narrowed the field to these two. Hackney Paper Box Company has 47 small plants, each with a white male personnel manager. There are no other management-level personnel employees in the company except at corporate headquarters where there are 10 management-level white male employees. Of Hackney's approximately 1,000 management-level employees only six are black, two are Mexican-American, and six are female. Prior to 1964 no management-level persons were from any minority group and there were no females in management.

Mr. Green's evaluation and summary of the qualifications of the two applicants are as follows:

I. June Triss
   a. Extremely intelligent but seemed to lack common sense.
   b. Master's degree in industrial relations from Cornell, a magna cum laude graduate.
   c. Three years' experience as an assistant personnel manager at a leading nonunion department store; no union relations experience.
   d. Mediocre references from Cornell and the department store.
   e. Ambitious—told the plant manager she would have his job in three years.
   f. Poor personality—informed Mr. Green she was interviewing Hackney, not Hackney interviewing her.
   g. The members of the management group in Philadelphia did not seem to like her.
   h. She has stated that she would sue the company for discrimination if she did not get the job.
II. Bob Young
   a. Three years of college as a personnel major but forced to transfer for economic reasons to a small liberal arts college in his home-

---

This case was prepared by Professor James C. Hodgetts of Memphis State University and is intended to be used as a teaching device rather than to show correct or incorrect methods of operations.

town. He received a degree in history and graduated in the middle third of his class.

b. Five years' experience as assistant personnel manager in a 500-employee unionized paper box plant.

c. Good references from his college and excellent references from the paper box plant.

d. Excellent personality—Mr. Green and all members of management with whom he talked at Philadelphia liked him.

e. Not very aggressive—Mr. Green doubted if he would ever progress very far in the company but believed he would be an excellent plant personnel manager.

Both Triss and Young had answered an advertisement in the *New York Times*. The advertisement set minimum qualifications of a college degree and three years' experience as an assistant personnel manager. The advertisement did not say what kind of experience as an assistant personnel manager and did not say union relations experience was necessary.

All of the Philadelphia managers were white males. The personnel department at Philadelphia consisted of the manager and a secretary. The plant manager and production superintendent had experience dealing with the union but this was primarily the job of the personnel manager.

Mr. Green has to make a decision this week so that the new personnel manager can spend some time with the retiring personnel manager before he leaves.

Discussion Question

What should Mr. Green decide? Why? Carefully explain.

3 Salary Discrimination at Acme Manufacturing

Joe Blankenship was trying to figure out what to do about a possible salary discrimination situation he believed he had in his plant.

Mr. Blankenship recently took over as president of Acme Manufacturing from the founder and president for 35 years, Mr. Bill George. The company was family owned and was located in a small eastern Arkansas

This case was prepared by Professor James C. Hodgetts of the Fogelman College of Business and Economics of Memphis State University as a basis for class discussion.

town. It had approximately 250 employees and was the largest employer in the community. Mr. Blankenship was a member of the family that owned Acme, but he had never worked for the company prior to becoming president. He had an MBA and a law degree, plus 15 years of management experience with a large manufacturing organization where he was senior vice president for human resources when he made his move to Acme.

A short time after joining Acme, Mr. Blankenship started to believe that there was considerable inequity in the pay structure for salaried employees. A discussion with the personnel director led him to believe that salaried employees' pay was very much a matter of individual bargaining with the past president. Hourly paid factory employees were not part of the problem, since they were unionized and their wages were set by collective bargaining. An examination of the salaried payroll showed that there were 25 employees, ranging in pay from that of the president to that of the receptionist. A closer examination showed that 14 of the salaried employees were female. Three of these were frontline factory supervisors and one was the personnel director. The other 10 were nonmanagement.

This examination also showed that the personnel director appeared to be underpaid, and that the three female supervisors were paid somewhat below any of the male supervisors. However, there were no similar supervisory jobs in which there were both male and female job incumbents. When asked, the personnel director said she thought the female supervisors were paid lower mainly because they were women, and Mr. George did not think that women needed as much money because they had working husbands. Also, she said she thought they were paid less because they supervised less-skilled employees than the male supervisors. However, Mr. Blankenship was not sure that this was true.

The company from which Mr. Blankenship had moved had a good job evaluation system. Although he was thoroughly familiar and capable with this compensation tool, Mr. Blankenship did not have time to make much use of this knowledge at Acme. Therefore, he decided to hire a compensation consultant from a nearby university to help him. They decided that all 25 salaried jobs should be in the job evaluation unit, that a modified ranking method of job evaluation should be used, and that the job descriptions recently completed by the personnel director were current, accurate, and usable in the study.

The job evaluation showed that there was no evidence of discrimination in the nonmanagement jobs, but that the personnel director and the three female supervisors were being underpaid relative to comparable male salaried employees.

Mr. Blankenship was not sure what to do. He knew that if the underpaid women supervisors took the case to the local EEOC office, the company could be found guilty of female discrimination and would have to pay considerable back wages. He was afraid that if he gave these employees an immediate wage increase large enough to bring them up to where they should be, the male supervisors would be upset and the female supervisors might comprehend the total situation and want back pay. Mr. Blankenship was told that the female supervisors had never complained about the pay differences, and they probably did not know the law to any extent.

The personnel director agreed to take a sizable salary increase with no back pay, so this part of the problem was "solved." Mr. Blankenship believed he had four choices relative to the female supervisors:

1. To do nothing.
2. To gradually increase the female supervisors' salaries.
3. To increase their salaries immediately.
4. To call the three supervisors into his office, discuss the situation with them, and jointly decide what to do.

Discussion Questions

1. Does Mr. Blankenship have only four choices? Discuss.
2. What action should Mr. Blankenship take? Carefully explain.

4 *Meritor Savings Bank* v. *Vinson*

A former Meritor Savings Bank employee, Michelle Vinson, brought suit against the bank and her supervisor, a vice president there. She alleged that the vice president and manager of one of Meritor's branches, Sidney Taylor, demanded sexual favors from her.

Ms. Vinson first met Mr. Taylor in 1974. On that occasion, she asked him if she might obtain employment at the bank. Mr. Taylor gave her an application, which she completed and returned the next day. Later that same day Mr. Taylor called to inform Michelle that she had been hired. Taylor served as supervisor of Vinson when she began her employment as a teller-trainee. She was later promoted to teller, head teller, and assistant branch manager. All information available indicates that her advancement was based upon merit alone. In September of 1978, Vinson informed her supervisor (Taylor) that she was taking sick leave for an indefinite period. On November 1, 1978, the bank discharged her for excessive use of that leave.

According to Vinson, she had "constantly been subjected to sexual harassment" by Taylor. At trial, she testified that when she was hired and during her probationary period as a teller-trainee, Taylor treated her in a fatherly way and made no sexual advances. Shortly thereafter, however, he invited her to dinner and, during the course of the meal, suggested that they go to a motel to have sexual relations. At first she refused, but out of what she described as fear of losing her job she eventually agreed. Vinson says that Taylor thereafter made repeated demands upon her for sexual favors, usually at the branch, both during and after business hours. She estimated that over the next several years she had intercourse with him some 40 to 50 times. In addition, Vinson testified that Taylor fondled her in front of other employees, followed her into the women's rest room when she went there alone, exposed himself to her, and even forcibly raped her on several occasions. These activities stopped after 1977, she stated, when she began and continued a relationship with a young man.

Vinson also claimed that Taylor touched and fondled other women employees of the bank and she sought to call witnesses to support this charge. However, although some supporting testimony was admitted, the court did not allow her "to present wholesale evidence" of a pattern and practice relating to sexual advances to other female employees. She was instructed that she might well be able to present such evidence in rebuttal. Despite the alleged repeated sexual advances, Vinson acknowledged that she was afraid of Taylor and therefore never reported his harassment to any of his supervisors and never attempted to use the bank's complaint procedure.

Taylor denied all charges made by Vinson. He denied allegations of sexual activity. He said that he never fondled her, never made suggestive remarks to her, never engaged in sexual intercourse with her, and never asked her to do so. He claimed that the sexual harassment accusations were the result of a business-related dispute. The bank also denied Vinson's allegations and asserted that the bank was not aware of any sexual harassment by Taylor. The bank claimed it did not know and could not have known given that the former employee made no complaint to Taylor's supervisors or through the grievance process.

Requirement

Carefully examine the facts presented in this case, study Title VII of the Civil Rights Act of 1964, and review the EEOC Guidelines on Sexual Harassment before you answer the questions posed below. *Do not* research the *Meritor Savings Bank, FSB* v. *Michelle Vinson et al.;* to do so defeats the purpose of this intellectual exercise.

Discussion Questions

1. Is the behavior described "illegal sexual harassment"?
2. Identify and discuss the factors you considered in responding to the first question.

---

5 *And Justice for All (A)*

During the late 1970s, Americans began to read about reverse discrimination cases. In a legal brief submitted, whites were declaring that their rights were being trampled upon when minority individuals were designated to be "underprivileged," "economically disadvantaged," or any of the other labels used to describe individuals who were members of protected groups who were underrepresented in the nations' most prestigious schools.

Two landmark cases on this subject are *DeFunis* v. *University of Washington Law School* (1971) and *Bakke* v. *Board of Regents and University of California (Davis)* (1978). In the former case, DeFunis, a white male, was denied admission to the University of Washington Law School while a number of minority applicants were admitted. The facts of the case reveal that Mr. DeFunis had somewhat higher Law School Admission Test (LSAT) scores and, in some instances, higher grade point averages than some of the minority students who were admitted. DeFunis brought suit against the school. However, when the case reached the U.S. Supreme Court, the Court declared the case moot because DeFunis had been admitted since the case began winding its way through the legal system and he was now about to graduate.

The reverse discrimination issue did not go away simply because the Court refused to rule on the *DeFunis* case. Later came the *Bakke* case. Allan Bakke, a white male, was a former engineer who applied to the medical school at the University of California (Davis). He was denied admission, in part, because of a dual admission program operated by the university. According to court documents, the 100 seats available each year to medical students was divided such that 20 of them were set aside for "economically disadvantaged." The 20 students selected were not directly compared to the whites in the 80-seat category. Bakke learned, with the help of certain anonymous university employees, that he had higher Medical College Admission Test (MCAT) scores than some of the minority group members accepted in the special category. In both these cases, attorneys for the whites who filed the lawsuits argued that the grades earned and the standardized test scores should be either the primary basis or the sole basis of the selection process. Skin color or membership in a particular group, in their judgment, should not influence the process. Whites, in effect, are harmed by a process that is influenced by such vital national goals as need for diversity of student body and the need to overcome centuries-old problems of racism.

Discussion Questions

1. Which are the most appropriate factors to consider in making graduate and professional school admission decisions? Explain.
2. Do you agree with the school's argument or the plaintiffs' arguments regarding the admission process?

And Justice for All (B)

Recent reports indicate that The Office of Civil Rights of the Department of Education is holding compliance reviews at Harvard and the University of California at Los Angeles to check for violations of the Civil Rights Act of 1964. Certain groups of students perceive that they are not being treated fairly. They are—or are perceived to be—too smart.

The University of California at Berkeley is a most obvious case in point. At this popular, prestigious institution, they simply do not have the space to accept most of its would-be students. For the fall of 1989, the school had 3,500 freshman places and 21,301 applicants! Competition for those spots, therefore, is extremely intense. Berkeley, however, has been extremely aggressive and successful in recruiting minority students. Berkeley's student body is now 48.5 percent white—giving whites less representation on campus than in the population of the state as a whole.

Berkeley has a convoluted, complex set of policies that are designed to avoid racism. However, Berkeley could change the ethnic mix of the student body more by relying strictly on grades and standardized test scores to determine admission. But, Asian-Americans are complaining that they are *not* getting a fair deal in admission to top-level colleges. One controversial study released in 1989 provides support for their contention. The school's academic senate found no systematic bias against Asian-Americans but suggested admissions policies may have kept out an estimated 18 to 50 well-qualified Asian students in each of the years between 1981 and 1987. By traditional standards of academic merit, Asian-Americans seem to have a justifiable case. In fact, the Berkeley chancellor apologized and promised to correct the problem. One concern of the school, however, is that more than 25 percent of the entering class will be Asian-Americans, although the minority makes up only 7 percent of California's population. The rejected Asian-Americans feel that test scores and grades should "speak loudest."

Discussion Questions

1. Which are the most appropriate factors to consider in making graduate and professional school admission decisions in light of the information presented in this section? Explain.
2. Do you agree with the argument of the school or plaintiff regarding the admission process?

6 Forest Park Corporation (B)

Bob Pelzer, manager of employment planning, almost swallowed his morning doughnut whole. The headline seemed to jump off the page— FOREST PARK MUST ACT TO CURB BIAS. The article continued with the story that the U.S. District Court had ordered Forest Park to start implementation of Judge Paul Kimble's plan to end practices of racial discrimination on hiring and promotion. He was just turning to the continuation on page 8 when his secretary buzzed to say that his boss, the director of employee relations, was on the phone. No point in putting it off. He picked up the receiver. "Dick, I was just reading the news; what does it all mean?"

Dick

I'll give it to you straight, Bob—we're in big trouble. Not only do we have to locate the managers for the textile expansion, but now we've got to get the EEOC people off our backs, too. I'd appreciate your input on this problem. Got any ideas?

This case was prepared by Professor George E. Stevens and Professor R. Penny Marquette. The case is disguised for obvious reasons.

Bob

I haven't had time to think about it, Dick. I haven't even finished the article in the paper. Have you got details on this mess?

Dick

You'll have a copy of the Atlanta EEOC report on your desk in an hour. I'm afraid you're going to have to think fast. We knew they were coming down, but I checked with the plant manager and the new personnel director, and I was assured that everything was in order—now this! After the review last week, I flew down to check things out personally and you wouldn't believe the things the old personnel director did down there! Applications "misplaced," selected jobs designated for minorities only, people promoted over other people regardless of seniority. . . .

Bob

It was *that* bad?

Dick

I'm afraid so. It's all said and done now. We have a new personnel director, and we've simply got to get on the right track. The president was on the phone first thing this morning, and he's asking some tough questions. I need answers—fast. That's where you come in. I need to know exactly how we go about selecting, developing, transferring, and promoting people at all levels, including professionals and managers. Prepare a report and get it to me by 12 tomorrow. I'm going to meet with the president at 3 tomorrow and that'll give me some time to study it.

Bob

Okay, Dick, you'll have the report in plenty of time.

Bob hung the phone up and sat back. Why, he wondered, did things always seem to happen at the worst possible time? The corporation was just beginning to expand its involvement in the textile industry. To meet the company's needs, Bob was working on a program to speed up hiring. His biggest headache was trying to find approximately 75 lower-range and middle managers. Now he'd have to stop working on the textile expansion and start worrying about equal opportunity.

Bob had come to Forest Park 10 years ago after earning his degree. He had developed a strong interest in corporate staffing systems and had held an internship one summer working closely with the human resource systems coordinator of a medium-sized firm. This experience had helped him land the job at Forest Park, and his interest and willingness to work resulted in rapid promotions. Now Bob is manager of employment planning. About the time he joined the company, it entered into a period of moderate but continuing growth. His internship experience had been with a company of 6,000 employees. When he joined Forest Park 8,000 people were employed, 2,500 in the headquarters building. That number had since grown to 12,000 workers, 7,500 of whom worked away from headquarters at 16 other domestic locations. The diversification into textiles would swell the employee ranks and the number of subsidiaries even further.

Only once in the past 10 years had Bob considered the possibility that the company's hiring and promotion policies might be discriminatory. He had been working with Pamela Gillis, the corporation's former EEO manager, and she had given him a special attrition report on female and black professionals at headquarters. On the surface it appeared that the company's policies were nondiscriminatory, but closer inspection of the records revealed a clear trend. Both blacks and women were paid slightly less than Caucasian professionals with comparable qualifications and tended to receive consistently lower performance ratings compared with white male peers. There seemed to be a critical three-year period during which these individuals decided whether to leave or stay. The report made the corporation look like a stone wall for women and minority professionals. They worked for a few years, got nowhere, and left. Bob had hoped to work with Pamela on it. Even though she seemed in too big a hurry, she did a good job. Unfortunately, after one particularly upsetting incident, Pamela also gave up on the company and left.

A young woman who identified herself as a university graduate with a major in accounting had applied for a job at the headquarters office. The receptionist gave her a clerical application to complete and, even after the woman questioned the appropriateness of the form—there was no place to list college degrees, just high schools and technical schools—the receptionist simply assured her, "Don't worry about it, just do the best you can."

The woman was interviewed, took typing and shorthand tests, and was offered a stenographer's job. Through it all, she never said a word in protest. Then came the notice from the Human Relations Commission that she had filed a complaint. Boy, he remembered, did we pay for that one! Here she was, a degreed accountant with a 3.5 grade point average and two years of experience, and we try to make a clerk out of her.

The knock on the door brought him back to the present. It was his secretary with Judge Kimble's plan. Sifting through the inevitable legal jargon, Bob outlined the essential requirements for the remedial program:

1. A listing would be made of all affected minority class members showing name, date of hire, and dates of all promotions with job classifications.

2. Assurances that the qualifications required of affected class members for transfer or promotion would not exceed the qualifications of the *least* qualified white male currently or previously employed in the job in question.

3. Assurances that affected class members would be provided training by the company, sufficient to ensure a fair opportunity to be successful in their new jobs. Should an affected class member show unsatisfactory performance after a reasonable amount of counseling and training, the employee would be returned to the previous position or to a position mutually agreeable both to the company and the worker, with no loss of pay.

4. Provide guarantees that each member of the affected class would receive individual counseling to ensure a thorough understanding of his or her opportunities under the remedial plan.

5. That the plan be implemented unilaterally, regardless of union agreement, although the plan should be discussed with the union in an attempt to reach an understanding and solicit its help in correcting the situation.

6. The completed plan must be submitted to the Equal Employment Opportunity Commission and be in operation by 30 days after EEOC's approval.

Bob carefully studied his outline, wondering aloud how he could possibly meet the many requirements. He had enough problems getting the managers for the textile operation, and Dick had already told him that a reasonable percentage of these people should come from minority categories. Where was he supposed to find the people?

In all honesty, he had to admit that a big part of the problem was the inadequacy of the existing personnel planning staffing system. Entry-level professionals were generally found in campus interviews by recruiting department staff. Beyond entry level, however, the system was a mess. Bob maintained a manual card file covering the whole company, but the cards were usually out of date and invariably incomplete. When departments had openings, they frequently suggested people to fill the new slots or promotions, and their recommendations were frequently acted on. Members of the recruiting department had contact with people at headquarters who might be good candidates for promotion, but these sources excluded people working at 16 other U.S. locations.

Bob leaned back in his chair and closed his eyes. The present personnel planning system would never meet the demands of the company for internal growth. The EEOC problem just aggravated the situation. The first step was done—identifying the problem. What, he asked himself, should I do now?

Discussion Questions

1. What problems does the corporation face in terms of staffing?
2. How would you evaluate Bob's performance as the corporation's staffing manager?
3. What alternatives are available for (a) attracting the staff necessary for the new textile expansion and (b) meeting the Affirmative Action requirements?

4. Which alternative do you consider best? Why?
5. Based on the details of Judge Kimble's plan, in what ways would it have been less costly (or more profitable) for the company to have developed a sound equal opportunity plan of its own and enforced it?

Negotiation with Employees

1 Employee Relations at the Washburn Division

The Washburn Division of the Cohack Manufacturing Corporation came into existence in August 1980 when Cohack completed building a new production plant at Crooked Tree, Montana. Crooked Tree is a small town in a rural resort area approximately 125 miles from Butte, Montana, the home office of Cohack Manufacturing.

The work force had grown to approximately 900 employees by July 1, 1986. They were recruited from Crooked Tree and the surrounding 10 counties. Almost all new employees were completely without past industrial experience. However, employment standards were high, and all persons hired appeared to have considerable potential. With only five exceptions, on July 1, 1986, all production supervisors in the lower three echelons of management had been promoted from within.

Washburn Division had the usual problems of all new plants plus the technological problem of a manufacturing process completely new to industry.

In January 1983, the plant was organized by the Amalgamated Workers of America after a long and costly strike. Good employee-management relations never returned. There were numerous changes in top management and union leadership. The union refused to follow the grievance procedure and demanded instant affirmative answers to all problems. The wildcat strike was frequent. Lower echelons of management suffered repeated abuses and threats from a limited number of employees. Sleeping, loafing, gambling, and even sabotage of production were not unusual. Higher management had, at times, failed to back lower management when it attempted to take disciplinary action.

This case was made possible by the cooperation of a business firm which remains anonymous. It was prepared by Dr. James C. Hodgetts of Memphis State University as a basis for class discussion rather than to illustrate either effective or ineffective administrative practices. The letter from the president appears as it did in the original except for changes in names and places that would reveal the company's true identity.

EXHIBIT 1

Cohack Manufacturing Corporation
Butte, Montana
July 29, 1986

To all Washburn Division employees:

As you know we have recently made many changes in the top-management group at Butte. There were also some changes made at Washburn. These were made because mistakes in the past had taken us to the point of bankruptcy. It was recognized that there were two (2) basic problems. One was the deterioration and lack of proper operating facilities, and the other was the small percentage of our employees who were seriously affecting our operating efficiency.

With regard to the first problem, this new management team immediately appropriated approximately four million dollars ($4,000,000) to improve facilities over the next three (3) years. Some improvements can already be seen; others will take time because of engineering and delivery delays.

Concerning the second problem, there are some employees who loaf, sleep, play cards, abuse and threaten our management, or just plain don't do the job they are being paid to do. We know, as you do, that no business can operate for long under these conditions. Their actions have caused us to reach the point where our operations are being seriously affected. When this happens, the security of everyone is threatened—we will not allow this to continue. Some feel that we were afraid to correct these problems. Nothing could be further from the truth. We honestly believe that since the future of so many employees and their families were at stake we, as management, had to first try persuasion and cooperation before resorting to disciplinary action. This approach has not been successful; in fact, matters have gotten worse.

In the interest of the job security of everyone concerned, we are hereby serving notice that we will no longer tolerate such things as sleeping, loafing, gambling, or game playing on company property, threats or abuse to management, or other interferences which affect production. Our management has the authority to take the necessary corrective measures to stop these practices.

We feel confident that most of our employees will do the job that has to be done. They performed magnificently in our recent production crisis. The only thing which good employees have to worry about is what the few bad ones can do to their job security. We ask for your cooperation in helping us make this a better, safer, more secure place to work. We are doing everything humanly possible and within reason to reach this goal.

C. J. Cohack, President

By the end of 1985, the Washburn Division had forced the Cohack Manufacturing Corporation to the verge of bankruptcy. Early in 1986 the company was able to borrow $4 million on the physical facilities at Washburn, and local top management was again changed. By July 1986 the technical problems were decreasing, but the human problems remained unchanged.

On July 29, 1986, the president of the company wrote the letter shown in Exhibit 1 to all Washburn employees with the hope that it might help to correct the situation.

Joe Grisson, human resources manager at Washburn, does not believe that Mr. Cohack's letter will do much good. To him this is just another threat that will not be backed up. He believes that there are only about 10 employees, all union officers or stewards, who are the ring leaders relative to the employee relations problem. Joe wants to start collecting concrete evidence that will enable the company to proceed with disciplinary action as permitted in the union-management agreement. Since all 10 employees have been given written reprimands, he wants to give all 10 employees disciplinary layoffs as soon as the company is sure they can defend their position, if the union decides to use the grievance and arbitration procedures. This was tried once before but when the union closed down the plant with a wildcat strike, the company let the employees return to work with back pay. Joe is certain the union will do the same again and when they do the company should take legal action against the union and fire the 10 ringleaders.

Requirement

Given the information presented, what specific personnel actions must Joe take? Identify the specific personnel problems to be addressed.

2 The New Union

Thomas Allen is the general manager of a medium-sized pharmaceutical manufacturing firm. About five years ago, the company moved its operations from the Northeast to the Deep South. Part of the rationale for the move was financial (better tax incentives, availability of land, etc.), but in addition the firm was seeking to operate without a union.

This case was prepared by Professor Paul J. Champagne, Old Dominion University.

Top management felt that moving to a site where unions had traditionally not been as strong might be the answer. Initially they were correct. For several years the plant had been able to operate on a nonunion basis. Recently, however, pressures have begun to build; there has been more and more talk about organizing a union. Nobody in management, including Allen, wants to see this happen. During the past few months, Allen has been wondering how he might handle this situation.

Joe Rockford, a production supervisor on the first shift, has told Allen of the experience of a local unionization of its workers. Allen decided to contact the manager, Jeff Welsh, of this other firm to see whether he can get any information. Allen and Welsh had the following conversation:

Allen

Mr. Welsh, I'm calling you because I've just heard of your recent experience with a union organizing campaign. I'm facing the same kind of problem, and I'm looking for ideas. How did you manage to defeat the organizers?

Welsh

I know the problem you're facing. Keeping a union out is always touchy. I'm glad you called.

Allen

What I really need to know is how do I proceed and still keep the NLRB off my back?

Welsh

OK, let me tell you about our situation. One of the things we found was that, surprisingly enough, money was not the most important factor encouraging our people to unionize. In fact, the more important issues seemed to be job security, confidence in management, and assurance of equal treatment. The organizers were making the pitch that a union could make management listen to the workers' problems and do something about them.

What I tried to do was convince people that we would listen to their problems and complaints. In effect, I was telling them that they did not need a union. Of course, I was very careful about how I got this information to the people in the plant.

Allen

That sounds real good, but how did you do it?

Welsh

I instituted an open-door policy.

Allen

A what?

Welsh

An open-door policy really isn't anything new, and it isn't that hard to start. It simply means letting your people know that when they have a gripe or a problem your door is always open to them. You are willing to listen and do what you can.

Allen

Sounds easy, but there must be more to it than that.

Welsh

Oh, sure. Keeping an open door is not as easy as it sounds. Let me tell you some of the key requirements I have for conducting an effective open-door policy.

1. Let the employees know about it. I use meetings, memos, face-to-face communication—any way that works.

2. When people come to see you, always talk with them right away. If you're pressed for time, make an appointment but always within a day or two. Never tell them to come back when you're less busy. If they think that you're putting them off, the whole thing may just seem like a gimmick.

3. After you've heard the complaint, ask for any additional information you need to act on it.

4. If you can't solve the problem on the spot, say so. Tell the employee that you'll take it up with your boss, and then be sure to follow through.

5. Always give the person some idea about when to expect an answer. If you can't get an answer within the time you've set, explain the delay personally.

6. Don't be afraid to send the employee to see your boss if it seems necessary. When employees' complaints are about me, I feel it's to everyone's benefit to open the door to higher management. Show them that you're not attempting to hide problems, and that they don't need a union to be heard by top management.

7. Finally, don't expect too much. People may be suspicious of your motives, and you'll have to start slow. Remember that your policy must not only be fair it must *seem* fair to the workers.

Allen

That all sounds reasonable, and really that is the way I've always tried to operate. Maybe I just haven't been explicit enough. Maybe I should openly communicate to the workers that this is my policy. Thanks, Jeff.

Welsh

It seemed to work for us. Give it a try. Good talking with you.

Allen does not want to see a union established. He feels that it would be of benefit to no one in the long run. But he is still concerned about what to do. He fears that even the approach suggested by Welsh might be construed as tampering by the NLRB. He also wonders whether Welsh's approach will work in his plant.

Discussion Questions

1. Do you have any suggestions for Allen? If you were faced with this problem, how would you proceed?
2. Once steps to organize have been taken, would the NLRB view this new approach as tampering? Can you see any way to get around this?
3. If it's true that Allen has operated with this open-door policy in mind all along, how can he now convince his people to take advantage of it and seek him out?
4. Should Allen try using someone else's solution?

---

3 *Southwestern Bell Telephone Company*

The chill of the late fall was starkly apparent the morning of December 10. The breath of the picketers rose like wispy smoke as they walked around the central telephone exchange in Kirksville, Missouri. The placards they carried were inscribed "Wilson Construction and Southwestern Bell violate area standards, Local 307 United Iron and Steelworkers of America." The word *strike* was not present on any of the posters. The steelworkers had been displaying their signs since 7:30 A.M., and it was increasingly obvious that they had no intention of removing themselves before 8 A.M., at which time the Southwestern Bell employees would normally report for work.

THE "INFORMATIONAL PICKET" ACTION

As noted by the placards, the picketers were representatives of Local 307 of the United Iron and Steelworkers of America (UISA), headquartered in Ottumwa, Iowa. During a meeting held the evening of December 9, it was agreed by the rank and file that they would erect an "informational picket" at the telephone office in Kirksville. Presiding at that meeting was William Johnson, president of the UISA local, and Ron Mikel, vice president and steward representing the Kirksville membership. The informational picket action was being taken due to the pres-

---

This case was prepared by Professor Chimezie A. B. Osigweh, Northeast Missouri State University, and James Ball, Southwestern Bell Telephone Company. Copyright © 1984 by Chimezie A. B. Osigweh.

ence of Wilson Constructors, Inc. of Lenexa, Kansas,[1] at Southwestern Bell's telephone office on Washington Street in Kirksville. Wilson Constructors is a nonunion general contractor that presented the low bid for the construction of a new microwave tower on top of the existing telephone building. Southwestern Bell Telephone Company must, by law, consider all bids submitted to it for new construction. The company cannot discriminate against bidders because they are either union or nonunion. The local steelworkers had been carefully monitoring the progress that Wilson was making on the tower project for several weeks. To this point all of the work performed had been in preparation for the actual handling and erecting of the steel tower.

On December 9, however, preparation work was not the steelworkers' concern. The first truckload of steel had arrived at the job site, along with a 15-ton crane on December 4. All attempts by Mikel to get Wilson Constructors to hire some of his people had failed. As a result, the union felt that its next course of action was to set up a picket line. A problem of *common situs picketing* was on its way: the operations of a secondary employer were being disrupted. The secondary employer was being picketed.

FROM THE WINDOW PANE

Jim Thompson, network service supervisor, switching (local service), and Jim Ball, network service supervisor, toll (long distance), watched the patrolling picketers through the windows of a large office inside the telephone building.

"Why did the company [Southwestern Bell] wait until it was too late to talk to these people?" Ball asked. Thompson answered with only a shake of the head.

Ball recalled many of the events of the last few weeks that had led up to the current situation. During a preconstruction meeting held in Kansas City on November 10, he and Thompson had stated that, once construction on the tower started, some kind of work action from the steelworkers local was almost 100 percent certain if Wilson did not use some union labor. They also informed the legal department representative that this particular union had a reputation for "busting heads" if anyone tried to cross its picket lines.

"Yes," Ball thought, "we've told them several times." But, given the present situation, that thought alone provided very little consolation.

As 8 A.M. approached, both supervisors felt crippled. "Is there anything that we can do to get these guys away from our employees' entrance?" Thompson asked.

---

[1]The state of Kansas is a right-to-work state.

"No," replied Ball, "the boss [Wes Storm—manager] said for us to hang loose until we see what legal has to say."

"Gee, that will take all day," responded Thompson. "You and I know that our craft people will not cross that picket line!"

About that time the phone rang. Ball put the call on the speaker so he and Thompson could both hear what Wes had found out from the legal department.

"OK," Wes began. "Legal is trying to contact the steelworkers' local office right now. The lawyers will attempt to get the picketers to clear the telephone employees' entrance so our people can come to work. Heck, their 'grievance' isn't with us anyway. It's with Wilson for refusing to hire some of the union steelworkers."

"Darnit, Wes," Ball countered. "Why didn't legal take Thompson and me seriously three weeks ago in Kansas City—when we told them that there would be trouble if Wilson uses strictly nonunion labor in our building?"

After a slight pause, Wes replied, "Nobody actually thought there would be any problems. We are building towers in Moberly, Sedalia, Chillicothe, and downtown Kansas City, and to this date we have not had any problems with any of the other local unions."

Just about that time, 7:55 A.M., another one of the office phones began to ring. Jim Thompson answered and talked for several minutes. He then hung up and returned to the speaker phone.

"That was one of our repeatermen [telephone craft title]," Thompson stated. "I'm sure it was Eldon Coy. He says that everyone is waiting over at Doughboy's Donut Shop to see what happens." They had contacted Scat Davis, president of their own union, the Communications Workers of America (CWA), local chapter, to see what the union wants them to do. But at that time they still had not heard from St. Louis headquarters about the next course of action.

"Eldon maintains," continued Thompson, "that regardless of what the union says, none of the Kirksville craft people have any intention of crossing that picket line. They think that someone will get hurt if they try to cross. They're a little scared."

"I understand that," Wes replied. "But they have to come to work, nonetheless. Legal says that this is only an informational picket set up against Wilson, and that it does not bind our people not to cross."

The legal staff had, indeed, added quick references to a certain National Labor Relation Board's (NLRB's) "Reserved Gate" doctrine, as well as to a *Denver* case, and to another *International Union of Electrical Workers (IUEW)* case.[2] But they did not elaborate. They had some more "checking into" to do before jumping to the conclusion that any of these applied to Bell's situation.

---

[2]According to the "Reserved Gate" doctrine, an employer who awards a bid to a

IN VIEW OF RESPONSIBILITIES

Eight o'clock came and went and still no telephone employees had come to work. Shortly after 8, another of the repeatermen called the office and asked if he and the other outside repairmen could report to their company vehicles and drive to their work sites. All company vehicles had been removed from the telephone exchange parking lot several weeks earlier because Wilson was using the company parking lot to store materials for the new tower. Therefore, the telephone vehicles were not on Southwestern Bell's property, but instead were parked in the municipal parking lot a few blocks away. This would allow some of the employees to report for work without having to cross the picket line.

John's request was, however, refused by Ball, his immediate supervisor. Wes supported Ball's refusal to grant the request. "The first floor of the telephone building is the reporting location, and not the front seat of a company vehicle," Wes stated flatly.

"Besides," added Ball, "it is the company's view that we, and not the union, should decide where the craft people report for work. We do not alter policy in order to allow union members to circumvent their contract responsibilities. In this case, the union is asking us to make an exception for them which could constitute a dangerous precedent should a situation like this occur again."

According to one member of the management staff, the union's responsibility in matters of this nature had been made clear under the "service interruption" provisions of the contract.[3] (See Exhibit 1.) Once it was determined that the picket was informational in nature, it was the union's responsibility to ensure that its members reported to work, whether or not picketers were present.

The picketers remained in place at *all* entrances until approximately 10:30 A.M. At that time, the picketing steelworkers were asked by their union to reposition themselves *only* at the entrances that had been

---

subcontractor should reserve an entrance for the subcontractor's employees. Because the subcontractor's employees can only get into the plant through the entrance, strikes against the subcontractor have to be picketed only at the entrance. The work done by the users of the Reserved Gate must be unrelated to the normal activities of the employer.

The *Denver* case probably refers to the Supreme Court ruling in *NLRB* v. *Denver Building and Construction Trades Council* [341 US 675 (1951), 95 L Ed 1284], while the *IUEW* case refers to *Local 761, International Union of Electrical Workers* v. *NLRB* [366 US 667 (1961), 6 L Ed 2d 592]. The student should locate these court cases and explore them to see how relevant they are to this case.

[3] 1980 Agreement of General Application, *Collective Bargaining Agreement CWA* (Southwestern Bell, Kirksville), p. 195.

EXHIBIT 1

Article II

Service Interruption

The Company and the Union recognize their responsibility in the interests of the public and the employees to avoid interruptions in telephone service. Accordingly, they will process promptly employee complaints and grievances which are subject to handling under the grievance procedures for the purpose of avoiding interruption of telephone service to the public and economic loss to employees from work stoppages.

Any employee complaint or grievance which is subject to handling under the grievance procedures shall be presented and heard promptly in accordance with the provisions of those procedures and the arbitration procedures, where applicable.

As to those employee grievances which are subject to arbitration, the Union, its officers, or representatives will not order or sanction a work stoppage or slowdown at any time.

---

clearly designated as those to be used by the "contractors only."[4] An agreement had been reached between the steelworkers and the company's attorneys.

THE 10 O'CLOCK SETTLEMENT

The agreement was reached between 10 A.M. and 10:20 A.M. By this time, all of the damage had already been done. The telephone employees (represented by CWA) who had refused to cross the picket line were docked for two and one half hours of pay, and the lost time was charged to their payroll records as unexcused absence. Unexcused absence is one of the criteria that help to determine whether employees receive a satisfactory or an unsatisfactory appraisal for their yearly performance. Their appraisal will, in turn, affect their hopes for transfer or promotion. It was not very surprising, therefore, that the employees involved had no intentions of accepting the unexcused absence charged to their records without a fight.

---

[4]These entrances had been so designated from the very first day that Wilson Construction arrived in Kirksville.

The first step was taken by Roger Elmore, union steward for the Kirksville telephone employees. Roger promptly informed the local CWA president, Scat Davis, of the situation, and that all of the telephone craftpeople at the Kirksville office wanted the unexcused absence removed from their payroll records. They also wanted to be reimbursed for the two and one half hours of pay that they had lost.

While Roger hoped that Scat would decide on an appropriate line of action, it was Roger's contention that this vexing and dangerous situation should have been averted by the company (Southwestern Bell) and the union (CWA). Failure to react according to the evidence of an imminent strike action, by both the company and the union, was clearly a case of negligence on both sides. Roger also contended that the failure of both sides to act in the face of this situation was a violation of Article III of the General Application section of the 1980 Collective Bargaining Agreement (see Exhibit 2). Moreover, he saw the refusal of the Kirksville CWA members to cross the steelworkers' picket line as the culmination of a month-long "ignore it and it'll go away" course of action.

EXHIBIT 2

Article III

Unusual Grievances

Whenever the Vice President of the Union (or in his or her absence, the Assistant to Vice President) informs the Vice President-Personnel of the Company (or in his or her absence, the Assistant Vice President-Labor Relations) that a complaint or a grievance exists which in the opinion of the Vice President of the Union involves a condition which constitutes a serious and immediate threat to the health or safety of an employee or group of employees and which in his or her opinion requires prompt handling, and it is mutually agreed that such a question of health or safety is in fact involved, then such complaint or grievance may be presented and heard at such level of the Grievance Procedure as the Vice President of the Union may select. The first meeting with respect to such complaint or grievance shall be held at a time and place to be agreed upon and as promptly as conditions permit; the two-week time limitation set forth in the Grievance Procedure shall be applicable. There shall be no obligation on the part of the Union to appeal such complaint or grievance to any higher level, and the grievance if arbitrable shall then be subject to the provisions of the arbitration procedures of this Agreement.

At any rate, tempers were reaching the boiling point, and the Kirksville employees were demanding that some action be taken. Subsequently, Scat Davis scheduled an emergency union meeting for the evening of December 15. The major item up for discussion by the membership was whether CWA should reimburse the Kirksville employees for their lost time out of the union's general fund, or whether the union would formally grieve the work stoppage and the subsequent withholding of pay.

Discussion Questions

1. How would you evaluate the activities of the Steelworkers, Local 307?
2. What options are available to the Communication Workers of America?
3. Evaluate the activities of Southwestern Bell.

4 The Discharge of Stanley Thompson: An Arbitrator's Dilemma

South Bay Corporation is a multimillion-dollar northeastern company engaged in manufacturing structural beams, engines, valves, and other support equipment for the petroleum industry. With recent interest in U.S. oil exploration, the corporation has experienced substantial growth through customer demand. This growth has caused the company to increase its work force in addition to working significant amounts of overtime to meet customer needs. Overtime requirements have been particularly heavy in the engine department, where mechanics and machine operators work long hours producing and assembling both standard and specially built engines for oil driling equipment.

Employees of South Bay have been represented by an independent union—South Bay Employees Association—since 1968. Labor-management relations are described as friendly, although during the past six months relations have become strained due to impending contract ne-

---

This case was prepared by Dr. George W. Bohlander, Arizona State University, and is based on an arbitration heard by the author. The company and individual names are fictitious.

gotiations. Grievance activity has increased 40 percent, and more cases are being finalized through the arbitration process. On December 10, 1979, the union requested the arbitration of a discharge case after repeated attempts to resolve the issue through the grievance procedure produced no results. The following facts and issues were presented to the arbitrator during the arbitration hearing.

FACTS OF THE CASE

The grievant, Stanley Thompson, had been employed by South Bay for six years. Thompson is an experienced and qualified engine mechanic, having worked 12 years in related jobs before joining the company in January 1974. At the time of his discharge, he was classified as a senior engine mechanic in the engine department. Thompson has received company recognition for his ability as an engine mechanic. His annual performance reviews are very good, and they acknowledge superior quantity and quality of work performance. He received a commendation letter on March 26, 1979, from his department manager for early completion of a job assignment involving a specially built engine.

During the first five years of Thompson's employment, his attendance record was excellent. He missed only one workday during this entire period.

However, the company maintains that, during the past year, Thompson has developed an excessive record of tardiness and absenteeism. Evidence submitted during the hearing shows that over a 10-month period—September 1978 through June 1979—the grievant was absent 9 full days, and he had 11 partial days of absence. On February 16, 1979, and again on April 10, 1979, Thompson received verbal warnings about his attendance problem. On May 25, 1979, he received a written warning notice about his excessive absenteeism. The written reprimand advised the grievant that continued absenteeism or "other evidence of lack of interest in job performance would not be tolerated and will result in termination of employment." Company procedures allow employees to respond to disciplinary action taken against them. When responding to the written warning, Thompson wrote on the note that he did not remember receiving prior verbal warnings. During the hearing, however, Thompson did testify that he had received one verbal warning prior to receipt of the written notice. Thompson claimed that his attendance problem was caused by the fact that his wife and young daughter had been critically ill.

After receiving the written reprimand on May 24, and up to his discharge on September 24, 1979, Thompson's attendance record shows an additional seven full days of absence, six partial days, and four incidents where he agreed to work overtime but did not report to work. His attendance record was again verbally reviewed with him on August 16, 1979, but no further disciplinary action was taken.

Thompson's discharge took place after an incident which occurred one Saturday morning. On Saturday, September 22, Thompson was working overtime due to the heavy work load in the engine department. At approximately 10:40 A.M., Thompson's supervisor, Tom Avey, while passing a window in the work area, observed Thompson sitting at his workbench with his feet up, reading a magazine. Avey did not approach or discuss the incident with Thompson at that time. At the time of the incident, the grievant was working on company time, and his lunch period did not begin until 11 A.M. Except for a slight disagreement over the exact time the incident occurred, Thompson admitted under oath to the conduct observed by his supervisor. Thompson does not, however, admit to loafing. Rather, his explanation for sitting at his work station was due to the need to receive parts for completion of a special engine. Without these parts, work could not proceed and no other jobs had been assigned to him. The parts were to be delivered from supply services at 1 P.M. that day.

Early Monday morning, September 24, 1979, Thompson's supervisor met with the manager of employee relations, Mrs. Gail Gorton, to discuss the incident observed on Saturday. After a brief discussion of Thompson's work record, it was decided to immediately terminate his employment. Thompson was given his discharge notice at 10 A.M., along with his final paycheck.

POSITIONS OF THE PARTIES

Company

The company maintains that Thompson was properly terminated according to the employment policies of South Bay. These policies were verbally covered with the grievant during his employment orientation, and they were listed in a handbook given to all new employees. The company argues that there are 19 different work infractions for which employees may be disciplined or terminated. Specifically, the company believes that Thompson violated rule number 9, "loafing or sleeping on the job," and number 17, "careless or inefficient performance or productivity." The company maintains that Thompson's admission of guilt, regardless of the reason, is sufficient to uphold the discharge. The company also believes Thompson's loafing is most serious since he was being paid time and a half for the Saturday assignment.

Given the gravity of the offense on September 22, Thompson's poor attendance record, and the proper application of the progressive disciplinary system over the past year, the disciplinary action which the company applied was reasonable and was properly within managerial discretion.

Grievant

Thompson maintains that the 19 causes for discipline spelled out in the employee handbook may result in termination, but that an infraction of any one cause does not mandate discharge. Due to the extenuating circumstances surrounding the incident on Saturday (i.e., unavailable parts), the actions of the company are too severe to warrant termination. Further, Thompson contends that the company neglected to properly investigate the Saturday incident prior to his termination on Monday. The grievant maintains that, when discharge is involved, the company bears the responsibility to consider any and all facts that could influence the extent of discipline. This should include a meeting with the employee to review his or her side of the story. Thompson believes that this omission is a general violation of industrial due process and a right of employees before discipline is administered.

Finally, the grievant argues that certain procedural errors were made during progressive discipline for his excessive absenteeism. Company policies state that, when employees receive written reprimands, at 45-day intervals or less, the company will investigate and counsel the employee until the problem appears to be corrected. This procedure was established to continually advise employees of how they stand in regard to achieving company standards. Therefore, based on Thompson's fine performance record, the procedural irregularities in applying progressive discipline, and the extenuating circumstances surrounding the Saturday incident—combined with the lack of due process—Thompson's discharge was not warranted and he should be reinstated.

CONCLUSION

The arbitration described above was conducted under the rules of the American Arbitration Association (AAA). All parties were given a full and fair opportunity to present witnesses and evidence. All witnesses testified under oath. According to AAA procedures, the arbitrator has 30 days from the close of the hearing to render his or her final and binding award.

Discussion Questions

You are the arbitrator and have heard the above case. Based on the facts presented and the arguments of each side, how would you rule?

Would you uphold or reverse the discharge of Mr. Thompson? You may wish to consider the following points before reaching your decision:

1. Thompson's attendance record.
2. Thompson's quantity and quality of work.
3. The progressive discipline given to Thompson and the manner in which it was administered by the company.
4. The discharge of September 24 and the facts surrounding the incident.
5. Management's right to discipline and discharge an employee for just cause.

5 *Inspiration Consolidated Copper Company*

BACKGROUND

Inspiration Consolidated Copper Company is an integrated natural resources company. Its principal business is the production and sale of copper from its Arizona operations, which include mines, smelter, refinery, solvent extraction, rod fabricating, and sulfuric acid plants. Inspiration also smelts copper-bearing materials for other producers and owns and operates a silver-bearing silica flux mine in Montana. Its exploration activities, which cover most of the western states and Alaska, are aimed at diversification, both geographically and among natural resources.

The company's Arizona facility, located in Miami, Arizona, is the only facility involved herein. At the Arizona facility, the company is party to several collective bargaining agreements, including one with the United Steelworkers of America, Miami Miners Union Local 586.

Failure to resolve the following grievance has required that it be submitted to an arbitrator. Your name was on the panel the American Association of Arbitrators sent to the parties, and they selected you to

This case was prepared by Felicia A. Finston. It was prepared as a basis for class discussion, rather than to illustrate either effective or ineffective handling of an administrative situation.

hear the grievance. You agreed and have just heard each party's position. Now you have to prepare your award.

The issue emerging in the instant case is: Did the company violate the collective bargaining agreement when it terminated the grievant, Douglas Peterson, on February 14, 1982? If so, what is the appropriate remedy?

CIRCUMSTANCES

Douglas Peterson, the grievant, had been employed by the company for approximately six years, prior to his termination in February 1982. At the time of his discharge, Peterson was classified as a steam plant operator in the smelter department.

The grievant's last day of work for the company was February 7, 1982. He was scheduled off on February 8 and was scheduled to work the B shift on February 9, 10, 11, 12, and 13. Following his regular work shift on February 7, Peterson was arrested and incarcerated and, subsequent to that date, was unable to report to work because he was in jail.

On February 11, 1982, Steven Slepian, the grievant's attorney in the criminal matters, telephoned Peterson's general foreman, who referred the attorney to Jim Yingst, the smelter production superintendent. Slepian told Yingst that Peterson had been incarcerated and that he was trying to obtain Peterson's release. Slepian asked Yingst what impact Peterson's failure to report for work would have on his employment status. Yingst replied that the company's policy dictated that a failure to report for work due to incarceration would be treated as an unexcused absence. Yingst informed Slepian that Peterson faced termination if he accumulated more than four successive days of absence. Although Slepian did not specifically request that Peterson be granted a leave of absence, the company treated the attorney's inquiry as a verbal request for a leave of absence.

On February 13, 1982, Peterson accumulated his fifth successive day of unexcused absence. In accordance with normal procedures, the company then processed his termination. Manny Casillas, a company labor relations representative, while processing the termination paperwork of February 14, 1982, showed Richard Guerra, one of the union's stewards, Peterson's termination papers. According to the company, when Casillas told Guerra that Peterson was being terminated, Guerra replied that Peterson was in jail.

No written request for a leave of absence was ever filed by Peterson or on his behalf.

The following week, Peterson's name was absent from the work schedules posted throughout the company's facility. On February 27,

1982, after the criminal charges against him were in the process of being dismissed, Peterson was released from jail. On that same day, Peterson called the company to check on his employment status. Peterson contends that he was told by the company that it would be necessary for the personnel representative to talk with labor relations and that he should call back. After additional unsuccessful attempts to determine his status on February 28 and 29, on March 3, Peterson filed a formal grievance protesting his termination. On March 4, he received official notice from the company that he had been terminated.

RELEVANT CONTRACT PROVISIONS

Paragraph 4.16 Discharge and Discipline

In the event an employee shall be discharged, suspended, or disciplined by the Company after the date of this Agreement, such employee shall be given full reasons for such discharge, suspension, or disciplining, in writing.

Paragraph 9.3 Granting of Leaves of Absence

Leaves of absence, without pay, may be granted for reasons such as jury duty and other good and sufficient reasons. Leaves of absence, without pay, for other good and sufficient reasons shall be granted to employees for a period up to thirty (30) days, which period may be extended by mutual consent.

Paragraph 9.4 Request for Leave in Writing, Separation of Employees, for Unauthorized Leave

Request for leaves of absence must be made in writing to the immediate supervisor, and each case must be considered on its merits. One copy of the leave of absence shall be given to the employee at the time the leave is granted and one copy to the Union. Upon return from leave of absence, the employee shall be reinstated without loss of his seniority rights. Leaves of absence shall in no way jeopardize the standing of rights of employees. Upon the employee's return, he shall be reinstated with seniority accumulated throughout his leave of absence. Employees absent for more than four (4) days, without having obtained a properly authorized leave of absence, shall be separated from the payroll.

The company's absentee program is described in Exhibit 1.

EXHIBIT 1 Absentee Program (adopted July 22, 1974)

TO ALL EMPLOYEES:

Please review the following procedure so that you are completely familiar with its provisions:

1. Excused absences will be granted only for:
   a. Prearranged absences for good and sufficient reason.
   b. Leave of Absence.
   c. Injury—immediate family or per contract.
   d. Sickness—immediate family or per contract.

A LEAVE OF ABSENCE may be granted for good and sufficient reasons by requesting a leave from this foreman in accordance with the applicable union contract. Employees, who because of emergency situations, are unable to arrange for a leave prior to the days needed may have a representative arrange the leave in accordance with the applicable union contract in their behalf by transmitting the required information to the department head.

2. Unexcused absences are those absences not covered in the above paragraph. The following steps will apply for unexcused absences:
   a. Each employee will be allowed two unexcused absences in any consecutive 12-week period.
   b. For the third absence, a written warning will be issued by the shift foreman.
   c. For the fourth absence, the employee will be interviewed by the department head or representative, and after investigation of the circumstances and absentee record, he will receive a second written warning if warranted.
   d. For the fifth absence, the employee will be interviewed by the department head or representative, and after investigation of the circumstances and absentee record, he may be subject to a five-day layoff.
   e. After receiving five days off, the employee may be discharged following the next unexcused absence.
3. Any employee can clear his record with 12 weeks without an excused absence. If the record is not cleared, the above sequence of steps will follow.
4. Consecutive days of 1, 2, 3, or 4 are to be counted as one absence.
5. The program will be administered as follows by all departments:
   a. Consecutive days of 1, 2, 3, or 4 are to be counted as one absence. On the fifth day, in accordance with the contract, employees are automatically terminated if they have not reported off.
6. The Company agrees to clear all absentee records as of the Date of Settlement (8/23/74).

COMPANY POSITION

The company contends that Peterson's failure to report to work for the five consecutive days without having obtained a prior leave of absence, coupled with Peterson's failure to provide a written request for leave of absence, formed the basis for its decision to terminate him.

To justify its action, the company relies on paragraph 9.4 of the agreement and a prior arbitration award involving this same company and union and issues as contained herein.

Paragraph 9.4 of the agreement clearly and unequivocally provides that a request for leave of absence must be in writing. It also provides that an employee who is absent for more than four days without having obtained a leave of absence shall be "separated from the payroll." As it has consistently done in the past, the company enforced the policy manifested in paragraph 9.4 and properly terminated Peterson.

At the hearing, the union argued that Peterson's termination was improper under the terms of paragraph 4.16 of the agreement (which relates to typical discharges) and points to the company's forms, used internally, to claim that Peterson was really "discharged" and that, therefore, paragraph 4.6 applies.

In this regard, the company refers to a prior arbitration, involving a Mr. Salvador Reco. Essentially, the issues raised in both the prior arbitration and the instant case are the same. However, Reco had filed a written request for leave of absence, which serves as further evidence of the propriety of the company's action in the instant case. In his decision, arbitrator Donald Daughten held that section 9.3 of the agreement gives the company total discretion in its determination of leaves of absence. In addition, arbitrator Daughten noted that the company has maintained its long-standing history of denying leaves of absence to incarcerated employees. As in the instant case, the union cited the company's internal documents in support of paragraph 4.16 as its defense to the grievant's termination. Arbitrator Daughten dismissed this argument and noted that the company views an employee that is separated from the payroll in accordance with section 9.4 as having quit.

Finally, arbitrator Daughten made it perfectly clear that paragraph 9.4 is controlling and gives the company the unequivocal right to terminate an incarcerated employee for more than four absences without having obtained a prior leave of absence. Due to the fact that arbitrator Daughten's decision makes no mention of the criminal guilt or innocence of the grievant, it is clear that criminal culpability is not a relevant factor in adjudging the propriety of a termination under paragraph 9.4.

It is standard "arbitration law" that a prior arbitration between the parties becomes part of the current agreement. Having lost the prior arbitration, the union cannot raise the identical issues before a new arbitrator (Reynolds & Reynolds Co., 67LA157, 1974.)

However, even if there has not been a prior arbitration, the company clearly acted in accordance with the agreement in separating Peterson from the payroll due to his failure to secure approval of a written request for leave of absence prior to being absent for more than four days.

UNION POSITION

The union alleges that the company acted in an arbitrary and capricious manner in terminating Peterson. The rationale forming its position is twofold. The union contends that the company's decision to terminate Peterson was premature in that Peterson's attorney, Steven Slepian, reported him absent on February 11, 1982, and thereby complied with the current absentee policy. In addition, on this same date Slepian requested a leave of absence to secure Peterson's job. The company denied this request and subsequently discharged the grievant on February 14, despite the fact that paragraph 9.3 plainly states that leave may be granted for good and sufficient reasons, and that, in the past, other phone requested leaves of absence have been granted. The fact that the company has, in the past, approved phone requested leaves serves to indicate its arbitrary treatment of the grievant.

In addition, the company's discharge of Peterson and subsequent failure to provide the benefits stipulated in paragraph 4.16 of the agreement constitute another violation of the collective bargaining agreement. Management's failure to notify Peterson of his termination, coupled with its failure to reinstate the grievant after he filed a grievance and provided documentary proof that the criminal charges against him had been dismissed, serves as proof of company capriciousness.

If the company were to have the sole right to deny a leave of absence, this would take away the right of an employee to grieve the company's decision. The very fact that paragraph 9.3 appears in the agreement gives credence to the union's contention that company decisions regarding leaves of absence are subject to both review and reversal.

The union requests that the grievant, Douglas Peterson, be reinstated to his former position with full back pay and restoration of all seniority and other job rights.

Discussion Questions

In this case, your award should contain:

1. Your rationale in finding on the merits of this case.
2. The degree to which you would grant the relief Peterson is asking or uphold management.

6 *Management Campaigns and Union Organizing at KCOM-KOHC Medical, Inc.*

BACKGROUND

It was February four years ago. A group of employees at the Kirksville College of Osteopathic Medicine, Inc., and Kirksville Osteopathic Health Center (KCOM-KOHC) approached some of the management personnel at the institution and informed them of a union organizing campaign being conducted by Service Employees International Union (SEIU), Local 50. The effort had been initiated during the summer of the previous year. SEIU's intent was to organize service, maintenance, and professional employees within a 12-month period, in the complex employing over 900 people. A representation election was eventually scheduled; but five years had elapsed after the initial campaign effort began.

THE TRAINING FACILITY AND THE HEALTH CENTER

Kirksville College of Osteopathic Medicine and Kirksville Osteopathic Health Center (KCOM-KOHC) were founded by Dr. Andrew Taylor Still,[1] in Kirksville, Missouri in 1892. KCOM, the first school of osteopathic medicine in the world and the Harvard of osteopathic colleges, offers a four-year post-baccalaureate training program that leads to a doctor of osteopathy (DO)[2] degree. It also offers a Bachelor of Science

---

This case was prepared by Chimezie A. B. Osigweh, Yg., Norfolk State University, with the assistance of Mark A. Morehouse, Service Master Management Services. The name KCOM-KOHC Medical, Inc., was chosen for its brevity to represent the organization and its hospitals, whose correct names appear within the first two pages of the text. About 4 percent of this material has been disguised and adapted. The material is meant to provide a basis for educational discussion and not to illustrate effective or ineffective handling of an administrative situation. I thank Karen C. Brown and Sylvester Jolley, Jr. for various degrees of research-related help. © Professor Chimezie A. B. Osigweh, Yg.

[1]Dr. Andrew Taylor Still is the recognized founder of the osteopathic field of medicine.

[2]A doctor of osteopathy (DO) is a medical physician enjoying rights and privileges of medical practice that are similar to those of a doctor of medicine (MD). However, there is at least one major difference between an MD and a DO. Whereas an MD traditionally

(BS) degree program in medical technology. The facility sponsors and houses numerous medical research projects in addition to its degree program.

The Kirksville Osteopathic Health Center began operating a few years after KCOM as the first hospital of osteopathic medicine. A part of the KCOM-KOHC complex, KOHC is a 254-bed hospital comprised of Kirksville Osteopathic Hospital, Laughlin Osteopathic Hospital, and several clinics. KOHC is a nonprofit organization that serves as the hands-on training unit for KCOM students.

WHEN WORKERS CALL: THE UNION AND ITS INVITATION

The Service Employees International Union (SEIU), an AFL-CIO affiliate, was headquartered in St. Louis, Missouri. The union was 230,000 employees strong and had been attempting to organize hospitals throughout the states of Missouri and Illinois. Its campaign efforts had been fairly successful, especially in the St. Louis area, where it had won a number of elections. Nationwide, SEIU had been more successful on the East and West Coasts than in the central section of the country. The union's activities were oriented toward people in the health care industry. Particular targets were service-type employees (e.g., dietary, housekeeping, and maintenance workers) as the union's name implied. In addition, however, SEIU was beginning to seek membership among professional employees such as nurses and lab personnel.

The emergency room personnel at KCOM-KOHC were the original group that contacted SEIU for assistance, although there were strong sentiments in favor of union presence in the nursing, dietary, housekeeping, and medical lab departments as well. Nurses in the emergency room felt that they received little recognition and were underpaid. All of the emergency room employees, like others in the KCOM-KOHC complex, were worried about rumored staff reductions and the status of their jobs. Grapevine discussions of impending layoffs at KCOM-KOHC had become something of a historical phenomenon. The hearsay had often turned out to be true. There were also major changes being implemented

---

relies on therapeutic measures (e.g., pills, drugs, surgery), DOs believe that these should only supplement the restoration of structural—and mental—integrity (which they achieve, for example, by the manipulation of the appropriate body parts). Thus, the DO prescribes fewer pills and injections, but nevertheless uses both physical manipulative and therapeutic (e.g., injections) measures. As a result, it is believed among some quarters that the DO is a more holistic medical practitioner, at least from a philosophical point of view.

within the complex that were ineffectively communicated to workers; these fueled concern with confusion.

Sensing that the workers were becoming increasingly dissatisfied with the existing employee program and work-related policies, management decided it was time to introduce some necessary changes. One example involved a concerted effort to improve the communication between employees and their managers, as well as between middle managers and top management. A number of communication-related seminars were sponsored to achieve this. Another example was the initiation of a wage survey, with the intent of overhauling the organization's compensation system.

These changes had been initiated by KCOM-KOHC, partly to forestall any of its workers' inclinations toward inviting a union. Indeed, the administration had always clearly voiced its opposition to the unionization of its employees even though, according to one employee, "no one could remember the last time KCOM-KOHC offered much to its workers in terms of good pay, benefits, and working conditions." Nevertheless, management's systematic, straightforward approach seemed to have kept the organization from alienating its employees. As one medical lab attendant noted, for example, "There's no one here in the organization or in the entire county who does not know that things have been pretty tight, financially, for KCOM-KOHC in the last several years." This time, however, the camel's back had been broken—not by a specific last straw, but by perennial cycles of underpayment and insufficient recognition for a job well done. As a result, some emergency room nurses secretly invited SEIU. Union officials at the St. Louis headquarters surveyed the workers' request and approved an organizing effort at KCOM-KOHC. In their assessment, the workers' concerns were with the types of issues with which "winning union campaigns" were made, and included serious problems of wages, communication, job security, staffing levels, and worker "floating" policies.[3] Later on, the employee grievance procedure would be another area raised by SEIU.

CAMPAIGNING FOR WORKERS' SUPPORT: THE FIRST YEAR

The campaign actually began in June, five years ago. The union initially acted by holding secret organizational meetings to acquaint union organizers with employees and to try to identify key people within the

---

[3]"Floating" involves rotating workers between various buildings of the organization as their services are required.

KCOM-KOHC complex. These people would be used to help promote SEIU by passing out pamphlets and starting word-of-mouth communications in general support of the union. If the organizing attempt proved successful, some of them would eventually become officers of the local union. SEIU representatives had somehow been able to obtain a variety of pro-union mailings. The union's effort at this point was to contact as many employees as possible, as a way of raising their awareness with regard to union presence.

Soon after the first contacts, the union began to ask KCOM-KOHC employees to sign authorization cards. The number of cards signed would indicate the magnitude of workers' interest in having SEIU, Local 50, represent them in collective negotiations with the employer. Union authorization cards were left on the tables in the cafeterias, lobbies, and near time clocks. A SEIU bulletin (Exhibit 1) stating wages, vacations, sick leave provisions, and other benefits that some SEIU members were receiving at other SEIU institutions were also placed at locations throughout the complex. It was at this point that some employees informed management of the increasing union activity at KCOM-KOHC.

EXHIBIT 1

SEIU Bulletin
Service Employees International Union AFL-CIO, CLU
Local No. 50

TO: All Hospital Employees

Service Employees International Union, AFL-CIO, CLC, is attempting to unionize all hospital workers in the states of Missouri and Illinois. Hospital workers' wages and benefits are far below those of other workers in the work force, and because of this, Local No. 50 will assist hospital workers in upgrading their wages and benefits. The following are a list of wages and benefits that are enjoyed by Service Employees International Union Members.

Wages

RNs	$8.09 per hour
Nurses aides	6.35
Dietary and kitchen employees	6.73
Housekeepers	6.52
Central supply	5.90
Laundry workers	6.04
Maintenance workers	6.74

Employees working the afternoon and midnight shifts shall receive more per hour for working these shifts.

EXHIBIT 1 *(concluded)*

All employees shall receive 50 cents more per hour when the hospital is short of help.

Employees working the weekend will receive (1-1/2) time and one half per hour.

Holidays

All employees shall receive 12 paid holidays per year: New Year's Day, Good Friday, Easter Sunday, Memorial Day, Independence Day, Mother's Day, Labor Day, Thanksgiving, Christmas, Employee Birthday, Personal Day, Father's Day.

  a. Double time and one half (2-1/2) shall be paid for all hours worked on a holiday.
  b. If employee is off on holidays, he/she shall receive pay for that day.

Vacation

All employees shall receive vacation as follows:

> 2 weeks after 1 year of service
> 3 weeks after 2 years of service
> 4 weeks after 4 years of service
> 5 weeks after 6 years of service

Paid Sick Days

All employees shall receive eighteen (18) paid sick days per year and three (3) paid personal days. Any unused sick days may be paid at the end of the year.

Funeral Leave

All employees shall receive five (5) paid funeral days per each family member.

Uniforms

Paid for or furnished.

Hospitalization

Paid hospitalization for employees and family.

Disability Paid

Employees will receive seventy-five percent (75%) of wages if off from work ill.

THE SECOND YEAR

Management was not aware of the union's presence at the complex until February, the following year. However, the administration wasted little time in preparing itself to defend against the union's campaign, when the organizing attempt by SEIU was brought to its attention.

One of the first decisions made by administration was the hiring of a management consulting law firm that had previous experience in anti-union tactics. This firm, Elliott, Kaiser and Freeman, whose main office is in Kansas City, Missouri, arrived within a matter of days and began to interview members of the KCOM-KOHC supervisory and management staff. The main purpose of these interviews was to determine how the supervisors and managers felt about the union campaign, identify what they felt were the key issues, and use the information to develop the type of training and support the supervisors and managers would need in order to prepare them to carry out the strategy that would be used by KCOM-KOHC.

At the first group meeting between the management consultants and the supervisory and management staff, supervisors and managers were given handouts on the "Dos and Don'ts of a union campaign," emphasizing what members of management could do and say, as well as what they could not do or say to employees during an antiunion campaign. Included in the handouts and discussed at the meeting were items such as those listed in Exhibit 2. Films of a firm dealing with a union campaign and of a strike at an inner-city hospital in New York were also shown. The importance of promptness in forwarding all the information and rumors heard to the attention of the administration was also discussed.

In April 1981, the union began to educate employees about their rights under the National Labor Relations Act by distributing letters explaining them. The first of these letters pointed out to workers that punitive actions by corporate management, such as terminating and transferring employees for union activity, were illegal. At this time, the union started to file unfair labor practice charges on behalf of KCOM-KOHC employees for all conceivable disciplinary warnings, regardless of how trivial. This was done in an effort to show KCOM-KOHC employees that the union was willing to fight management for them. The union also hoped to use up the management consultant's time by giving the consulting firm too many unfair labor practice charges to defend. To further persuade employees of the union's good intentions, a letter from the president of SEIU, William Stodghill, was posted which stressed the intent of the union to be that of improving patient quality care through increasing staff.

Early in May, a class on union authorization cards was given to management personnel. Its purpose was to enable managers to answer questions that were often raised by some employees about authorization cards. Discussed also were different approaches the union could use to ask workers to sign cards and whether or not each could stand up under the law. The class culminated in a test on when an authorization card could be viewed as valid or invalid by the National Labor Relations Board. Examples of the reviewed items were as follows:

Union Organizer: "Don't be a renegade. Sign the card just like eveyrone else. If you do, you won't have to pay either regular dues or initiation fee."

Employee: "That sounds pretty good to me. I'm always looking for a bargain."

Valid   [*Invalid*]

Union Organizer: "Well, it looks like you could be the lucky person. We need one more person to get an election at this facility. If you sign this card, we can go down to the Labor Board and ask for an election."

Employee: "Well, I'm not saying I'll vote for the union, but I'll sign to get an election."

[*Valid*]   *Invalid*

The union responded by preparing and mailing a one-page leaflet to employees entitled, "Have you heard this message yet?" This leaflet posted and addressed seven questions that the union felt would be raised by management. It consisted of counterarguments to standard management objections during an organizing campaign and included statements such as: "All the Union wants is your dues money," and "The Union will be run by outsiders." The leaflet was poorly timed to the extent that the issues it raised had not been originated by management, and thus, prematurely opened a can of worms; it began to raise and address questions that had not yet been raised by management. Therefore, it provided management a perfect opportunity to bring out the administration's views and responses to the raised questions.

On May 8, Dr. H. Charles Moore, president of KCOM, sent a memorandum to all employees appealing to them not to sign the union authorization cards. In addition, Dr. Moore's memo stated in part: "We do indeed have problems and are working as quickly and as positively as we can to work out those problems. We ask that you bear with us during this time of change and we believe that our future together will be positive and rewarding to all." He went on to explain that if employees were patient with KCOM-KOHC during the turbulent times, both worker and employer would benefit more if unencumbered by a union.

On May 19, the vice president and administrator of KOHC, Mr. William Greene, sent another memo on union authorization cards to the employees. Mr. Greene's memo used a question and answer format to discuss items such as what a union authorization card is: whether or not it obligates employees (it does); what the union does with the signed cards (to seek an NLRB certification election and/or to try to force the employer to recognize it without an election); the types of pressure workers are subjected to so as to get them to sign union cards (while

---

EXHIBIT 2 Some Things the Employer Can or Cannot Do during a Campaign

The "Cans"	*The "Cannots"*

1. Tell the hospital employees that if a majority of them select the union (an outside organization), the hospital will have to deal with it on all their daily problems involving wages, hours, and other conditions of employment. Advise them that the hospital would prefer to continue dealing with them directly on such matters.

2. Tell hospital employees that you and other members of management are always willing to discuss with them any subject of interest to them.

3. Tell the hospital employees about the benefits they presently enjoy, all of which may have been obtained without union representation. Avoid promises or threats, either direct or veiled.

4. Tell the hospital employees how their wages, benefits, and working conditions compare favorably with other hospitals in the area, whether unionized or not. Information should be factual.

5. Tell the hospital employees some of the disadvantages of belonging to a union—such as the expense of initiation fees, monthly dues, fines, strike assessments, and membership rules restricting their personal freedom. Quote from the specific union's constitution and by-laws granting the union power to impose punishment and discipline against its members.

6. Tell the hospital employees there is a possibility that a union will call a strike or work stoppage even though many employees may not want to strike and even though the employer is willing to bargain or has been bargaining with the union. Inform employees that any strike can cost them money in lost wages.

1. Promise hospital employees a pay increase, promotion, betterment, benefit, or special favor if they stay out of the union or vote against it.

2. Threaten loss of jobs, reduction of income, discontinuance of privileges or benefits presently enjoyed, or use intimidating language which may be designed to influence a hospital employee in the exercise of his or her right to belong, or refrain from belonging to a union.

3. Threaten or actually discharge, discipline, or lay off a hospital employee because of his or her activities in behalf of the union.

4. Threaten, through a third party, any of the foregoing acts of interference.

5. Threaten to close or move the hospital, or to drastically reduce operations if a union is selected as a representative.

6. Spy on union meetings (parking across the street from a union hall would be suspect.)

7. Conduct yourself in a way which would indicate to the hospital employees that you are watching them to determine whether or not they are participating in union activities.

8. Discriminate against hospital employees actively supporting the union by intentionally assigning undesirable work to the union employee.

9. Transfer hospital employees prejudicially because of union affiliation.

10. Engage in any activity favoring nonunion hospital employees over employees active in behalf of the union.

sweeping under the rug the equally important right not to join a union); the difficulties of getting rid of a union; and how to revoke a signed card (simply, by writing the union and asking it to withdraw the signed authorization card). One of the interesting revelations underscored by Mr. Greene's memo was that SEIU had won an election a few years earlier at Jefferson Memorial Hospital in nearby Festus, Missouri. Some years later, the employees at Jefferson Memorial were very disenchanted with the union and voted to get rid of it. However, this was done after the union had already dragged its suffering members through an unpopular strike of over one year in duration.

KCOM-KOHC administration, feeling that communication between the employees and the frontline supervisors and managers was a key point, continued to have seminars on better communication skills for supervisory and middle-management personnel. They were encouraged to discuss with the employees any issue that would arise in their everyday dealings on the work site.

By the end of May, management had also put into effect the *Hotline*, an anonymous call-in service for workers. The purpose of the *Hotline* was to improve communication between the employees and administration. An employee could call the *Hotline* and ask a question without having to leave his or her name. Once a week a printed edition of the *Hotline* was given to all of the employees and the questions asked the previous weeks and the answers were given. This was the beginning of a management-supported, employee-oriented weekly newsletter called the *Health Center Hotline*.

Early in August, the union sent a letter to the employees that was co-signed by Mr. William Stodghill, president, and Mr. Kevin Gallagher, business representative, of SEIU, Local 50. In this letter it was stressed that the intent of the union was to improve the quality of patient care by increasing staff, and to improve wages, benefits, and working conditions and to create a functional grievance procedure. This letter also contained a cartoon to demonstrate the strength of the union. The union was hopeful that the cartoon, which made a caricature of management's powerlessness in the union's presence, would show KCOM-KOHC employees that they had nothing to fear from management as long as they had the union behind them.

A CONTRACT SAMPLER

On August 17, KCOM-KOHC management responded (to SEIU's letter of early August) with a letter to the workers from Mr. William Greene. This letter began by indicating that the union was an *outsider* to the local community, the medical complex, the ways of life of the people who worked in the complex, and to the effective running of a health care business. Mr. Greene lamented that it would be a tragedy to be represented by "someone" who did not "know anything about 'our Health Center,' and [hadn't] ever taken the time to find out." He characterized the union's statement of intent to "improve patient care by increasing staff" and to achieve "optimal patient care" by decreasing patient load per employee as "empty promises." He illustrated by pointing out that the organization's nurse staffing problems were due to a nationwide shortage of licensed nursing personnel, which KCOM-KOHC had attempted to ease through a widely publicized nurse recruitment and retention program. Further, he underscored that no union could possibly guarantee the hiring of additional licensed nursing personnel anywhere that he was familiar with. But this was not all.

Mr. Greene admitted that in terms of wages, benefits, and working conditions, KCOM-KOHC needed a great deal of improvement, and explained why a wage and salary study was already being conducted by the organization. However, he revealed that even at that, the complex "looked good" compared to contracts negotiated by the union at other medical facilities and hospitals. Reference was made to the terms of a contract that had been negotiated and signed between SEIU (representing the housekeeping employees at St. Louis University Hospital in St. Louis, Missouri) and Service Master Industries (a contractor that was the primary employer of those employees at the hospital). Mr. Greene did not excerpt and attach any specific parts of the contract to his letter. Instead, copies of the entire contract were given to supervisors and managers who, in turn, passed them along to workers. In addition, copies were kept in the Employee Relations Office by Mrs. Sueanna Hannah, director of employee relations. Employees were also encouraged by their supervisors to go to the Employee Relations Office to look at the contract.

All workers who inspected the contract found comparisons similar to those in Table 1. The wages earned by housekeepers at St. Louis University Hospital were generally lower than those that already existed at KCOM-KOHC. In addition, the SEIU contract with Service Master Industries revealed wages that were by far lower than those publicized by the union, in Exhibit 1, as typical results of its negotiations.

Furthermore, all benefits announced in Exhibit 1 as representative of SEIU agreements were considerably higher than those on the signed contract. One of the most talked about benefits in the contract concerned sick pay. Under the SEIU/Service Master Industries contract, an employee would not receive sick pay for the first day he or she called in sick, unless the individual was hospitalized. Thus, if a full-time employee was ill on Monday and Tuesday without being hospitalized, he or she would only be paid for Tuesday. On the other hand, the individual would receive pay for both days under the prevailing terms at KCOM-KOHC.

TABLE 1   Comparisons Based in a Contract Sampler

Minimum Wage Rates Effective June 1

Length of Service	SEIU/SMI* Contract per Hour	KCOM-KOHC† Per Hour
Start	$3.65	$3.85
After 60 days	3.75	4.00
After 1 year	3.90	4.15
After 3 years	4.00	4.25
After 5 years	4.10	4.45
After 10 years	4.20	4.60

*The SEIU/Service Master Industries contract stipulated that employees with ten (10) years or more of service on June 1 would receive the indicated rate or forty cents (40) per hour over the current rate, whichever was higher.
†Reported here are approximations of prevailing wage rates at KCOM-KOHC, for the same category of workers (housekeepers), at the time. They are based on estimations by KCOM-KOHC managers.

Management personnel kept referring back to this contract throughout the campaign. For example, it was often underscored that the cost of living was very high in St. Louis, a large city of a few million people, compared to small Kirksville, a city of only 17,000. Yet KCOM-KOHC workers had relatively better wages, benefits, and work conditions, even if marginally so.

HOPE NEWS OR NEWSLETTER WARS?

The union began its own newsletter in late August. The publication was called *Hope News* and did not appear regularly. "Hope" originally stood for "Help Our Patients and Employees." Later on, it would also stand for "Help Our POOR Employees." Because SEIU had its local headquarters in St. Louis, it found itself having to fight the "outsider" image. For example, management often referred to the union as an outsider that did not understand the local problems of the Kirksville area. Hope was an attempt to improve the union's *outsider* image by associating familiar names with SEIU. Although the union had about half of the workers interested in organizing, many of the rest were still uncertain about what the union would do to their local work life. The others seemed to have been afraid of change in general, and particularly those underscored by the presence of the union. To show those with doubts that the union had become part of the local community, the newsletter contained comments from employees of KCOM-KOHC concerning working conditions, recipes for cookies and salads, and other such items from the local people. Comments in the *Hope News* would also be used to raise issues such as grievance procedures, floating, and acuity levels. *Acuity level* was a factor used to decide the number of nursing personnel that would work a particular shift on a particular floor. It was based on the type and seriousness of the patient's illness. For example, the number of nurses assigned per cancer patient may be higher than for a routine tonsillectomy.

FLOATING THE PERSONNEL

The floating issue grew in importance, and it became obvious to management that the strength of the union was in the nursing department. Nurses were the employees most often asked to float between buildings. In fact, floating was not even a policy in some departments such as dietary and housekeeping. The purpose of floating employees, from management's point of view, was to spread the work load evenly throughout the medical complex. For example, if the 5-South wing had four nurses, three aides, and three patients, and 2-South had two nurses, one aide, and six patients, then one nurse and one aide from 5-South would be floated to work on 2-South. The union, on the other hand, maintained that it was harassment to make employees work at areas that they were not permanently or originally assigned to. The union stated that more employees were needed to overcome the practice of employee floating. The nurses themselves felt it unfair that they were moved around when other employees were not. Furthermore, they were bitter about being originally hired to work on particular floors by virtue of their specialties, and then "forced" to work outside their primary skill areas.

THE TALK, LISTEN, AND COMMUNICATE COMMITTEE (TLC)

Not all classifications of KCOM-KOHC workers felt as strongly for their own self-interest motivations to unionize, as the nurses at this point in time. As a result, a splinter group emerged around the months of August through November. Several employees had started being upset with the union and decided to form a committee of their own. Indeed the committee was neither originated by, nor connected in any way as a stooge to either SEIU or the KCOM-KOHC management. Rather, the group was an independent movement started by a certain Tom Auxter and a handful of his friends. Its purpose was to solve problems of the organization within the organization and without the benefit of a union. This committee sent two letters to the employees, in a membership drive, during this period. The letters read in part:

WE ARE THE EMPLOYEE COMMITTEE THAT CARES! WE KNOW that we can work with the staff, physicians, administration, community, with each other and with you to make KOHC the best possible health center. WE THINK it's time for the union to leave us alone so that we can all work together to improve the things that we all care about . . . JOIN US, and let's work together to get things done for KOHC and each other!

Out of this employee committee grew the Talk, Listen, and Communicate (TLC) Committee. This committee, which is still functioning (as of data collection date), meets with administration to communicate suggestions and concerns that have been given to them by their fellow employees. The union contended that the employee committee was actually initiated by the administration of KCOM-KOHC, but lacked concrete evidence to that effect.

ECONOMIC AND FINANCIAL HARDSHIPS

During this entire year, KCOM-KOHC experienced severe financial troubles. Like many other health care organizations in the country, the patient census had dropped well below the normal average. The cost of new equipment, supplies, and other expenses had skyrocketed. When this was combined with the fact that medicare and medicaid reimbursements to the institution no longer covered the costs laid out by the institution, KCOM-KOHC had to absorb over $2 million in bad debts that it could not pay. Some managers estimated that the organization was already about $1.5 million in the red. Because the financial picture of KCOM-KOHC was anything but rosy, management announced in late November that no merit increases would be given to employees of KCOM-KOHC for one year, beginning on December 1.

On December 2, the union sent a letter asking the employees to consider the fact that they would be receiving no pay increases and that the practice of floating was still taking place. The union stated that it could negotiate regular wage and benefit increases if given the chance. Sections of the letter read as follows:

NO pay increases for (the entire next year)?
NO overtime pay for working a holiday?
NO reimbursement . . . for completing the LPN training program?
A floating policy still in effect, whereby employees are moved back and forth between the two hospitals without advance notice and NO reimbursement for gas?
NO disability insurance?
NO hospitalization coverage while you are not working?

And after all of this the (administration) hires a management consultant to conduct a "compensation study" for . . . computing new wage rates that (management) claims it can't afford to pay anyway???

The union did not know how bad the financial situation of KCOM-KOHC had become. After several weeks of discussion and planning between management and the institution's board of directors, a plan to reduce KCOM-KOHC's expenses was developed. A main component of the plan called for the reduction of 140 full-time equivalents from the KCOM-KOHC personnel.

The decision on which employees would be terminated was based on employee seniority within the individual's current department at the time. In addition, all part-time positions were eliminated in each department before any full-time employee was terminated. On December 10, those people that represented the 140 full-time equivalents were told that they were in positions that had been declared excessive by the institution, and therefore their services were no longer needed. Each of these employees was given two weeks' severance pay and was also paid for any unused vacation and holiday time. Unemployment compensation would not be contested by the institution for any of the excessive personnel that had been terminated.

SEIU had something of a field day with the mass terminations that were taking place. During the three months prior to the December 10 dismissals, the union had been losing much of its support among the employees. The mass discharge was just what the union needed to bolster its waning campaign. Employees began to question their job security. Rumors of more mass terminations began to spread like wildfire.

A QUESTION OF IMAGE

In late December, Mr. William Greene sent to all employees a "facts versus rumors" handout. His foremost intent was to put an end to some of the rumors concerning additional terminations; but the handout also attacked the union as being an outsider. Mr. Greene pointed out that the union's closest office to KCOM-KOHC's location was in St. Louis—about 260 miles away from Kirksville. Further, he indicated that "SEIU (was *NOT* really SEIU), but SEIU-RWDSU." [RWDSU stood for Retail, Wholesale, Department Store Employees Union (New York City).] In addition, his letter uncovered that SEIU, Local 50, had 19 members on its executive board out of which only 1 was a hospital employee. Based on this and similar revelations, the letter left the workers with a question: How could SEIU, Local 50, be "your union?" Mr. Greene encouraged the employees to call the *Hotline* to get factual answers to any other uncertainties they may have.

During the last few weeks of December, SEIU's representatives were being quoted on an almost daily basis in the *Kirksville Daily Express,* the local newspaper, and on the local television and radio stations. The mass terminations and the need for union protection of KCOM-KOHC employees were the main topic. This left the union with the feeling of having the local press behind its cause. However, that was not and did not translate to the strong endorsement the union had hoped for. Public opinion did not take a swing for the worse against KCOM-KOHC, as the union had hoped for. The fact, however, was that due to perennial hardships, KCOM-KOHC had been receiving a great deal of local bad press for several years. This had consistently produced a curious mixture of low public image and immense public sympathy for the organization. In a sense, therefore, hearing negative remarks concerning KCOM-KOHC had become "old hat" in the Kirksville community. Thus, a dismayed SEIU official lamented that the union's strategy of getting the local press on its side was not as helpful a tool as in other SEIU campaigns he had been associated with.

THE THIRD YEAR

The union petitioned for an election and on January 18, a representation hearing commenced in Kirksville before the National Labor Relations Board (NLRB). The purpose of the hearing was to determine the right of the KCOM-KOHC employees to be represented by SEIU, Local 50, for purposes of collective bargaining. An issue of *Hope News* came out at this time encouraging the employees to keep faith and to stand up for their rights. This edition of the newsletter also questioned management's tactics and implied that the institution could not be trusted to tell the truth. For example, it stated that "Mr. Greene is lying when he claims that SEIU is not really SEIU." It explained that a merger between SEIU and RWDSU had been proposed, but final action could not be taken on it until a convention in May or June. It further argued that perhaps the merger would, nevertheless, be an advantage to workers in the medical and health care industry.

THE BARGAINING UNIT CONTROVERSY

The representation hearing took much longer than anyone had anticipated. Due to a scheduling problem, the hearing was on recess for several days and then reconvened on February 16. SEIU took the position that there should be two bargaining units—one for professional and the other for nonprofessional workers. The professional unit would include the registered nurses and the medical and X-ray technicians. Everyone else would be in the nonprofessional unit. The union argued vigorously for including only KOHC employees and no KCOM workers in the bargaining units.

KCOM-KOHC management took the position that three bargaining units were needed in order to represent each of the professional, service and maintenance, and nonprofessional groups of employees. The professional unit would be made up of the same group of workers proposed by SEIU (i.e., RNs, medical, and X-ray techs). The service and maintenance unit would include nurses' aides, maintenance, housekeeping, and dietary employees. The nonprofessional bargaining unit would include all other employees. In addition, the administration argued that clerical personnel should be included in one of the three bargaining units and that all employees (KCOM and KOHC) were to be included in the bargaining units.

The biggest battle during the hearings centered around the inclusion of KCOM employees. The union contended that KCOM was a separate organizaton by itself and had no connection with KOHC in any shape or form. To support this premise, the union called numerous witnesses in an attempt to establish that KCOM and KOHC could each function on its own, without any support or help from the other.

Management's lawyers also called numerous witnesses to provide evidence that KCOM and KOHC were two arms of the same private organization. The KCOM-KOHC lawyers began by establishing that traditionally, the dietary, housekeeping, and maintenance departments all functioned between both KCOM and KOHC. Further, Mr. Don Hunter, director of budgets, presented data showing that the budget was based on the operation of KCOM-KOHC as a whole and that separate budgets were not prepared for each arm of the organization. Testimony was given on the fact that some departments, such as audiovisual, did work for both units. Moreover, a number of departments, such as X-ray and medial lab, testified that some pieces of equipment were shared between their departments at KOHC and the research labs at KCOM. It was noted that all employees' checks were issued by the same organization, and that the institution's major regular newsletter, the *Intercom*, was distributed to all employees and also stated on its cover that it was the biweekly "KCOM-KOHC" newsletter. Finally an examination of the corporate organizational structure during the hearings underscored that KCOM-KOHC had the same board of directors, and that Mr. William Greene, vice president of KOHC, reported to Dr. H. Charles Moore, president of KCOM.

A manager at KCOM-KOHC later explained why the administration wanted all KCOM-KOHC employees included in the bargaining units.

Union support was much stronger among KOHC employees than in the ranks of KCOM employees. Besides, the management's lawyers felt that if all employees were in the unit the chance for a union victory would be greatly reduced. A labor relations expert added that it was quite possible that the union did not have enough authorization cards signed to warrant an election by all KCOM-KOHC employees; hence the union's unequivocal contention for the exclusion of KCOM employees.

Management also felt that three bargaining units would decrease the chance for a union victory. In a three-unit bargaining structure, nursing aides would fall into the service and maintenance employees unit. Nursing aides had become a union strength, while union support among service and maintenance employees had begun to slide downhill. This meant that in an election, the pro-management support of the service and maintenance employees could cancel out the strength of the nursing aides. The clerical personnel also hoped to dilute the union vote in the nonprofessional unit. Tactical or fortuitous? The waiting begins!

The representation hearing ended in late February. The union sent out a *Hope News* in late March. This issue of the newsletter contained several comments from KOHC employees about the right to organize and the benefits of a union. It also contained a section entitled "The Pope's on Our Side," which discussed the pope's view of working conditions in Italy and the pope's belief that workers have the right to organize. An appeal to vote yes on election day was included. The union and its supporters were confident that an election would take place around the middle of April. Little did they know that the long wait had just begun.

April came and no election date had been set. Meanwhile, the management lawyers had been hatching their own "grand design." They had filed a brief with the regional office of the National Labor Relations Board in Kansas City, Missouri, requesting that the *SEIU, Local 50 KCOM-KOHC* case be heard and decided upon by the nation's National Labor Relations Board (i.e., the national board) in Washington, D.C. Management's lawyers stated in their brief that due to the difference in opinion on the number of bargaining units and on whether all employees should be in the bargaining units, as well as the fact that few decisions on bargaining units at colleges of medicine had ever been made, it was in the best interest of the union and the institution to have the national board make the ruling. Shortly after this brief was filed, both the union and the institution were advised that the regional National Labor Relations Board had passed on their case to the national board.

The union's campaign officers were upset by this new development. SEIU had been telling the employees to "hang tough," because an election was near. Now, however, the election date would be delayed by, well, a few months more; or so it was thought.

THE SECOND CONTRACT SAMPLER

During the first week of May, the administration began to distribute to the management staff copies of an agreement between SEIU, Local 513, and Mount Carmel Medical Center in Pittsburgh, Kansas. This was soon after the union had mentioned the contract as one of those it had negotiated for a unit of registered nurses in an issue of the *Hope News*. Management had observed that the SEIU/Mount Carmel contract compared with the SEIU/Service Master Industries contract, and therefore contained wages, terms, and conditions that were not as good as those prevailing at KCOM-KOHC at the time—even though, as the union would later clarify, the Mount Carmel contract reflected a twelve percent (12%) wage increase.

On May 13, the union sent to the employees a letter signed by William Stodghill, president of SEIU, Local 50 (and addressed to "Dear KCOM, Inc. employees"), concerning the Mount Carmel Medical Center contract. The union called attention to the fact that the contract established an Educational Reimbursement Program for registered nurses (RNs); a shift differential of thirty-five cents (35) per hour in the afternoon and forty-five cents (45) per hour for the night shift; pay for being on-call or on standby time and one-half if actually called back to work; and a general 12 percent raise in wages. The letter expressed that "The Mt. Carmel contract, which covers 77 Registered Nurses, is far from the 'best' the union had negotiated for its 230,000 members in the United States and Canada." Furthermore, it stated that "It is ridiculous to waste time and energy worrying about someone else's contract. Each facility negotiates its own contract. Language which KCOM, Inc. employees find unacceptable in other Union contracts does not have to end up in your contract." Thus, the letter also attempted to underscore that the workers could refuse to ratify any contract negotiated by the union, if they did not like its terms. This was the first time that SEIU specifically addressed any piece of correspondence to "KCOM, Inc. Employees." All future union letters and memos would follow the same example, in an effort to establish a better relationship with KCOM employees that the union had previously snubbed.

THE UNFAIR LABOR PRACTICE CHARGE: A DOUBLE-EDGED SWORD?

When the union started filing unfair labor practice charges against KCOM-KOHC about one and a half years ago, its intent was at least threefold. First was to provide the workers some quick evidence of the fine job SEIU could do in their defense; second was to overwhelm and distract management's "antiunion" consultants by confronting them with a barrage of cases to deal with; and third, to provide some martyrs for the union's cause by seizing on some unjust, ill-conceived, recklessly reactive, or vindictive disciplinary actions by the organization. As a result, the union eagerly filed more than 25 unfair labor practice charges by the end of June during the second year. The number of the charges exceeded 60 by May of the third year and dealt with a variety of KCOM-KOHC disciplinary actions, ranging from warnings and suspensions to terminations.

The first major wave of decisions was received by July of the second year, from NLRB's regional office in Kansas City. Not even one disciplinary action by KCOM-KOHC was reversed. (This was one of the events that preceded the formation of the TLC committee.) The union followed up with two actions. First, SEIU appealed the findings of the regional NLRB office to the National Labor Relations Board's national office in Washington, D.C. Second, the union distributed a leaflet toward the end of July, attacking the campaign strategies of management's "antiunion consultants" and suggesting to the workers that they were not receiving better wages because all of the money was being spent on the consultants. The leaflet read in part:

> Big business's attack on the labor movement is occurring on many fronts. The prime movers in this attack are an army of lawyers and consultants whose major purpose is to help business maintain outlandish profits by preventing workers from organizing. But the consultants constitute a Big Business of their own—bringing in up to $1,000.00 a day for their services.

The second major wave of decisions was received in early May, during the third year, from NLRB's Kansas City regional office. The regional NLRB ruled against five of the organization's disciplinary actions and ordered it to reverse or correct them. However, the union could not enjoy the victory. Winning only five reversals in almost one and a half years and after filing more than 60 unfair labor practice charges was not something to brag about. Besides, management was immediately appealing the decisions to the NLRB, which meant that SEIU could not take credit for the victory yet.

Management's legal consultants decided in June to discontinue the fight against the five reversals of management disciplinary actions. The lawyers felt that even though they could probably win four of the charges, it was not worth the time and money it would take to contest the decisions. Therefore in July, KCOM-KOHC was required by the NLRB to post the findings of unfair labor practices for a period of 30 days.

The posting of the NLRB findings created little discussion among the employees. Most employees would begin to read the announcement and then would say "big deal" and walk away. Union supporters did little to spread the word of their small victory. They were apprehensive that some employees might ask about the other charges that the union was unable to reverse. Besides, by initiating an appeal in May and then dropping it by early July, KCOM-KOHC management allowed the findings to slip out through the grapevine and, thus, diffused the punch which the release of the news would have had otherwise.

It was during the month of July that KCOM-KOHC received word that the National Labor Relations Board in Washington, D.C., had upheld the findings of the regional board in Kansas City, concerning the termination of a housekeeping employee in January that year. The Kansas City board ruled that KCOM-KOHC had just cause to terminate the employee. Both union and management officials conceded that this was the most important of all the unfair labor practice charges. Indeed, management and its legal consultants viewed the case as the only important one of the charges. First, it was the only termination case that was directly related to the presence of the union. Second, the worker was discharged soon after he was found sharing and distributing union cards and discussing union organizing activities during work time. Management based its arguments on the grounds that he was negligent in his own duties, while at the same time disrupting the performance of other workers. Third, he was one of the most outspoken supporters of the union. On the night that the employee was terminated, he made several statements that the union would protect him and he would be back on the job in a few days. At a union meeting the next day, he was used as an example of a poor employee who was abused by management and was terminated for supporting the union. When KCOM-KOHC publicized its victory in this case, the union once again began to lose employee support. Several employees began to question just how much protection the union could really give them. Shortly after, several of the stronger and more vocal union supporters began to quit their jobs at KCOM-KOHC and to work or look for jobs in other organizations.

Late July saw another issue of *Hope News*, asking the employees to remain united and faithful to the union's cause. It contained an open letter from William Stodghill and described the "long and hard" union fight by the SEIU-supported employees of Baptist Hospital in Beaumont, Texas. The union-organizing effort in Beaumont had lasted for almost 16 months.

STRATEGIC REPOSITIONING

As August approached, management and its consultants decided to slightly change their strategy. Seminars and classes on communications and management techniques would continue on a regular basis. The administration believed that the seminars had been improving the quality of the institution's supervisors and managers, and that continuing them would be in the best interest of all. Management also decided to hire a training manager for KCOM-KOHC. This person would not only develop and give seminars for the supervisors and managers, but would also develop a new employee handbook, an employee orientation program, and other training programs for the employees.

Any new unfair labor charges would be fought, as in the past. However, the union had not filed any charges for several months.

Management would no longer answer any union letters, memos, or announcements that would appear in the future. For example, from August (of the third year) to April (of the fourth year), the union sent out two issues of the *Hope News*. In neither case was there any response from management. Management personnel also ceased to discuss the union and its activities with the employees, unless it was absolutely necessary. Supervisors would no longer encourage discussions about the union.

Any changes taking place at KCOM-KOHC continued to be communicated to the employees by letter and through the TLC committee. For example, if a change were to be made in the insurer for KCOM-KOHC employee health insurance, a letter would communicate the information to the employee.

In addition, management planned to write more letters to the employees to enable them to become more comfortable with receiving letters from the administration. As one KCOM-KOHC manager explained, the purpose was to preempt the time when a letter-writing campaign against the union would become necessary.

A PERIOD OF QUIET WAITING: THE FOURTH AND FIFTH YEARS

The campaign remained extremely quiet through the early part of the fifth year. Management was very faithful to the strategic repositioning which it adopted in August, during the third year, and never mentioned SEIU. The union filed no additional unfair labor practice charges. An issue of *Hope News* appeared in April; only one or two more appeared in the fourth year.

The lack of an election date added to the lack of campaign activity. Some observers speculated back in April during the fourth year that an election would be held by November. However, December came and went, but there was no election. Meanwhile, more and more union supporters were leaving the employ of KCOM-KOHC. The organization, itself, was hiring new employees who were not familiar with the union or what it stood for. The compensation study had been completed and management approved and established the new salary and wage structure. Workers also began to use the employees' grievance procedure that had existed but was rarely used in the past and found that in some cases, management was willing to reverse a disciplinary action.

Word was finally received by April, during the fifth year, that the selection date had been set for June 28. The management and union teams pondered their respective plans of action for the next few weeks.

Discussion Questions

1. How would you describe, from a collecting bargaining perspective, the internal environment at KCOM?
2. Is it likely that an organizing campaign will be successful? Explain.

Managing a Difficult Employee

1 Paying the Bills at Fidelity Bank

Elgin Davis, controller at the Fidelity Bank of Florida: "I've had about all I can take of these court orders for the garnishment of employee wages. I just got one for C. B. Dappert yesterday. Fidelity shouldn't have to be responsible for an employee's private life and the debts they accumulate. If the people want to buy furniture, cars, stereos, and other items they can't afford we shouldn't have to serve as bill collectors!"

"Mr. Davis, I couldn't agree more. The worst group are these deadbeat dads! In our administrative services department, the word processing staff is always talking about fathers who agree to pay child support but look the other way when they leave the attorney's office or the judge's courtroom," Sheila Porter said.

After Sheila expounded further on the problem of dads who refuse to pay, Lonnie Smith interjected his belief that some of the dads are denied visitation rights so that's why they don't pay. It took Elgin some time to restore order in the conference room. He explained that he had called the supervisors together to discuss the wage garnishment situation and to ask for their cooperation and quick response when a writ of garnishment is received. He told them: "We don't receive these writs on a day-to-day basis but often we have had delays in responding to these writs in the past. The first result is that we have worried employees who learn second-hand that the monies are not being sent. The store or court clerk then sends threatening letters to the employee. In some instances, employees know they face the risk of being sent to jail on contempt of court charges. So, we cannot afford to have these things 'fall through the cracks.' We must see it as our duty, not some privilege we benevolently provide."

After further discussion the meeting was adjourned. Before adjourning, however, there was discussion about the right of the bank to fire people whose wages were subject to garnishment. Certain supervisors felt they had a right to discharge the employees. Other supervisors felt that to discharge these employees was only "pouring salt on their wounds." No one knew for sure if company representatives could take such action.

Discussion Questions

1. Discuss wage garnishment.
2. What is it?
3. What rights and responsibilities do employers and employees have concerning garnishment?

---

2 *The Right Nurse for the Job*

Frances Matthews, the director of clinical services at Appalachian Home Health Services, Inc. (AHHS), was concerned. AHHS needed to hire a nurse quickly. One of the staff nurses had just handed in her resignation because her husband was being transferred out of state. The nurse who was leaving gave AHHS two weeks' notice, which complied with the agency policy; however, it still left the agency in a bind. Frances knew that recruiting and interviewing of home health nurses was a time-consuming process, and even after a nurse was hired, several weeks of orientation were usually required before the nurse could perform independently. She knew that all of the regular staff were working to capacity, and that the loss of even one nurse at this time would have major implications. She walked over to Kate Hennessey's office to discuss the situation. Kate was the director of administration services. Frances and Kate had started AHHS four years ago as a partnership. Together, they made all final hiring decisions.

Frances knocked on the door, saw that Kate was sitting at her desk, and walked in. "Sue is leaving. She sure picked a bad time to move!" She laughed halfheartedly and said, "We need to replace her quickly. Do you have any brilliant ideas?" Kate sighed, and responded, more in the form of a statement than a question, "We don't have any decent applications on file, do we?"

"Nope."

"Great. Well, let's get our ad into the paper today, maybe something will turn up."

This case was prepared by Professor Kathryn H. Dansky, doctoral student, The Ohio State University. Copyright 1989, Professor Dansky.

Appalachian Home Health Services, Inc., is a private, not-for-profit home health agency, located in a rural area of a midwestern state. The stated purpose of AHHS is to provide health care services at home, to elderly and disabled individuals, and to persons with a short-term, specific health care need that could be handled at home.

AHHS is a "fee-for-service" health care organization; it provides in-home services, then bills for the services, either to a public or private insurance carrier (e.g., medicare, medicaid, Blue Cross/Blue Shield), or the patient directly. AHHS receives all (100 percent) of its revenue from billed services. As a private organization, it does not receive government subsidies or tax support.

Competition in the home health field is intense, particularly in rural areas where the need for service fluctuates. Because services are expensive to provide, it is critical for agencies to generate a volume of visits sufficient to cover fixed expenses plus make a small profit. Competition for the AHHS comes primarily from Care One, Inc., a multicounty operation that has been established in the area for well over 10 years. AHHS surpassed Care One in total number of visits after its second year of operation and has been steadily growing. Many of the physicians in the area, however, continue to use Care One, and they receive more referrals from nonlocal hospitals than does AHHS.

AHHS currently has 32 employees: 15 registered nurses (full-time and part-time), 8 nursing aides, 1 physical therapist, 1 speech therapist, and 7 administrative staff. All but two employees at AHHS are female.

REFERRALS FOR SERVICE

Most of the business generated for AHHS is in the form of referrals. Hospitals (social workers, discharge planners), account for over 70 percent of patient referrals; of this total, approximately 85 percent are from the two local hospitals, and 15 percent are from out-of-town hospitals. The second most frequent source of referrals is the general public; former patients, potential patients, family members, clergy, and so on may request services directly. Approximately 20 percent of referrals come from this source. A small number of referrals come directly from physicians. Although this source is less than 10 percent of the total, it is important to the AHHS, because of the power and status that physicians have in the community.

PATIENTS WHO RECEIVE HOME HEALTH SERVICES

Most of the individuals who receive in-home care are elderly. They usually have a chronic illness that requires monitoring, or have a need for rehabilitation therapy following an acute episode, such as a stroke or hip fracture. Some patients are disabled, and require ongoing therapy at home. Some are convalescing from a hospital stay, and need short-term care (e.g., dressing changes). Others have a special type of medical care need that does not require hospitalization, such as intravenous antibiotics or chemotherapy.

Most of the patients cared for by AHHS are indigenous to the area, live in the country (some without running water or bathrooms), and are religious. Although not all patients fit this description, it is fairly safe to say that the patient population is elderly, traditional, and conservative.

THE ROLE OF THE HOME HEALTH NURSE

The registered nurse is the central caregiver in the home health field. The nurse must be able to function independently and comfortably in the patient's home, and must be capable of performing a wide variety of clinical procedures (e.g., injections, inserting catheters, obtaining specimens). Furthermore, the RN is considered both a "case manager," and a "gatekeeper," in the coordinating medical, health, and social services (see Exhibit 1 for job description). This position requires high-level skills in nursing and communications. Nurses with a BSN (Bachelor of Science in Nursing), plus experience in home health or community nursing are usually sought for these positions.

After Frances left, Kate asked the office manager to run off a copy of their standard classified ad for a home health nurse, and take it out to the local newspaper's office. The next day, the newspaper carried the ad in the classified section. (See Exhibit 2.) The advertisement ran for three consecutive days. Applicants were requested to call the office, or to send a résumé to the director of clinical services.

AHHS received two responses to the advertisement. One was a résumé from a student at a nearby technical college. The college had a two-year (associate degree) registered nurse program, and the applicant was in the last quarter of her second year. Frances read over the résumé. She knew, from past experience, that RNs from two-year programs lacked many of the skills needed for this type of work. She decided not to interview this applicant.

The other applicant, Margaret Jenkins, called to express interest in this position. The conversation was pleasant and informal, since the women knew each other. Margaret had lived in the area all of her life, had family there, and was well known for her community activities.

Margaret Jenkins was a registered nurse with a BSN from a local university. She had been working for the past eight years for Dr. Edward Smith, a general practitioner in town. Prior to that time, she had worked at the state mental health center. References from both employers indicated that she was hardworking, responsible, professional, and got along well with patients, staff, and physicians.

EXHIBIT 1   Job Description

Registered Nurse

Definition:

The registered nurse administers skilled nursing services to patients in accordance with a written plan of treatment established by the patient's physician. The incumbent is directly responsible to the nursing supervisor, and ultimately to the director of patient services.

Qualifications:

1. Graduate of an approved school of professional nursing.
2. Current license to practice as a registered nurse in Ohio.

Responsibilities:

1. Conducts initial patient assessment and evaluation.
2. Evaluates the ongoing needs of patients on a regular basis.
3. Initiates the patient's plan of treatment and any necessary revisions.
4. Provides those services which require substantial specialized nursing skills.
5. Initiates appropriate preventive and rehabilitative nursing procedures.
6. Prepares and maintains clinical notes.
7. Coordinates care with allied health professionals.
8. Informs the physician and other personnel of changes in the patient's conditions.
9. Counsels the patient and family in meeting nursing and related health needs.
10. Participates in in-service and continuing education programs.
11. Supervises and teaches other nursing personnel.

Eighteen months ago, Margaret was involved in a domestic violence situation in her home. During an argument with her husband, according to the press, Margaret was physically attacked and the argument ended in the death of her husband. Margaret was charged with murder. During the course of the trial, most of the details were made public. Episodes of violence had occurred previously, resulting in a separation of Margaret and her husband, with a restraining order against the husband. Margaret testified that on the night of the fatal argument, she was home with her two children when he appeared and threatened all three of them. While he was beating her, she managed to pick up a kitchen knife, and killed him. The court convicted her of involuntary manslaughter and sentenced her to 10 years in prison. While she was in prison, her attorney petitioned for early release, based on her standing in the community and the fact that she was the sole support of two young children. Also during this time, several concerned friends led a successful campaign to have her nursing license reinstated. The State Board of Nursing had revoked her license to practice nursing (standard practice for convicted felons).

EXHIBIT 2   Classified Advertisement
_____

The following ad appeared in the classified advertising section of the local newspaper.

> Registered nurse in Home Health Agency. Position available immediately. Ohio license required. Must have own transportation. Prefer candidate with home health/community health experience. Call AHHS, 1–614–555–1212, or send résumé to Box 163, Anywhere, U.S.A. E.O.E.

Margaret's immediate concern was finding employment. Dr. Smith, her former employer, was semiretired, and not able to rehire her. When she saw the AHHS ad in the paper, she thought it was her answer. Now that she had her license back, she could begin working immediately.

THE INTERVIEWS

Because of Margaret's good work record, and because no other suitable applicants were available, Frances asked Margaret to come in for an interview, and set up an appointment for that afternoon. The procedure at AHHS was for all RN applicants to be interviewed first by the nursing supervisor, and then by the two directors, Frances and Kate.

Margaret Jenkins walked into the AHHS offices and greeted everyone warmly. A Caucasian woman of average height and weight, she appeared to be in her mid-30s. She was on time, was dressed appropriately, and looked a little nervous. Barbara, the nursing supervisor, introduced herself and led her into the conference room. A half hour later, Barbara brought Margaret to Kate's office, where the second interview would take place. Barbara went in first and briefly summarized her interview. Although she had a positive overall impression, she was concerned about Margaret's lack of experience with home health procedures, particularly interviewing and assessment skills. (Since this part of the job was so important to the overall plan of care, it was essential that RNs have experience in this area.) She then left the office and Margaret went in.

Margaret sat down with Kate and Frances. The three women discussed AHHS policies, and general personnel issues, including benefits. It was clear that Margaret had the abilities and skills needed, she knew the geographical area well, and could communicate effectively with area physicians. Her only weakness was that she did not have home health experience. Her personal life was not discussed, but she did remark at one point, "You know I really need this job." At the end of the interview, Frances thanked her for coming, and said, "You do meet many of the qualifications, but I'm not sure if you're the right person for this job." Margaret smiled grimly and said, "I wouldn't blame you if you don't want to hire me." With that, she picked up her things and walked quietly from the office.

Frances and Kate looked at each other. "I don't know," Kate said. "I don't know either!" responded Frances. They usually based their hiring decisions on qualifications, plus "intuition" and usually agreed on an applicant's suitability. This case was different, however, and neither was sure whether they should hire Margaret Jenkins.

Discussion Questions

1. What specific factors must the directors consider in deciding whether or not to hire Margaret Jenkins?
2. If AHHS does not hire Ms. Jenkins, does she have grounds for legal action?
3. What could AHHS have done to increase the number of applicants?
4. What selection devices did AHHS use? How valid are they? What other methods could they use?

SUGGESTED READINGS

Arvey, R. D., and R. H. Faley. *Fairness in Selecting Employees*. Reading, Mass: Addison-Wesley Publishing, 1988.

Caldwell, D. F., and W. A. Spivey. "The Relationship between Recruiting Source and Employee Success: An Analysis by Race." *Personnel Psychology* 36 (1983), pp. 67–72.

Klimoski, R., and M. Brickner. "Why Do Assessment Centers Work? The Puzzle of Assessment Center Validity." *Personnel Psychology* 40 (1987), pp. 243–60.

Latham G. P.; L. M. Sarri; E. D. Pursell; and M. A. Campion. "The Situational Interview." *Journal of Applied Psychology* 65 (1980), pp. 422–27.

Taylor, M. S., and D. W. Schmidt. "A Process Oriented Investigation of Recruitment Source Effectiveness." *Personnel Psychology* 36 (1983), pp. 343–54.

3 The Courtland Hotel (A)

BACKGROUND

The Courtland Hotel has been in operation for nearly 15 years. It operates in the central Florida area near the numerous and popular theme parks. The Courtland Hotel is considered one of several luxury resorts. It is owned by a very prestigious European hotel corporation, and it is managed by officers who are located in Houston, Texas. The Courtland has 400 rooms, two restaurants, a lobby bar called The Lamplighter, and a nightclub/lounge called After Hours. Many parts of The Courtland have been renovated over the past few years. The renovation was done so that the hotel would remain competitive with new hotels in the area.

The Courtland's market consists mostly of middle-class families who take annual vacations together. The hotel is price-competitive for this target group and the management believes in the philosophy of "the best value for the dollar spent. . . . " Also, The Courtland offers many "extra" services to their guests including free coffee and newspaper each morning, health club privileges, room service, in-room safes, and in-room stocked minirefrigerator.

Many of these services are the brainchild of the present general manager, Peter Starke. Starke has been the general manager for approximately three years. This is considered to be a record at The Courtland. One hotel veteran believes that there have been about 20 general managers over the past 15 years. This is a very high number, but not so high in the hotel business. Employees at all levels of a hotel—from maids to managers—tend to "drift" from one property to another during their respective careers. Hourly employees often will change jobs for one that pays just 10 cents more per hour, even if the overall benefits are not as good. Wages are often an incentive for managers as well, but more often prestige, power, and the freedom to manage are more important factors. Peter Starke had learned to play the corporate game; that is, he knew the balance of following corporate directives and subsequent red tape, and managing his property like he wanted. He believed in a "personal style of management" and an "open-door policy" with all members of his staff. He made an effort to learn the names of all 200 employees at The Courtland.

Peter Starke reflected on the lessons learned at a recent meeting of the Florida Hotel & Motel Association. The association estimated that,

---

This case was prepared by George E. Stevens and Amy Harding, University of Central Florida graduate.

of the state's 50,000 hospitality jobs, as many as a fifth, or 10,000, are going begging. Most of those positions are entry level. One speaker at the meeting estimates the industry will need 500,000 new workers by the year 2000, yet hoteliers have failed to tap adequately two large pools of talent: older people and disabled individuals. Peter was wondering what he might do to tap into the pool of 60 million Americans older than 50. All studies indicate that these people have fewer absences and accidents than younger workers and are highly motivated. Peter also noted that there might be something he could do to consider for hiring from the local pool of the nation's 35 million disabled adults. He thought about these workers as he concerned himself with the lack of motivation and commitment, turnover, and absenteeism he noticed in some of his employees. Although The Courtland had experienced a high employee turnover rate, there were still many employees who had been with the company for 10 years or more. Some of these employees truly enjoyed their work; some stayed for the better-than-average benefit package; others stayed because they have attained a certain level of seniority in their own departments. While it is true that many of these employees are considered valued members of the "team," there are several who cause problems among their co-workers. These problems are often initiated by these senior employees who display the attitude that they are "permanent" employees of The Courtland. This often causes disciplinary problems, as these employees feel that they are "above" directives from their immediate supervisor or department manager. Co-workers often feel that they, too, are above any new rules or procedures that are instituted by their superiors.

THE MISSING JUICE

As he was leaving the banquet area of the restaurant, Wally Reiff was approached by his supervisor, who had observed him hiding a six-ounce can of orange juice under his coat. After he was stopped, Wally dropped the juice on the floor and left the premises. The next day, when approached by management regarding the incident, the employee denied that he had attempted to steal the juice. Wally was fired, and he filed a grievance.

The union maintained that the company failed to establish "beyond a reasonable doubt" that the grievant had stolen the juice or even seen the container on the floor. Firing, the union said, should not be considered because of the nominal value of the stolen juice. The punishment was not, in the union's judgment, commensurate with the crime. The union also argued that while the grievant was a low-seniority employee with a poor disciplinary record, it was improper to discharge him due to theft.

Requirement

You are the arbitrator. Would you uphold the company's decision to dismiss or would you reverse it? Explain your ruling.

The Courtland Hotel (B)

THE FUNERAL

Many of the hotel employees attended the memorial service for their former comrades at the hotel. It was an unfortunate and tragic situation. On payday Fridays a bunch of employees would walk down to the local branch bank to cash their checks. Last Friday was no different at first. Unfortunately, tragedy struck. While waiting in line to cash their checks, two employees found themselves in the line of fire when a bank security guard went berserk. The bank's lobby was full of people, most in a somewhat festive mood as they waited to have their checks cashed. When the shooting had subsided, eight people were wounded and three were dead. Of the three who died, two were from the hotel and the other person was a bank employee.

After the memorial service was held it was learned that the survivors of both hotel employees who had died made clear their intention to sue the bank. They now want to talk to an attorney. It was their intention to sue the bank because they shouldn't hire "dangerous people." Someone found out that the bank guard had a lengthy arrest record. Other employees were surprised to hear that a lawsuit was being considered. Their friends at the bank said that the bank routinely does background checks on their employees. Judy Ryder, who works at the hotel's front desk, knew people in the bank's personnel office. According to Judy, the personnel director was always complaining that the privacy laws really made it difficult to investigate the background of prospective employees, and the new polygraph law took away an important tool that the bank had relied upon. She said that the bank had just started using paper-and-pencil-type honesty tests.

Discussion Questions

1. In general can a company be held responsible for the actions of an employee? If so, under what conditions?
2. Can the bank be held responsible for the behavior of this bank guard? Explain your answer.

The Courtland Hotel (C)

TENDING THE BAR

In February of 1989 a new food and beverage director was hired at The Courtland. Brett Simpson had worked previously as an assistant food and beverage director and dining room supervisor with other large hotels in the area. Simpson quickly met all his staff members including Barbie Danforth, the head bartender at the hotel's bar, After Hours. Barbie had, as was the case with other bartenders, worked initially in the hotel's Lamplighter Restaurant. So, she was proud to become the head bartender after five years of experience at The Courtland. Simpson knew that there was a need to make some changes in the beverage department but did not feel rushed since he believed that Barbie was "holding down the fort."

Penny Martin had been a bartender at The Courtland for three years, second only in number of years to Barbie. Penny was a rather plain looking girl who tended to bring her problems to work in that she was often rude or curt to patrons. For this reason, unlike many of the other bartenders, she did not have any "regulars." However, Penny enjoyed certain special privileges from Barbie because they had outlasted so many other employees. These privileges included schedules tailored to fit her other appointments, and all of her shifts at After Hours, behind the bar. This did cause some resentment among newer employees, but Barbie had the attitude that the others could "take it or leave it." Despite these problems, After Hours enjoyed high revenues and the bartenders usually tipped out at $50–$100 for each girl per night. Of course, the norm for these tipped employees was that they only declared about $10.

Later in the year, Penny learned that she was pregnant, and was due to deliver in early December. She was happy about this but was also somewhat distressed since she had recently separated from her husband. She knew that she would have to support herself for an indeterminate length of time but felt she could manage given her tip income. Penny said nothing to anyone about her pregnancy until she began to show. Penny and Barbie had no discussion about the possible problems her pregnancy might cause if Penny continued as a bartender. Barbie knew, however, that it was not doing anything for business. Simpson and Starke made no attempt to transfer her. They were aware of the recent court cases and the need to treat expectant mothers fairly.

In early September, Penny asked Joyce McDonald, front office manager, about possible openings in the front office or in the reservations office. Penny accepted the only available position for someone who was untrained and did not want to stand for long periods of time—PBX switchboard operator. The job was at the same hourly rate as her previous position but there was no opportunity to earn tips. The actual rate for the job was $1 an hour less but Penny's pay rate was not changed because the job in question was about the only practical one for someone pregnant.

After a couple months on the job, it was obvious that Penny was a very poor operator. Despite intensive training and the emphasis Joyce placed on being pleasant and congenial, Penny refused to comply. The desk clerks and others complained about Penny's demeanor and her failure to be cooperative, even when they asked her to do simple tasks. Soon Peter Starke, the general manager, heard of these problems. He personally received complaints from hotel guests, too. Joyce repeatedly warned Penny about her behavior. In fact, she counseled her, verbally warned her, and prepared a written warning which was placed in Penny's file. It seemed to do no good.

In November, Penny informed Joyce that she would take maternity leave from November 20 until six weeks from her expected date of delivery of December 5. At the same time, another employee, Ann Lyle, planned her maternity leave for an expected delivery date of December 1.

After giving birth to her baby on December 10, Penny contacts the new food and beverage director, Barry Cotton. Barry has had only limited contact with her, and that when she was on the switchboard. He is surprised when she asks if there are openings in the beverage department. He, not knowing her background, honestly replies that there are no openings. Penny does not accept Barry's word. She contacts Barbie (who does not return Penny's calls). Peter Starke, when he learns of the situation, fills Barry in on Penny's past history with The Courtland. Penny next calls Joyce McDonald about work. Against her better judgment, Joyce gives in after Penny begs her for work.

Penny returns to work on December 24, 1989. Her attitude has *not* changed. It is obvious that she was dissatisfied with having to return to the switchboard. She made sure that everyone in the hotel knew of her displeasure. The verbal and written warnings began all over again.

In January, Cotton received a notice from the state that Penny had filed a sexual discrimination suit against the hotel and named Cotton as the chief defendant. Penny claimed that she had been discriminated against on the basis of her sex because she was not able to reclaim her former position as a bartender when returning from her maternity leave. She also claimed that McDonald had forced her to return early from her leave, but that she had let Ann Lyle stay home for her total six weeks after childbirth. Cotton and McDonald were outraged by these fabrications. Starke was particularly upset because he felt that The Courtland had acted as a fair and responsible employer in Penny's case. Starke immediately contacted his superiors as well as the corporate legal staff.

Although they had dealt with many cases of disgruntled employees, they were not entirely familiar with how to handle a sexual discrimination case.

Penny continued to work at The Courtland until one particularly nasty and vexing confrontation with another employee. The verbal altercation with the executive housekeeper was witnessed by several people. Penny was suspended for three days. She demanded a meeting with Joyce McDonald and later Peter Starke to protest her treatment. At a meeting with both Joyce and Peter, she was insubordinate to both. She directly confronted each person, screaming and cursing at both. Finally, her actions had gone too far. Peter terminated her on the spot.

Discussion Questions

1. Did Penny have a strong case against The Courtland?
2. Was it a coincidence that Joyce submitted more warnings on Penny *after* she had filed the case against the hotel?
3. Was Starke justified in his dismissal of Penny?

---

4 The Ottumwa Education Association

Ottumwa High School (OHS) assistant football coach Mike Taylor was suspended after he threw a chicken into the annual OHS homecoming bonfire on Tuesday, September 7. High school principal Ed Sammons stated that some OHS students brought the chicken to the rally but did not intend for it to be killed. Taylor, who also teaches physical education at Evans Junior High, said the incident was not planned. In a prepared statement for the public and the media, Taylor stated: "I had no prior knowledge that a chicken was going to be brought to the bonfire. The chicken was handed to me. I took the bird, held it up, and threw it down beside the fire hoping it would run off and be forgotten. Someone brought the bird back to me, and, to avoid any more abusive actions to the chicken, I wrung its neck and threw it into the fire."

This case was prepared by Professor Chimezie A. B. Osigweh, Norfolk State University, and Curtis Campbell, Iowa Department of Correctional Services. These authors acknowledge the assistance of Penny Richards and Linda Dudgeon. Copyright © 1984 by Chimezie A. B. Osigweh.

David Howard, OHS activity director and head football coach, said that he (Howard) was helping supervise the crowd at the time and did not see the chicken being cast into the fire. The chicken had been painted blue, the school color of the Cedar Rapids Jefferson J-Hawks, the homecoming opponent of OHS. Taylor had been known as a practical joker. Last year, he jumped over the homecoming bonfire. In concluding his statement, Taylor said, "I wish to express my heartfelt apologies to the Ottumwa Community School District, the school, the students, and anyone else in the community offended by my actions."

SCHOOL BOARD ACTION

Ottumwa Superintendent of Schools Richard Kennedy suspended Taylor on the morning of September 8 after learning of the incident the evening before. The suspension by Kennedy was in effect until Taylor could meet with the school board during a closed session that same afternoon, at which time the exact duration of the suspension, or any other disciplinary action, would be determined. Superintendent Kennedy recommended to the board that they suspend Taylor without pay for one week. On a vote of 5–2, the board voted to carry out the punishment recommended by the superintendent.

Board member Tom Renquist said that three options were discussed at the closed session meeting: to fire Taylor, to give him a one-week suspension, or to give him a two-week suspension. Renquist stated that the two-week suspension was his idea, but he backed down because he thought the one-week penalty was also fair. "I think termination is far too severe. It was something done hastily, and the man feels very badly for it. But we needed action because the action was inappropriate. Our action was appropriate."

Board members Ardith Hudson and Angela Lopez voted against the suspension after an hour of discussion. Hudson stated that she would have voted to fire Taylor if given the chance. "It's a matter of principle," she said. "It's nothing personal, and I would have voted the same way for anyone doing that kind of thing. I abhor violence of any sort, and this was an act of violence. It was conduct unbecoming a teacher. They should set a good example for the students. We are trying to teach that we should not be a violent society." Hudson further stated that she believed Taylor was sorry and that there were "extenuating circumstances" involved. Nevertheless, she believed that consistency in decision making is important. Lopez, the other board member who voted against the suspension, declined to comment, saying that the matter was discussed in executive session where it belonged and the discussion was not meant for the public's ears.

"It's something he'll (Taylor) think about," said Renquist. He continued: "[Taylor has] done a lot for this community, and he is a good teacher. It was a no-win situation. Some will say it's too severe, some will say it's not enough. I'm glad it's over." Taylor accepted the suspension, relieved that it was over, or so he thought.

BACKGROUND

The Ottumwa Education Association (OEA) was formed in 1975 as a result of a new state law that gave collective bargaining rights to public employees in Iowa. The OEA represents approximately 330 teachers within the Ottumwa Community School District. The OEA is the only recognized bargaining unit for all teachers. The OEA is a local affiliate of the Iowa State Education Association (ISEA), which has a branch office in Ottumwa. The ISEA is a state affiliate of the National Education Association (NEA), which has a national membership of over 1.7 million teachers. The ISEA represents approximately 30,000 teachers within its ranks. As provided by law, the school district may have only one recognized bargaining unit representing its teachers. However, membership is optional.

Union Position

Even though Taylor, who is not a member of the OEA, accepted his suspension voluntarily and says that he was treated fairly, the OEA filed a written grievance against the school system. The OEA believes that the disciplinary action taken against Taylor violated the teachers' contract, which implies that discipline must be either a reprimand or a firing. The OEA contract does not include any specific information regarding the issue of teacher discipline. According to OEA officials, both the OEA and the district would have to mutually agree to bargain the item before any discipline issue can become a negotiable item. Thus far, the district has refused to bargain teacher discipline.

The OEA has continued to pursue the grievance even though Taylor has asked that it be dropped. According to Connie Johnson, OEA president, the complaint was not filed on behalf of Taylor, it was filed on behalf of the OEA. "It's a situation that involves our contract," contends Johnson. "Really, it's against our contract to have a teacher out there bargaining alone on the side." The association is not specifically objecting to the disciplining of Taylor but to the fact that wages were withheld during the suspension. It also does not matter that Taylor is not an OEA member. "By law, we have to negotiate for members and nonmembers; he is covered by our contract," said Johnson.

David Knight, a member of the ISEA field staff in Ottumwa, stated: "We feel an obligation under the contract to enforce it, and I really don't see that the threat of a lawsuit is going to stand in our way. If OEA and ISEA buckled to lawsuit threats now, we would lay ourselves open to similar threats in other cases." Knight also stated that the grievance was signed by President Johnson for the association, not Taylor. "The grievance is owned by the OEA," he explained, "and it addresses a situation that circumstantially involves Mike Taylor."

The association also contends that the only instance when a teacher may be suspended under Iowa law, and then with pay, is pending a hearing before the school board when the superintendent has recommended that the teacher be terminated. This statement is based in part on Chapter 279.27 of the Code of Iowa, which indicates that:

> A teacher may be discharged at any time during the contract year for just cause. . . . The superintendent may suspend a teacher under this section pending hearing and determination by the board.

In addition to the Iowa code, the OEA is also basing its case on a 1979 Iowa Supreme Court case. The court's reversal opinion in *McFarland* v. *Board of Education of Norwalk Community School District* 277 N. W. 2d 901 reads, in part, that:

> The school board did not act to terminate the teacher's contract in discharge proceedings but decided only to suspend a teacher without pay prior to a discharge hearing.

Taylor's Position

Taylor states that he has not joined the OEA because he does not agree with the way the organization is handled. According to Taylor, "I feel sometimes they don't hold the teacher's interest in mind as much as their own [the OEA officers]." Charles Henning, Taylor's attorney, has sent a letter to Johnson suggesting that his client will not allow the OEA to continue to use his name in pushing the grievance. The association is failing to represent Taylor as required, because he is opposed to contesting the suspension.

"I have warned them that they better do it right or face the consequences," Henning said. "I told them to stop." Henning would not elaborate what the "consequences" might be, but he explained that Taylor has a legal argument against the OEA.

Henning partially bases Taylor's case on two sections of the Iowa code. Chapter 20.7 permits public employers to "suspend or discharge public employees for proper cause." Chapter 20.18 outlines the grievance procedures, and states, in part, that:

> An arbitrator's decision on a grievance may not change or amend the terms, conditions, or applications of the collective bargaining agreement. Such procedures shall provide for the invoking of arbitration, and in the case of an employee grievance, only with the approval of the public employee.

Taylor, of course, does not approve of the grievance and has insisted that it be dropped. Taylor believes that the issue was between him and the school board and that the matter is settled to his satisfaction. An arbitrator has scheduled a hearing on the matter for April 27, seven months after the beginning of the incident.

Discussion Questions

1. What are the major problem areas in this case?
2. What options are available to the following major participants: the Ottumwa High School Board, Ottumwa Education Association, and Mike Taylor?

5 *Harding Space, Inc.*

KEEPING 'EM HONEST

Harding Space, Inc. (HSI) is a medium-sized firm located in Melbourne, Florida. The firm essentially has been a subcontractor on many large aerospace contracts which have been acquired by firms such as Rockwell International, Martin-Marietta, and Harris Corp. In 1989, the newly elected Bush administration sought ways to bring the federal budget in compliance with the Gramm-Rudman Act. Although it was unlikely that full compliance would occur, it was certain that certain cutbacks in spending would be necessary. Military, social, and space programs would all be affected. With the cutback in many of the National Aeronautics and Space Administration programs, Harding anticipates declining revenues. In anticipation of these cutbacks the firm is

---

This case was prepared by George E. Stevens with the assistance of Cathie S. Stango, MBA, Golden Gate University.

looking very closely at ways to cut labor and other significant costs. Sick leave, medical and hospitalization, as well as long-term disability policies and other payments for time not worked, are all being carefully examined by the financial officers.

"Have you seen our most recent telephone bills?" the company's controller asked supervisors at the department heads meeting. In reviewing telephone bills over the most recent three-year period, he had noticed a 150 percent increase in the size of the monthly bill and a substantial increase in the number of long-distance calls. The controller informed the group that the supervisors' gentle prodding, posted rules, and memoranda circulated to employees asking them to curb long-distance phone calls and to eliminate personal calls just seemed to have no effect. At present he had no way to identify the culprits, but he had an idea for them to consider. "If someone is speaking five times a day with a friend who works across town or making long-distance calls to relatives, the company cannot find out." He wanted their feedback before he moved to implement the plan. "Every time I look at a telephone on someone's desk, it looks like a blank check."

After the announcement of the company's new telephone monitoring system was made, a great debate ranged among employees as to whether the company had a right to track calls made by employees. The new system consists of software for personal computers and a cable connecting the PC to the telephone system. The system tells the employer who was called, how long the worker spoke, and how much the call cost. Some employees, especially managers, approved of the company's actions. These employees believed that keeping tabs on personal calls made from the office should not be a problem, as long as it is the company that's doing the paying for the calls.

Many employees, however, felt that the company had overstepped its boundaries. They felt that it is bad enough that they work under surveillance by way of TV cameras, but now some management type wants to listen in on their calls. These employees believed that the worker is entitled to personal privacy in the workplace and at home. A company spokesman acknowledged that the potential for going overboard does exist, but he did not believe that the company would use the system to check up on employees. He felt that the company would probably track only those calls that exceed $10 or some other limit.

What the spokesman didn't say was that the company was planning to use other electronic monitoring techniques to observe worker performance, to guard against materials thefts, and to provide security. Hindsight is 20-20, he thinks, but he wishes the company had carefully thought about the ramifications of the planned and recently implemented surveillance techniques. He almost said out loud, "Thank goodness we don't have a union!"

Discussion Questions

1. What rights of privacy do employees have while on the job?
2. Should employers be restricted in their ability to monitor calls made by employees while at work? Why or why not?

---

6 *Ben Franklin Hospital (A)*

The patient, a 42-year-old Philadelphia woman, ended up on the doorsteps of Ben Franklin Hospital, so to speak. She was brought in to the emergency room by paramedics. The paramedics said the woman informed them that she was infected with the virus that causes acquired immune deficiency syndrome. It is not clear whether AIDS was a factor in the treatment the woman received. What is clear is that her blood pressure was dangerously high—230/120 compared to a normal level of 140/90 or lower—and that her heart rate was elevated. She was taken to Ben Franklin Hospital by paramedics shortly after midnight on November 14, 1989, after she dialed the 911 emergency number for help. According to state officials who later investigated the case, no treatment whatsoever was provided. The state licensing agency claims that the hospital refused to treat the indigent emergency room patient and then paid a taxi to take her to Philadelphia General Hospital (PGH). A Ben Franklin Hospital administrator claimed the hospital *did* examine the woman but failed to document her care. He claimed that the hospital provided the taxi because the woman wanted to go to PGH where she had been treated in the past.

Philadelphia General Hospital is a large, city-owned and -operated hospital in the City of Brotherly Love. It has 650 beds, has all of the departments one would find in a general, public hospital of its type that's located in a metropolitan area. Unfortunately, PGH has some of the same problems that have beset other metropolitan hospitals. The patient load continues to increase at a rate that is much faster than the hospital's ability to acquire resources (human, equipment, money). When the for-profit hospitals in the area decide that ability to pay is a "test" prospective patients cannot meet, these patients often become the victims because the for-profit hospitals turn them away.

Unlike the many half-empty hospitals around the country, PGH is bustling. At least 25 percent of its patients occupy "public beds"—admitted under medicaid or with no resources at all. For those without resources, their care may be paid for by the city government or simply written off by the hospital. The length of stay at PGH averages 12 days, much longer than the national average, because poor people who come in are usually sicker than the middle class. The poor may not eat properly, their living conditions may be unhealthy, they don't have access or can't afford preventive care, and there are those individuals who are irresponsible about caring for themselves. With the hospital's location being in easy walking distance of the University of Pennsylvania and Drexel University, those among the poor who live in nearby Powelton Village and the surrounding area are well served. In the immediate area the poor and the rich are compressed together.

Discussion Question

1. What rights to admission do indigent patients have? Discuss in terms of the various *types* of hospitals.

Ben Franklin Hospital (B)

Ben Franklin Hospital, unlike Philadelphia General Hospital, is an investor-owned (for profit) hospital. It has 358 beds. Nearly every form of surgery and treatment is offered at its facility. There is a psychiatric center, cancer and physical rehabilitation facilities, a gynecology building, a day-care center, and some apartments for medical residents. The 374 doctors are certified to admit patients. Technological expense in medicine is significant. However, labor is the hospital's greatest cost. More than 55 percent of the typical hospital bill is for staff—and that *excludes* doctors! Hospitals such as Ben Franklin require doctors, nurses, pharmacists, technicians, orderlies, accountants, lab technicians, cooks, maintenance crews, and so forth, all day every day. During the 1970s the number of hospital beds grew quite rapidly. Then came the 1980s; between diagnosis-related groups (DRGs) and the advent of less debilitating forms of surgery, the call for beds declined. In recent years, however, the hospital's census has fallen drastically. The hospital finds itself bigger than it needs to be and it is forced to manage its costs better. Charlotte Wilson, unit coordinator, really had her hands full. Never could she recall having such problems scheduling registered nurses, technicians, and others needed for various operating rooms. The problem seemed not to be associated with the nature of the operations, the days of the week, or the time of day when scheduled. Everyone worked long, hard days at the hospital but the work schedule was in no way different than it had been in recent months. Of course, turnover is *always* a problem, but what else is new! Recent efforts to attract and retain nurses with the offering of "bounties" had proved successful. These bounties allowed current employees to get a special bonus if they identified people in scarce job categories (e.g., registered nurses) and these folks were actually hired. In addition, payment for training and education both on and off the premises as well as the on-site child-care facilities had really reduced absenteeism and turnover. After weeks of struggling with the problem she decided to let Cheryl Ransburg, director of the operating rooms, know about the extent of the problem. Exhibit 1 provides a partial Ben Franklin Hospital Organization Chart.

Cheryl and Charlotte talked about the coverage problem at length. They decided that Cheryl should take a more direct approach in seeking a solution to the problem. Informal discussions with circulating technicians and circulating nurses did reveal a pattern. In general, many of them were reluctant to work with Dr. Benjamin Cooper. Dr. Cooper has had admitting privileges for at least nine years. In fact, he is responsible for about 20 percent of the elective pulmonary admissions.

After three weeks of quietly investigating the matter, the pieces began to fit together. Selected hospital staff came to see Cheryl and offered to provide information if they could be assured of confidentiality and anonymity. Several people knew that Dr. Cooper was in trouble. Rumors were persistent. He loved to snort. He was hooked on "snow." At first he tried to hide his habit but after awhile he seemed not to care. People knew that he had a razor blade, pocket mirror, hypodermic needle, and other possible drug paraphernalia in his office desk. Some co-workers mentioned that his marriage had fallen apart over his dependence on drugs but he clung tightly to his job. Not much could be ascertained from his physical appearance. He was tireless, seldom ate, and his pupils did not seem quite normal in size. Without his medical practice, there was no possible way that Ben could support his habit. Dr. Cooper and Ms. Ransburg had maintained a good working relationship but the information she received was corroborated by too many people. Something had to be done. A medical doctor who does drugs could put himself, his patient(s), and the hospital at great risk.

Discussion Questions

1. What should Ms. Ransburg do?
2. What's the likelihood that disciplinary action will be taken against Dr. Cooper?
3. Are personnel or other laws relevant?

EXHIBIT 1 Ben Franklin Partial Organization Chart

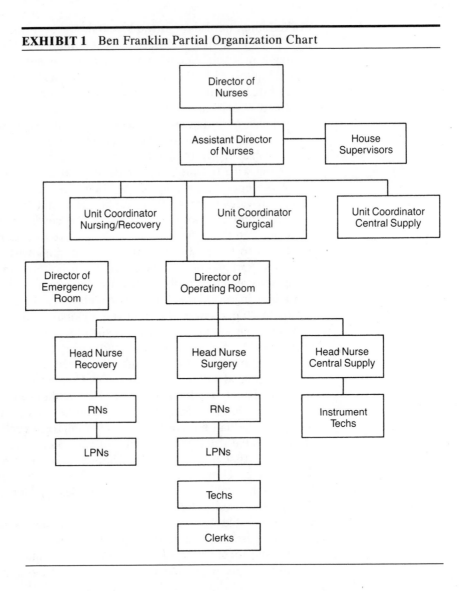

Ben Franklin (C)

Judy Ryder had been in nursing for 15 years. She knew that one of the occupational hazards people in the profession face is that of drug dependency. From her perspective this society looks the other way when it comes to so-called legal drugs. Folks don't go to jail for possession or abuse of alcohol unless they harm someone, as in automobile accidents. Even then the sentence may be lighter. Judy has seen legal drugs as an issue from a different perspective. She has always worried about the overprescribing of drugs and a failure on the part of some doctors and patients to be knowledgeable about the effects of certain drugs' interaction. Fortunately, pharmacists are playing a greater role and taking the initiative in explaining to patients what effect certain drugs have and whether they should be taken with other drugs. Judy also knows that some patients abuse stimulants, depressants, and other common drugs. Patients have been known to complain to different doctors about their (rehearsed) symptoms, then collect prescriptions to take to the pharmacist of their choosing.

Judy's greatest fears have less to do with the situations described above and more to do with other professionals in her own field. She knows that nurses and doctors have access to various medical cabinets. If one wants something to keep him or her going, that person knows just which medication will do the trick. What starts out as something innocent—just a pill to keep the energy flowing—becomes a habit that gets out of control. The people who get "hooked" tend to deny their dependence and many can mask the fact that they have an abuse problem. Unfortunately, the habit does not disappear. Sooner or later, behavior changes or the ability to function on or off the job suffers. However, the changes may be difficult to detect.

Judy hated to be the one to break the news to the director of nursing, but she knew that she would have to report her friend and co-worker, Pat Clement. They had worked together at the hospital for 11 years. Pat had marital problems. She has been a single parent with the responsibility of raising three children. Handling the demands of family and a nursing career was difficult for her. When she realized that Judy knew about her thefts from patients, she just told Judy that the patient would not miss the reduction in dosage and Pat wanted to get something to "calm her nerves."

Discussion Questions

1. What action should be taken (from a personnel perspective)?
2. What's the likelihood that Pat will be disciplined?
3. Are any personnel laws relevant here?

Employee Discharge/ Turnover

1 Making Partner in an Accounting Firm

Public accounting firms and law firms provide an ideal setting to study and attempt to model promotion opportunities. Such firms hire highly motivated, task-oriented achievers who put many, many hours into getting the job done. During the past decade there has been a dramatic rise in the number of women who have entered the professions that these firms represent. Specifically, large gains in the number of employed female professionals have occurred in law schools, business schools, medical schools, schools of architecture, and schools of accountancy, among others. However, the fact that women gain entrance into the organization or a profession does not ensure that upward mobility will follow. Significant inroads are being made in many industries. However, the female workers in many occupations continue to encounter the glass ceiling writers now talk about.

THE ANN HOPKINS CASE

In 1978 Ann Hopkins was hired as a senior manager in the Washington office of Price Waterhouse. Price Waterhouse is one of the giant nationwide firms that dominate the public accounting field. Prior to the merger of certain large accounting firms (e.g., Arthur Anderson and Arthur Young), Price Waterhouse was one of the so-called Big Eight, a major player on a nationwide basis. The senior manager position is a position of high responsibility and visibility, and one that makes tremendous demands upon one's time. Coming in at such a high level would seem to indicate that the firm both acknowledged Ann Hopkins' competence and had high expectations of her. A senior manager is one step below the highest rank—that of partner. Typical levels of progression in an accounting firm range from the lowest (staff accountant or junior accountant, senior accountant, manager, partner, and managing partner) to the highest rank. The partners share in the revenues derived by the firm. Both they and senior managers have the responsibility of attracting new and repeat business for the firm.

In 1982, Ann Hopkins was nominated for promotion to partnership. She was the only woman among 88 candidates that year. Her record was outstanding. Despite the demands that go with raising three children, she had helped bring in between $34 million and $44 million in business to the firm. In addition, she had billed more hours in the preceding year than any of the other 87 partnership candidates.

The road to partnership, however, is fraught with peril. The results *were* excellent. Written evaluations uncovered perceived problems. Specifically, brought into question was the femininity, personality, and attire of Ann Hopkins. Questions were raised both verbally and in writing by certain (male) partners. She received written evaluations that described her as "macho," harsh, and foulmouthed to co-workers. According to a report in *Time,* a partner said she needed to take a "course at charm school." After her candidacy for partner, the decision was delayed for a year. A partner who supported her candidacy advised her that she might improve her chances if she "learned to walk, talk and dress more femininely . . . wear makeup, have her hair styled and wear jewelry."

Hopkins remained with the firm for another year or two. Later, she left the firm and brought suit, contending that the promotion process had violated Title II of the 1964 Civil Rights Act. This act prohibits job discrimination.

One aspect of the *Hopkins* case dramatizes a dilemma women in professional positions face. Firms ask women to walk a narrow line between appearing serious and seeming overly severe. Those who have worked in male-dominated occupations expect women to act both feminine and businesslike. Males may not realize that they are sending out a conflicting message. Brenda Taylor, a former assistant state attorney in Florida, learned that dress codes and one's taste in clothes can cause problems. Taylor had a penchant for short skirts, designer blouses, ornate jewelry, and spike heels and colored hosiery. In general, the law permits officers to establish dress codes, so long as they impose equivalent restrictions upon both sexes. Taylor's office has such a dress code, which mandates conservative dress for all. An issue not addressed is captured in a statement by Prof. Mary Coombs of the University of Miami, "Almost anything you wear runs the risk of looking like you're trying to appear just like a man, or too feminine."

Discussion Questions

1. Do partnership organizations (e.g., law, business, architecture) differ in personnel decision making from the other business organizations?

2. Are partnerships to be exempt from provisions of nondiscrimination or equal employment opportunity laws?
3. What actions can companies or individuals take to avoid the conflicting messages mentioned in this case?

2 Food King Super Markets, Inc. (A)

"Charlie, I am getting too old for this job. Supervising today's young people is putting lots of gray hair on my head!"

"Joe, when you're bald like me, you might prefer *any* color hair to having no hair at all. I'm just kidding. I wonder myself sometimes why I waste my time and energies trying to supervise these employees."

"Tell me what happened . . ."

THE STORY

The city of Sanford's Food King Super Market had developed a grooming policy 15 years ago. The policy included a dress code which made explicit how employees, whether full-time or part-time, should dress. Over the years, applicants were told about the dress code and made aware of the company's expectations. Those who were hired were reminded of the dress code. Attire was not a major problem. Oh, occasionally someone would forget his or her uniform; the supervisors and managers expected that out of their predominantly teenage work force. In recent years, the "punk" hairdos and scuffed jeans look was out so the dress code/attire problem was a nonissue.

The year 1989, however, became the year of notoriety for Food King. They didn't want the publicity but they got it anyway. The first complaint involved Sylvia Foreman, a black cashier who had been with the supermarket chain since 1987. She was an extremely competent, reliable, and friendly employee. Sylvia managed the high stress and grumpiest of customers with ease. For all of 1987 and 1988 she was a model employee. The problem was her hairstyle. Charlie constantly reminded his cashiers that they were very critical to the success of the store. They were, in Charlie's words, "the last line of defense" between the customer and the store when there was the potential for a complaint. Apparently, at least one regular customer violently objected to Sylvia's new hairstyle. During the latter part of 1988 Sylvia had taken to having her hair tightly braided in a cornrow hairstyle. Her co-workers were noncommittal about it at first, but over time they grew to like it. Sylvia was an attractive person who got along with her fellow employees. Her behavior toward others did not change. However, the complaint letters stating an objection to the hairstyle came in on a regular basis. Finally, Charlie felt compelled to act. He did not find her appearance objectionable, but if a customer or customers objected—

Following a progressive discipline approach starting with a verbal warning, he proceeded to discipline Sylvia. In the end, he gave her an ultimatum—"get rid of the cornrows or face dismissal." Sylvia refused. She was terminated on March 19, 1989.

It did not take long for the summons to arrive. Sylvia felt that the cornrow hairstyle had no effect on her ability to do her job as cashier. Her attorney claimed the company was overreacting to the complaints of one or a very few customers. The dress code was too vague and she was not informed previous to formal discipline interviews that any rule was violated. The real troublesome issue though was her claim that the requirement banning the hairstyle had a racial connotation because the requirement was more likely to affect blacks or other minorities since few whites wore their hair in the cornrow style. Charlie wondered what the company would do. He was interviewed by the company's counsel, but they didn't volunteer any information as to the strategy they would take.

Discussion Questions

1. What should Charlie have done?
2. How would you have handled this situation?
3. Was the dismissal appropriate? Explain.

Food King Super Markets, Inc. (B)

The Sylvia Foreman case was not the only dress code/grooming issue the food market chain faced in 1988. The Chris Carter "problem" occurred in Casselberry, Florida. One little round object was the focus of attention in the local newspapers. When the object in question is an earring in a young man's ear, people sit up and take notice!

Joe Newsome was one of Food King's most experienced managers. This was his fourth managerial stint. He had been manager of the Casselberry Food King store for five years. He had devoted most of his time and energy to the problem of handling the administrative duties related to the store. He left the day-to-day operation of the store to his subordinates. He had been pleased with the development of his assistant store managers. His ability to develop people was evidenced in the upward mobility of so many of his people over the years. The stickiest problem he faced in 1988 was a *people* problem. Often, he lectured his assistants that the people problems were the problems that really tested the mettle of those who manage. "Working with data and with things was simple by comparison," Joe claimed.

In July of 1988 Chris Carter applied for a position at Food King. Chris was only 16 years old. Chris was hired as a bag boy. He was a good student and appeared to take orders well. He got the nickname Odd Job because he willingly did a little bit of everything from assisting customers with their packages and taking loaded shopping carts to the customer's car to bagging groceries and helping with stock. He appeared to be a fast learner. Everyone liked him, but when he started wearing his earring during working hours, he lost a few friends. His peers had no problem with the ornamentation, but not so for his supervisors. Chris argued that he had a right to wear the earring. He wanted to know why he was being persecuted. As he stated, "No one bothered women when they wore earrings."

After discussing the earring situation with his assistant managers, managers at other stores, and the food chain's personnel director, Joe decided to send Chris home. He told Chris he would have to remove the earring before he could return to work. Chris refused and hired an attorney. Chris's attorney was a member of a law firm that was well known for its handling of Title VII (Civil Rights Act of 1964) cases. A sex discrimination complaint was filed with the Equal Employment Opportunity Commission and the Florida Commission on Human Relations. The case is currently being investigated by these agencies.

Requirement

Considering the facts of this case, is the company's position legally defensible? How would you have handled this situation? Explain.

3 The Dallas Computer Caper—A Newspaper Account[1]

Richardson, Texas—at about 3 A.M. on a Saturday morning, Joe Di-Maggio Sykes broke into the offices of WWPA, Inc. and UGP, Inc., and sat down at his old terminal. He signed on and signed off. He immediately signed back on with a three-day-old security password that let him perform his job—computer security officer. He then erased 168,000 payroll records on the company's Zenith System 326/38 and invoked a time bomb intended to erase records on a monthly basis. Sykes had been fired three days before, on September 18, 1989.

In a case that was initially considered too technical to pursue, a jury, including three computer professionals, convicted Sykes on a felony charge of harmful access to a computer last week. He faces up to 10 years in prison.

Computer security experts agree that the case will likely not deter this criminal activity, but the precedent may persuade more law enforcement officials to pursue computer criminals.

NOT CLEVER ENOUGH

While Sykes may have been clever about covering his audit trail, the break-in and a coincidental weekend work session of a fellow programmer led to his discovery.

"He was having continual conflict with the company and anticipated being fired," said David Bob Johnson, Dallas county assistant district attorney. Johnson said that the time bomb was created in a new account, which Sykes gave a name beginning with the letter Q—the same letter that begins account names provided in IBM software—so it would remain undetected. Sykes apparently used it to create a program that gave it security clearance. According to Johnson, he tied this program, which was intended to erase files, to legitimate files and put it on a time switch.

The company, an insurance and brokerage firm, made a cursory check of the accounts after Sykes was fired but did not find the hidden account, according to Johnson. Computer system officials at the company would not comment.

Saturday morning, after Sykes's break-in, a programmer came into the office to figure out how a new bonus system would affect the com-

---

[1]The names and places used in this case are, for obvious reasons, fictitious but the events described are real.

pany's payroll. Johnson said that every time the programmer ran the simulations, the payroll came up with zeros, signaling that the initial payroll deletion had occurred. This led the company to shut down the computer for two days to cleanse the system, a move that allowed the time bomb to be discovered.

Johnson, who had little past experience with computers, said he wanted to pursue the case even though the district attorney thought it was too technical to try and was willing to negotiate out of court. The jury was more technical than most, Johnson said; it included one systems analyst and two computer designers.

Also, the case was not attractive to the prosecution because the actual damages were rather small; the county only proved $12,000 in damages for downtime and the cost to fix the payroll accounts.

"In the scheme of things, it was not a large loss. But 550 people didn't get their checks for a week or two, and if the program had gone off as planned, it would have created havoc," McCown said.

SHOW SOME SPINE

The conviction most likely will help other prosecutors overcome an apparent fear of prosecuting high-tech crime cases, Johnson said.

"One of the most pressing needs in the criminal area of viruses is the education of attorneys," said John McAfee, chairman of the Santa Clara, California-based Computer Virus Industry Association. McAfee noted that there has been a rapid increase lately in requests for virus-related information from police organizations.

The *Sykes* case is thought to be the first to win a felony conviction. A 1985 case involving a similar time bomb planted by a disgruntled employee in Minneapolis only involved a misdemeanor, although the original charge was extortion. Sykes was sentenced on October 21, 1989.

Requirement

Identify and discuss the personnel issues raised by the situations described in this case.

4 *Western Lighting and Electric Co.*

The Western Lighting and Electric Co. is a company of 210 employees. It had made its mark in the southeast corner of Pennsylvania. In addition to supplying power to a limited number of customers in counties surrounding Philadelphia, it sold some electrical appliances to consumers and dabbled in the sale and manufacture of some consumer goods. Unfortunately, in recent years it has had to rely on the power supply aspect of its business to generate revenues to offset losses in the Consumer Goods Division. The principal reasons for these losses were the overwhelming consumer acceptance of foreign products, especially those from Japan and Korea and the incredible price competition that high-import tariffs seemed not to affect. The result: continued loss of market share, movement back to its basic business, and belt-tightening that has led to a reduction in the work force. However, heavy losses continue.

"Mark, I am telling you, we *have* to cut back! We have attempted to rely on attrition but it is just not working. After three years of being benevolent, it's time for folks here to face the harsh reality of the bottom line. You and Paul Silas came up with a fantastic early retirement program for these old guys nine months ago, yet few of them wanted to take advantage of it. I just don't understand it. Many of them might as well be at home tending their gardens for all the good the slow-moving old farts do us!"

"Jim, I really think that you are losing your objectivity on this one. These folks have given us 20 or more good years of service. I don't think that it's right to just cast them out. Where would we be without the technological breakthroughs of Pete Johnson, Robert Wells, and John Corrigan, for example? All of those guys started here when they were in their 20s. The oldest is John at 59."

"Jim, you're my boss and you're my friend. In fact, I am glad that you will make the decisions. You certainly seem more objective and positive about these guys than I am. It is too bad that I am not convinced. These old clowns might have made contributions years ago but when is the last time one of them had something patented? Age *is* a problem. I'd get rid of the lot of them. You can sit around and wait for them to croak if you want. By then our business will be in bankruptcy. One word of advice: Fire the bunch of them. They are slow, obsolete, and our most expensive employees, from a compensation standpoint."

Just one year after the discussion between Mark and Jim, a downsizing plan was implemented. This plan was based upon employee performance evaluation data, projected labor cost data for all job categories, seniority, and anticipated profitability of various units. Jim knew that regardless of the work force reduction strategy taken, there would be opposition. Someone would be hurt. He tried to make the selection scheme as objective, consistent, and impersonal as possible. The end result would be that approximately 45 people would be terminated. The *headache* came a great deal sooner than he expected.

Several older employees were terminated. At a recent EEOC hearing, these discharged employees testified that their supervisors made derogatory comments, like "old farts" and "old clowns," and argued that these statements were evidence causally linking their termination to prohibited age discrimination. Jim was really worried because he knew that a number of supervisors, not just Mark, felt this way. Although he developed his reduction in the work force scheme without using age or seniority as a negative factor, he knew that the termination decisions were based upon his model.

Discussion Questions

1. Should Jim be worried? Why or why not?
2. Do these remarks provide sufficient evidence that the decisions were discriminatory?

---

5 *Arizona Highway Patrol*[1]

The Arizona Highway Patrol (AHP) has a long, proud, illustrious history and a reputation for having a professional, well-trained group of officers. Most of the officers turn down opportunities to make more as city police officers or county sheriffs so that they can be an integral part of the most highly respected police officers in the southwestern United States. The job of patrolling the many hundreds of miles of state highway is a difficult one. Officers, traveling alone, cover many miles a day checking motor vehicles for near compliance with posted speed limits. When it comes to speed, the judgment is made on the basis of the weather and road conditions as well as the speed of other traffic. Informally, officers allow drivers to exceed the speed limit to some degree, especially in the wide open spaces that is much of Arizona. Arizona

---

[1]The names, places, and organization used in this actual case are disguised for obvious reasons.

does have its contrasts though—from the desert landscape of Tucson to the mountainous terrain of Sedona or Flagstaff. Other major duties of these officers are to identify unsafe trucks hauling goods through the region, assist motorists who need help, and determine if individuals are bringing plants or other contraband into the state.

Over the past 10 to 15 years the composition of the AHP has undergone significant change. More women, Hispanics, native Americans, and blacks have been added to the force. Increased development and growth in the Phoenix and Tucson areas has led to a need to increase the size of the Arizona Highway Patrol and to provide more of a concentration of officers in the troops around these two metropolitan areas.

"I know he's a hard worker and a good officer, but I want him dismissed anyway. . . ." So ordered Major Ted Herbert to Captain Mark Peters.

BACKGROUND

Tom Woodson joined the Arizona Highway Patrol about three and a half years ago. Tom had a spotless record. In fact, his personnel file at the headquarters shows his work was above average and that supervisors considered him "a hard worker," "professional, eager to learn, dedicated and very personable." Such a record is not surprising since Tom's parents are officers elsewhere in Arizona and he has been a police "brat" for as long as he can remember. Law enforcement is his life and he would love to continue his career.

Tom didn't want notoriety or publicity but what he got was a scandal. Tom never thought that he would see his name in headlines but there it was, part of the lead story in *The Phoenix Gazette:* "Bisexual deputy forced to resign." He was a good officer who worked well with others and had no difficulty in doing his job. He had the respect of his fellow officers and that of his neighbors, associates, and friends. Now, this story might change all that.

In April of 1989, during an investigation conducted by Mesa Deputy Sheriff Paul Butler, Jr., Woodson admitted he had had a homosexual affair with a man about one and a half years before. Woodson also told investigators he has had numerous relationships with women. The report concluded that "Woodson's chosen sexual preference could compromise his position as a highway patrol officer and public servant. His decision . . . could bring dishonor or disrepute to the AHP Commander, who "holds that homosexuality is unnatural, immoral, and inexcusable."

An internal investigation, which led to Woodson's dismissal, was begun when Mesa police Captain Fred Ware told internal investigators that Woodson had a sexual encounter with another man. AHP spokesman George Solomon said the officer's sexual preference is not congruent with the standard of behavior we'd like to see in a member of our state highway patrol. We informed Tom that termination was a definite possibility but he would have the option to resign. The department also told him that the case could become public if he refused to resign, was fired, then chose to fight the decision. "If you have a drinking problem, a drug problem, you beat your wife, write bad checks, or you're a homosexual, you'll have problems in this agency," Solomon said.

When interviewed by the press, Woodson took issue with the views of his former employer. He said that his sexual affairs were with consenting adults while off duty. He did not believe that the Arizona Highway Patrol had a right to investigate his private life.

"If they want to investigate me because they heard little kids were involved or I was doing something on duty, I'll take my medicine. But I didn't do anything wrong," he said. According to Solomon, the major concerns of AHP were along those lines—whether the activity was conducted while on duty and whether it involved minors. The internal report, however, states that there were never any allegations that Woodson was engaging in sex while at work or with children. Solomon also claimed that the AHP does not screen out homosexuals or bisexuals in hiring. He said there is no written policy preventing their employment.

After consulting with an attorney, Bill Peterson, Woodson has decided to withdraw the resignation he submitted on April 27 (less than a week ago). He wants to be reinstated. On advice of his attorney, if the AHP refuses, Woodson will sue to get his job back. According to Peterson, AHP "doesn't have a leg to stand on. . . . This threat of termination is not legally defensible. They should be ashamed to discharge an otherwise competent highway patrol officer because of his sexual predilections. The AHP has violated some of his basic civil liberties."

When the attorney completed his interview with the media, he spoke off the record to a couple of associates. He noted that court rulings on the rights of homosexuals have been mixed. Certain recent cases (since about 1986) have wound their way through the federal courts. Peterson stated his belief that the Arizona Constitution specifically protects privacy.

EPILOGUE

Members of the state's two largest metropolitan (Phoenix and Tucson) areas' Fraternal Order of Police (FOP) voted by a 2-1 margin to support Woodson in his bid to gain reinstatement to his job as a highway patrol officer. Two of the Arizona Highway Patrol's top administrators abstained from voting but more than 800 of the state's troopers are members of these two FOP groups. According to veteran officers, this is the first time in anyone's memory that FOP lodges had taken a stand opposing a commandant's action.

Several troopers, in fear of losing their jobs, spoke off the record to reporters. They said they personally oppose homosexuality. But they said they support Woodson's right to do as he pleases with his private life as long as his off-duty activities are legal and do not interfere with work. These officers believe that the commandant has overstepped his duty to enforce state laws and was regulating the morality of his state troopers. This action against Woodson, they said, set a bad precedent that could affect other deputies—homosexual and heterosexual—in the future.

Not everyone disapproved of the commandant's decision. The following excerpt is typical of some of the recent mail received by the commandant:

"The gay situation is a travesty—a holy sin, the same today as when the Bible was written. When sin walks in, we have pestilence (AIDS), much degradation. All morals are cast out. We used to arrest on sodomy cases. . . ."

Another person wrote: "I stand in prayerful support of your recent action. . . . How can a state trooper live an openly immoral or even amoral lifestyle and then protect my family from the activities associated with prostitution and pornography?"

Requirement

Research this issue, the relevance of sexual preference as grounds for dismissal. How would you rule if you sat as a judge to hear this case? What factors would you consider in making your decision?

---

6 Jergins Department Store (B)

"Working in the back room has never been a problem for me. Once in awhile we have an irate customer but usually I can shake that off as part of the job. This, however, is the first time that I've ever been injured on the job."

WHAT HAPPENED

John Haviland joined Jergins in January 1987. He took his job seriously. He worked in the customer package pickup area. He was a quick learner. In no time at all he had mastered the filing and inventory system for merchandise ordered and later delivered to the Coral Gables store. As a package/materials handler for Jergins, he had earned good performance evaluations. The evaluations were a tribute to his competence and good-natured manner of getting the job done. His supervisor, Charlie Winner, was convinced that John worked hard when you watched him but took things easy when the boss was out of sight. Charlie just thought that John was a guy who spent most of his time thinking up ways to get out of work so for Charlie to give John a good rating suggests others' feedback about John is quite positive.

A recurrent problem in the loading dock area had never been addressed. Over the years, the Miami heat and humidity took its toll on the rubber seal surrounding the loading dock door. During the summer, heavy thunderstorms would lead to a great deal of rain in a very short period of time. The result of these torrential rains was that puddles of water formed inside the bay area. Peter Smith, one of three package handlers, informed Charlie of his concern about possible injury to anyone working in the area when the floor near the loading dock was wet. Charlie told Peter to mind his own business and get back to work.

In January, one month into the start of his third year on the job, John made Peter's nightmare become a reality. While moving a customer's television and video recorder off a cart and into position for loading, John slipped on a wet spot. His feet flew from under him and he landed hard on his back. At first, he thought that he was fine but when he tried to get to his feet, he knew that he had a serious problem. He felt sharp pains in the lower back area. John was off duty for nearly seven work days. When he returned he brought a doctor's note which stated that there was damage to discs in his lower back and that his lifting should be restricted to no more than 50 pounds. John asked the personnel manager to transfer him. The personnel manager called Charlie Winner. Charlie informed him that the job could not be done by someone with the stated lifting restriction. John had made a case for his transfer or retention in the same job. He said that heavy lifting was only required a small percentage of the time and there were other workers in the department who could lift for him; therefore the employer could accommodate without undue hardship. From John's perspective, he saw himself as handicapped and believed that the company was required to accommodate him. Unfortunately, the company's decision was to terminate John. They felt no need to accommodate the employee.

Discussion Questions

1. Should John be treated as handicapped?
2. What obligation does the company have to accommodate him?

7 Drinking His Job Away[1]

"Do you know how many days of work you've missed over the last two or three years?" Harry Harvey, supervisor of the purchasing department, could contain himself no longer. "I'm tired of covering for you, Clarence. You have been slipping, slipping, slipping for a long time. I have talked to you until I've become blue in the face. Despite all the verbal and written warnings you refuse to stop your drinking. This is official: Your dismissal is imminent. Anyone who can miss 389 days in three years deserves the opportunity to find a job elsewhere." Three months later, after repeated verbal warnings, Clarence, an 11-year veteran of the National Marine Fisheries Service, was fired.

WHAT HAPPENED

Clarence Peterson, 47, served as a purchasing agent for the National Marine Fisheries Service, a federal agency in Madison, Wisconsin. Family and financial problems had really been difficult for him to handle over the past few years. He had one thing after another go wrong. The worst of the financial setbacks was the Black Thursday on Wall Street when he took a $38,000 loss. He had recently bought some stock short and it had started to rise in value when the bottom fell out. Repeated calls that day to his stockbroker went unanswered. By afternoon, additional attempts to reach the stockbroker were met with a constant busy signal.

His marriage of 25 years abruptly ended three years ago. No one could describe the shock and utter despair he felt when his wife calmly informed him that her lawyer would be getting in touch with him about the divorce decree. Clarence didn't realize that his marriage was in trouble! He asked himself why he had been so blind to what was going on. His three kids were going to go with their mother. He wasn't exactly thrilled that he would have occasional visitation privileges.

The divorce and loss of his children seemed to devastate him and cause him to lose interest in his job. Nothing seemed to matter anymore. He began to drown his sorrows in a bottle. He drank alone; he drank with others. Co-workers and friends began to notice that he had become more than a "social" drinker. Some even asked if he could "handle it."

---

[1]The names of the individuals and organization are fictitious but the situation described is based on an actual incident.

Clarence's drinking got out hand. Everywhere he went he took a bottle. Finally, he started bringing a bottle to work each day. At the dismissal hearing, Clarence admitted to drinking a pint of gin a day while at work. He claimed that he could control his drinking and, whether he drank or not, he could maintain good performance. What he did not acknowledge is that concerned co-workers and subordinates served as "enablers" who helped him to get his job done, took telephone messages when he was too inebriated to do so, gave excuses when he was indisposed, or otherwise helped him get through his workday.

As the years went by it became increasingly obvious that he could not do the job. Friends grew tired of pinch-hitting for him. In fact, some co-workers became downright resentful of having to cover for him. His $48,000 mistake on a purchase order served as the impetus for his dismissal. The 389 days missed from work over the last three years didn't help his case at all. The dismissal hearing was held shortly after the auditors uncovered the $48,000. At the hearing, the employee's attorney claimed that his client was sick. His alcoholism was an illness requiring treatment—not dismissal. The attorney also argued that although many people told Clarence that he should stop drinking, no formal counseling took place. "Rehabilitation, not retribution, should have been the order of the day," the attorney claimed. "My client had a crippling disability and the agency failed to make reasonable accommodation. Federal agencies, more so than do local or state agencies, have a special duty to assist handicapped workers."

Discussion Questions

1. What issues does the case raise?
2. Should an employee miss 389 days over a three-year period yet still retain his job?
3. Should alcoholism be treated as a disease? How would you rule in this case?

8 Consultants' Advice at WTAM—Channel 4[1]

WTAM encountered great difficulty in its attempts to compete with the current news leader, WCAU-TV. WCAU is the pride of CBS's southeastern U.S. market. The Tampa-based affiliate consistently places first in all the "sweeps." The station's stranglehold on first has been very frustrating to other local TV competitors. WCAU's dominance has been most pronounced in the news department. No one has been able to unseat the evening and late night news teams from the number one perch over the last four years. These competitors have *not* stood idly by. The turnover rate among the anchors and others on the evening and nightly news teams has been astronomical.

For many, many years WCAU was the doormat of the sweeps process. The competing television stations, WPIX and WTAM, had taken turns as leader in the region. In fact, until 1982, WCAU trailed both stations in the viewer ratings process. Bill Baxter, the original owner of WCAU, encountered financial difficulties. He then decided to sell out to a new owner. The highest bidder for the station was the flamboyant, hard-driving Charlie Stevens. Dr. Stevens had spent much of his life as a professor at the University of South Florida. He later became Dean of the College of Business Administration. His financial moxie, personal contacts he had developed and nurtured over the years, and his wife's inheritance enabled him to purchase the station. Charlie had become accustomed to success. He was one of those city fathers who got in on the ground floor of Tampa's incredible growth spurt of the 1970s and 1980s. He had purchased a great deal of real estate, and his financial holdings had multiplied dramatically as well. He was, as he liked to say, fond of "winning." The station was *not* a toy. He wanted it to be the best. He told all the employees at their very first meeting under his ownership that he "took no pride in being the Avis of the television industry."

Charlie was willing to recruit the best even if it meant raiding neighboring stations. He spent thousands on promotions and marketing of the station, its programs, and its television personalities. During the early years of his ownership there was rapid turnover. He established a new top-management team beginning with the station's general manager. His "real baby" was the evening news. During 1982–84, he tinkered constantly with that program, and program format changes were made. He experimented with anchors and co-anchors, and he changed the key

---

[1]The names, places, and organizations identified have been disguised. The personnel situation is real.

people who delivered the news, weather, and sports. Most of his efforts were designed to change the image of the television station. He was determined to see the station become number 1 in viewer audience. The 1984 ratings results placed WCAU in first place for the first time in over a decade. Dr. Stevens did anything and everything needed to remain at the top of the local television market. Not unlike other station management, Charlie relied upon consultants to provide marketing suggestions and to gather marketing research. However, Charlie was a maverick. He was as likely to implement their recommendations as he was to discard them. He liked the motto "if it ain't broke, don't fix it."

WCAU's efforts left the other Tampa television stations in a panic. They did not know what to do. Their corporate owners weren't happy being also-rans in the television sweeps. These stations tried rather drastic moves in an effort to entice viewers away from WCAU. In some instances, move lineups, use of syndicated programs, and evening schedule changes were made. Each of the stations has modified its news format as well. Nothing has worked. WTAM is just a station. If anything, their most recent move may have helped WCAU strengthen its hold on first place.

The consultants have spoken. The surveys have been done. The ratings over the past two years have been carefully examined. *Somebody* from the evening news team must go. The news team consists of two co-anchors, Gerald Rising and Michelle Murray, weather forecaster Al Donnelly, and sportscaster Ray C. Jurgensen. They all knew that the ratings weren't what they should be. None of them knew why they were so low. The team itself had changed in recent years. People who worked for WTAM viewed the team as being a pretty good one—with one notable exception.

The exception was Al Donnelly. Not only was he popular with the station's television audience but everybody at the station liked him. His personal mark of distinction and touch of individuality was his neatly trimmed beard. (Few in the industry dared to break the unwritten rule of "no facial hair.") Al was really good at what he did. He brought to the team an air of professionalism, a touch of humor, and the knack of interjecting a remark or two that made people feel that he was talking to them.

A LOOK AT AL DONNELLY

Al Donnelly is a native of Fort Wayne, Indiana. He has had two loves—sports and meteorology. For many years he wrestled with the need to balance his dual loves. He wasn't a great athlete, but he certainly had accumulated his share of trophies and medals as a high school star at a Class A (small) school. He learned very quickly, however, that sports offers a very short-lived career with risk of injury hanging over one's head. A rather mediocre college athletic career helped reinforce his decision to become a weatherman. He did earn four letters, two each in baseball and basketball, but competing for a varsity position at an NCAA Division III was not all that difficult.

Since earning his Bachelor of Science in Physical Sciences degree in 1979, Al has worked for three different TV stations during the past nine and one half years. His first job, which took place at a television station in Indianapolis, left much to be desired. He was more of a gofer than a weather person. The station was small and ranked number three out of the three local stations. One value of the station was that he was more of a generalist. He had the opportunity to learn how everything works. It provided a nice overview of television—from management to the lowliest (but essential) technician. He learned quite a bit.

The experience helped him land a full-time position doing the weather for a top-rated station in Toledo, Ohio. He thoroughly enjoyed his work at WTOL-TV. Despite the severe winter weather and the depressed state of the economy during his first two years there, he turned down two employment opportunities. As he gained in stature at the station, he watched Toledo begin its slow but steady recovery. Business opportunities such as the retention of the Jeep plant, revitalization of downtown and the water front area, and the attraction of new industry including the city's first mini-mill for steel production, helped keep Al in Toledo. When the offer to join WTAM came along, however, Al decided that for professional reasons it was the best thing to do. He also decided that the Florida weather would not be too hard to tolerate. So, in 1986 he joined Tampa, Florida's WTAM-TV. He'd been in the business for seven years and had become a very competent, seasoned veteran.

WORDS TO A COLLEAGUE

"There's nothing wrong with my beard. I don't even want to hear that malarkey! In fact, many of the viewers who write to me take time to compliment me on having such an attractive beard. Some say that they don't care what the consultants and so-called experts say, the beard should stay; the consultants should go! From my perspective, the smart boys raise the beard issue, but it is really a straw man. They just want to justify the big bucks they get. They haven't got a clue as to what is wrong. There is no concrete evidence that I'm the cause of the news program's persistent low ratings.

"I know that I am not the problem. No one person, especially not the meteorologist [who is responsible for weather reports], makes or breaks the evening news program. The program format, the personalities and competence of the anchor, co-anchors or production crew, or strength of the news-gathering function, have a much more dramatic impact upon ratings.

I have watched news anchors come and go so often during my years here that it looks like a trapdoor instead of a softly contoured chair that should be their homes when they are on the air. These previous changes and my gut lead me to believe that the real problem may be management malfeasance. However, I have learned that being forthright around here is a sure ticket to somewhere else. Clearly, there's little security in this business. Clive Thomasson, my counterpart at WCAU, warned me not to sign an employment contract that included a noncompete clause. [See Exhibit 1.] I wish that I had listened. Today I received my 'pink slip.' The owner terminated me. He believes the consultants know what is best. I asked what it was that I did wrong. He said that he had no complaints with me regarding my performance, just that it was time for a change. Obviously, the accumulation of wealth doesn't mean that you are smart. I'm not happy about the situation. I don't think I should just be gotten rid of. I'm going to talk to my attorney about my discharge to see what recourse I have."

EXHIBIT 1   Employment Agreement

Employment Agreement

EMPLOYMENT AGREEMENT (this "Agreement"), dated August 17, 1989, is between Television Station WTAM, a Delaware corporation (the "Company"), and Al Donnelly (the "Employee").

WHEREAS, the nature of the Company's business is broadcast media in a highly elastic market and the Company has provided significant compensation to the Employee, the parties enter into this Agreement.

I, Al Donnelly, of Plant City, Florida, in consideration of my employment by Television Station WTAM–Channel 4, and the consideration of the premises and the mutual covenants contained herein, the parties agree as follows:

1. *Employment and Acceptance*

    The Company has hired the Employee to work in the position of meteorologist or weather forecaster on the station's nightly and early afternoon news programs. This employment is not guaranteed to last a specific, determinant length of time. The employment may be terminated with or without cause at any time.

2. *Duties and Authority*

    During this unspecified term of employment the Employee shall devote his full time and energies to the business and affairs of the Company. The Employee agrees to use his best efforts, skills, and abilities to promote the Company's interests and to serve as meteorologist or weather forecaster and to perform such duties as may be assigned to him by the Company's management. The Employee shall, as part of the employment agreement, perform his job in an exemplary manner, obeying all rules, regulations, procedures, and policies established by management.

3. *Compensation*

    3.1   As base compensation for all services to be rendered by the Employee of the Company pursuant to this Agreement, the Company agrees to

EXHIBIT 1 *(continued)*

pay the Employee, during the term of his employment, a salary ("Salary") at the rate of $90,000 per annum, payable in equal biweekly installments, subject to increase during the term in accordance with the Company's salary review policies as in effect at the time of employment.

3.2 In addition to the base compensation specified above, the Employee shall be entitled to receive a bonus (the "1989 Bonus") determined in accordance with the Fall 1989 TV news program "sweeps" results.

3.3 The Company shall pay or reimburse the Employee for all reasonable expenses actually incurred or paid by him during the term of employment in the performance of services to the Company under this Agreement, upon presentation of expense statements or vouchers or such other supporting information as the Company may require.

3.4 The Employee shall be entitled to all rights and benefits for which he shall be eligible under any pension, group insurance and other forms of insurance, as well as other "fringe benefits" which the Company provides for its professional and managerial employees. Without limiting the generality of the foregoing, the Employee shall be provided, at the Company's expense (including fuel, lubricants, maintenance, and insurance) an automobile of the same make and model (or comparable) as is now provided to him by the Company.

4. *Termination*

4.1 In the event of (i) the Employee's willful, material and bad faith failure to perform his duties hereunder, (ii) the conviction of the Employee of (x) any felony, or (y) of any lesser crime or offense involving the property of the Company or any of its subsidiaries or affiliates, (iii) the gross misconduct by the Employee in connection with the performance of his duties hereunder. These items constitute, among others not stated, "for cause" reasons for dismissal. The employee so terminated forfeits any rights to unaccrued benefits. The company shall have no further obligation to make any payments to, or bestow any benefits on, the Employee from and after the date of said termination, other than payments or benefits accrued prior to the Date of Termination.

4.2 If the Employee shall die during the Term, the Employee's employment under this Agreement shall terminate, except that the Employee's legal representatives shall be entitled to receive the compensation provided for hereunder to the last day of the month in which the Employee's death occurs.

4.3 If the Employee becomes disabled during the term so that he is unable substantially to perform his services hereunder for an aggregate of 6 months within any period of 12 consecutive months, this Agreement may be terminated by the Company. Such termination shall be determined by resolution of the Company's Board of Directors after the expiration of said six months, and shall be effective upon written notice to the Employee of the adoption of such resolution. The compensation due the employee hereunder shall be paid through the last day of the calendar month in which such termination shall have become effective.

EXHIBIT 1   *(continued)*

4.4   In the event the site of the Employee's employment is relocated outside of Hillsborough, Osceola, Seminole, or Orange Counties, the Employee shall have the right to terminate this Agreement, and following such termination shall be entitled to receive six months salary.

5.   *Protection of Confidential Information:*
Non-Competition

5.1   The employee shall not divulge to anyone, either during or at any time after the termination of his employment, any confidential information concerning the Company and its subsidiaries and affiliates or its or their customers. The Employee acknowledges that any such confidential information is of great value to the Company and its subsidiaries and affiliates, and upon the termination of his employment the Employee shall forthwith deliver up to the Company all documents, memoranda, and other data in his possession relating thereto. The Employee shall not, either during, or at any time after the termination of his employment, make any public or private statement reflecting adversely on the Company and its business prospects or otherwise disparage the Company. The employee shall not, either during his employment or during the first 18 months after the termination of his employment, solicit or encourage any employees of the Company to leave the employ of the Company, consult with any such employee with respect to other employment opportunities, or on behalf of any future employer, hire or offer to hire any person while he or she is an employee of the Company.

5.2   The Employee shall not directly or indirectly appear in the position of meteorologist, weather forecaster, or other on-the-air capacity on any television station program within a restricted area of 90 miles radius of Tampa. This geographical restriction applies to major television markets (e.g., Orlando) as well as smaller markets (e.g., Lakeland) and covers a period of 18 months after the date of termination of the employee's employment, whether this termination is with or without cause. This covenant on the Employee's part shall be construed as an agreement independent of any other provision in this Agreement; and the existence of any claim or cause of action on the Employee's part against the Company, of any kind whatsoever, shall not constitute a defense to the enforcement by the Company of this covenant. The Employee shall be entitled to seek or arrange for any such position, ownership interest or association, so long as it does not go into effect until the expiration of this Agreement's stipulations. In addition to any other right and remedy it may have, at law or in equity, the company shall be entitled, upon a proper showing, to an injunction enjoining or restraining the Employee from any violation or threatened violation of this Section, provided, however, that the foregoing shall not prevent the Employee from contesting the issuance of any such injunction on the grounds that no violation or threatened violation of this Section had occurred. If any of the restrictions contained herein shall be deemed to be unenforceable by reason of the extent, duration, geographical scope, or other provisions hereof, and in its reduced form, this Section shall then be enforceable in the manner contemplated hereby.

EXHIBIT 1   *(concluded)*

---

6. *Intellectual Property*

The Company shall be the sole owner of all the products and proceeds of the Employee's services, including, but not limited to, all materials, ideas, concepts, formats, suggestions, developments, arrangements, packages, programs, and other intellectual properties that the Employee may acquire, obtain, develop, or create in connection with, and during the Employee's employment, free and clear of any claims by the Employee (or anyone claiming under the Employee) of any kind of character whatsoever (other than the Employee's right to receive compensation hereunder).

7. *General*

7.1   This Agreement shall be governed by and construed and enforced in accordance with the laws of the State of Florida without regard to the principles of conflicts of laws thereof.

7.2   This Agreement sets forth the entire agreement and understanding of the parties relating to the subject matter hereof, and supersedes all prior agreements, arrangements and understandings, written or oral, relating to the subject matter hereof.

7.3   The invalidity or unenforceability of any provision or provisions of this Agreement shall not affect the validity or enforceability of any provision of this Agreement, which shall remain in full force and effect.

IN WITNESS WHEREOF, the parties have executed this Agreement as of the date first above written.

TELEVISION STATION WTAM CHANNEL 4
By: _____

_____
Al Donnelly

_____

Clive Thomasson had talked to Al about employee noncompetition clauses. Although the concept wasn't new to Al, he had never been asked to sign a contract with such a clause. Since his arrival at WTAM, Al has signed a contract that has an employment-at-will clause and a noncompetition clause. The employment-at-will clause makes clear that the employee serves for an indeterminant period and that he or she may be terminated "for good cause, no cause or a cause morally wrong provided that cause does not violate a statute. . . ." The noncompetition clause bars the former employee from working in the same career field for a competing television station in the same geographical region.

Discussion Questions

1. Discuss the employment relationship between Al Donnelly and WTAM–Channel 4. In particular, examine the employment agreement. Pay special attention to noncompetition and employment-at-will clauses. What personnel issues does this agreement raise?
2. What factors should a television station consider in determining whether to dismiss or retain a television personality?

Part 2

Incident Cases and Role-Playing Exercises in Human Resource Management

Section A

Incident Cases and Role-Playing Exercises: A Discussion

Paul and Faith Pigors observed that sometimes cases do not simulate reality as well as they might.[1] They believed that this was so because cases can give the impression that all the material necessary to deal with a situation is given at one time. In fact, they argue, usually problems unfold over time and require the problem solver to act to gather more information than is first given.

Thus, the Pigors advocated the use of the *incident* case method. The method works like this[2]:

Step 1: A short statement or incident (usually 100 words or so) is presented to the participants.

Step 2: Each participant examines the incident and asks, "What's going on here?" The participant tries to decide the main issues at stake.

Step 3: The participant formulates a series of questions which are essential or useful in solving or coming to grips with the case. Usually these questions focus on the who, what, when, where, and how of the incident.

Step 4: The focus becomes: What is the most important issue here, and what needs to be decided and done right now?

Step 5: The case as a whole is examined, and all major issues are dealt with.

---

[1] Paul Pigors and Faith Pigors, *Case Method in Human Relations: The Incident Process* (New York: McGraw-Hill, 1961).

[2] Ibid., pp. 142–45.

Thus, the incident method is similar to cases, but in some ways different. Typically, this is how an incident case is handled:

In Step 1, each participant reads the incident alone and makes notes about his or her reaction to it. He or she also answers the questions in Step 2. Then, the participant discusses the conclusions of Steps 1 and 2 with a small group in the class or seminar. Typically, this is a group of three to five persons. Together they come to agree on Steps 1 and 2, at least initially, and formulate the questions in Step 3.

When Step 3 is completed, the discussion leader for the group is chosen by the group. It is suggested that this role rotate among the members from time to time. This leader calls over the person conducting the session. The discussion leader asks the questions the group formulated of the person conducting the session. He or she has additional information available about the incident, and thus, this simulates the search for information in the real problem-solving experience.

At this point, the groups formulate the responses to Steps 4 and 5. Finally, there is a group discussion of all the groups in which all the ideas developed are examined. This process involves more active participation by all present and is a useful learning experience in most cases. The incidents given in this text involve a variety of problems and settings, as was true with the case situations.

Incidents

1 Franklin's Department Store

The Franklin's Department Store branch at Scottsdale Avenue and Broadway had been in business for 16 years. It was a very good volume store that more than held its own when it came to sales. The store's close proximity to Arizona State University in the city of Tempe certainly didn't hurt. The store got its fair share of sales from a portion of the 40,000 students in the neighborhood. In addition, the location was a good one. Scottsdale Avenue was one of the busiest streets in the Tempe, Phoenix, and Scottsdale areas. The store is one of eight in the Phoenix metropolitan area. Although its sales have increased somewhat, store size in terms of square footage and work force has remained constant since 1988.

The store's previous manager, Roxana Bacon, had done an outstanding job of cutting costs by managing employee turnover well, using appropriate recruitment sources and methods, and keeping pilferage and spoilage to a minimum. Her reward for her excellent performance was a promotion to a regional management position. All the employees at the Scottsdale store were happy for her *until* they met the new department store manager.

Rick Cohen, the new store manager, is a native of Los Angeles. Coming to Arizona from a California store was just one more stop in his climb to the top of Franklin's. He was an ambitious sort who let nothing stand in his way. From top management's perspective, they liked the fact that he was a highly motivated, intelligent, and determined workaholic who kept himself in top physical condition. Tennis and jogging were two of his greatest loves. His motto was "work hard and play hard." After two weeks on the job, Rick issued a memorandum to all employees appealing to them to get in shape. Specifically, he mentioned that lower medical costs and higher productivity could be obtained if employees exercised and ate nutritious meals. Within one month Rick had issued individual memoranda identifying each employee's proposed weight given that person's height.

Bob Johnson, a 6-foot, 3-inch, 300-pound department store salesman, knew he was in big trouble. He broke into a cold sweat every time he saw Rick approach. Bob had been given orders to lose 90 pounds in six months. Bob had been able to shed only 49 pounds, and he feared for his job. The six-month grace period ends next Friday. Bob was not the only fearful employee. The new boss, whom all described as a "health nut," had all the store's overweight workers in a tizzy. Several had been informed of their pending terminations. The reason: It was unlikely that they could meet his weight mandates.

Sure enough, Bob lasted another two weeks, then received his pink slip. Off the record, Rick believed that not only were there savings in terms of medical care expenditures and lost time, but those who are obese, in his mind, possess undesirable characteristics. In Rick's view, the overweight are lazy, slothful, and dishonest. He told employment agencies not to send overweight candidates to him because "fat people steal."

Quite a few employees, among them some who are not overweight, believe that the store manager is overstepping his bounds. They feel that Rick is discriminating against those who are heavy. "The focus should be on whether the person does a good job, not whether he is good looking," was the view of many workers. The "fatty" dismissals seemed hard to prevent. No one could think of any laws or regulations that protected someone who was discriminated against on the basis of his/her weight. One person recalled a man being denied a job at a health club because he didn't have a muscular build and another health club applicant was rejected because he was overweight. In each case, the employer argued that the people did not project the image a health club needed their employees to project. Neither looked like the "after" in a health club commercial, so the employer turned them down because they would destroy the club's credibility and make it difficult to recruit clients.

Employees later learned that one fired employee had gone to an attorney who admitted that there were gaps in the law that could make obese workers vulnerable to discrimination in the workplace. The attorney also mentioned that employers were not required to give a reason for dismissal so those cases are even more difficult to win.

Discussion Questions

1. Under what conditions does an employer have a right to dismiss a person because of an employee's overweight condition?
2. Are there are federal laws that prohibit discrimination on the basis of obesity?

2 *The Contract Settlement*

You are the plant manager of a large chemical plant of a multiplant, multiproduct company. Some of the company's plants are union, some are not. Your company has the typical wage-salary structure, with wages and salary structures determined by such factors as area rates, economic conditions, law of supply and demand, starting wage and salary rates, and the like.

Your union plant has recently negotiated a three-year contract for hourly employees. The contract calls for total increases, including fringe benefits, or a total of 25 percent over the three-year period. You and other members of your management team feel the contract is a generous one, and the workers voted overwhelmingly to accept it. You felt, with a sigh of relief, that now you could devote more of your time to long-range planning, particularly on cost-reduction methods to permit your plant to continue to remain competitive in spite of the increased labor costs.

Today you received a shock in the form of a committee of salaried employees consisting of technical supervisory personnel. The committee had asked for a meeting with you, and in the course of the meeting had outlined a number of grievances. First of all, very few of them had received, in recent years, pay raises of an equivalent percentage to the contract increases. Also, the hourly workers consistently received overtime and other premium pay equal to approximately 15 percent of their regular income, so many of the skilled workers made more annually than the engineers and supervisors. Many of the committee members were very belligerent and resentful, and you could tell that they had discussed this problem among themselves before asking for the meeting.

Without making any specific concessions, you agreed to look into their grievances and to meet with them again in two weeks. Meanwhile, at your suggestion, they selected a committee of their members to study the problem and to present some specific suggestions at the next meeting.

Outline the analytical and action steps you will take between now and the next meeting.

Prepared by Professor Henry F. Houser, Auburn University at Montgomery.

3 Fat Is Fabulous

Sarah Burns told herself that she was not going to quietly walk off and simply accept the college's decision. She had been passive long enough. All of her life people have been discriminating against her because of her size. Enough is enough. She knew what she weighed—280 pounds— down from the 328 pounds she weighed when her former nursing college forced her to resign. Sarah had been in a state of shock and inertia for six months. She was devastated that her college saw fit to pressure her to leave. Overweight since childhood, Sarah notes that she has endured a lifetime of discrimination, beginning in kindergarten where she bore the brunt of classmates' jokes. Some students called her Tubby or Fatso. According to Burns, "Fat is an OK word. I think this is an important issue. I don't think people really accept the fact that society can be very cruel."

Sarah believed that the college's explanation for forcing her to resign from the school's nursing program was bogus. They claimed that they had made an agreement with her. The agreement: Maintain her good academic standing, lose two pounds a week and keep in contact with faculty who had the responsibility of monitoring her diet. A school spokesman claimed, "We were trying to get her to do two things: one was helping her to address her condition of morbid obesity. Two was in terms of the academic requirements. She flunked a course because she could not successfully integrate information related to diet and nutrition."

Later, she enrolled at another nursing school. There she completed all requirements of the program, and she now serves as a pediatric nurse. After consultation with an employment law attorney, she filed a lawsuit. No verdict has been rendered but arguments for both sides have been heard. Before the verdict was reached a friend brought news of a former Xerox Corporation employee who had filed discrimination charges. The woman, who weighed 249 pounds, claimed that her weight in no way detracted from her performance as a marketer for the copier-duplicator giant. The woman lost her case in trial court but has appealed the decision.

Discussion Questions

1. Does a school have a right to dismiss a student because of his/her physical condition, in this instance, obesity?
2. If so, what basis does the school have for such a decision?

4 St. Luke's Children's Hospital

You are the director of facility services for a 600-bed urban hospital located in a large southwestern city. Your unit is responsible for cleaning all patient rooms, maintaining all public areas, removing ordinary trash from offices and laboratories (hazardous materials are handled separately), and making various physical repairs. There are about 150 people in the facility services unit. This includes yourself, 2 assistant directors, 11 supervisors, 7 clerical workers, 35 skilled craftspeople (electricians, plumbers, painters, etc.), and about 90–100 unskilled cleaners and janitors.

The skilled craftspeople are represented by five different trade unions (all AFL-CIO affiliates). Most of the craftspeople are male (70 percent). Their ages range from mid-30s to early-60s (St. Luke's doesn't hire apprentices). About half are white, 35 percent Hispanic, and 15 percent black. They come from all over the city and suburbs. Their wage and benefits package is comparable to local industry packages and much better than other local hospital packages.

The unskilled cleaners are represented by a rather militant local of an AFL-CIO affiliated industrial union. Almost all of the cleaners are women (88 percent). They range in age from teens to late-60s, although most are between 25 and 45. More than half are single parents. About 60 percent are black, 35 percent Hispanic, and 5 percent white. Most live in the city, within two miles of the hospital. Their wage and benefits package is one of the best in the city—better than most local industry packages.

Absenteeism for both groups is getting out of hand. People don't show up when they are scheduled to work. During the last three months, daily absenteeism for the craftspeople averaged 15 to 20 percent. For the cleaners, daily absenteeism is running at 20 to 24 percent; these rates are three to four times higher than the national averages. In order to ensure that you can cover any given shift you have been overscheduling by about 20 percent. In other words, you have to schedule 50 people a day on a day shift to make sure that 40 will show up, or 25 people on an evening shift to get 20, or 12 on a night shift to get 10.

Maintaining buffer staff is expensive. Most employees receive full pay for the days they miss, because of vacation day, sick day, and personal leave provisions of the various union contracts. Employee benefit costs accrue even when the person is absent. The hospital's chief financial

---

This case was prepared by Professor Donald P. Rogers, Rollins College.

officer has been tracking your payroll costs and considers them excessive. You need to do something to reduce labor costs without reducing levels of service.

Discussion Questions

1. What reasons do workers have for not showing up for work?
2. What can you do to motivate them to show up?
3. Is absenteeism really the problem in this case?

5 *The New Mexico Railroad "Red Light" Case*

The history of the New Mexico R.R. system dates back to 1871 when the idea was first envisioned by D. B. (Gizmo) Jackson. During this period of time there was an increasing need to "link" widespread regions for trade and transportation. Formal organization was completed on September 6, 1872, and the name of the company was changed from the Albuquerque & Santa Fe System on November 24, 1875.

Paul Hearn comes into the personnel office one day. He has always loved trains and his lifelong dream is to become a train engineer. Hearn completes the employment application, passes a screening interview, and he gets the highest score that anyone has earned on the railroad's fireman test. (The position of fireman leads, with experience, to the job of engineer. An engineer is required to be able to distinguish red, green, amber, blue, and white traffic signals.) In addition, he takes and successfully passes the company's comprehensive physical examination. The two of you talk salary and benefits. You have done everything just short of hiring him when you notice that he did *not* pass all parts of the physical examination. He has failed Ishihara's test, a pattern of different color dots forming figures, but he passed a "bright color" test. Even though he failed Ishihara's test, the examining physician recommended that he be accepted for the fireman training program. This recommendation has been passed on to the railroad's chief medical officer who informs you that he would like to overrule the examining physician and declare the applicant unfit for service on engines. The chief medical of-

This case was prepared by Professor George E. Stevens with assistance from Paul Stephenson, Paulius Birutis, John Dottore, Steve Droze, Brad Glass, Laurie Shapek, and Diane Wharton, all of whom are students at the University of Central Florida.

ficer reminds you that "... as a carrier, it has an extraordinarily high duty to ensure the safety of its passengers and that the rejection of Hearn would be based on company standards that are justifiable and reasonable.

Discussion Questions

1. Do you let the examining physician's recommendation stand or do you reverse the decision? Explain.
2. What factors should you consider in making your decision?

6 *The Cleaning Woman*

When Cheryl Green of Rockville, Maryland, realized that she was just too hurried and too harried to keep her house clean she came up with the perfect solution—hire someone. She didn't need to have someone perform those duties every week so she hired a woman to clean her house on a biweekly basis. Cheryl paid Carole Washington, the housekeeper, $50 once every two weeks to do the cleaning for her.

Carole was especially pleased to have Mrs. Green for an employer. Mrs. Green faithfully paid her employee's social security. Carole had previously been "burned" by an employer who failed to do so despite the fact that the employer deducted the employee's contribution from her paycheck. Mrs. Green also kept track of sick leave and holidays. These efforts were even more remarkable given that Mrs. Green lived on a very limited budget. Paying Carole $1,300 a year really strained her financial resources. The working relationship between the two women was excellent. Carole believed that her working relationship was more than satisfactory. Cheryl was convinced that she was doing everything the law required.

She was not. To her amazement, the Rockville woman received a letter informing her that she was a lawbreaker. Mrs. Green was told that she was violating Maryland's worker's compensation law. The Maryland law covers any employee who is paid at least $250 a quarter in wages. The employer must buy a worker's compensation policy that costs $350 a year. (Carole is paid $1,300 a year.) Mrs. Green finds herself in an unenviable position. She can hardly scrape up the $1,300 in wages needed but now she must pay additional money if she is to comply with the law. She must decide whether to continue to employ Carole illegally without paying the policy premium or risk going into debt if she wants to keep her cleaning lady legally. The former option means risk for the employer should the employee become injured. In this case, the employer did act in good faith. There was a communication breakdown between the Maryland Workmen's Compensation Commission and the insurance companies. Each thought that the other would notify the employer-client about his or her obligations.

Requirement

Research your own state's workers compensation law. When you do see these laws, tell how those laws differ from the ones described here. Do such laws actually protect the worker?

7 *The "Great" Professor*[1]

Dr. Harvey Davis, a professor of management, has taught at the University of Southwest Florida since 1980. During this time he has gained tremendous recognition from students for being a dedicated, caring, and knowledgeable instructor. He spends hours with students. He helps them with their student organizations and assists students who need encouragement in the classroom. In fact, for the last two years, Dr. Davis has been chosen recipient of the Teacher of the Year Award. To Dr. Davis' credit, the recognition has not been based on a popularity contest. Student evaluations are examined, a special midterm evaluation and a student evaluation are done, student interviews are conducted, and the professor's teaching is observed by a team consisting of students, faculty, and administrators.

Today, you receive the results of an investigation initiated by the Federal Bureau of Investigation. While investigating charges of misrepresentation and mail fraud concerning administrators of an Arizona university, it was determined that 73 individuals bought their degrees from a diploma mill. "Dr." Davis is among those individuals identified in the FBI report. The report reveals that Davis bought two degrees from the same institution. He did no academic work for either. Basi-

---

[1] The names of the university and people listed are fictitious. The personnel issues described are real.

cally, he paid a fee and, in return, was given fabricated transcripts, diplomas, and even parking decals. Your first inclination is to fire him and then have the university sue him for fraud.

Requirement

Research this type of case. Determine what action(s) you should take to handle this specific situation and to possibly avoid recurrences of this type in the future.

8 *Tastee Donuts, Inc. (A)*

Michael Creighton, owner of two Tastee Donuts shops in Tampa, Florida, felt great about the revenues generated by his businesses. When he opened his first shop five years ago, he was afraid that donut lovers might be loyal to Mr. Donut and other established franchises. Fortunately, his fears were never realized. He had done a great job of identifying and studying factors most crucial to the success of his business. He had identified capital, location, promotions, advertising, overhead costs (e.g., rental fees), equipment, and staffing as the most critical factors. Now he is the proud owner of two money-making shops which employ a total of 12 employees, 6 in each shop. His turnover has been high but he has been able to hold onto his doughnut makers and he has been able to easily replace those who work the counter, drive-in window, and operate the register. Most of his employees are women. About half of the women are married. The single ones tend to be in their 20s and attractive. Mr. Creighton wants women who meet all his criteria—job related and nonjob related.

Creighton had believed that 1989 would be a great year. According to his timetable, this would be the year that he doubled his shops and eventually doubled his profit. Now, he's afraid that 1989 could be the year that he loses it all. His greatest fear could be realized. He knows better than anyone else that he sees the culprit each time he looks in a mirror. He just couldn't keep his hands off his workers. He was always saying things of a sexual nature to his employees. Until Arlene complained, no one had had the guts to file a complaint. Her repeated attempts to get him to stop the jokes, touching, and other objectionable behavior failed. She told him that she was going to the local office of the Equal Employment Opportunity Commission. There she would file a sexual harassment complaint. Arlene said that she had met with a couple of his former employees who would provide depositions supporting her case. According to Arlene, she had learned from a personnel class that she could file a complaint under provisions of Title VII of the Civil Rights Act of 1964 and EEOC guidelines. Over the years, Creighton had come to believe that a sort of contract existed between himself and his "girls." If they wanted to work for him or wanted a raise then they had to go out with him when he wanted. Much of the turnover was caused by voluntary resignations or his firing of those who did not want to "cooperate."

Discussion Questions

1. Which laws cover unlawful sexual harassment?
2. Is Michael Creighton violating the Civil Rights Act (1964), the EEOC's guidelines, or any other statute that might cover sexual harassment?
3. What legal recourse, if any, does Arlene have?

Tastee Donuts, Inc. (B)

"Look, Phil, I could fire you! We run a very small operation here so every worker is doubly important. I can't have people taking time off for weeks at a time even if it is for jury duty. Now, it looks like you're going to be involved with a grand jury case that will keep you occupied for weeks. You can demand your full salary and declare your right to serve jury duty but I want you to know two things: (1) Your salary will be reduced by the amount of money you're paid for being a juror; and (2) if this thing goes more than three weeks you can consider yourself fired."

When Creighton hung up the telephone, Phil's angry retort still echoed in his ear. Phil Richards threatened to get an attorney immediately if Creighton took any type of adverse action against Phil. Richards said Creighton put him in a classic Catch-22 position. To do so to an employee is grossly unfair. He claimed that he was just doing his patriotic duty. Creighton felt that he had a business necessity reason for terminating Phil should the trial go on because accommodation should only go so far. If Phil was in prison, Creighton reasoned, he could replace him, so why should this situation be different? After all, a small operation has practically no slack. Everyone had to be present in order to get the job done. Just to be on the safe side though, the store owner decided to talk to a labor attorney friend about the situation he now faced.

Discussion Questions

1. Did Creighton make a good personnel decision?
2. Does an employer have a right to pay an employee's salary less the amount paid by the court for jury duty?
3. Can an employee be fired because of jury duty commitment?

9 Fort Pierce Truck Personnel Company

The Fort Pierce (Florida) Truck Personnel Company is a subsidiary of Worldwide Corporation of Pennsylvania. The Florida company's principal business is long-distance hauling up and down the Eastern seaboard. In 1988, the trucking company hired its first woman driver, Gina Hall.

Mrs. Gina Hall, a former corporate accountant, gave up her white-collar job in Elizabethtown, Pennsylvania, in 1986 to enroll in tractor-trailer school. There she met her husband, Harry, who was a 20-year veteran of the road. Harry was certified to teach truck driving in Pennsylvania and Florida. When Gina and Harry met, he was an instructor and she was a student at the MTA Truck Driving School in Elizabethtown. During the summer of 1988, the Halls decided to apply for driving jobs with Fort Pierce Truck Personnel Company. They did so on the advice of a friend who was a company employee. During the period 1986–88 she gained experience with three different trucking companies.

As a strategy, the couple decided to have Harry apply for a job there first. However, when Gina returned her husband's completed application to the company, the office dispatcher asked her where her application was. She told the dispatcher that she had not completed one. After learning of her driving experience, the dispatcher encouraged her to do so. Harry was hired in one day and put on the road the next. She waited 40 days to be hired. The company representatives stipulated that she would work primarily with her husband. There were a series of delays until finally she called the operations manager in Pennsylvania to ask if her being a woman was a problem. The manager said no. She next had to pass an extremely difficult road test. (Her husband was not subjected to any road test.) Before she could be hired though, she faced an interview by a headquarters manager who flew down from Pittsburgh. Finally, in October 1988, she was hired officially as the company's first woman driver. On her first day the dispatcher told her that they needed a driver to substitute for a sick team member and asked her if she was ready to go, right then. She would have been riding with another man, and the manager said right in front of her that he did not want to face that issue yet. So, someone else was assigned. According to Gina, "Trucking is a tough business. Being a woman driver clearly puts me at a distinct disadvantage." Despite the perceived disadvantage, she was earning $500 a week with the company. In late November an event occurred, she says, that led to the dismissal of both her and her husband Harry. On a trip to Paoli, Pennsylvania, the Halls met a southbound company team that shouldn't have been where it was. "We knew when that team left the Fort Pierce terminal—we were there—and there was no way they could be where they were on the road without grossly exceeding the speed limit," Gina said. "Not only that, they were off route, on the wrong interstate." During their visit to Worldwide headquarters in Pennsylvania, the Halls reported the incident to a company official. After they returned to Fort Pierce the next day, they were fired.

When the couple asked why there were being fired, they were told that they did not have "a Worldwide attitude" and that their performance was poor. The company spokesman refused to define the poor performance. Later, the dismissal decision was referred to a Worldwide grievance committee. That committee refused to hear her complaint. Afterwards, she decided to seek legal recourse. She retained an attorney to represent her when she presented her case before the state's deferral agency, the Florida Commission on Human Relations. In the 1989 hearing concerning her dismissal, the company stated that they terminated her at the end of her 30-day probation period "as a result of her poor performance." The briefs submitted by the company stated that "Gina Hall's team was taking too much time to complete a trip."

Gina counters Worldwide's claims by saying the company's subsidiary discriminated against her by:

- Hiring her as someone who occasionally would ride and drive with drivers other than her husband, then refusing to allow her to work with anyone but her husband because other drivers' wives complained.
- Subjecting her to sexual harassment by telling her that "all she had to do was show appreciation and play along."
- Firing her at the same time they fired her husband, who they considered to be a whistle-blower, because she became a personnel problem without him.
- Only once did a dispatcher inform her team that they took too long to make a trip. Their destination dispatcher, however, said that there was not a problem. This delay was caused by a truck that was not road-

worthy. Gina wrote up 10 safety violations on the vehicle when she returned from the trip.

- At no time were the Halls given a written time schedule to follow.

Discussion Questions

1. If you were the hearing officer in this case, how would you rule and why?
2. Are there federal or, in the case of Florida, state laws that would prohibit the company from discharging either Gina or Harry or both?
3. Under what conditions may a company legitimately fire a whistle-blower? Do any of those conditions exist here? Explain.

Section C

Role-Playing Exercises

This section also contains a series of descriptive settings that can be used as a basis for role-playing. Role-playing has some similarity to case studies and incident cases; that is, the individual or group assesses the data presented in the exercise. The problem is isolated, possible causes are considered, and attempts are made to solve the problem.

At this point, however, individuals are chosen to represent each of the key persons in the exercise. Each role-player absorbs all he or she knows about the role to be played. The person attempts to determine how the role-occupant would respond to problem solutions.

Then the role-players come together. They react to each other as the persons in the exercise would likely react to the approaches made by the focal persons. Role-playing allows the participants and observers to simulate how various solutions to problems might be concluded. The involvement of the role-players provides a new dimension to learning experiences in personnel administration.

1 Stringing the Applicant Along

A. Preparation for role-playing.
1. This case illustrates the difficulties of stringing an applicant along and keeping interest up when there are second thoughts about joining the company.
2. Background material is read aloud to all.

Prepared by Professor Allen J. Schuh, California State University, Hayward, California.

3. Participants are divided into groups of three (one or two groups may contain two persons in order to handle groups not divisible by three).

4. This case has two roles: Chris (recruiter) and Jean (applicant), and an observer. Group members should decide role assignments among themselves.

5. After reading the instructions, role-players should set them aside and act their parts in a natural way.

B. The role-playing process.

1. At the instructor's signal, the Jeans will shake hands with the Chrises, signifying the start of the role-playing. From this point, players will act in their roles for about 10 minutes.

2. Observers watch and prepare to report; be as unobtrusive as possible.

BACKGROUND INFORMATION

This case involves Chris, a recruiter, and Jean, a prospective recruit. Jean will soon graduate from college. Jean has yet to hear, after two weeks of waiting, on qualification for the management training program and the starting date. Right now, other firms are pressing for acceptance to their offers and there is a chance to work for a public utility.

Two years ago, a brother graduated from college and got fast answers to job offers. Every time Jean called Chris, there's another delay. There are some new pressures so why not stop in to see Chris to try to expedite matters. We join the scene as Jean walks into Chris's office and they shake hands.

ROLE FOR CHRIS

You are a recruiter in a large organization, but despite the size of the office, you've got your own stable of steady customers. For over two weeks, Jean has been stopping in or calling every few days with a seemingly endless variety of questions. At first, the eagerness was refreshing—not many recruits are that gung ho—but now it's a drag. You've already explained the application procedure several times, but Jean seems too impatient. Lately, though, Jean is asking more questions and seems less eager; and because of your quota situation, you know you've got to keep up interest. Last time Jean was in, you heard about the other opportunities but you can't quit now. If only the papers would come through. Until they do, you are determined to keep interest up, so hang in there.

ROLE FOR JEAN

For the last two weeks, you've been talking with Chris about a position. Soon you will graduate from college and you want to make some firm plans. Processing of your application has been slow, and besides all the delays, you're now getting pressure from several people to withdraw your application because it would require you to relocate to another geographical area. Your loved ones seem to be on an emotional bandwagon. They say that if you went with another firm you wouldn't have to relocate or travel as much. You didn't have an answer for this one, so you've stopped in to see Chris once again.

All these things are building on you, and you are wondering if you are doing the right thing in waiting for your application to be processed with Chris's company.

INSTRUCTIONS FOR OBSERVERS

You are overhearing a conversation between Chris (recruiter) and an applicant named Jean. Make a report on the following:

a. Chris's behavior and attitudes in the early, middle, and late parts of the exercise.
b. The way you would have felt if you were Chris.
c. The way you would have felt if you were Jean.
d. What would you do if you were assigned the role of Chris?

2 Follow-Up Recruiting Effort

A. Preparation for role-playing.
1. This case features a follow-up recruiting effort on a good prospect. Two years earlier, the applicant had rejected your offer in favor of another firm's offer of employment.
2. Background information is read aloud to all.
3. The class is divided into groups of three, and three roles (Pat, recruiter; Terry, applicant; and observer) are assigned by mutual agreement of the group members.

Prepared by Professor Allen J. Schuh, California State University, Hayward, California.

4. The roles should be played spontaneously, after reading the role instructions. *Players should not read each other's roles.*

B. The role-playing process.

1. Each group starts on signal and plays each case segment as directed. Total time will be 15 minutes.

2. Observers watch and prepare to report.

BACKGROUND INFORMATION

This case involves three follow-up telephone calls from Pat to Terry, a young person who two years ago rejected the firm's offer in favor of other employment. The telephone calls are independent. Each contact has a different outcome. After these segments are completed, a final scene takes place in Pat's office. We listen first, however, to a telephone call.

ROLE FOR TERRY

About two years ago you graduated from a local college and took a job with a small company which manufactures various kinds of electronic equipment. You took this job after a great deal of soul searching because it looked like a great opportunity.

The first part of this exercise is divided into three segments, each one representing a telephone call to you from Pat, a recruiter you got to know and like when you were trying to decide which job offer to accept. Pat will be "calling" to see how you're getting along in your job; and each of the three times you will have a different answer.

1. On the first call say you're happy with your work, but the training wasn't very good and your boss is a problem.

2. On the second call say you are completely happy with the job, your supervisor, your co-workers, and you know you made the right decision. But offer to get together for lunch sometime.

3. On the third call say you're not sure about your decision anymore because the job isn't very challenging. The people are fine, but you don't seem to be getting anywhere.

The second part of this exercise is set in Pat's office where you've come in to talk about your career. Let Pat try to sell you again, but don't be an eager buyer. Remember, another company could be worse than your current employer.

ROLE FOR PAT

You are a recruiter in a personnel department in a smaller city. Several years ago you became acquainted with Terry, a sharp young person who was graduating from a local college. You had high hopes for a recruitment but at the last minute the applicant accepted other employment after a great deal of wavering. Today is a slow day in your office and on these occasions you go through your follow-up file. You've decided to call Terry to see how the current job is going.

The first part of this case is divided into three segments, each one representing a telephone call to Terry. Your purpose in calling is the same each time, to consider a new employment offer from you. Assume that each call you make to him is the first one in six months. Terry will have a different answer each time. Each "phone call" should last two to four minutes.

Following the telephone calls, the second part of the exercise is set in your office when Terry comes in to talk once again about your company. Good luck in your recruiting.

INSTRUCTIONS FOR OBSERVERS

This exercise allows you to pretend you are wiretapping three telephone conversations between Pat (recruiter) and Terry (applicant), and then you will eavesdrop on a meeting in Pat's office. The first three segments of the exercise involve telephone conversations in which Pat calls Terry to find out how the job has gone; and to see whether Terry might now be ready to switch companies, after finding out that the present employment has some drawbacks.

Focus your attention on Pat's approach. For each of the "calls," what could be done differently? Summarize your reactions to the telephone calls after all three have been completed.

Segment Four is set in Pat's office. Note these things:

a. Pat's opening and the development of appeals.
b. How you would react if you were Terry.
c. Whether Pat pushes too hard, given that Terry has already come into the office.

3 *Turning Down an Eager Applicant*

A. Preparation for role-playing.
   1. In this exercise, participants will be asked to role-play a case involving an eager but unacceptable applicant.
   2. Participants are divided into groups of three (one or two groups may contain two persons in order to handle groups not divisible by three).
   3. In each group, one participant takes the role of the recruiter, another takes the role of the applicant, and the third acts as observer (in two-person groups, the observer is omitted).
   4. When all have completed reading the instructions and background material, the role-players will set aside their instructions and prepare to act their parts in a natural way.
   5. Observers should be ignored by the role-players and should make themselves as unobtrusive as possible.
B. The role-playing process.
   1. The applicants are asked to turn away from their groups. At a signal they will return, indicating their arrival at the personnel department. From this point in, participants will act in their roles.
   2. Role-playing ensues for about 10 minutes of interaction.
   3. Observers watch and prepare to report.
C. Reports from observers and participants.
   1. The observer reports with references to the instructions to the observer.
   2. The applicant (Bobby) reports on how they felt as they talked with recruiter Kim, especially when they learned of rejection.
   3. The Kims report on what they would do differently next time in similar circumstances.

BACKGROUND INFORMATION

The case involves recruiter Kim and an applicant named Bobby. Bobby will soon graduate from college. Bobby is a conscientious student who gets slightly better than average grades, is a persistent worker, and does a good job of career planning. Two-and-a-half-months ago, Bobby met Kim on campus and began to talk seriously about joining the company.

Prepared by Professor Allen J. Schuh, California State University, Hayward, California.

After two interviews, Bobby took the screening tests and completed the application, which has been pending for several weeks now. At this point, Bobby has just decided to drop in on Kim in the personnel department to see if any word has been received on the application.

ROLE FOR KIM

For the past two-and-a-half-weeks, you have been recruiting Bobby for the company. In today's in-basket you found a memo indicating that Bobby's application had been rejected by the prospective department manager. Your task now is to contact Bobby and give the bad news, a task which is especially difficult because Bobby is quite eager to join the company.

ROLE FOR BOBBY

On the spur of the moment, you've decided to drop in at the personnel department to talk with Kim about your pending application. It's over two weeks since the application was filed, and you are especially eager to get official word of your acceptance since you've told all your friends about the company. Also, you know how pleased your parents will be because one of them is now employed with the company in another division.

You are about to be told by recruiter Kim that your application has been rejected, an outcome you didn't expect and cannot accept. Your task is to give Kim as hard a time as you can. Make Kim uncomfortable. As far as you know you meet all the qualifications. Kim had led you to expect acceptance. Maybe an error has been made somewhere. Maybe Kim was just stringing you along. You don't know the reason for taking so long to find out, and you don't care about it, you just want to know what went wrong.

INFORMATION FOR OBSERVER

You are overhearing a conversation between Kim, a recruiter, and an applicant Bobby. Make special note of the following:

a. The manner in which recruiter Kim leads up to and breaks the bad news to Bobby.
b. The way you would have felt if you were Bobby.

    c. What Bobby did that made Kim seem to feel uneasy.

    d. The ways Kim tries to accommodate Bobby's disappointment. Do not enter into the discussion in any way. Learn what you can by "listening in."

4 The New General Supervisor

You have just been promoted to the position of general supervisor, department two, of Colby Manufacturing, Inc. Your department is one of three manufacturing departments reporting to a manufacturing superintendent.

Colby employs 250 people, as revealed by the organization structure, and most of them work in manufacturing. Table 1 presents a demographic breakdown of the company; Exhibit 1 shows the organization structure of the company.

You joined Colby as a manufacturing supervisor in department one in June 1978, after graduating with a bachelor's degree in business from a southwestern U.S. university. After one year, you were transferred to a similar position in department three. Your recent promotion (January 1982) was a result of your excellent performance as a supervisor. You seem to be well known and well liked in most parts of the organization, although there appeared to be some resentment (especially among the nonsupervisory employees) when you first joined the organization. Apparently some of the veteran employees disliked having to work for a newly hired, white woman, aged 22.

TABLE 1   Company Breakdown

	Supervisory			Nonsupervisory		
	Total	*Women*	*Black*	*Total*	*Women*	*Black*
Accounting	1	—	—	3	—	—
Personnel	1	—	—	2	—	—
Sales	1	—	—	10	—	1
Purchasing	11	—	—	1	—	—
Manufacturing	19	1	2	210	105	110

Note: There are 50 black women.

This exercise was prepared by Professor Ronald W. Clement, Murray State University.

EXHIBIT 1   Organization Chart for Colby Manufacturing, Inc.

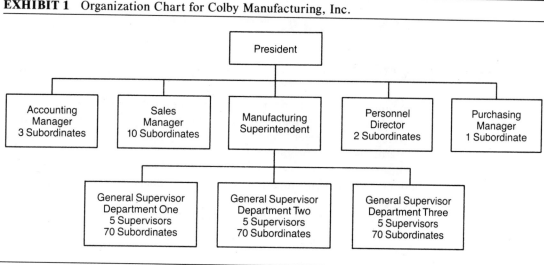

Now that you have been promoted to the position of general supervisor of department two, you have heard new rumors of discontent about working for a woman. These rumors regard the attitudes of your two new peers in departments one and three, and two of your subordinate supervisors in department two.

Although you do not consider yourself to be a militant feminist, you are concerned that there are so few blacks and women in supervisory positions in your firm. Although no charges of discrimination have been filed against Colby Manufacturing, you believe that this is a likely possibility, especially in manufacturing. Even your department could be the focus of such a charge.

You would like to investigate to determine whether or not the firm is in violation of equal employment legislation. If you find that a real problem exists (and it probably does), you would like to propose a way to correct the situation.

Discussion Questions

1. How would you go about investigating the extent of the problem (e.g., to whom would you speak? What records or procedures would you check?).
2. Assuming you conclude that the changes for discriminatory charges are great, what action would you propose? To whom? How?

5 *Termination Interview: The Pink Slip Exercise*

BACKGROUND INFORMATION

The pink slip has long been a signal of employment termination. It can be quite a psychological blow to a person to hear this phrase: "Your services are no longer required." Naturally, the termination may cause desperate financial problems, too.

On the organization's side of the ledger, there are any number of situations in which termination—the pink slip—is necessary. From the perspective of an individual manager, there may be no choice in the matter. It may simply be the manager's job to pass along the bad news to the other person. The experience may be associated with anxiety, regret, and guilt.

Because many people have not had experience terminating an employee, some guidelines are offered:

1. The manager's major task is to be clear in letting the person know that he or she has really been terminated.
2. The other person may try to reverse the decision, but this is not possible. The manager can save unnecessary argument if the finality of the decision is made very clear.
3. The manager wishes to communicate the terms of the termination clearly, including the effective date, information about severance pay (if any), information about other benefits and rights, and other information.
4. While the manager may wish to help the person find a new job, that help could be postponed for now. The other person probably needs to absorb the fact of the termination for a while.

In short, the termination interview is primarily a one-way communication from the manager, in which he or she presents the facts and checks to see if the other person understands those facts. The termination interview need not be lengthy. Ten minutes is probably enough time.

This exercise was prepared by Professor Jack L. Mendleson, Arizona State University.

THE EXERCISE

Two or three rounds of multiple role-playing are best. The group should be divided into small groups of three. The instructor will tell you how the three roles will be allocated:

Note: The regional manager should read *only* the "role for regional manager." The store manager should read *only* the "role for store manager." The observer should read *both* roles and "observer instructions." NOW STOP READING! Do not read on until assignments have been made.

Instructions

1. Be sure you know which role you are to play.
2. Read your assigned roles carefully and decide what you plan to say to the other person in playing your part.
3. Set aside the papers. The observer should sit to the side and should not intrude.
4. Conduct the interview for 10 minutes.
5. The observer should report his/her findings to both people, and for all three should discuss how the interview went, and how you felt about it.
6. The instructor may have further instructions for you.

ROLE FOR THE REGIONAL MANAGER—(*Not* to be read by the store manager)

Today you have an unpleasant job. You must terminate X, a store manager with 15 years of service.

This store manager has been warned many times about his/her customer relations. He/she promises to work on it but never seems to improve. He/she was sent to a Dale Carnegie course and to an executive program in human relations at the local university. Some of it may have helped, but only temporarily.

You don't want to get into all the old disagreements again. You want to terminate the manager. Here is what you want to do:

1. Let X know that this is the end of the line. There is no appeal. X is terminated. This is his/her last day on the job.
2. Follow the guideline of procedures in the attached memo from the director of personnel.
3. Let X know that you personally are willing to help him/her find a new job with another company.

4. Prepare yourself as best you can to deal with whatever X may say. He may be mad at you, the company, or the world. He may yell or cry.
5. Review the performance summary for X.

One thing in your favor is this: The termination should not come as a big surprise for X. He/she has been warned many times. He/she will not be the first store manager to be terminated.

A performance summary for X is attached.

When you have studied the materials and have an idea of what you need to say, call the store manager into your (imaginary) office and discuss the termination with X. Limit the meeting to about 10 minutes. Address X by his or her real first name.

MEMORANDUM—(*Not* to be read by the store manager)

To: (You), Regional manager
From: Marion Karline, Corporate Director of Personnel
Subject: Termination of X, Store Manager

It is always a difficult task to terminate someone with long service. I hope I can help you a little in this assignment. Let me review the corporate policies and procedures with you. It is essential these be followed to the letter.

1. Today is X's last day at the store. This is company policy for terminated people so they don't damage other people's morale. He/she should be instructed to turn in all keys to the regional office at the end of his/her shift today.
2. In lieu of notice, he/she will be given two-weeks' full pay.
3. Then he/she will receive the regular severance. It is two-weeks' pay for every year of service. In this manager's case, that means 30 weeks of full pay. The checks will continue to be deposited in the person's checking account.
4. The company's portion of insurance premiums will be paid until X accepts a new, full-time position or until the end of the 30 weeks, whichever comes first.
5. If X has any questions about these severance arrangements, he/she may phone me at 555-0007 or visit me in my office.
6. I am knowledgeable about jobs in this industry and will help X find a new job if he/she wishes. I also have some ideas on résumés, interviewing, and the whole job search process. I have known X for a long time, and we have a friendly relationship. I really want to help.

FOR THE REGIONAL MANAGER—(*Not* to be read by the store manager)

Performance Summary for X, Store Manager

Hired in January, 15 years ago, as a stock person.
Worked up through numerous positions, becoming store manager 10 years ago.

Performance as Store Manager

Rated as an adequate manager through last year. Continuously rated "not immediately promotable."

Last year, with the new corporate policies regarding customer relations, X was rated low on customer relations, while ratings for performance against quota and cost savings continued as before, adequate but not outstanding.

X was informed three times during the year that his overall performance was rated unsatisfactory, mainly because of his inadequate customer relations. X was shown the complaints received by several customers about his rude behavior in dealing with refunds and exchanges.

X has met with the regional manager on three occasions about customer relations and once with the corporate director of personnel. X was coached carefully and specifically over a period of one year.

ROLE FOR THE STORE MANAGER—(*Not* to be read by the regional manager)

You have been with the ABC Stores for 15 years and have been a manager for the last 10 of those years.

You are about to meet with your boss, the regional manager. This may be the day you get fired. You've been warned about customer relations a lot, but you just don't agree with the company's liberal policy.

You would hate to be fired. Your spouse is out of work, and you are sole support for your three kids. You have always worked here at the store. You don't know any other kind of work. You have no idea what you might do for a job if you lose this one.

If the regional manager does talk about firing you, talk him/her out of it. After all, the company owes you something for your 15 years of loyal service.

If the manager finally does fire you, you're not going to take it without telling him/her off.

Call the regional manager by his/her real first name.

OBSERVER INSTRUCTIONS

1. Study the regional manager's role with him/her. Do *not* give advice.
2. Keep notes on how well the interview progresses:

   How clear is the communication of termination?

   What is the regional manager doing or saying which *detracts* from the message?

   How would you characterize the regional manager's behavior?
   - Rough (too harsh, etc.).
   - Too soft, wishy-washy.
   - Professional.
   - Friendly.
   - Helpful.
   - Others.

   How would you assess the regional manager's overall success in the meeting?
   - Very effective.
   - Effective.
   - So-so.
   - Not every effective.

   What feelings do *you* have for the store manager?
   - No sympathy, he got what he/she deserved.
   - Strong sympathy for him/her.
   - Other.

Part 3

Other Exercises and Experiences in Human Resource Management

The following is a series of exercises to be completed by the user of this book. Some of them are cost-benefit exercises. They require the participant to calculate specific costs of a personnel function, to calculate or infer its benefits, and to recommend whether to continue the activity. If it is to be continued, the participant must specify the future form or approach.

The other exercises require the participant to take part in data gathering before analysis takes place. In some of the exercises, the participant enters the field, observes, and gathers and analyzes the data. In others, the participant interacts with other participants in the classroom or other settings. The exercise takes place and analysis and recommendations follow. Both of these approaches have in common participant input to the exercise before analysis can take place.

The purpose of these exercises is to provide the participant the opportunity to put his or her knowledge of personnel activities to work. Not only are participants building their decision-making skills in these exercises but they are also developing some more specific skills in designing and evaluating such activities as human resource planning, recruitment and selection programs, performance evaluation systems, work scheduling, and compensation and benefit plans. The participant will realize there is still much work to be done after the decisions are made and also will realize some of the problems involved in implementing the decisions. Participants find these specific skills useful, because most managerial positions are involved in implementing and evaluating personnel policies and programs.

Cost-Benefit and Field Exercises

1 Job Description Exercise

Job analysis is a term that is applied to the systematic study of work in industries. It is the process of identifying by observation, interview, and study all of the significant worker activities and requirements for a specific job. It is the identification of the tasks which comprise the job and of the skills, knowledge, abilities, and responsibilities that are required of a worker performing a specific job. (See Exhibit 1.) It has many purposes, some of which are:

1. To establish job specifications.
2. To determine wage structures.
3. To resolve issues of comparable worth and equal pay.
4. To determine qualifications to be used in employee selection.
5. To derive training programs.
6. To identify job parameters so that performance appraisal can be based on job duties and tasks.
7. To design or restructure jobs.

EXHIBIT 1

Position Description

---

1. **Identification**
   Job title _____ Code _____
   Alternative title _____ Date _____
   Department _____ Analyst _____
   Name of incumbent _____

Prepared by Vandra L. Huber. Copyright © 1984 by Vandra L. Huber. This exercise is an adaptation of class materials originally prepared by E. J. McCormick and William E. Scott, Jr.

EXHIBIT 1   *(concluded)*

2. **Job Summary**

3. **Supervision**
    A. *Supervision Received*
    Immediate supervision _____   Overall supervision _____
    Direction only _____   Understudy _____

    B. *Supervision Given*
    Coordinates systems _____   Supervises assistants _____
    Supervises work group _____   Supervises fellow workers _____
    Number of departments or units supervised _____
        List: _____
        _____
        _____

    Number supervised:
    Full-time employees _____   Part-time employees _____

4. **Work Performed**
    Descriptions:

5. **Training and Experience**
    A. *Previous Job Experience* (desired/or necessary, or both)
    B. *Schooling and Training*
        1. General Schooling
        2. Special Training
    C. On-the-job Training

6. **Working Conditions** (specify percent of time exposed to conditions)
    ____ Inside   ____ High Temp   ____ Toxic Conditions   ____ Odors
    ____ Outside   ____ Low Temp   ____ Vibration   ____ Dust
    ____ Noise   ____ Fumes   ____ Poor Ventilation   ____ Other
    ____ Slippery Floors   ____ Moving Objects
    ____ Electrical Shocks
    Remarks:

7. **Physical Demands** (specify percentage of time)
    ____ Lifting   ____ Pushing   ____ Standing   ____ Other
    ____ Carrying   ____ Pulling   ____ Sitting
    Remarks:

8. **Relation to other jobs**
    A. Promotion from_____
    B. Promotion to_____
    C. Transfer to and from_____
    D. Temporary assignments_____

While job analysis can be conducted in many different ways (i.e., interviews, structured questionnaires, behavioral sampling, participant-observation), the culmination of the analysis is a written description of the job. Sometimes called the *job specification,* the job description is a written statement of purpose, duties, equipment, working conditions, and relation of a particular job to other jobs. While job descriptions may detail many different aspects of a job, nine functional areas are primary. They include:

1. Identification.
2. Job summary.
3. Supervision.
4. Work performed.
5. Training and experience.
6. Working conditions.
7. Job hazards.
8. Physical demands.
9. Relationship to other jobs.

IDENTIFICATION

Job title. Record in this space the name by which the job is usually known. When jobs are known by various titles, the most commonly known title should be used. A list of common job titles is contained in the *Dictionary of Occupational Titles,* which is published by the U.S. Department of Labor.

Code. In this space write the job code that is listed by the Department of Labor.

Alternative title. Some jobs in an organization have more than one job title. If this is so, for the position you are examining, write in the alternative title in this space.

Department. Because organizations may have individuals performing similar identical work in different departments, it may be important to identify for which department the job is performed. This may be critical in determining wages since job incumbents performing jobs of the same title may in actuality be performing different work (i.e., a secretary in the legal department may prepare briefs, while a secretary in another department may prepare accounts receivable records).

JOB SUMMARY

(Complete this section after all other sections.)

The purpose of this section to define the job, pointing out the basic factors that differentiate this job from other jobs. The writing should be concise, complete, and accurate. In this section, action verbs should be used to summarize:

1. What the worker does.
2. How the worker does it.
3. Why the worker does it.

In describing "what" the worker does, include physical and mental actions. In describing "what," avoid such general terms as *prepares* or *operates* because they cannot give a precise picture of the job. Record "how" the work is done, including the machinery and tools used, job knowledge applications, and decisions. Finally, record "why" the worker does the job—in other words, the purpose or expected result or product.

SUPERVISION

In this section, the supervisory relationship is specified. Place an X next to the appropriate descriptor specifying the *amount* of supervision received.

Immediate supervision. Applies to jobs with detailed instructions given to worker and frequent monitoring of work outputs. Applies to well-structured situations with little deviation from established work procedures.

Overall supervision. Worker receives overall supervision but is responsible for determining work procedures within a broad area of operations.

Concerning the *supervision given,* record:

1. Number of departments supervised.
2. Number of workers supervised.
3. Job titles held by employees who are supervised.

Then put an X next to the *nature* of the supervision given.

Directions only. Worker is permitted to do work without any type of direction or instruction and with little work inspection.

Understudying. This is a special supervisory relationship. Usually associated with job coaching or apprenticeships. The objective is for the subordinate to learn the duties of a higher-level job.

Coordinates operations. Coordinates an organization or phase of operations within an organization. Gives general directions.

Supervises work group. Supervises individuals in a work group. Individuals who fall in this category usually have supervision as a primary job task or duty.

Supervisor's assistants. Supervision is an incidental part of other primary duties. A professor who supervises a secretary is an example of someone in this category.

Working supervisor. This person operates as a worker-supervisor. The individual performs work that is comparable to that performed by the workers he or she supervises. An example is an office manager who coordinates and distributes work to other secretaries.

WORK PERFORMED

In this section, the duties and tasks that the worker (sometimes called a "job incumbent") performs are recorded. Complete statements beginning with action verbs should be utilized. Each descriptive statement should describe *what* the worker does, *how* the worker does it, *why* the work operation is performed, and *what tools and equipment* are used. The writing style should be uniform. Begin each sentence with a verb in third-person singular. Avoid unnecessary words or words that have more than one meaning. Avoid vague terms, such as *performs* and *coordinates.* Be specific.

Break each job apart into its relevant duties. You may wish to summarize, under each duty, the specific tasks which comprise that duty.

Time. Because it is important to determine which job tasks are the most important, you also need to identify the amount of time devoted to each task. Use multiples of 5 for the percentage. Use "N" for those operations requiring less than 5 percent of the time. Some job cycles involve hours or days, some, weeks and some, months. Record the percentages of time for each operation in the same manner, regardless of the length of the cycle. List first the job tasks that take the most time and follow with those of decreasing time importance. If time figures cannot be calculated, explain why not. Be sure to specify what time dimension you are using when you figure the percentages.

TRAINING AND EXPERIENCE

In this section, it is important to carefully describe previous job experience and the schooling and training necessary to perform well on the job. You should describe the training and experience necessary to do the tasks that comprise the job, rather than the specific training that the job incumbent possesses. Your description should include:

A. *Previous job experience.* Describe the type, amount, and level of previous experience that is considered necessary and desirable. Differentiate between *desired* and *required* experience.

B. *Schooling and training.* Schooling and training refers to job-related knowledge that is not acquired on the job. Required job training is the minimum amount of training necessary to perform the job acceptably.

General schooling refers to education of a general academic nature that contributes to the worker's ability to follow instruction and to acquisition of knowledges, such as computer languages or shorthand. This education refers to what is acquired in liberal arts programs of a high school.

Special training refers to job-oriented training, which may be obtained through apprenticeship, business colleges, and correspondence courses. You should list the specific courses, such as bookkeeping, machinist apprenticeship, and so on.

On-the-job-training refers to skills acquired on the job. It is training beyond that obtained from experience in other jobs or from special training programs. For example, an accountant may have to learn the specific account receivable processes used by the firm. Specific skills that must be learned on the job should be *listed* (e.g., two weeks required to learn computer monitoring procedures).

WORKING CONDITIONS

In this section describe the environment in which the work is to be performed. List the approximate percentages of time the worker is exposed to each condition. Be specific when describing the environment that the work will be performed in. Add clarifying statements, such as "works in temperatures ranging from 40 to 65 degrees." If time percentages cannot be accurately estimated, use "O" for "occasionally" and "F" for "frequently."

JOB HAZARDS

Each work environment contains special dangers (e.g., molten steel or a line drive) both inside and outside (e.g., a windowless swinging door to a fast-food kitchen). Conditions to be observed and noted may include high temperatures, fumes, rickety shelving, waxed floors, and . . . the list can be endless.

PHYSICAL DEMANDS

Record the percentage of time the workers performing the job spend lifting, carrying, pushing, and pulling. For lifting, indicate the amount in *pounds*. Be sure to indicate the percentage of time spent standing and sitting and list other physical demands as necessary for the successful performance of the job.

RELATIONSHIP TO OTHER JOBS

If the job is an established career path or promotional sequence, then it is important to indicate the relationship between the job being analyzed and other jobs. *Item A* indicates the position from which workers are promoted. If the job traditionally is associated with promotion to a particular position, this should be noted in *Item B*. If there are no advancement possibilities, such a fact should also be noted. *Item C* should include the titles of jobs to which the worker may normally be laterally assigned within the department on a permanent basis. *Item D* should be used to list the titles or job specifics to which the worker may be temporarily assigned or transferred (i.e., proofreader to paste-up artist).

2 A Field Study of Business Recruiting Practices

Different companies in different areas of the country use varying sources to obtain their employees. Most texts provide a model which describes these practices and one is duplicated in Table 1. You will notice that each category has one additional column, which is the point of this exercise.

First form a group of three to four persons, then elect one of your group to be the spokesperson. Call a business in your area (preferably a larger business with several hundred employees) and speak to the personnel manager or a knowledgeable person in the personnel area. Ask this person the following question: What (internal, external) sources of recruits do you use for your (blue) (gray) (white) (managerial, technical, professional) employees? You will probably find that you may have to mention a few of the sources to aid them in understanding what you are

Prepared by Jerry L. Wall. Copyright © 1982 by Business Publications, Inc. Reprinted by permission of Business Publications, Inc.

TABLE 1   Sources of Recruiting Various Types of Employees

Sources	*Blue-Collar*	*Gray-Collar*	*White-Collar*	*Managerial, Technical, Professional*
Internal:				
Job posting and bidding	X	X	X	
Friends of present employees	X	X	X	
Skills inventories	X	X	X	X
External:				
Walk-ins, including previous employees	X	X	X	
Agencies				
Temporary help				
Private employment agencies			X	
Public employment agencies*	X	X	X	
Executive search firms				X
Educational institutions:				
High school	X	X	X	
Vocational/technical	X	X	X	X
Colleges and universities				X
Other:				
Union	X			
Professional associations				X
Military services	X			X
Former employees	X	X	X	X

*Normally called U.S. Employment Services.

referring to, and you will probably find it most advantageous to divide the questions into internal versus external by level of job.

The professor will make sure that each group in the class obtains information from a different business and thus maximizes information obtained and minimizes time lost for the business. Check the chart each time the business mentions a source and be careful not to imply that they are right, wrong, or different from others in the responses they give.

When the personnel representative has finished all of the questions, quickly compare your findings with those listed as "usual." Notice any differences and ask the personnel representative why he or she does not use that source. Write down any comments the representative makes in the space provided on the next pages.

COMMENTS

Discuss the comments obtained within your group. Does your group agree or disagree with the commentary about that source? Jot down your feelings:

Are there any characteristics of your labor market that the businesses have mentioned that would cause it to vary from the average? If so, note these below:

Each group of the class should now be given an opportunity to present and discuss their findings. Do you find substantial differences between groups? If so, note these below as the groups make their presentations:

Discuss in the class how any common differences from the model in the text reflect characteristics of the local labor market. Examples:

Discuss how any individual company differs from the local average (or the text model). Could such differences reflect company idiosyncrasies? Discuss how these can emerge and indicate your responses below:

3 Standard Interview Form

(You may look back and forth between the application and this interview form during the interview. Make all of your notes only on this form. With young applicants, start the interview with education. With older applicants, you should start the interview with work history.)

Applicant's Name _____ Date of Interview _____
Interviewer _____

Education and Activities

a1 Tell me about the grades you made in high school (and college).

a2 Compare grades in your major versus overall/first-year versus last-year attendance.

a3 Why did you go to college?

a4 Why did you go to this particular college?

b1 How were your college expenses paid?

b2 Are all of your full-time and part-time jobs reported on the application form?

b3 What were your housing arrangements? What were your responsibilities?

c1 Were you in any student activities? Which ones? (List them if they are not reported on the application form.)

c2 How did you get into these?

c3 Did these organizations have any special purposes? How effective were they at those purposes?

c4 How much time did they take?

c5 What responsibilities did you have?

c6 How effective were you? Give some examples.

c7 Any connection with any of these now?

c8 How well did you get along with the other people in these activities?

d1 Were there any courses in college you did not complete?

d2 Did you change your major while in college?

d3 When did you study?

d4 How much did you study?

d5 What did you think of your teachers?

d6 How would you evaluate your overall effectiveness as a student?

Prepared by Allen J. Schuh, California State University, Hayward.

e1 Did you participate in any sports?

e2 What did you think of your coaches and teammates?

f1 How did you spend your weekends during the academic year?

f2 How did you spend your summers while going to college?

f3 Was there anything you particularly liked/disliked about your school years?

f4 Were there any experiences in school that have been particularly helpful since leaving school?

Military Experience

g1 What is your present situation with regard to military service?

g2 If you have been in military service, start at the time you entered service and describe your different jobs.

g3 What were your responsibilities? How effective were you at these jobs?

g4 Was there anything you particularly liked/disliked about your military experience?

g5 Were there any experiences in the service that have been particularly helpful since leaving the military?

Work History and Experience (start with first full-time employment)

h1 What was the first full-time job you had?

h2 When was that exactly?

h3 What other jobs did you consider at that time?

h4 Why did you take the one you did?

h5 How do you feel now about your experiences with them?

h6 Why did you leave?

h7 When was that exactly?

h8 What did you do between jobs?

h9 How did you decide to go with the next company?

Note: cycle h2 to h9 for each job.

h10 What are you looking for in your next job?

Specific Job Activities (start with the most recent employment)

i1 What did you do on this last job?

i2 How effective were you at that job? Give me some examples of your effectiveness.

i3 Describe any record-keeping.

i4 What kind of hours did you have?

i5 How much and how often were you paid?

i6 How much and what kind of travel was involved?

j1 What other people did you work with?

j2 Were there any people you worked with who disliked you?

j3 How well did you report?

j4 To whom did you report?

j5 How often and what did you report?

j6 How did your supervisor know what you were doing?

j7 How well did you and your supervisor get along?

j8 Did you get things done correctly and on time? In general. Specifically.

j9 Did you need to work much overtime?

Your Next Job

k1 Have you discussed this possible job change with (family)? What was the reaction?

k2 How do you and your family feel about your working nights?

k3 How do you and your family feel about your working weekends?

k4 What would be your reaction to being confronted with a mistake that others thought you committed? Has this ever happened? How did you handle it?

Note to interviewer:

Consider the following for Sales, Management, Scientist, and Engineer positions.

Family Responsibilities

l1 Describe for me the neighborhood where you are presently living.

l2 How long have you lived there?

l3 Why did you decide to live there?

l4 How well do you get along with your neighbors?

l5 How do you feel about education?

l6 What do you do around the home? Lawn/house/car?

l7 Do you have any hobbies? What/where/how often/with whom?

l9 What kind of vacations do you take (what do you do)? Describe the last one.

l10 How much time do you spend each week reading: books/magazines/newspapers?

l11 How much time do you spend watching television: favorite programs/those you like less well?

l12 How do you feel about the doctors and hospitals available to you?

Social Life

m1 How often do you entertain?

m2 How often do you go out?

m3 How do you usually spend your lunch time?

m4 How do you spend weekends and holidays?

Social Mobility

n1 What organizations do you belong to?

n2 How long have you been a member?

n3 Why did you join these organizations?

n4 Have you held any offices or been on any committees? What were your responsibilities? How effective were you?

Insurance

o1 What life insurance policies do you have?

o2 How about other forms of insurance?

o3 When did you have your last physical examination?

o4 Any illnesses during the last year?

o5 Any minor chronic conditions? (allergies, lower back)

Financial Picture

p1 What do you think about the income from your present job? How about income from other sources? (How permanent is the source?)

p2 Do you have a checking account? Who handles it? What is its balance?

p3 How do you feel about charge accounts and credit cards?

p4 What kinds of automobiles do you have (make/model year)? How were these cars purchased?

p5 How do you usually pay for major items?

p6 Are your parents/in-laws living? What is their health? Do they get any financial help from you? How much? How often?

p7 Is there any chance that any of them would need to live with you during the next year? How would you handle that?

p8 Do you have any financial obligations of any kind that have not been discussed?

The Future

q1 What would you like to be doing five years from now?

q2 How much money would you like to be making five years from now? Why this amount?

q3 What kinds of people would you like to be working with five years from now?

q4 What kinds of people would you like to associate with socially five years from now?

q5 What do you believe is an ideal job for you?

q6 What do you plan to do after you retire?

Note: Deficiencies in interpersonal relations, motivation, trustworthiness, responsibilities, and effectiveness.

---

4 Friends Can Get You in Trouble!

Arthur Nelson smiled expansively at his guest and remarked, "Yes, I do run a tight ship here. I'm very proud of the way I took over this personnel department and made it one of the best around. You can't fault the way I moved Rondo Manufacturing from a 15 percent a year turnover to about 1 percent. That speaks well of my efforts in the company as a whole, too."

Ron Clark looked at his friend and said, "I wish I was in as good shape as you, but this EEO thing really has me bothered." Ron was referring to the fact that he had just received a notice from the State Fair Employment Practices Commission that his company had been charged with discrimination by a minority male. He was expecting a visit from the state EEO investigator in two weeks. "I remember the guy, I talked to him but I could see he really didn't fit in. He'd just moved to town and didn't know anyone in the plant or in town. And you know how close-knit my work groups are."

Prepared by Jerry L. Wall. Copyright © 1982 by Business Publications, Inc. Reprinted by permission of Business Publications, Inc.

"You know that reminds me of the way I combated the attitude and motivation problems in my company, too," Arthur remarked. "You remember that we discussed how letting the workers pick who they wanted to work with and recommend their friends for employment would work wonders for morale. And sure enough, it did. Why, that's all we use now!"

"You're right, those recommendations from friends and promotions from within have totally satisfied our employment needs for several years now, too," Ron sighed. "I really can't understand what's wrong with letting your employees pick who they want to work with. It seems to be a great motivational tool, but I have a feeling that's what the state EEO people want to talk to me about. And, Arthur, I have a hunch you may be next in line!"

Do you think there's some truth to Ron's observation on the appropriateness of recruiting from within? Why?

Discussion Questions

1. What are the characteristics, advantages, and disadvantages of the following:
   A. Promotion from within:

   B. Using recommendations from friends:

2. Under what circumstances would these be acceptable sources? Unacceptable?
   A. Acceptable:

   B. Unacceptable:

3. What sources would be more acceptable in terms of providing equal employment opportunity and demonstrate positive recruiting efforts?

5 *Looking at Résumés*

Your organization has an opening for manager of accounting, a department head position with mid-level management responsibility. The job is a high-stress one, since the incumbent must supervise some 25 professional and clerical employees handling diverse duties. The manager of accounting reports directly to the president, who is a hard-nosed stickler for detail. The president manages with a tight rein and expects not only perfection but immediate solutions to problems.

A newspaper advertisement of the position has yielded, unfortunately, only one response. The following résumé was received in this morning's mail. Because the organization has had a great deal of difficulty filling this job in the past, and turnover in the job has been frequent, you want to give this résumé your immediate attention to see whether the applicant should be hired before he gets away.

Discussion Questions

1. Do you think the applicant is qualified for the job?
2. What additional information would you like to know before answering question 1?

RÉSUMÉ

NAME:	GEORGE JONES
ADDRESS:	715 Judy Drive Nashville, TN Telephone: (123) 456-7890
PERSONAL:	Born 11-6-32 (Nashville, Tennessee) 5'11", 185 lbs.
	Married to Ola Mae Jones 4 children, born 4-20-52, 10-5-58, 2-15-60, 8-2-71
EDUCATION:	H.S. Diploma, Jackson High School Jackson, Mississippi, 1951
	BS Degree, University of Southern Tennessee, 1962. Double Major: Accounting and Business Administration
	MS Degree, Business, California State University, 1978

Prepared by Professor John E. Oliver, Austin Peay University.

PhD Degree, Business Administration, University of Mississippi, 1981.

Certified Public Accountant—Mississippi and Tennessee

Special Courses: "Growth Through Acquisition and Merger Seminar," National Association Wholesalers, 1972.

"Sales Management Seminar," National Association Wholesalers, 1968

PUBLICATIONS AND RESEARCH:

"Transportation Rates," coauthored with Joe Smith.

Paper to be presented to Southwest Marketing Association, Atlanta, Georgia, March 1985

Currently doing research in the area of cash budgeting practices in small organizations.

TEACHING EXPERIENCE:

Undergraduate: Principles of Accounting, Intermediate Accounting, Advanced Accounting, Accounting Standards, Cost Accounting.

Graduate: Specialized Accounting Problems, Theory

Seminars and Special Courses: Program Budgeting Seminar, Florida Department of Health and Rehabilitation, CPA Review Course (Practice), Certified Professional Secretary Review (Accounting).

PROFESSIONAL ORGANIZATIONS:

American Institute Certified Public Accountants
American Accounting Association
American Society Traffic and Transportation
Tennessee Society Certified Public Accountants (member, scholarship committee)

COMMUNITY ACTIVITIES:

Former member of Jackson Junior Chamber of Commerce
Former President of Jackson Exchange Club, 1971 (Club won National Big E Award for Excellence during my term of office)
Jackson Chamber of Commerce activities:
    Director 1971–1972
    Member of Wholesale-Retail Promotion Committee
    Chairman—Community Minimum Wage Clinic, January 1970
Salvation Army Building Fund Committee, 1980
Dawn of Hope, Nashville, Tennessee
    Member—Sheltered Workshop Committee, 1983–1984

WORK EXPERIENCE:

August 1951 to
December 1951

SEARS, ROEBUCK & CO., Jackson, Mississippi
<u>Sales Clerk</u>

January 1952 to
January 1955

EQUITABLE LIFE ASSURANCE SOCIETY, Nashville, Tennessee
<u>Assistant Teller Cashier's Office</u>

1955
1956

USAF, Korea & Japan
<u>Personnel Specialist</u>. Worked at Wing Headquarters level.

October 1965	SOUTHERN DRUG COMPANY, Jackson, Mississippi <u>Accountant—Operation Manager, Sales Manager Secretary &</u> <u>Treasurer and share in General Management</u>.
	I am familiar with all phases of Wholesale Drug House operation and have supervised a warehouse employing 33 people. Directed the installation of data processing Unit Record Equipment in 1974. I was responsible for the activities of 10 salesmen, two buyers, and shared in top management decisions. I have visited several wholesale drug firms and have been active in trade associations.
June 1978 to March 1981	Graduate Student, University of Mississippi
March 1981 to July 1983	Assistant Professor, Accountancy, Tennessee College, Nashville, Tennessee
September 1983 to Present	Associate Professor, Accountancy, Tennessee College, Nashville, Tennessee
TRADE ASSOCIATIONS ACTIVITIES:	Past President, Southern Drug Club, 1973–74 Served four years as Secretary, Drug Travelers of Mississippi. (Auxiliary organization to Mississippi State Pharmaceutical Association.)

6 A Problem of Orientation

You are Phil Myrich, personnel manager for Wiedno Manufacturing. The plant manager has just asked you to come in to have a talk concerning what he considers an unacceptable rate of turnover in the plant. During the last year you have had approximately 60 percent of your new-hires leave within the first six months. The plant manager has asked you to find out the reason for this problem. When you return to your office, your secretary informs you that Adam Wright, an automatic lathe operator who was hired only two months ago, is scheduled for an exit interview in the next few minutes. You decide to do the exit interview yourself, rather than let the assistant personnel manager, Julie Rogers, do it as she usually does.

Prepared by Jerry L. Wall. Copyright © 1982 by Business Publications, Inc. Reprinted by permission of Business Publications, Inc.

The information you gather is:

Adam reported for work the first day as requested at 8:30 A.M. He met initially with your assistant personnel manager who started by giving him a "pep talk" that was aimed at convincing him the company was a good place to work. Next she read him the job description and gave a brief explanation of his new duties. He was told to get a cup of coffee at the coffee shop next door and return at 10 for a general orientation meeting which he and several other employees would attend.

During this meeting the following subjects were covered:

1. Time clock requirements.
2. Lunch hours, coffee breaks, and rest periods.
3. Overtime policies.
4. Pay.
5. Attendance, tardiness, and absenteeism.
6. Their immediate job hierarchy.
7. Insurance, pay, medical, and other administrative forms.

They were given a walking tour of the plant, covering all areas and facilities. As each new employee was taken through his respective department he was introduced to his new supervisor. Upon completion of the tour, the group was met by each supervisor they had met earlier who escorted them back to their new departments.

The supervisor then explained the daily routine and showed Adam around the department. When possible on several occasions, co-workers were stopped for introductions but were not interrupted at their work. The supervisor then gave Adam some on-the-job training on the automatic lathe, observed his performance for a while, then was called away. Adam saw him again the next day for a few minutes when the supervisor slapped him on the back and asked how things were going. When Adam started to ask questions he was told, "Don't have time to talk now, have an appointment. Ask Joe over there." After Adam approached Joe with the question, Joe called over a group of other workers and the group teased Adam for his dumb question for almost an hour. This harassment and teasing has continued since. Adam now feels that he is out of place in the group, because they constantly ridicule him, and he simply wants to leave.

Although the information above is sketchy, you should be able to identify several things that went wrong with this orientation. What are these?

Discussion Questions

1. How do you believe that this orientation could be improved?
2. What should be covered and in what order?

7 *Behaviorally Anchored Performance Evaluation*

INSTRUCTIONS

1. During the next two weeks, observe both your teachers' (all classes) and fellow students' performance.

Develop a list of critical incidents of college teacher performance and a list of critical incidents of student performance.

Each list should contain 20 behavioral examples; some of the examples should illustrate good performance, and some poor performance. Each of the examples should describe actual behaviors you have observed.

2. Once you have your 20 examples, group the examples into 2–4 dimensions that appear to be key dimensions of student or teacher performance.

Hand in a list of the dimensions, a brief definition of each of the dimensions, and, under each dimension, list the critical incidents illustrating that dimension.

Assign each example to only one dimension.

List separately any critical incidents that don't seem to fit under any of your key dimensions.

Do the above steps separately for student performance and teacher performance.

3. Use the following five-point rating scale to rate each of your 40 critical incidents on the dimension to which you have assigned it.

5—Excellent performance on this dimension.
4
3—Average/adequate performance on this dimension.
2
1—Poor performance on this dimension.

List your incidents in order from excellent (**5**) to poor (**1**) under each dimension.

4. Rate yourself on each of your student dimensions and justify your rating. Use the incidents you have rated above to help you make your ratings.

Prepared by Vicki S. Kaman, Colorado State University.

5. Rate your professor (me) on each of your teacher dimensions, justify, and hand in with your homework on a SEPARATE PAGE.

Discussion Questions

1. What is difficult about rating job performance? How does the process used in the exercise help you do a better job as a rater?
2. How could you improve upon this process to make it more reliable? More valid? More acceptable to raters and ratees?

---

8 *A Field Study of Training*

Visit several industrial or nonprofit or governmental organizations in your locality that have several hundred employees. Try to obtain answers to the following questions and enter the information in the matrix below by check marks.

1. How long does the initial training period for your blue-collar (low-level) worker last?
2. How long does the initial training period for your technical and professional workers last?
3. How long does the initial training period for your supervisory and managerial workers last?

LENGTH OF TRAINING PERIOD

Check those which apply:

	Less Than 2 Weeks	2 Weeks to 1 Month	1 Month to 2 Months	2 Months to 3 Months	3 Months to 4 Months	More Than 4 Months
Blue-collar						
Technical, Professional						
Supervisory, Management						

---

1. What types of training do you use for your blue-collar (low-level) employees?
2. What types of training do you use for your technical and professional workers?
3. What types of training do you use for your supervisory and managerial workers?

TYPES OF TRAINING PROGRAMS

Check those which apply:

	(Low-level) Blue-collar	*Professional Technical*	*Supervisory Management*
Apprenticeships			
Vestibule			
On-the-job training	⨉	⨉	⨉
Coaching and counseling			
Transitory/anticipatory experiences			
Self-improvement programs			
Transfers, rotations			
Off-job training	⨉	⨉	⨉
Conference, discussions			
Programmed instruction			
Computer-assisted instruction			
Simulation approaches			
Management development	⨉	⨉	⨉
Training			

TYPES OF TRAINING PROGRAMS *(concluded)*

Check those which apply:

	(Low-level) Blue-collar	*Professional Technical*	*Supervisory Management*
Role-playing			
Synectics			
In-basket techniques			
Management games			
Case methods			

Discussion Questions

Within your group and class, try to answer the following questions. Later these will be discussed by your teacher.

1. Did you notice any tendencies on the average length of blue-collar training as it compared to the other two?
   Technical and professional training as it compared to supervisory and managerial training?
   Why do you think these phenomena occurred?
2. What tendencies did you notice on the part of variety of training for blue-collar versus other employees?
   For technical and professional training versus supervisory and managerial employees?
   Why do you believe this occurs?
3. Did you notice any differences by the type of company you went to? What were these?

9 A-1 Appliances, Inc.

A-1 Appliances is a medium-sized manufacturer of small appliances located in Pomona, California. The firm employs 1,500 persons. A-1 also has a plant in Phenix City, Alabama, and Sandusky, Ohio.

Recently, the firm has been trying to hire a new plant manager for the Sandusky plant. Because of the importance of the position, the firm has used multiple selection techniques. The techniques include: (1) interviews, (2) tests, (3) honesty tests, (4) graphology, and (5) references. A brief description of the candidates is given in Exhibit 1.

A-1 has had about an average profit and growth record for the industry. But Sandusky has been the real problem plant. Costs are high, and there has been a history of labor strife there.

Each of the applicants was interviewed by five executives at A-1. Then the executives were asked to rank the applicants in their order of

---

EXHIBIT 1   Biographical Data on the Candidates

1. **Charlie Reddick,** assistant plant manager at Sandusky. Age 48. Education: B.S., B.A., Kent State University; M.B.A., University of Akron. Has always worked for A-1 except during military service.

2. **Nathalee Williams,** assistant plant manager at Phenix City. Age 51. Education: A.A., Cuyahoga Community College. Has worked for A-1 for 10 years. Prior to that, worked for two other appliance manufacturers (six and four years, respectively), and before that a variety of other jobs.

3. **Ron Taylor,** assistant plant manager at Pomona. Age 41. Education: B.A. in political science, Yale University. Has four years' military experience. Worked in appliance sales for competitors for three years and had production experience for competitor for five years. Has worked for A-1 for six years.

4. **George King,** plant manager of a small plant for a very aggressive competitor. Age 36. Education: B.S. in engineering, University of Central Florida. Has been employed at present company for 10 years, three as plant manager. Has four years' military experience.

5. **Mark Dappert,** former plant manager of electrical equipment firm which went bankrupt in Toledo. Age 58. Education: Attended University of Toledo's college of business; no degree. Worked for prior employer all of his working life. Ran a successful plant for this company, which failed for other reasons.

TABLE 1 Preferences for Candidates by Five A-1 Appliances Executives

	Candidates				
Interviewers' rankings	*Reddick*	*Williams*	*Taylor*	*King*	*Dappert*
President					
James Cox	5	3	1	2	4
Vice president—personnel					
Dale Young	3	2	1	5	4
Vice president—production					
Kenneth O'Connor	2	5	3	4	1
Plant manager, Sandusky					
Stanley Hale	4	3	5	1	2
Plant manager, Phenix City					
Ernest Butler	5	1	3	2	4

preference. The results of these rankings are given in Table 1. The results of the intelligence tests are given in Table 2.

In terms of personality analysis drawn from interpretation of revised thematic apperception tests, the psychologists ranked the individuals as follows: (1) King, (2) Dappert, (3) Reddick, (4) Williams, and (5) Taylor. One of the psychologist's comments was that "King and Dappert are quite competitive and ought to take charge well especially when faced with a real challenge."

The honesty tests analyses indicated that most were thought to be honest, although the analyst had some questions about King. The analyst remarked "that he placed little faith in the paper-and-pencil honesty tests; he liked the old-fashioned polygraphs when he wanted to get at the truth."

Requirement

You are Dale Young. Prepare a recommendation for a decision by Kenneth O'Connor and James Cox. Document your choice with systematic analysis.

The revised version of the TAT contains pictures of men and women. The original TAT contained only pictures of men.

The graphologist was asked to analyze an essay written by each in long-hand entitled "The Challenge in Appliance Manufacturing Today." She was asked to select a person most likely to initiate change in a difficult established situation. Her recommendations were:

TABLE 2   Intelligence Tests Results at A-1 Appliances

Candidate	Test (1) score	Test (2) score
Reddick	127	133
Williams	118	121
Taylor	123	128
King	130	131
Dappert	110	115

Outstanding .... King, Dappert, Williams
Acceptable .... Taylor
Not acceptable .... Reddick

Reference letters were favorable to all candidates.

10 Philadelphia Streets Department

The Philadelphia Streets Department, because of recent litigation filed against it, must find ways to dramatically increase the number of females in skilled and semiskilled classes. The department has maintained an antiwomen stance for at least the past 35 years. For example, the department has allowed female stereotypes to stand as the reason for refusing to hire women for the job of garbage collector. The belief was that the work was too dirty and that women could not do the heavy lifting required. In recent months, however, Elaine Taylor, an applicant who was turned down without an opportunity to attempt the physical lifting tests, has filed a class action suit.

The department would like to continue to refuse to hire women but they also know that a token number of women can be hired at little cost to the department thanks to a federal government grant and the lifting of a brief hiring freeze. At present, the department needs to hire 25 new employees. If past practice is followed, 50 employees will have to be hired to have 25 effective ones. The total training cost amounts to $2,250 per employee.

It has been proposed that testing might improve this employment record. For administering and using the test, the cost will be $77.50 per applicant. Table 1 presents data on the percentage of applicants who score various levels on the test and the percentage of applicants likely to be successful at various predictor-score levels.

TABLE 1 Employee Selection and Personnel Costs

Frequency	10	20	30	40	50	60	70	80	90	100	110
						20					
20						X					
19						X					
18						X					
17					16	X	16				
16					X	X	X				
15					X	X	X				
14					X	X	X				
13				12	X	X	X	12			
12				X	X	X	X	X			
11				X	X	X	X	X			
10				X	X	X	X	X			
9				X	X	X	X	X			
8				X	X	X	X	X			
7			6	X	X	X	X	X	6		
6			X	X	X	X	X	X	X		
5		4	X	X	X	X	X	X	X	4	
4		X	X	X	X	X	X	X	X	X	
3	2	X	X	X	X	X	X	X	X	X	2
2	X	X	X	X	X	X	X	X	X	X	X
1	X	X	X	X	X	X	X	X	X	X	X
Score	10	20	30	40	50	60	70	80	90	100	110
Percent	2	6	12	24	40	60	76	88	94	98	100

High	10	20	30	40	50	60	70	80	90	100	110	
								16	12	6	4	2	
								X	X	X	X	X	
							20	X	X	X	X	X	
								X	X	X	X	X	
								X	X	X	X	X	
								X	X	X	X		
								X	X	X	X		
								X	X	X			
						16		X	X	X			
							X	X	X	X			
							X	X	X	X			
							X	X	X	X			(50) successful
					12		X	X	X	X			
						X	X	X	X				
Criterion						X	X	X	X			50	unsuccessful
measure						X	X	X	X				
					6	X	X	X	X				
				X	X	X	X						
				X	X	X	X						
				X	X	X	X						
			4	X	X	X	X						

TABLE 1   *(concluded)*

		X	X	X	X	X					
		X	X	X	X	X					
	2	X		X	X						
	X	X		X	X						
Low	X										

Percent	2	6	12	24	40	60	76	88	94	98	100

Predictor

Requirements

Calculate the best predictor scores designed to minimize costs and maximize the number of best applicants to get 25 successful employees. Is the garbage collector's position only a "man's job?"

Experiences in Human Resource Management

1 Discrimination in Preemployment Inquiry

The following application blank is a composite of several application blanks all of which were still in use within the last few years (see Exhibit 1). Several of the questions should not have been asked because of their tendency to discriminate against protected groups. *Before* reading the section following the application blank entitled "Guidelines about Preemployment Inquiry," examine the application blank and circle those items you believe should *not* be asked. After completing the application blank, count the number of separate questions you circled and enter that number in the blank at the bottom of the page (the last line). Then read the instructions at the end of the exercise.

GUIDELINES ABOUT PREEMPLOYMENT INQUIRY

Address

Permissible:	What is your current address? How long have you lived in this city or state?
Discriminatory:	Where have you lived? How long have you lived in this country? Do you own (rent) your home? Who lives with you?
Comment:	Information needed to contact applicant is generally acceptable, but do not go beyond this.

Age

Permissible:	Age should be asked only when a bona fide occupational qualification (BFOQ) (i.e., necessary to do the job).

continued on page 354

Prepared by Jerry L Wall. Copyright © 1982 by Business Publications, Inc. Reprinted by permission of Business Publications, Inc.

EXHIBIT 1

APPLICATION FOR EMPLOYMENT

EMPLOYMENT DESIRED

Position _____ | Date you can start _____ | Salary Desired _____

Are you employed now? _____ | If so may we inquire of your present employer _____

Ever applied to this company before? _____ | Where _____ | When _____

PERSONAL DATA

Date _____

Name_____ | Tel. No. _____
Last   First   Middle initial | area code

Address_____ | Soc. Sec. No. _____
No.   Street   City   State

Previous address_____ | Date of birth _____
No.   Street   City   State

Own home _____ Rent _____ Board _____ Live with parents _____

Are you a U.S.A. citizen? _____ If not, type of visa _____ | Marital Status: ☐ Single ☐ Engaged ☐ Married ☐ Divorced ☐ Widower

Number of exemptions claimed for withholding tax purposes? _____ (Include self)

If married, spouse's name _____ | Does spouse work? _____

If yes, what type of position _____ | Name of company _____

No. of children _____ Names and ages of children _____

Color of hair _____ Color of eyes _____ Dependents other than wife or children _____ | Years lived in this metropolitan area _____

If related to anyone in our employ, state name and department _____ | Referred by _____

In case of emergency or illness, whom should we notify? _____

Relationship _____ Address _____ Tel. No. _____
Street   City   State

EDUCATION

	Name and Location of School	Years Attended	Date Graduated	Degree Granted	Kind of Course, Major Subjects, Honors Received, Cutline as completely as possible
Grammar School				//////	
High School					
College					
Trade, Busniess or Correspondence School					

If you graduated from college, university, business school or institute within the past few years, what was your overall scholastic grade-point average? _____ Graduate School _____ (Please indicate ratio 3.5/4 0 etc.)

Extra-curricular activities & honors (social, scholastic, athletic) _____

Courses completed High School or College

	Yes	No		Yes	No		Yes	No
Algebra	☐	☐	Calculus	☐	☐	Mechanical Drawing	☐	☐
Geometry	☐	☐	Physics	☐	☐	Accounting	☐	☐
Trigonometry	☐	☐	Chemistry	☐	☐			

Do you type? Yes ☐ No ☐ Words per minute _____ | Subjects of special study or research work _____

Do you write shorthand? Yes ☐ No ☐ Words per minute _____

Have you had any training or experience in machine accounting? (Key punch, Sorter verifier, etc.) Yes ☐ No ☐ | What machines? _____ What were your duties? _____

EXHIBIT 1 *(continued)*

EMPLOYMENT HISTORY

List All Past Employment - Last Employment First, etc.

Dates of Empl.		Name of Past and Present Employers and Addresses	*Describe Kind of Work and Duties	What Was Your Monthly Salary or Hourly Rate	Why Did You Leave?
From Mo./Yr.	To Mo./Yr.				
		Name			
		Street			
		City			
		Name			
		Street			
		City			
		Name			
		Street			
		City			
		Name			
		Street			
		City			

OTHER EMPLOYMENT NOT SHOWN ABOVE: _____

INDICATE MACHINES YOU HAVE OPERATED
☐ DRILL ☐ MILL ☐ ENGINE LATHE ☐ TURRET LATHE ☐ AUTOMATIC LATHE ☐ GEAR CUTTING MACH. ☐ GRINDER ☐ WELDER ☐ PRESS ☐ SHEAR ☐ OTHER ☐

HAVE YOU EVERY BEEN DISCHARGED FROM A POSITION? Yes ☐ No ☐
IF THE ANSWER IS YES GIVE DETAILS.

FOR WHAT KIND OF WORK ARE YOU BEST SUITED? _____   WHAT WORK DO YOU PREFER? _____

Have you worked for any of these employers under any name other than previously indicated? (Yes or No) _____

If now working may we contact your present employer? _____

MILITARY

NONE ☐	SERVICE BRANCH	DATE OF ENTRY	DATE OF DISCHARGE	HIGHEST RANK HELD	TYPE OF DISCHARGE

WHAT WERE YOUR DUTIES?   SELECTIVE SERVICE CLASSIFICATION

HAVE YOUR EVER ASKED FOR OR RECEIVED A DISABILITY PENSION? Yes ☐ No ☐   SERIAL NUMBER   SPECIAL TRAINING

LOCAL BOARD NUMBER AND ADDRESS

Special Training _____

Military Occupational Specialty

MEDICAL

HEALTH	HAVE YOU EVER HAD ANY DEFECTS OR TROUBLE WITH:					HEIGHT

		Yes	No		Yes	No		Yes	No		Yes	No		Yes	No	
EXCELLENT ☐																
GOOD ☐	SIGHT	☐	☐	POLIO	☐	☐	HEART	☐	☐	BACK	☐	☐	RHEUMATIC FEVER	☐	☐	
FAIR ☐	HEARING	☐	☐	DIABETES	☐	☐	KIDNEYS	☐	☐	LUNGS	☐	☐	VARICOSE VEINS	☐	☐	WEIGHT
POOR ☐	BONES	☐	☐	ASTHMA	☐	☐	RUPTURE	☐	☐	BLACK OUTS	☐	☐	OTHER	☐	☐	

HAVE YOU EVER BEEN IN A HOSPITAL FOR TREATMENT OR OBSERVATION? Yes ☐ No ☐ WHEN? _____

FOR WHAT? _____
LIST ALL ACCIDENTS, OPERATIONS OR SERIOUS ILLNESSES YOU HAVE HAD.

ARE YOU NOW TAKING ANY MEDICINES OR INJECTIONS? Yes ☐ No ☐ FOR WHAT? _____
HAVE YOU EVER RECEIVED WORKMEN'S COMPENSATION OR DISABILITY PAY? Yes ☐ No ☐ FOR WHAT? _____

EXHIBIT 1 (concluded)

GENERAL

Have you ever been arrested?_____For what reason?_____

HAVE YOU EVER
BEEN CONVICTED   Yes   No   IF YES,
IN A COURT OF LAW? ☐   ☐   WHERE?_____ WHEN?_____

WHY?_____ FINAL
ACTION _____

Have you ever been a member of the Communist Party?_____

List civic, professional or social organizations of which you are a member _____

WHAT ARE YOUR HOBBIES
OR INTERESTS?

FOREIGN LANGUAGE ABILITY

	SPEAK	READ	WRITE
FRENCH	☐	☐	☐
GERMAN	☐	☐	☐
ITALIAN	☐	☐	☐
SPANISH	☐	☐	☐
	☐	☐	☐

The following space is provided for any additional information about your background you may wish to include _____

List below name, address (in the U. S.) and occupation of father, mother, husband or wife. Indicate if parents are deceased.

Name	Relation-ship	Address if Living in U. S.	Occupation	Where Employed if Employed in U. S.
	Father			
	Mother			
	Husband or Wife			

If you have brothers or sisters employed, indicate where (if employed in U. S.)_____

REFERENCES : GIVE BELOW THE NAMES OF THREE PERSONS NOT RELATED TO YOU, WHOM YOU HAVE KNOWN AT LEAST ONE YEAR.

	NAME	ADDRESS	BUSINESS	YEARS ACQUAINTED
1				
2				
3				

SIGNATURE

I UNDERSTAND THAT ANY FALSE OR MISLEADING STATEMENTS MADE BY ME ON THIS APPLICATION MAY PREVENT MY EM-PLOYMENT OR MAY BE CAUSE FOR DISMISSAL IF HIRED. I HEREBY AUTHORIZE MY FORMER AND PRESENT EMPLOYERS AND OTHERS TO GIVE ANY INFORMATION THEY HAVE REGARDING ME, OR MY EMPLOYMENT WITH THEM AND I RELEASE THEM AND THEIR COMPANIES FROM ANY LIABILITY FOR DAMAGE RESULTING THEREFROM. I HEREBY CERTIFY THAT I AM NOT A MEMBER OF ANY ORGANIZATION DEEMED SUBVERSIVE TO THE INTEREST OF THE UNITED STATES GOVERNMENT. I FURTHER UNDERSTAND THAT EMPLOYMENT, IF OFFERED, WILL BE CONTINGENT ON MY SATISFACTORILY PASSING A PRE-EMPLOYMENT PHYSICAL EXAMINATION GIVEN BY THE COMPANY.

SIGNATURE _____

Number of separate items circled after reading Guidelines: _____

Number of separate items circled prior to reading Guidelines: _____

(subtract) Knowledge Factor: _____

Discriminatory: How old are you? When were you born? Show your birth certificate or driver's license. (Any age-related question.)

Comment: Proving age to be a BFOQ is difficult but possible under certain circumstances in which age can be directly linked to job performance. Proof of age after hiring can be required.

Birthplace

Permissible: None.

Discriminatory: Asking birthplace of applicant, parents, spouse, other close relatives.

Comment: These relate directly to ancestry and national origin in most cases.

Character

Permissible: If related to sensitivity of the job (e.g., cashier, teller), inquiry as to specific convictions and dispositions is acceptable sometimes. Provide the names of character witnesses.

Discriminatory: Inquiry as to arrest record or conviction record if not directly job related.

Comment: Arrest or conviction records, or both, particularly for minor offenses would be difficult to prove as job related. Federal, state, and local laws may provide more guidance in certain cases.

Citizenship

Permissible: Do you have permission to work in this country? If you are *not* a citizen of the United States, do you intend to become one?

Discriminatory: Are you a citizen of the United States? Are you a naturalized citizen? Are your parents natural or naturalized citizens? When did you acquire citizenship?

Comment: Proof of citizenship, visa, and the like can be required *after* employment, but inquiry into this area prior to employment should be carefully limited.

Commitments

Permissible: Do you have any social, family, or economic commitments or responsibilities that would prevent you from performing the normal and routine duties of this job?

Discriminatory: Questions over marital status, dependents, spouse's job, child-care arrangements.

Comment: Care *must* be taken that these questions are asked of *both* men and women and that answers given are weighted similarly.

Credit Inquiries

Permissible: None unless specifically job related.
Discriminatory: What charge accounts do you have? Where do you bank?
Comment: In most cases these kinds of questions would be very difficult to prove as job related.

Disabilities

Permissible: Inquiry as to whether any disabilities exist which would interfere with ability to do specific job applied for. Inquiry as to whether there are jobs or activities that applicant should not be considered for because of handicap.
Discriminatory: Do you have any handicaps or disabilities? Have you or your family ever had any of the following diseases? (List)
Comment: Disabilities should be taken into consideration with regard to placement but general inquiry should be avoided. Disabilities should be related only to ability to do job applied for by job analysis.

Education

Permissible: What specific academic, vocational, technical, or professional education have you had which specifically relate to the job?
Discriminatory: Broad questions over education that have little or no relevance to job in question. Questions with regard to the racial or sexual composition of schools attended.
Comment: Any inquiry into education should be limited to that proven to be necessary to perform the job applied for.

Emergency Notification

Permissible: Name and address of person to be notified in case of emergency.
Discriminatory: Inquiry as to relationship of person listed to applicant and why this person was chosen. Who do you live with?
Comment: Although it could be argued that this is not necessary preemployment information, it could be equally argued that this information could be used to contact the prospective employee or that an accident could happen while the individual is on company premises during the selection process, hence necessary.

Experience

Permissible: Questions as to work and travel experiences when relevant.
Discriminatory: Questions as to why travel took place? Questions as to experiences with discrimination in previous jobs.
Comment: Inquiry should be limited to work experiences or travel that specifically relate to job requirements.

Financial Condition

Permissible: Probably none unless related to job (e.g., owning a car) might be necessary for an outside sales job.

Discriminatory: Almost all inquiry as to finances, rental, or owning of home or car, debts, mortgages.

Comment: Questions of this sort usually have greater impact on minorities and females, hence should be avoided.

Height and Weight

Permissible: Certain jobs may have height or weight requirements based on performance standards.

Discriminatory: How tall are you? What do you weigh? Are you within the weight classification for your height (chart)?

Comment: Jobs should be examined on a case-by-case basis to make sure these requirements are valid and cannot be avoided since these discriminate against persons of Hispanic or Asian background and against women.

Marital Status

Permissible: None.

Discriminatory: Are you (or have you been) married, single, divorced, separated, widowed, engaged? Do you have any dependents? What are their ages?

Comment: Questions of this type should be avoided as they are major problem areas.

Military Background

Permissible: What (federal or state) armed services training, education, or experience have you had which relates to this job?

Discriminatory: Were you honorably discharged? Attach a copy of your DD 214 (discharge papers) to application blank. Have you served in any foreign armed services?

Comment: Inquiry should be limited to military experience relevant to job, and questions over general military experience should be avoided.

Name

Permissible: What is your name? Do we need information in addition to your name (e.g., nickname, assumed name) to check your application blank? Have you worked for this company under another name?

Discriminatory: Has your name been changed? Give us your maiden name. Have you ever worked under another name? What are your aliases or nicknames?

Comments: Any inquiry in addition to that necessary to merge employee records or perform a suitable background check should be avoided. Females cannot be compelled to use their husbands' names upon marriage but can be required to use that name appearing on their social security records.

National Origin

Permissible: Can you read, write, or speak a foreign language, and how fluently (when required by a specific job)?

Discriminatory: How did you acquire your language ability? What is your ancestry? What is the ancestry of your spouse or parents? Do your parents or spouse speak foreign languages? What is your national origin?

Comments: Inquiry into language ability must be integrally related to job performance. Under very rare circumstances, a spouse's language ability might be job related if family foreign travel were involved.

Organizational Memberships

Permissible: What professional organizations do you belong to that relate to this specific job? Do you belong to any other organizations that specifically would relate to ability to do this job (e.g., community service, fraternal, social—not including those who exclude persons on the basis of race, color, religion, sex, or national origin)?

Discriminatory: List the organizations to which you belong. Do you belong to any country clubs, lodges, religious orders, fraternal orders?

Comment: Under certain circumstances organizational memberships may be directly related to the job (e.g., professional or organizational memberships). Unless an inquiry can be specifically related to some characteristics of job performance, it should be avoided.

Photograph

Permissible: None.

Discriminatory: Affix a recent photograph to your application blank. You may, if desired, affix a photograph to your application.

Comment: Photographs can be required only after employment. A request, even at the option of the applicant, should be avoided since this implies preference.

Pregnancy

Permissible: When asked of *both* sexes: What do you think your tenure on this job will be? Are there any reasons why you expect to miss a substantial amount of work in the foreseeable future?

Discriminatory:	Are you pregnant? Are you going to have children in the near future? When are you going to have your children?
Comment:	In general, questions in the medical or pregnancy area should be avoided. You would be engaging in sex discrimination if you refused to hire a woman *solely* because she was pregnant. This would be a condition that only applied to one sex, hence discriminatory. The same logic would apply to future family plans.

Race/Color

Permissible:	None.
Discriminatory:	Color, complexion, coloration, race.
Comment:	Questions in this area should be strictly avoided. Hiring a black based on the lightness of skin is also a discriminatory practice.

References

Permissible:	How did you find out about this opening? Who referred you to this opening? Please give character or work references.
Discriminatory:	Give us credit references. Stipulations as to the economic or social class of required references.
Comment:	Some inquiry into this area is permitted to allow background investigation to take place and to determine the effectiveness of recruiting measures.

Relatives

Permissible:	Do you have any relatives employed here or by a competitor? Do you have any close relatives employed by firms we regulate?
Discriminatory:	What are the names, ages, and addresses of your children, parents, etc., not employed by this company?
Comment:	The use of a "nepotism" rule either to eliminate or select personnel should be carefully examined to make sure that it does not adversely affect protected groups. If protected groups are not represented in the work force, this will usually keep them out.

Sex

Permissible:	Only when sex is a bona fide occupational qualification (BFOQ).
Discriminatory:	What is your sex? Marital status? Do you have domestic responsibilities limiting your availability during evenings and/or weekends (unless weighted equally as to response).
Comment:	Typical grounds for proving sex to be a BFOQ are: Authenticity and genuineness (e.g., actors or models), sex

appeal (e.g., certain entertainment jobs), or public morality (e.g., locker room attendant).

Social Security Number

Permissible:	In private sector and for sensitive or law enforcement jobs in public sector. (See Public Law 93-579.)
Discriminatory:	Only in public sector as above.
Comment:	*Failure* to fill in the SSN should not be used to discriminate against a person particularly since the federal government holds it is *not* necessary preemployment information. It is required by law *after* employment, however.

Now that you have read the Guidelines, go back through the application blank and circle those items you missed the first time but in actuality are discriminatory. Now recount those items circled and enter the improved score on the line immediately before the last line on the page. Subtract your first score from your second. Have you improved your performance? The subtracted number represents a knowledge of this problem-prone area.

Discussion Questions

Discuss as a group why a company gathers background information on prospective employees. Outline your thoughts below.

1. Which part of the selection process would probably be more appropriate in making final selection decisions concerning higher level managerial and professional positions—the application blank or the interview? Why?
2. Which part would probably be more appropriate for selecting blue-collar workers for an assembly line? Why?
3. Could you design a contingency application blank that would meet the guidelines you just read? How would it look?

2 The B.I.T.C.H. Test

Black Intelligence Test of Cultural Homogeneity

Name _____ Age _____ Date _____

Grade _____

DIRECTIONS: Below are some words, terms, and expressions taken from the black experience. Select the correct answers and put a check mark in the space provided on the right of the test sheet. Remember, we want the correct definition as black people use the words and expressions. There is no time limit. Ten minutes should be sufficient time to complete the 20 items extracted from the full 100-item test. **Go ahead.**

		a	b	c	d
1. Bread					
(a) Something to eat	(c) Religion	1. ____	____	____	____
(b) Weapons	(d) Money				
2. Crib					
(a) An apartment	(c) A job	2. ____	____	____	____
(b) A game	(d) Hot stuff				
3. Deuce-and-a-quarter					
(a) Money	(c) A house	3. ____	____	____	____
(b) A car	(d) Dicey				
4. Do rag					
(a) The hair	(c) Washing	4. ____	____	____	____
(b) The shoes	(d) Tablecloth				
5. The eagle flies					
(a) The blahs	(c) Payday	5. ____	____	____	____
(b) Movie	(d) Deficit				
6. Gig					
(a) A job	(c) A car	6. ____	____	____	____
(b) Being discriminated against	(d) Jogging				
7. Gospel bird					
(a) A pheasant	(c) A goose	7. ____	____	____	____
(b) A chicken	(d) A duck				

Prepared by Robert Williams, Washington University, St. Louis. Copyright © 1971 by Robert Williams.

a   b   c   d

8. Hawk
   - (a) Rain
   - (b) Sunshine
   - (c) Water
   - (d) Cold wind

8. ___ ___ ___ ___

9. Heavy cat
   - (a) Fat
   - (b) Arrogant
   - (c) Depressed
   - (d) Intelligent

9. ___ ___ ___ ___

10. Hog
    - (a) Bad person
    - (b) A car
    - (c) Animal
    - (d) A whiskey still

10. ___ ___ ___ ___

11. Jaws are tight
    - (a) Hungry
    - (b) Excited
    - (c) Angry
    - (d) Frightened

11. ___ ___ ___ ___

12. Lay dead
    - (a) Do nothing
    - (b) Sneaky
    - (c) To lose
    - (d) Deep

12. ___ ___ ___ ___

13. Member
    - (a) Church goer
    - (b) Black
    - (c) White
    - (d) Foreigner

13. ___ ___ ___ ___

14. Nose opened
    - (a) Flirting
    - (b) Teed off
    - (c) Deeply in love
    - (d) Very angry

14. ___ ___ ___ ___

15. On my case
    - (a) Sitting on my luggage
    - (b) My lawyer
    - (c) Taking my money
    - (d) Criticizing me

15. ___ ___ ___ ___

16. Rags
    - (a) Clothes
    - (b) Wornout
    - (c) Brake
    - (d) Poor

16. ___ ___ ___ ___

17. Sapphire
    - (a) Black preacher
    - (b) Black woman
    - (c) Dish of soul food
    - (d) Hair style

17. ___ ___ ___ ___

18. Stone fox
    - (a) Bitchy
    - (b) Pretty
    - (c) Sly
    - (d) Uncanny

18. ___ ___ ___ ___

19. T.C.B.
    - (a) That's cool, baby
    - (b) Taking care of business
    - (c) They couldn't breathe
    - (d) Took careful behavior

19. ___ ___ ___ ___

	a	b	c	d

20. What had went down
    - (a) To throw someone off
    - (b) Being confused
    - (c) To say what is happening
    - (d) To say someone had died

20. _____ _____ _____ _____

---

3 Agronomics

You are director of personnel for a small manufacturing company, Agronomics. Recently you have heard increasing complaints about pay in your organization. Upon investigation, you discover that most of the complaints deal with alleged internal inequities (i.e., with situations in which employees feel that their salary is out of line in comparison with the amount of work that they do). You also have heard rumors that the blue-collar workers in your company are attempting to organize. They feel that their wages are consistently lower than those of unionized workers in other companies. Finally, you've just received word from the Department of Labor that Sara Rynes, one of your more vocal feminists, has filed a complaint alleging that Agronomics is violating the Equal Pay Act. She claims that she is being underpaid for performing the same job as her co-workers because she is a woman.

In attempting to confront these problems, you have had your assistant collect the following data:

A. Job descriptions. (Your professor will give you directions on this. If you generated a job description during the job analysis exercise, you might use it here.)
B. A point evaluation system to determine the relative worth of these positions (Form A).
C. A record sheet on which to record the point totals for the key organizational jobs (Form B).
D. A personnel inventory sheet which lists the names, age, sex, organizational and job tenure, performance rating, and current salary of all employees in the relevant job categories (Form C).
E. Wage and salary survey ranges for the positions (Form C).
F. Description of how to operate mini-tab.

Prepared by Vandra L. Huber. Copyright © 1984 by Vandra L. Huber.

PART I—JOB EVALUATION

5 pts.   **1.** Calculate the point value of each job. The job descriptions are on file in the library. Record the results of your point evaluation on Form B. List the lowest point total and move to the highest.

5 pts.   **2.** Now that you have experience with the point evaluation system of job evaluation, briefly (one page or less) summarize the positive and negative aspects of this method. What problems did you encounter in using the system?

PART II—USING THE COMPUTER

Using the information discussed in class and the mini-tab handout, you are now ready to find out about the wage structure of Agronomics. After logging into the computer, enter the point totals into the mini-tab's memory. What you are doing is creating a new variable called "c9." Remember that when a job has more than one incumbent, you have to type in the point total for each person. If you run into trouble, type HELP.

Now you are ready to begin looking at the data.

5 pts.   **3.** Using the plot command, plot the relationship between point total and salary. Label this graph "Question 3—Job Evaluation."

Computer commands: height 20, plot 'salary' 'points'.

10 pts.   **4.** What does the graph tell you about the wage structure of Agronomics? Identify any problems you see with the wage structure.

5 pts.   **5.** To acquire an overview of the organization, calculate the means for each of the quantifiable variables.

Computer command: mean 'age'.

5 pts.   **6.** While the information in question 5 is useful, it does not tell you if there are differences between males and females. Because questions concerning the pay of males and females have been raised by Sara Rynes, it would be useful to determine if there are any male/female differences. Therefore, you should calculate separate means for males and females. Label this output "Question 6—Male and Female means."

Computer command: Table 'sex';
    mean 'salary';
    mean 'age';
    mean 'firm yrs';
    mean 'job yrs';
    mean 'rating';
    mean 'points'.

This will make a table for you, listing the means on each variable by sex.

5 pts. **7.** What do you now know about males and females in the organization? What are the key differences? If you found differences in salary point total, which variables (excluding sex) might be responsible for the differences? Summarize your findings (one page).

5 pts. **8.** While this information is useful, it does not tell us how closely related or important these variables are. Therefore, the next step is to look at the correlation between the variables. Remember that a number closer to ± 1 means the two variables are highly related, and that a number closer to 0 means the relationship is weak. Positive correlations mean that, when one variable increases, the other variable also increases. When the correlation is negative, when one variable increases, the other decreases. Calculate the correlation between all of the quantifiable variables (c3–c9). Label this output "Question 8—Correlations."

Computer command: Correlation c3, c4, and so on.

5 pts. **9.** Explain what the results tell you about the relationship between the variables. Which ones are strongly related and which ones are not? How do the results compare to what you think the relationship between salary and the other variables ought to be? Discuss (1–2 pages).

10 pts. **10.** You now have available a great deal of usable information on which to make some decisions. In a professionally written and formatted memorandum (five pages or less), summarize your findings as they relate to the equity complaints detailed in the opening paragraph of the case. Be sure you detail key problems with the page structure and equity. Make specific recommendations in terms of what you would do to correct the problems. You have been given $20,000 to adjust *annual* salaries, should you have found any problems in the organization.

Extra credit:

10 pts. Compute a regression equation using age, organizational and job tenure, sex, and performance rating to predict salary. Label this output "Extra Credit." What does the regression equation tell you about the relationship between these variables? What happens to your salary if you are a male versus female? How does your age affect your salary? What effect does your performance rating have on salary? On other factors?

Now follow your recommendations that are detailed in Part III of the exercise. Create a new variable (c10), which will represent the new salaries after you have used the $20,000 to adjust individual salaries. Call the new variable "Newsal." Now calculate a regression equation where the other variables, age, tenure, sex, rating are used to predict these new salaries (c10). Label this output "Extra Credit with Adjustments." Do your proposed changes in the salary structure correct the problems you reported? Discuss (1–2 pages).

FORM A

Job Evaluation Manual

A. Education/Formal Training

This factor measures the extent of education or knowledge required by the worker to perform the job successfully. The education or knowledge may be the result of formal schooling or district-sponsored educational courses.

Degrees	Points
1. None required	20
2. Grammar school (8th grade)	35
3. Two years high school or equivalent	50
4. Four years high school or equivalent	75
5. Partial college: One year	90
Two years	105
Three years	120
6. College graduate	150
7. Postgraduate (master's level)	175
8. Postgraduate (PhD level)	200

B. Job Experience/Informal Training

This factor measures the time required by the worker to learn how to do the job, or the experience necessary to perform the job competently. Produced work should be of a quality and quantity to justify

FORM A   *(continued)*

continuous work employment. Avoid confusing experience with formal education. Use same point scale for on-the-job training and apprenticeships.

One week	20	One year	90
One month	35	18 months	100
Two months	45	Two years	110
Three months	55	Three years	130
Six months	80	Four years	150
Nine months	85		

C. Nonsupervisory Responsibility

These factors measure the degree of responsibility placed on the worker for materials, equipment, buildings, safety of others, money, confidential data, and so on. The activity may consist of transporting, stocking, loading, unloading, maintaining, cooking, and the like.

Great responsibility:	11–125
	10–115
	9–105
Moderate responsibility:	8–90
	7–80
	6–70
	5–60
Little responsibility:	4–40
	3–30
	2–20
	1–10

D. Supervisory Responsibility

These factors measure the responsibility to absorb and carry out policies, rules, and regulations, to understand worker psychology, and to maintain satisfactory human relations within the scope of the supervisor's jurisdiction.

Great responsibility:	11–70
	10–60
	9–50
Moderate responsibility:	8–40
	7–35
	6–30
	5–25
Little responsibility:	4–20
	3–15
	2–10
	1–5

FORM A   *(continued)*

E. Mental Effort

Measured here is the degree of intellectual attention and concentration required by the job.

Vital:	11–100
	10–90
	9–80
Important:	8–60
	7–50
	6–40
	5–30
Basic:	4–20
	3–15
	2–10
	1–5

G. Physical

Physical factors measure and compare endurance, fatigue, and strength under normal or abnormal conditions. Also relates to expenditure of physical exertion inherent in the job to be performed at a normal pace. Consideration must be given to muscular exertion required for material handling, use of tools, and operation of machines. Also, consider weights when the job requires pushing, pulling, or lifting; frequency of weight handling, speed, and time required to complete a job are equally important.

Vital:	11–200
	10–185
	9–170
Important	8–150
	7–135
	6–120
	5–105
Basic	4–85
	3–70
	2–55
	1–40

H. Working Conditions

These factors measure the environment and general conditions under which work is performed. Consider disagreeable features, such as cold, dampness, darkness, dirt, dust, fumes, grease, glare, heat, noise, oil, use of respirators, vibration, and other disagreeable conditions surrounding the job to which the worker is exposed.

FORM A   *(concluded)*

Vital:	11–200
	10–185
	9–170
Important:	8–150
	7–135
	6–120
	5–105
Basic:	4–85
	3–70
	2–55
	1–40

FORM B

Job	*A* Educational training	*B* Job experience	*C* Nonsupervisory responsibility	*D* Supervisory responsibility	*E* Mental effort	*F* Mental fatigue	*G* Physical effort	*H* Working conditions			Total points

FORM C Agronomics: Personnel Inventory Sheet

Name C1	Job Title C2	Age C3	Sex C4	Firm Yrs. C5	Job Yrs. C6	Rating C7	Monthly Salary C8	External Salary Range	Total Point C9
1. Jimmy Jones	1. Janitor	24	0	2	3	5	2,500	1,000 to 2,000	
2. Henry Smith	1.	30	0	5	5	5	2,800		
3. Patsy Williams	1.	34	1	4	3	4	1,400		
4. Sara Jones	1.	22	1	2	3	5	1,200		
5. Walt Ratcliff	1.	50	0	12	8	1	1,800		
6. Henry "Hank" Sims	2. Pre-press supervisor	59	0	16	12	2	4,200	3,200 to 4,500	
7. Mike Rich	2.	36	0	20	16	4	3,400		
8. Chris Smith	3. Litigation associate	32	1	15	15	3	2,800	3,000 to 5,000	
9. Tom Selleck	3.	45	0	15	10	3	4,000		
10. Bruce Jenner	3.	34	0	5	5	4	3,000		
11. Chris Everett	3.	24	1	1	1	4	2,500		
12. Bob Sterns	4. Commercial advertising	44	0	10	8	3	3,500	2,500 to 3,500	
13. Denny Gioia	4. director	40	0	10	10	2	4,000		
14. Ed Locke	4.	44	0	8	6	3	3,900		
15. Frederick Herzberg	4.	36	0	10	9	5	2,900		
16. Phil Podsakoff	5. Market research analyst	35	0	10	5	2	3,500	3,500 to 4,200	
17. Jo Churey	5.	36	1	15	8	3	2,800		
18. Pay Mayo	5.	25	1	5	3	4	2,900		
19. Henry Smith	5.	45	0	20	10	2	3,800		
20. Pat Kelley	5.	30	0	20	7	5	4,200		

FORM C *continued*

Name C1	Job Title C2	Age C3	Sex C4	Firm Yrs. C5	Job Yrs. C6	Rating C7	Monthly Salary C8	External Salary Range C9	Total Point C9
21. John Boudreau	6. Process control engineer	38	0	8	8	1	3,600	3,400 to 4,200	
22. George Milkovich	6.	52	0	25	15	5	4,200		
23. Denny Organ	6.	35	0	19	16	4	3,600		
24. Lynn Johnson	6.	49	1	20	14	5	3,900		
25. Sara Smith	7. Internal development	28	1	8	4	3	1,800	1,500 to 3,000	
26. Harold Loew	7. specialist	50	0	20	8	3	3,400		
27. Joan Benoit	7.	30	1	5	8	5	2,000		
28. Bob Risley	8. Senior financial analyst	52	0	22	12	3	3,200	2,400 to 3,600	
29. Fel Foltman	8.	66	0	25	10	3	3,200		
30. Susan Taylor	8.	38	1	8	3	4	2,800		
31. Janet Near	8.	25	1	2	1	5	2,400		
32. Henry Longfellow	9. CEO	47	0	10	10	2	6,000	4,000 to 10,000	
33. San Bacharach	10. Staffing specialist	30	0	2	2	4	1,800	1,400 to 1,800	
34. Pam Tolbert	10.	23	1	1	1	5	1,800		
35. Sara Rynes	10.	29	1	4	2	4	1,500		
36. Don Kane	10.	44	0	12	6	3	2,200		
37. Billy Lee	11. Shipping & receiving	42	0	10	6	3	2,400	1,500 to 2,200	
38. Janice Byer	11.	35	1	8	4	4	2,000		
39. Mike Krolewski	11.	40	0	15	10	3	2,200		
40. Bill Todor	11.	35	0	10	8	5	1,800		
41. Marcia Miceli	11.	22	1	2	2	4	1,200		

Sex codes—0 = Male; 1 = Female.
Performance rating—1 = low performance; 5 = High performance.

4 Women as Managers Scale

Please give your personal opinion concerning attitudes toward women in business. The statements below cover many different and opposing points of view. You may find yourself agreeing strongly with some of the statements, disagreeing just as strongly with others, and perhaps uncertain about others.

Rating Scale

1 = Strongly Disagree
2 = Disagree
3 = Slightly Disagree
4 = Neither Disagree nor Agree
5 = Slightly Agree
6 = Agree
7 = Strongly Agree

To the left of each statement is a blank space. Using the numbers from 1 to 7 on the above rating scale, mark your personal opinion about each statement in the blank that immediately precedes it. Remember, all that is wanted is *your* personal opinion. A rating of one (1) would mean that you *strongly disagree* with the statement, whereas a rating of seven (7) would mean you *strongly agree* with the statement. For example:

————— It is especially important that all workers be paid on the basis of their performance.

If you strongly agree with this statement, you should place the number 7 in the blank before the statement. In other words, the stronger your agreement with the statement, the higher the number you should select. Please respond to all 21 items.

————— 1. It is less desirable for women than men to have a job that requires responsibility.

————— 2. Women have the objectivity required to evaluate business situations properly.

————— 3. Challenging work is more important to men than it is to women.

————— 4. Men and women should be given equal opportunity for participation in management training programs.

————— 5. Women have the capability to acquire the necessary skills to be successful managers.

The WAMS was developed by Lawrence H. Peters, Southern Illinois University, James R. Terborg, University of Oregon, and Janet Taynor, Purdue University, Copyright © 1974 by Lawrence H. Peters.

_____ 6. On the average, women managers are less capable of contributing to an organization's overall goals than are men.

_____ 7. It is not acceptable for women to assume leadership roles as often as men.

_____ 8. The business community should someday accept women in key managerial positions.

_____ 9. Society should regard work by female managers as valuable as work by male managers.

_____ 10. It is acceptable for women to compete with men for top executive positions.

_____ 11. The possibility of pregnancy does not make women less desirable employees than men.

_____ 12. Women would no more allow their emotions to influence their managerial behavior than would men.

_____ 13. Problems associated with menstruation should not make women less desirable than men as employees.

_____ 14. To be a successful executive, a woman does not have to sacrifice some of her femininity.

_____ 15. On the average, a woman who stays home all the time with her children is a better mother than a woman who works outside the home at least half-time.

_____ 16. Women are less capable of learning mathematical and mechanical skills than men.

_____ 17. Women are not ambitious enough to be successful in the business world.

_____ 18. Women cannot be assertive in business situations that demand it.

_____ 19. Women possess the self-confidence required of a good leader.

_____ 20. Women are not competitive enough to be successful in the business world.

_____ 21. Women cannot be aggressive in business situations that demand it.

Note: Directions for scoring the WAMS and an explanation of its meaning will be provided by your instructor.

5 *The Supervisor's EEO Reality Test*

This quiz is designed to help you sharpen your on-the-job understanding of how EEO and related laws affect your everyday decisions.

	True	False
1. It is ill-advised to discuss details of employment benefits with applicants.	T	F
2. If a supervisor is sued for attempting to sexually harass a subordinate, for permitting sexual jokes or remarks, or allowing co-workers to post nudes or pin-ups (creating a "sexually intimating atmosphere"), the employer is the one who may be liable for substantial monetary awards.	T	F
3. It is ill-advised to give employees discharged for poor performance overly rosy references for a new job.	T	F
4. Since job offers can be delicate negotiations, they are best made in private between the offering supervisor or manager and the applicant.	T	F
5. To avoid a surprise panic or hysteria, it is advisable to keep employees informed about a co-worker who has AIDS.	T	F
6. It is acceptable to require AIDS-infected employees to wear special items of clothing or equipment.	T	F
7. When layoffs are required, you may select those who will remain based on your company's future needs rather than on the employee's past performance.	T	F
8. The "T-Form" is used to prevent ill-advised disciplinary discharge, promotion, or other personnel-related decisions.	T	F
9. The safest way to prevent lawsuits over testing and avoid hiring mistakes is to test applicants before you involve them in other parts of the screening process, such as personal interviews.	T	F

	True	*False*
10. Your written company policy or union contract providing time off for religious observances or flexible scheduling is sufficient reasonable accommodation and frees you from responsibility for taking any additional steps.	T	F

6 New Position Simulation

You are the human resource manager of a rapidly growing high-tech firm in the local metropolitan area. One year ago, your firm had 45 employees; currently there are 225 full-time employees on the payroll, and the plans include expansion to 400 within the next 12 months. At the present time you have one subordinate: a recruitment/selection specialist. You have now been given authorization to hire a compensation analyst. Your objective is to develop appropriate support materials and to hire the proper person.

You have a bachelor's degree in business from the local state university and maintain close contact with the school. You are aware of the development of the human resource program in their business school, and you have been told by a faculty member whom you respect that a number of good candidates are available. Further, this professor has a strong background in compensation and has imparted a great deal of this knowledge to the students. Thus, you have decided to attempt to fill the position from among this year's crop of human resource management graduates. As a result of this decision, education, motivation, and intelligence will become more important selection criteria than experience.

This position provides an opportunity which rarely exists with old positions—all human resource tasks can be developed without having to correct past errors or worry about the incumbent's reaction. You seek to take advantage of this situation and to develop a comprehensive job manual for a compensation analyst before you make a hiring decision. Thus, your set of tasks includes the following:

1. Write a job analysis (description, specification, evaluation) for the compensation analyst job.
2. Develop a recruitment strategy (advertisements, posters, and the like) for the job.

Prepared by Alan Cabelly, Portland State University. Copyright © 1984 by Alan Cabelly.

3. Develop selection criteria for the position.
4. Produce an application blank.
5. Write a brochure for prospective candidates.
6. Develop an interview guide or other methods, or both, of selection (related to selection criteria).
7. Develop a compensation range for the position.
8. Produce a benefits package.
9. Develop performance appraisal criteria (related to the job description) and an appropriate appraisal format.
10. State how this person would be trained by you (remember—this is a person with academic learning and little experience).
11. Describe the career path for the successful applicant.
12. Interview applicants.
13. Make a selection decision, along with the associated compensation decision.
14. Write the appropriate letters of acceptance/rejection.

OTHER INFORMATION AND SUGGESTIONS

The pool of applicants includes all members of your class. Each student will interview with two companies; each team is to interview exactly two times as many applicants as it has team members (thus, a five-person team will interview 10 applicants). At each interview, at least two team members must be present. All interviews will be arranged by the instructor.

All students are to take the interviews *seriously*. This includes punctuality, appropriate dress, appropriate interview rooms, preparation, and so on. Although résumés are not required, the better students will have given one to their prospective employers a few days before the interviews occur. In cases of borderline grades, being selected for a job will increase the course grade.

FINAL REPORT

A comprehensive professional report which describes the entire exercise and critically analyzes your efforts is expected. It should include all *relevant* appendixes (e.g., job description, blank interview guides, etc.). The truly outstanding report will be *comprehensive, analytical,* and *professional.*

1. *Comprehensive.* The report should show that the team went through all the steps discussed in the project description. Incomplete reports are unacceptable.

2. *Analytical.* Thorough analysis of all decisions is expected. Describe why and how you made your decisions. State what should have been done differently and why (it is better to analyze your errors than to ignore them and *hope* the instructor will not find them). Be certain to provide an overall analysis of the project. Reference to *academic* and professional journals, as well as to practitioners, is generally useful.

3. *Professional.* Students at your stage of academic career should be able to present a truly professional report. Method of presentation is often as important as content. Your report should be structured appropriately (main text, bibliography, appendixes, etc.) and be pleasing to the eye.

Part 4

In-Basket Exercises

Section A

In-Basket Exercises:
A Discussion

Introduction to the Use of In-Baskets

This section introduces the last group of exercises: in-basket exercises. An in-basket is a series of items such as letters and telephone calls. This group of materials is designed to simulate the kind of material a supervisor or manager, such as a personnel manager, would receive in a workday.

As suggested by Terri Burchett in a *Personnel Journal* article of May 1987, supervisors, managers, personnel professionals, and others who are engaged in personnel decisions can make costly mistakes. Those mistakes having to do with personnel policies (e.g., lack of knowledge about disciplinary policies, the impact of setting precedents, understanding union-management relations, overtime policies, benefits, etc.) can result in costly errors. The result may be grievances, improperly or inaccurately paid wages, and subsequent lawsuits. It comes as no surprise, therefore that most managers understand the importance of properly orienting those involved in personnel practices and procedures, whether in one-on-one meetings or by means of an organizationwide program.

Those who make personnel decisions are a diverse lot. The group may include experienced, long-tenured employees who, for the first time, have a supervisory role or those who are industry or corporate newcomers, team leaders, administrators, or executives. One tool that has proven invaluable in helping people understand the importance of personnel policies (without boring the learners to death or insulting their intelligence) is the in-basket exercise. Trainers or other personnel

---

Many thanks to Professor Walter A. Bogumil, Jr., University of Central Florida, for his discussion of in-basket exercise grading (which appears in the *Instructor's Manual*) and his contribution of five in-baskets. Each of these in-baskets is 10 to 12 items in length. The intent of the smaller in-baskets is to provide the instructor with greater flexibility not normally provided by having to use 25–30 item in-baskets.

professionals may create in-basket exercises of personnel issues in which trainees may work on simulated policy-related concerns. "Reality" or relevance comes from the process of developing in-baskets which cover issues that the trainee is likely to find in his or her *own* in-basket.

The construction of an in-basket exercise is not very difficult. For each such exercise four basic steps must be followed: (1) define the general type of problem, (2) define the setting, (3) draft the appropriate materials, and (4) make the exercise realistic. I believe the in-basket contributors have properly followed each of these four crucial steps.

THE EXERCISES

The first part of the exercise consists of a description of the managerial setting and the role the participant will play. Next, the actual material waiting for the manager on his or her desk is provided.

These items are presented in the order in which they were received. It is your responsibility to sort out out those which are the most pressing from those which can wait a bit. Typically, you will be given a time limit within which you must complete the work.

The professor will describe how he or she wants you to proceed with the data. In addition to the letters and phone calls provided, it is possible that during the exercise you will receive additional phone calls and memoranda. For, when you are on a job, no one hands you all your work for the day and then leaves you uninterrupted until you are finished.

Remember that you must place yourself in the situation described. When you have completed what you would do and in which order of importance, this can be compared with norms developed for the exercise. You should learn how you react to the time pressures and how well you make decisions in the usual less-than-full-information environment in which most managers work.

Section B

In-Basket Exercises

1 Ashland Regional Hospital

The Ashland Regional Hospital is a nonprofit hospital that employs 600 employees. It was established by Kenneth Appleton, one of the current members of the board of directors. You are Scott Larson, the personnel director. You accepted this position six months ago. Rumor has it that there was a problem with the previous personnel director which no one will discuss. You have only recently turned the department around and operations are now running on an even keel. However, at this time you must go on your first out-of-town meeting since you assumed command. You have only one hour in your office and must consider all of the items in your in-basket before departure. You will return to your office one week from today (Friday, January 30).

ITEM 1

To: Scott Larson

From: Madge Garrison, Selection Officer

Subject: Flunked Exam

Date: January 27

Mr. Jon Adams, who was applying for the job of lab tech, did not pass his physical exam. We explained to him that it was a condition of employment to pass the physical. Well, he became quite upset and wants to file for workers' compensation. He threatens that if he is not allowed to file for it he will go to the press. Please advise as to how to solve this problem. I need an answer as soon as possible.

Prepared by Professor Walter A. Bogumil, Jr., University of Central Florida.

ITEM 2

To: Scott Larson

From: Lois Huners, Business Office Director

Subject: Pay Inequity

Date: January 26

One of the telephone operators, Donna Rebel, who worked for us for seven years, came to me to complain about one of the other telephone operators who was recently hired. The new employee earns only 15 cents less per hour than Donna. She is fuming mad. I told her I would get back to her after I talked with you. Please call me within a day. Thank you.

ITEM 3

To: Madge Garrison

From: Sandra Lockheed, Nursing Supervisor

Subject: Hiring of Nurses

Madge, you and I have talked on numerous occasions about the selection process for nurses. Obviously you were not listening. I am still getting people in my department who lack the experience we need. I will not stand for this any more. I am tired of training these people. If the problem is not corrected I will go over everybody's head.

ITEM 4

To: Scott Larson

From: Bonnie Alderman

Hope your trip is exciting. Have a good flight and learn lots of good ideas for us all.

ITEM 5

Phone message

Mr. Wilder, the administrator, called at 4:36 P.M. Wants you to call him back. Did not say what it is in reference to.

ITEM 6

To: Scott Larson

From: Andrew King, Controller

Subject: Upcoming Budget

I thought I would take the opportunity to remind you that the annual budget time is approaching (February 15). Since this is your first budget here at ARH I might offer you some tips on our budget system. Give me a call.

ITEM 7

To: Scott Larson

From: Judith Spencer, RN

Subject: Supervisor

I am having a problem with my supervisor. I am afraid to say anything, especially since her mother-in-law is the department head. She does not treat me fairly and I don't know why. I have repeatedly asked for weekends off and I never get them. I was not hired to work every weekend. She did not give me a good performance appraisal a week ago, and when I refused to sign it she yelled at me and told me there were other people out there who wanted my job. Please help. I do not know what to do.

ITEM 8

To: Scott Larson

From: Sharon Newman, Personnel Assistant

Subject: *Employee Handbook*

The new revised editions of the *Employee Handbook* have just arrived. But, before we can hand them out, you are required to read it and make sure everything is in order. Mr. Wilder called and is anxious about getting them out to the employees. Come by and pick up a copy. I tried to drop one off yesterday afternoon, but you had already left.

ITEM 9

To: Scott Larson

From: Madge Garrison, Selection Officer

Subject: Sandra Lockheed

I know you are aware of the situation with Ms. Lockheed. I feel that I am between a rock and a hard place. I need to satisfy the employment requirements, but I also need to satisfy the minority hiring goals. I'm damned if I do and damned if I don't. I feel the real problem is Ms. Lockheed; I think she is prejudiced. I cannot prove it, but I think that is the real problem. Don't let her go over your head on this matter.

ITEM 10

To: Scott Larson

From: Joseph Wilder, Administrator

Subject: Personnel Convention

Scott, I would like very much for you to get together with me after you return from your convention. I am interested in what is going in the human resources field. I've never sent a personnel director to a conference before; you are the first. Good luck.

Item No.	Priority	Action Information

_____

_____

_____

_____

_____

_____

_____

_____

2 Sayers, Inc.

Sayers, Inc., is a retail department store located in the southeastern United States. It is a part of a large chain of stores that have a very centralized and bureaucratic structure. Advertising and marketing decisions and strategies are formed at headquarters. Recently, the accounting department was pared down and also centralized. Sayers, Inc. has more than 250 employees.

You are Larry Reed, the head of your store's personnel department. Having arrived early, you are in the process of clearing your in-basket before a day-long meeting.

Instructions

You have one hour to go through the items. Place a priority on each item and what action you would take for that item. Delegating is not a course of action you may take. The purpose of this in-basket is to test your abilities as a personnel manager in pressured and difficult situations. An organization chart is provided for you in Exhibit 1.

_____

Prepared by Professor Walter A. Bogumil, Jr., University of Central Florida.

EXHIBIT 1   Sayers, Inc.—Organization Chart

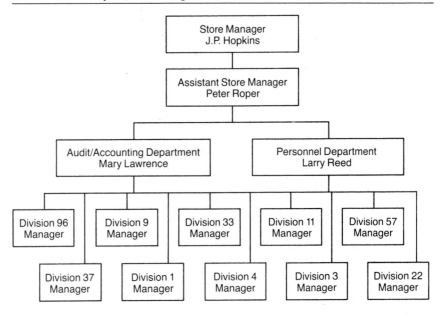

ITEM 1

To: Larry Reed

From: Peter Roper

Re: Company Picnic

As you know, our company picnic will be in just three weeks. Please make the necessary arrangements for location, catering, activities, and decorations. We would also appreciate an extra effort in advertising this event to our employees so they will be able to attend. J.P. and I feel you will do an excellent job for our employees.

ITEM 2

To: Larry Reed

From: Marge Brown, Training Assistant

With the installation of courtesy cards at the registers we have found that customers are complaining about salesclerks not knowing where the merchandise is located in the store. I feel we should have all employees tour the store once every six months so they can be more helpful to our customers. I would appreciate any suggestions you might have in helping to correct this problem.

Thanks, Marge

ITEM 3

To: Larry Reed

From: Mary Lawrence, Auditing Department

Once again part-time employees are working between 31–39 hours. If we let this continue, part-timers will be able to claim they should receive the benefits we give to full-time employees. Your personnel staff should add scheduled hours from the divisions to see if they are correct. Apparently the total hours shown for each employee are inconsistent with what they are actually working. I know you will appreciate this information. See you in the meeting.

ITEM 4

To: Larry Reed

From: Tracy Sinclair

I'm very concerned because I have heard rumors of a union organizing attempt. I can't believe that morale is so poor and conditions so bad that the employees would actually consider this. I just thought you should be aware of these rumors and would like to help if I can.

ITEM 5

Dear Mr. Reed:

I'm very upset that my raise was an increase of only $0.10 per hour. For an entire year of hard work I feel I was very unjustly treated. I also believe that it has something to do with the fact that I am a black woman. In any event, I am considering moving to another job.

Sincerely,
Cynthia A. Toth

ITEM 6

Hey Larry,

Tina called you earlier and said please call her as soon as possible!

Jo

ITEM 7

To: Larry Reed

From: Bob Reyes, Personnel Assistant

Several employees have inquired about scheduling their vacations during our peak season. I have explained that our company policy specifies that vacations are to be taken in the off-season. I would also like to send out a companywide memo reminding employees of this policy. I made an exception for one employee and evidently the other employees are resentful of this exception, even though it was for a good reason. Just wanted to keep you informed of the situation.

ITEM 8

To: Larry Reed

From: Marion Hughes [Mr. Hopkins' secretary]

Mr. Hopkins would like for you to send out memos to all of the employees who are not taking their required meal periods and breaks. This needs to be expedited due to the Federal Wage and Hour Laws.

ITEM 9

To: All Divisions and Department Heads

From: J. P. Hopkins, Store Manager

I will be holding a general meeting on Friday, December 13. Please make the necessary arrangements in your schedule for that day as the meeting is expected to last the greater part of the day. The meeting will be centered around the previous quarter's sales data for our store. Come prepared.

ITEM 10

To: All Sayers, Inc. Personnel Managers

From: Mr. Charles Cross, Director of Personnel Relations

This is to advise you of a change in procedure concerning our profit sharing plan for employees. As of January 1, 1990, all employees are required to reaffirm their decision to waive participation in the program. If at this time they decide to take advantage of this plan, they will be able to sign up. Forms to implement this new procedure will be arriving at your store in the coming weeks. In one week I will send a follow-up letter to advise you of specifics.

Item No.	Priority	Action Information

3 The Constructor Corporation

The Constructor Corporation is engaged in the construction industry. It works mainly for the Florida state government. It is located in downtown Orlando and has 5,500 unionized employees working for it.

The primary work for the government consists in the development and construction of state highways and community roads. The company also develops private projects such as small complexes and buildings.

You are Rafael Velasquez, Constructor's director of personnel. The day is Monday morning and you are to leave for Los Angeles in three hours. You will not be in for the rest of the week. Therefore, you have to take care of your in-basket in the time remaining before you leave.

Instructions

You have two hours. Read your in-baskets and rank them in the order of priority you consider appropriate. At the end of the exercise, give a short, written explanation reasoning the order of your priorities and suggesting the courses of action you believe should be taken.

ITEM 1

To: Rafael Velasquez, Personnel Director
From: Robert Johnson, Civil Engineer Department
Re: Mary Cash

My cousin, Mary, just came out of management school and she is in town now. She is looking for a job in her field and I asked her to talk to you. Would you please see what she has to say? I would really appreciate it.

ITEM 2

To: Rafael Velasquez
From: Andy Right, Special Project Director
Re: Violation of Weingarten Right

One of our supervisors caught an employee, Bill Landmark, stealing tools from our toolroom. I called Bill into my office and questioned him. He

---

Prepared by Professor Walter A. Bogumil, Jr., University of Central Florida.

wanted to have the union steward present but I denied it; I was not aware that his request was a legal one. Now the union is contacting me. Please call me immediately and help me with this matter.

ITEM 3

To: Rafael Velasquez
From: Jim Butt, Director of State Projects
Re: Low Morale

We may be facing a low morale problem with the workers involved in the construction of the expressway. The other day Steve Zakka, the coordinator of the road program, waved his paycheck in front of all the workers in a showing off manner. The workers got pretty upset and came complaining to me. They said that unless Zakka apologized to them, they would go and work somewhere else. I talked to Zakka, but he denied the accusations. Now the employees' pace of work is not the same. Their morale seems to be low.

   Rafael, this is a $30,000,000 project. I do not need to tell you how important it is to finish it on time (November 1991). I know you attended a seminar dealing with problems like this one. Please let's have lunch tomorrow and discuss the issue.

ITEM 4

To: Rafael Velasquez
From: Peter Castle, Paving Department
Re: Immigration and Naturalization Office

Mr. Sanchez, the responsible fellow I talked to you about was working illegally for us. He was using a fake social security number. Immigration contacted me yesterday and a representative will be here tomorrow inquiring about the matter. What should I do? Give me a call. We need to be prepared right away!

ITEM 5

OFFICE OF THE PRESIDENT
CARL ALLEN

To: Rafael Velasquez, Director of Personnel Management

I have drawn up a sketch concerning the company's new policy about searching employees to prevent theft. I would like you to give me your opinion. Enclosed is the sketch. [See Exhibit 1]

EXHIBIT 1   Sample Memo Explaining Employee Search Policy

Subject: Policy Statement
Regarding: Theft
Attention: All Employees
Effective: Immediately

The company has a responsibility to its customers, shareholders, and employees to provide protection for its property. To discharge that responsibility, a security program is being instituted and a security department has been formed to implement the program.

Among the tasks the department will be expected to perform will be the development of a program to detect theft. Since many of the tasks this new department will perform have been handled at the district or division level in the past, it is important that a systemwide review of company policy be published so no confusion or misunderstanding concerning the company's policy will occur.

Removal of company materials, tools, or equipment from company premises without proper authorization is considered to be theft and is viewed by the company as a most serious matter.

Personnel operating in the field may occasionally, with management approval but without written authorization, carry tools outside normal working areas to expedite service in case of an emergency. During normal operation, approval for removing company property from company premises should be in writing and obtained from the employee's supervisor. When necessary, approval can be obtained from security coordinators or other management personnel if the regular supervisor is not available. For example, on evening or night shift and cases except emergencies, a supervisor, security coordinator, or manager must be aware of the items being removed and must give written approval for the removal.

Unless specifically stated in the approval, authorizations will be effective only for the date the items are to be removed and will not be considered an approval for future removal of items. In the generating stations an approval can be in the form of a gate pass. In other operating areas the approval should be in the form of a written, signed authorization from the proper person.

Company property will be considered to be removed without authorization if found in the possession of an employee who cannot provide proof that the property is legitimately in his or her possession. Disciplinary action, which may result in discharge, will be taken in all instances.

No distinction will be made between bargaining unit and nonbargaining unit employees in instances of discipline for theft. The company is confident that the vast majority of its employees will welcome positive efforts to control costs and eliminate unnecessary loss through an active security program. It is the responsibility of all company employees to cooperate and assist in the programs.

Chairman, President, and
Chief Executive Officer

ITEM 6

To: Rafael Velasquez

From: Kenny Brown, Vice President, Finance Department

Re: Budget

What happened with the budget for your department? I don't have it here in my office and the meeting is tomorrow. Please send me your final budget revision as soon as possible, because otherwise, it may be reduced for 1990.

ITEM 7

Rafael Velasquez
Director of Personnel
Constructor Corporation
Orlando, FL

Dear Mr. Velasquez:

At the University of Central Florida we prepare tomorrow's managers. Our core of management studies includes such classes as personnel management and personnel management issues, and even though we try to teach in an environment which reflects that of managers, we cannot supply the total managerial expertise reflected by a person holding a position as important as yours.

Mr. Velasquez, we invite you to give a presentation about your expertise in managerial issues. We will be glad to have you among our most important collaborators and believe me, your help will be greatly appreciated. You will be happy to have given the managers of the future a little bit of your knowledge.

Mr. Velasquez, please do consider this invitation. We look forward to hearing from you in the near future.

> Sincerely yours,
> Veronica Eldford, Ph.D.
> Chair, Management Department
> University of Central Florida

ITEM 8

To: Rafael Velasquez
From: Alice Michaels
Re: Drugs

My secretary found drugs in Ralph Brook's desk. Ralph has been my loyal assistant for two years, and I am very concerned about him. I tried to talk to him, but he refuses to. I do not want him to be harmed, but I do not want the FBI here either.

I asked my secretary not to comment about what happened to anyone, but you know that the grapevine works very fast. I do not know what to do. Please advise me.

ITEM 9

December 9

Rafael:

The president, the vice president, and I are going to have dinner this weekend at Mario's. We are going to discuss the construction for a new complex of apartments here in Orlando, and are interested in the lot of land you have in the suburbs.

We would like you to join us. Please call me to make the arrangements.

J. Payne

ITEM 10

To: Rafael Velasquez
From: Tracy Jones, Personnel Department Secretary
Re: Sexual Harassment

Two days ago, Mr. Smith, secretary of the office of special projects, called me into his office so that I would bring him some important papers. When I got there, a representative of Ace, Inc. was talking to him. I was invited in, introduced, and, without any reason, Mr. Smith sexually humiliated me in front of the Ace representative.

Mr. Velasquez, I would like to talk to you before you leave. This is not the first time it has happened. I have thought about resigning or even calling the EEOC, but I have been working for this company for six years, and I would not like to end it all like that. Please advise me.

Item No.	Priority	Action Information

4 Burton Electronics

Burton Electronics is a small manufacturing company located in Binghamton, New York. The company has 300 employees and manufactures electronic components for telephones, computers, aircraft, and appliances. Its customers include major manufacturers, both foreign and domestic. Burton's organization chart as it relates to this exercise is shown in Exhibit 1.

The company was founded in 1964 by Ken Burton, and has developed a reputation for its high-quality products. Burton has shown a profit for the last 18 years. However, a financial analysis shows a downward trend in sales over the last three years. The company has not yet been successful in reversing this trend. The decline in sales has led to labor force problems in that some employees have been overworked in efforts to complete projects on schedule while employees in other departments were idle because new projects were not started.

Richard Benson, the company personnel director, retired eight months ago after 16 years with Burton. Helen Wilcox, a bright and experienced personnel director, was hired to replace him. She immediately began to work on the uneven work load and developed a system of transferring or loaning employees interdepartmentally. Although the problem is not completely resolved, it has improved substantially.

Employee turnover is high in both the manufacturing and research and development departments. Helen suspects that the high turnover in R&D is directly related to the decreased sales. She feels that if the R&D division were more productive and innovative, the salespeople would be more successful.

Helen's staff consists of her secretary, Ellen McKervey, and two assistants. The assistants, Anthony Cerratani and Kay Wallenberg, are both business students at the State University of New York at Binghamton. They work full-time during the summers and part-time during the school year. Mr. Burton is a strong believer in encouraging students to work while attending college and thinks that both the company and the students benefit from their experience with the company.

Today is Monday, December 2. Helen has just returned from a two-week vacation. Exhibit 2 shows the calendar for the month. The following items were in her in-basket when she arrived at work.

Prepared by Professor Walter A. Bogumil, Jr., University of Central Florida.

EXHIBIT 1   Burton Electronics

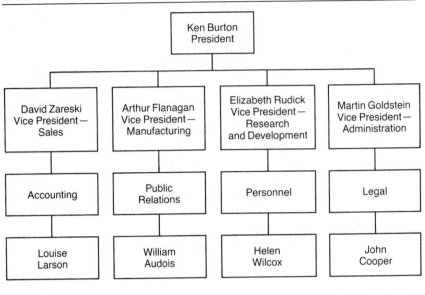

EXHIBIT 2   Calendar

| December | | | | | | |
S	M	T	W	T	F	S
1	2	3	4	5	6	7
8	9	10	11	12	13	14
15	16	17	18	19	20	21
22	23	24	25	26	27	28
29	30	31				

ITEM 1

BURTON ELECTRONICS
Interoffice Memorandum

To: Helen Wilcox
From: Raymond Greenfield, Foreman (Manufacturing)
Date: November 22
Subject: Suggestion Plan

What's going on with your suggestion plan? In the last six months I've submitted eight very useful suggestions. I know that at least five of my men have also submitted suggestions. We haven't heard any response at all. It sure makes you feel like you're wasting your time. How about getting on the stick so we can improve the way this company operates.

ITEM 2

BURTON ELECTRONICS
Interoffice Memorandum

To: Helen Wilcox

From: Anthony Cerratani

Date: November 27

Subject: On-the-Job Accident Statistics

1989 Year-to-Date On-the-Job Accident Report

Dept.	Jan.	Feb.	Mar.	Apr.	May	Jun.	Jul.	Aug.	Sep.	Oct.
Sales	0	1	0	2	0	0	1	1	0	0
Manufacturing	9	11	12	16	13	15	17	23	16	19
R&D	2	1	1	0	0	1	0	0	0	1
Administration	0	0	0	1	0	0	0	0	0	0

I found the manufacturing accident rate startling and felt I should bring it to your attention.

Should I investigate further?

ITEM 3

BURTON ELECTRONICS
Interoffice Memorandum

To: Helen Wilcox

From: Lucy Koski

Date: November 29

Subject: Unfair Working Hours

This is to inform you that I am planning to contact the local office of the Wage and Hour Division.

I have been required to work unpaid overtime by my boss, Mr. Flannigan, many times over the last six months. I worked the overtime without complaining because I thought I would be rewarded in other ways, such as a raise. No rewards have ever come.

Earlier this week I told Mr. Flannigan that I am no longer able to work 12-hour days without getting overtime pay. He responded by telling me, "You'll work the hours you need to in order to get the job done. And if you can't handle the job, there are other secretaries in the company who would love to have your job."

I have not taken a vacation this year because I was planning to take it the last two weeks of December. Now Mr. Flannigan tells me that there is too much work in the office for me to take a vacation.

I want you to be aware of the situation when you are contacted by the Wage and Hour Division office.

ITEM 4

BURTON ELECTRONICS
Interoffice Memorandum

To: Helen Wilcox

From: John Craig, Unit Manager, R&D

Subject: Salary Increase for Gary Wilson

Date: November 25

I am writing to request a policy waiver. Our policy states that the maximum annual salary increase is 10 percent. In my department, that is not always practical. With the shortage of engineers, we really have to compete with other companies in order to keep our good people.

Gary Wilson has been offered a job with another company here in Binghamton. It will take a substantial salary increase to keep him. He is one of our most motivated and creative engineers and we cannot afford to lose him. I am asking for a 15 percent raise for Gary in my 1990 budget.

Please send your okay as soon as possible so I can get back to Gary.

ITEM 5

BURTON ELECTRONICS
Interoffice Memorandum

To: Helen Wilcox

From: Ken Burton

Date: November 29

Subject: Employee of the Month Program

I have heard that other companies have been very successful in motivating their employees by implementing employee recognition programs. These programs are said to increase employee commitment and morale.

I would like to see an "Employee of the Month" program instituted here at Burton Electronics. I have a few ideas and would like to discuss them with you.

Please see me the week of December 2 so we can begin setting up this program. We should aim to have it in effect by January 1.

ITEM 6

BINGHAMTON CENTRAL HIGH SCHOOL

November 22, 1989

Ms. Helen Wilcox
c/o Burton Electronics
1386 Riverside Drive
Binghamton, NY 13905

Dear Ms. Wilcox:

The Future Business Leaders Club of Binghamton Central High School would like to invite you to be the guest speaker at our January meeting. The meeting will be held Thursday, January 23 at 3:30 P.M. at the school. We would like you to discuss "The Changing Role of the Professional Personnel Manager."

We believe that your presentation will be quite informative for us because our club members plan to either major in business in college or go into business for themselves.

We hope you will be able to accept this invitation. Our sponsor, Mrs. Mary Watson, will call you soon for confirmation.

Sincerely,
Kathryn Dahulich

ITEM 7

BURTON ELECTRONICS
Interoffice Memorandum

To: Helen Wilcox
From: Bill Sullivan
Date: November 25
Subject: Morale

I need your help with a morale problem.

I have a deadline of December 27 to finish my current project. In order to meet that deadline, I am having to ask my employees to work overtime. They just refuse, and seem to feel that if we don't finish the project on schedule it's not their problem. According to the Union Contract, I can schedule overtime if I don't get enough volunteers. But with the bad attitudes around here, I'm almost afraid to take that step.

What should I do?

ITEM 8

BURTON ELECTRONICS
Interoffice Memorandum

To: Helen Wilcox

From: Jack Day, Foreman (Manufacturing)

Date: November 21

Subject: Larry Smith

I have a serious problem with one of my employees. I would like you to help me if you can.

Larry Smith appears to have a serious drinking problem. He's been with the company 13 years and until the last 2 years he has been a satisfactory worker.

I have tried talking to him about his drinking, but he continues to deny he has a problem. I have even talked to his son who works in another department here at Burton. He told me that whenever it seems like his father is doing better, something happens to make him slip up. Larry has even come to work intoxicated a few times. I have sent him home, but I am concerned that he is becoming a bad influence on the other welders.

Is there anything more I can do or is it time to dismiss him?

ITEM 9

To _Helen Wilcox_

Date _11/27_ Time _3:20_ ☐ AM ☒ PM

WHILE YOU WERE OUT

M _RS. Watson_

of _Binghamton Central H.S._

Phone (_____) _675-4001_
Area Code   Number   Extension

TELEPHONED	✔	PLEASE CALL	
CALLED TO SEE YOU	✔	WILL CALL AGAIN	
WANTS TO SEE YOU		URGENT	
	RETURNED YOUR CALL		

Message_____

_BM_

Operator

ITEM 10

BURTON ELECTRONICS
Interoffice Memorandum

To: Helen Wilcox

From: Dave Zareski

Date: November 20

Subject: Training Salespeople for the International Market

We are planning to expand our niche in the overseas market. I would like to have my salespeople trained in "dealing with the foreign customer."

We currently sell to West Germany, but I know my people are working at a disadvantage because they were never trained on the differences between a German and an American customer.

We would like to expand our marketing territory to include Saudi Arabia and Japan. Can you pick a training package for me? Items I would like to see included are:

- Social and Business Customs
- Key Words in the Language
- Key Cities
- General Orientation to the Country

We are planning to send some of our people to a conference in Japan in April, so if you can have this ready by March 1, I would be most appreciative.

Call me if you have any questions.

ITEM 11

BURTON ELECTRONICS
Interoffice Memorandum

To: Helen Wilcox
From: Martin Goldstein
Date: November 27
Subject: 1990 Budget

Our company's annual budget meeting will be held January 2. Since this will be your first budget for Burton Electronics, I would like to meet with you the week of December 16 to review your plans.

Please contact me to set up a meeting time.

Item No.	Priority	Action Information

5 *Good Motors Corporation*

You are J. Metcaff, executive vice president of human resources for the Good Motors Corporation. In one hour you must catch a flight out of Detroit to testify at the Senate subcommittee hearings on human resources. These are the items in your in-basket. Today is December 14, 1989, and if you are not out of the office by 11:00 A.M. you will miss your flight.

ITEM 1

MEMO

From: Frank Smith, President

Subject: Upcoming labor negotiations

Date: December 14, 1989

J., we need to get together to discuss the possibility of "snapbacks" in the April labor negotiations. Where are we with regard to the rest of the industry? With the Ross Perot buyout the company is cash poor and we need to develop a strategy (as you suggested last year) to prevent the UAW from demanding full return to the previous year wage and benefit progression.

ITEM 2

PHONE MESSAGE

From: John Barnett, International Representative, UAW

Date: December 13, 1989

Called—Will call back.

ITEM 3

LETTER
MEULLER, MINSK, CORNREICK, & CASEY PA.

Dear Mr. Metcaff:

Prepared by Professor Walter A. Bogumil, Jr., University of Central Florida.

We are representing the International Brotherhood of Teamsters Local 5592 in regards to the matter of NLRB case no. 86–11264–04. As you will recall the NLRB has called for an Unfair Labor Practice hearing on the 8(a)(5) charge (refusal to bargain in good faith) associated with the negotiations which took place October last. The Administrative Law Judge (Smith) has scheduled the hearing for January 13, 1990. Before we go into the hearing, we, as appropriate to discovery hearings, are requesting a list of financial data (list to follow) regarding your corporation's assertion of inability to pay requested wages demanded during the negotiations.

Sincerely,
David Cornreick, Esq.

ITEM 4

LETTER

Carol Lobsinger
University of Central Florida
P.O. Box 25000
Orlando, FL 32816

Dear Mr. Metcaff:

I am a student in labor relations at the University of Central Florida in Orlando. In a recent edition of *Time* Magazine, I noted that you will be in the Orlando area during the third and fourth weeks of December. Coincidentally, this time period is when our professor has scheduled labor negotiations for our class. Could you make time in your busy schedule to come to our class and address us in the intricacies of the Good Motors 1989 labor agreement which we have been assigned to renegotiate? I can be reached at (407) 555-5505. I sincerely hope that you will be able to assist us in this project.

Sincerely,
Carol Lobsinger

ITEM 5

MEMO

From: John Singleton, Director
          I.R. Lordstown
Subject: Plant Productivity
Date: December 8, 1989

J., the year-end productivity data are coming out of our computer and I must warn you that the numbers are not at all good. From preliminary information it seems that we will be running unfavorable labor rate and usage variances substantially above last year. Before the president sees the information, I would like to fly up to see you and discuss strategy for dealing with this problem.

Regards,
John

ITEM 6

SUBPOENA

You are herewith ordered to appear before Administrative Law Judge Bernard Smith and bring with you any and all documents associated with NLRB case No. 86–11264–04 on January 13, 1990, at the Municipal Justice Building, 538 Van Dike Blvd., Detroit, Michigan, at 9:00 A.M. Failure to comply with this subpoena will subject you personally and the corporation to a contempt citation under the provisions of U.S. Code 49–997 and 49–998.

ITEM 7

MEMO

From: Fred Stevens, Assistant Vice President, Human Resources
Subject: Smoking Policy
Date: November 15, 1989

J., we finally finished a NO SMOKING policy for approval by the president. I believe that the corporate attorney's office has removed some serious impediments and that we are ready to implement the policy as of January 1, 1990. Will you please review the policy statement and pending your approval we will have the document reproduced for distribution corporatewide with the last paycheck in December.

ITEM 8

LETTER

BATTON BARTON DERSTEIN AND OSBOURNE
Marketing Consultants

Dear Mr. Metcaff:

As you are aware, the firm of B.B.D. and O. has represented the Good Motors Corporation successfully for the past fifteen years. At this time we are reviewing our accounts and find that the corporate human resources function has yet to avail itself of our services which are provided on a retained basis to your corporation. Mr. Mendelson of our senior staff will be calling upon you in the near future to discuss the possibilities of a corporatewide human resources advertising campaign which would certainly boost the public image of GM as well as indicate your commitment to the social issues of the day.

Sincerely,
Robert Batton

ITEM 9

LETTER
ASSESSMENT DESIGNS INC.

Dr. Cabot Jaffe
5000 Maitland Center
Orlando, Florida

Dear J.:

The time has come in our continuing contract with Good Motors for ADI to assess the potential of the vice presidential level of your human resources staff. As you are aware, ADI has assessed all section seven levels of management at GM and provided developmental as well as effective promotional advice to the corporation over the last four years. At this time it is necessary that you select five members of your top staff for the completion of the program starting January 3, 1990. Regards to you and your family for the holiday season. I understand that it is snowing in Detroit.

Cabot

ITEM 10

PHONE MESSAGE

From: Jeff Kunneth, *The Detroit Free Press*
Subject: Verification of quote
Date: December 14, 1989

Text: It is my understanding that you made a statement at the Greater Detroit Chamber of Commerce meeting this morning to the effect that Good Motors has had its most profitable year yet and you would be damned if you would share the corporate profits with the UAW in this year's contract negotiations. I would like your comments regarding this statement for a banner heading and follow-up story for tonight's newspaper.

Item No.	Priority	Action Information

6 Continental Parcel of America

INSTRUCTIONS

For the purpose of this exercise, you are to consider yourself to be Chris Barr. The company you work for is Continental Parcel of America, an air freight service specializing in rapid pickup and delivery of various immediate supply parcels between commercial companies throughout the United States. Central headquarters are located in Baltimore, Maryland, with four area headquarters over the United States, and districts falling within these areas.

Until this week, you have been the assistant manager in the Decatur, Georgia area, Atlanta district. On Monday, January 7, you were notified that you were being immediately transferred to the position of city station manager in New Orleans, Louisiana, in charge of the eastern section. The present manager, Robert Morgan, suffered a sudden heart attack and is not expected to return to work. His assistant manager, Jeffrey Farnsworth, has not had enough experience to assume the position of manager. Because of this emergency situation, you have flown into New Orleans for the weekend on Saturday night, January 12, to familiarize yourself with the station. You must return to Decatur to complete some urgent final work in your present position and will not be able to return permanently to New Orleans until Thursday, January 17, at the earliest.

You are now in your new office. It is Sunday, January 13. You have been unable to contact your predecessor, Robert Morgan, because he is in the intensive care unit of the hospital. Your efforts to reach the district director, Patrick Bennett, were unsuccessful because he and the administrative manager, J. J. Stewart, have flown to Baltimore. You would like to take care of as much as possible before returning to Decatur. You will not be able to take any work back with you because of your heavy schedule and your plane is due to leave in one and one half hours.

Material has been left for you in your in-basket by the secretary, Doris Moses. This consists of letters, memoranda, reports, and so on. There is also a calendar, organizational chart, and policy manual. Your files are locked and the secretary has the key. You are unable to make any outgoing phone calls because the switchboard is closed.

Since you will be out of town, all actions should be handled in the form of written memos, letters, or notes to yourself or others. (You may want to use the in-basket memos to write on.)

Remember, all actions you deem necessary should be in writing. You now have one and one half hours to complete all necessary work.

EXHIBIT 1

JANUARY						
Sunday	Monday	Tuesday	Wednesday	Thursday	Friday	Saturday
		1	2	3	4	5
6	7	8	9	10	11	12
13	14	15	16	17	18	19
20	21	22	23	24	25	26
27	28	29	30	31		

EXHIBIT 2

FEBRUARY						
Sunday	Monday	Tuesday	Wednesday	Thursday	Friday	Saturday
					1	2
3	4	5	6	7	8	9
10	11	12 Lincoln's Birthday	13	14	15	16
17	18	19 Mardi Gras	20 Ash Wednesday	21	22	23
24	25	26	27	28		

EXHIBIT 3 Eastern Section

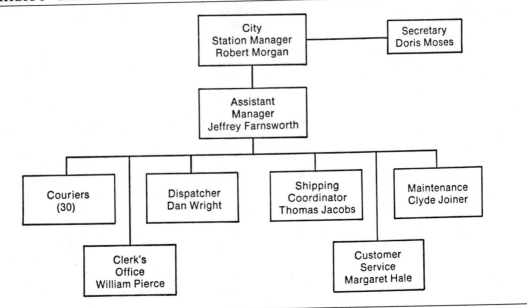

EXHIBIT 4 Continental Parcel of America, HQD Louisiana District, New Orleans

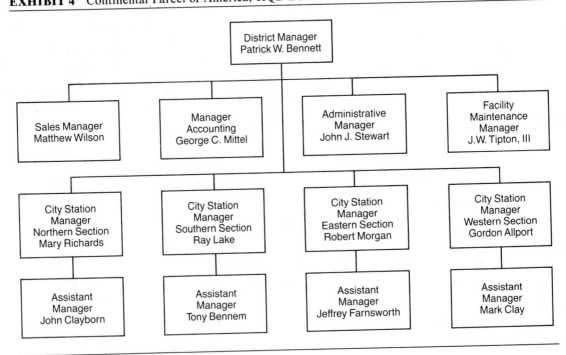

CONTINENTAL PARCEL OF AMERICA
Policy Manual
Table of Contents

SECTION I Letter from the President

Dear Fellow Employees:

It is with great pleasure that I send this revised policy manual to you. The reason I say this is because the necessity of having to update our manual represents an important stage in the growth of our company. In addition, this reflects the vast amount of progress Continental Parcel of America has made since our first day of operation.

The main thought I wish to express, however, is that even though a policy manual is a set of rules, it is not a "set of don'ts." Instead, this manual serves as an extension of the genuine interest CPA expresses for their employees.

One of our utmost concerns is that all of our employees are treated with the same fairness and equality. In order to accomplish that goal, it is imperative to have a framework by which day-to-day situations can be handled. With this framework and your cooperation CPA will remain a rewarding place to work.

Keeping your best interest in mind, I suggest that each of you become familiar with this new manual. Not only will it aid you in learning the benefits which CPA provides but it will also inform you of the changes in your job areas. While some of these changes will require a brief period of time for adjustment, the changes will result in less complicated job duties and a more efficient use of your time.

Finally, I would like to express my appreciation to everyone for their dedication and motivation in their work. Without these two factors CPA would not be experiencing the amount of success that we now have. Each employee of CPA can share with me the pride in our accomplishments to date. It is with the contributions of everyone that we can continue to proceed on the course of and determine the future progress of Continental Parcel of America.

Alan C. Norton
President

SECTION II   Employment

A. DETERMINATION OF EMPLOYEE NEEDS

The acquisition of all employees will first start with a determination from headquarters as to whether or not a need exists for a new employee.

Two alternatives are provided for this determination. First, a periodic check will be made at the headquarter's level and, if the need is determined, the appropriate manager will be notified. Second, at any time, an individual manager may request this determination. All requests will be handled through the Operations Division.

B. PROCEDURES FOR THE ACQUISITION OF NEW RECRUITS

There are three phases of processing new recruits. Phase one is conducted by company headquarters in determining and confirming the need of a recruit. Phase two is conducted by the Personnel Division at city headquarters. This phase includes the screening of initial applications for employment, checking references, verification of past employment and educational histories, and processing physical examination records.

Periodically, personnel will send lists of approved candidates to managers and, if necessary, managers may request approved candidate lists. The third phase is conducted by the manager who will be the immediate supervisor of the employee. This consists of personal interviews with approved candidates after review of the candidate data from personnel. The decision to hire rests with the manager.

C. NEPOTISM

The policy of hiring and promoting the best qualified individuals shall extend to the relatives of CPA employees, except that in no event may relatives report to each other, nor may husbands and wives have the same supervisor.

D. EEO

It is the policy of Continental Parcel of America to extend equal employment opportunities to all qualified persons including handicapped individuals, disabled veterans, and veterans of the Vietnam era without regard to race, color, sex, religion, age, or national origin. To deny one's contribution to our efforts because he/she is a member of a minority group is an injustice, not only to the individual but to the company. It is, therefore, the intent and desire of the company that equal employment opportunity be provided in employment, promotions, wages, benefits, and all other privileges, terms, and conditions of employment.

SECTION III   Training and Evaluation

A. ORIENTATION

While Continental Parcel makes every attempt to hire and promote the best qualified individuals, it realizes that each job may have special and unique methods, language, and requirements to be learned. In order to facilitate this learning and to effect maximum productivity from all employees, each newly hired or promoted employee will complete a one-week training and orientation course.

B. FIELD TRAINING

After completion of the orientation program, all employees, each newly hired or promoted employee, will complete a minimum two-day training program at each respective individual's job location. It shall be the manager's responsibility to meet this requirement.

C. PROBATION AND EVALUATION

A probation period of one year is required for each newly hired or promoted employee. During this time, each individual will be evaluated, by a performance appraisal, on a quarterly basis. The performance appraisals shall be handled through the individual's immediate manager.

SECTION IV   Benefits

A. VACATIONS

Continental Parcel of America provides vacations with pay for all eligible employees for the purpose of rest and recreation. CPA is convinced that both the employee and the company benefit thereby and employees are better prepared for the coming year. Each employee will be responsible for notifying his respective manager one month in advance of the preferred time period. No more than two employees from a work group, size 10 or more, may take vacation at the same time. No more than one employee from a work group, size 9 or less, make take vacation at the same time. Due to manpower needs, no employee shall be granted vacation during the time period of December 1 to January 15.

B. HOLIDAYS

Certain days of religious and historic importance are observed by the company as paid holidays in accordance with special eligibility rules.

The following holidays are observed by the company and eligible employees will receive holiday pay accordingly:

New Year's Day   Thanksgiving
Memorial Day   Christmas
Independence Day   Drifting holidays (three
Labor Day   unscheduled drifting holidays)

One drifting holiday will be designated by the manager and selected from among the following days:

Day after New Year's
Friday after Thanksgiving
Christmas Eve
Day after Christmas
New Year's Eve

C. OVERTIME

All overtime in any department or work group will be divided equally among all the respective employees unless the employee elects not to take the overtime.

D. HEALTH AND OTHER BENEFITS

Each full-time employee of CPA is entitled to certain insurance programs and retirement programs. These benefits are to aid the employee as well as CPA. The above programs are outlined in the *Employee Handbook*.

SECTION V Customer Service

A. CUSTOMER COMPLAINTS

All customer complaints received by telephone shall be directed to head-quarters' complaint office via a toll-free number. However, any complaints which cannot be handled sufficiently at this office will be referred to either the respective city station complaint officer or the city station manager. All written communications regarding complaints will be handled by the appropriate city station and the respective manager or complaint officer.

B. CUSTOMER DELIVERIES

All customer pickups and deliveries are to be made or arranged to be made according to the dispatcher's daily work load. Under no circumstances should any delays occur for deliveries. All delays resulting in failure to meet TOP PRIORITY deadlines (the sender specifies all TOP PRIORITY deadlines) or failure to meet daily route completion deadlines shall be investigated thoroughly with the courier involved.

C. CUSTOMER DISCOUNTS

Customer discounts are provided to large-volume shippers. The rate for both TOP PRIORITY and standard deliveries is 5 percent. Any requests for discounts must be referred to headquarters for approval. Under certain conditions, the discount rate may vary; however, changes in the discount rate occur only for exceptional occasions.

D. SPECIAL DELIVERY ARRANGEMENTS

Special arrangement considerations for pickups of packages are not the normal procedures for CPA. Only under exceptional circumstances of large volumes of parcels is this procedure changed. When under contract agreements, special arrangements are not considered unless an adjustment in the contract price occurs.

E. COLLECTION FOR SERVICES

Billing and collection for services is the responsibility of the city headquarters' accounting department. Any complaints or requests for information should be referred to that department. Pickups will be stopped within one month of a customer's nonpayment of account. The accounting department is responsible for notifying the customer and each station on the decision to discontinue customer service.

A. RESTRICTIONS OF PARCELS

1. Weight Limits. CPA restricts the weight of parcels it handles. Parcels can weigh no more than 50 pounds. No parcels exceeding 50 pounds will be accepted for delivery unless one week's prior notice is given. With prior notice given, a single parcel may exceed this limit by another 50 pounds. There are no limitations restricting the total weight of parcels from a single shipper other than no single shipper may send over 300 pounds per day to a single consignee.

2. Size Limits. CPA also restricts the size of parcels it handles. Parcels can measure no more than 30 inches in width or height and 70 inches in length. No parcel exceeding these measurements will be accepted unless one week's prior notice is given. With prior notice given, a single parcel may measure up to 45 inches in width or height and 85 inches in length.

3. Parcel Bundling. Any parcels being shipped to a single consignee may be bundled for ease of handling. However, if parcel bundling occurs, the above weight and size limits are required.

4. Parcel Shipping Costs. The rate for shipping parcels is determined by two factors, distance of travel and weight. The rates for shipping parcels are listed in the *Customer Handbook*. Additional costs are required if a parcel exceeds the parcel restrictions.

5. Parcel Acceptances. All city stations are ultimately responsible for accepting only those parcels meeting the parcel restrictions. Therefore, if any parcels exceeding these restrictions are accepted by a city station or courier, the proper overcharge will be deducted from a city station's budget.

B. VEHICLE SERVICING

All vehicle servicing is the responsibility of both the respective city stations and couriers. Therefore, regular maintenance shall adhere to the specifications stated in the Owner's Manual of the vehicle.

C. VEHICLE SAFETY

It is the responsibility of both the city station manager and the courier that company vehicles are safe to operate. Any problems which may endanger the welfare of a courier, the care of the vehicle, or the care of the shipment must be corrected, immediately, at the least possible cost.

D. ACCIDENT REPORTING

For insurance reasons, all accidents involving either employees, vehicles, or both must be reported to headquarters within 48 hours.

E. COURIER DELIVERY REPORTS

All courier delivery reports must be filled out properly and turned in by each courier, at the end of the day. After this, each city station's clerical staff shall transfer the appropriate data and send it to headquarters within the next 24 hours.

F. ALTERATION OF DELIVERY ROUTES

If at any time the need arises that requires a route to be changed, technical services at headquarters shall be notified. At no time should a city station manager arbitrarily change a delivery route without first receiving assistance from headquarters.

G. EMPLOYEE REPRIMANDS

If for any reason an employee does not uphold CPA's regulations, then that individual shall be issued a *written warning* upon the manager's discretion of the need of a warning. An employee who receives three *written warnings* within six months shall be subject to suspension.

ITEM 1

MEMORANDUM

To: Chris Barr, City Station Manager

From: Doris Moses

Date: January 9

Welcome to your new job. I have gathered some material that you may need to handle immediately. Since Mr. Morgan's untimely illness, things have gotten a little disorganized.

The letter to the staff was written by Mr. Morgan and he intended its submission to staff personnel immediately. If this, along with the tentative vacation schedules for January and February are satisfactory, please sign them. I will circulate the letter and inform the people that you have granted all vacation requests.

I will be glad to do anything I can to help. Just let me know. I am looking forward to meeting you.

Doris Moses

Doris Moses

Participant Action

1. How important is this item?

_____

_____

_____

2.   What should be done about this item?

_____

_____

_____

ITEM 2

MEMORANDUM

To: All Personnel
From: R. Morgan, City Station Manager
Date: October 28
Subject: Policy Manual

As you may be aware, the company has recently published a new policy manual which apparently will be used to control all future operations.

This manual represents a departure from our previous methods of conducting business and I am required to have each member of the staff become familiar with the contents of the new manual. Therefore, I expect each of you to review the manual and take the necessary action to ensure compliance.

R. Morgan

Robert Morgan
Manager, New
Orleans
Eastern Section

CC: Patrick Bennet

Participant Action

1.   How important is this item?

_____

_____

_____

2. What should be done about this item?

_____

_____

_____

ITEM 3

MEMORANDUM

To: Robert Morgan, City Station Manager

From: W. Pierre, Administrative Department

Date: December 18

Subject: Performance Appraisal Reviews

The period for the courier's quarterly performance evaluation is now over a month past due for several employees. The merit raise program, driver of the month, and driver of the quarter are seriously impeded without these reviews. Since part of company policy is to recognize those drivers with outstanding records, I do hope this information will be forthcoming.

The two reviews, which did arrive at my office, were turned in on the old review forms. As you are aware, the new policy changes within CPA included a new form. I am forwarding performance data, and will send you the new review forms if needed.

William Pierre

Participant Action

1. How important is this item?

_____

_____

_____

2. What should be done about this item?

_____

_____

_____

ITEM 3a   Courier Quarterly Summary Report, 3d Quarter, 66 Work Days

Truck No.	Route No.	Name of Driver-Courier	Total Days Absent	Total Times Tardy	Total Hours Over-time	Accidents per Million Miles	Average Pickup and Deliveries per Day	Avg. Miles per Day	Truck Maint. Cost (Cents per Mile)
PA-4A	1	R. Sizemore	2	2	77	2.36	16	245	$0.29
PA-7X	5	C. Stark	3	1	76	1.50	19	265	0.41
PA-9S	6	R. Sullivan	1	0	74	1.32	21	290	0.30
PA-1A	10	O. Kimball	5	63	75	5.0	16	228	0.20
PA-9Q	11	J. Brown	8	2	80	6.80	19	242	0.18
PA-5R	13	H. Shrewsberry	10	8	69	4.61	13	220	0.50
PA-9R	15	C. Bedsole	2	0	75	4.15	19	265	0.28
PA-14R	16	O. Messick	8	4	78	5.61	18	250	0.22
PA-19S	18	G. Dillon	10	12	51	4.16	10	116	0.36
PA-1S	20	D. Stover	4	2	60	7.12	16	230	0.69
PA-2F	25	K. Nordan	3	3	74	4.10	19	261	0.30
PA-11A	30	J. Fincher	1	2	68	4.91	25	320	0.14
PA-6R	4	R. Rockey	4	1	40	1.65	18	260	0.68

ITEM 4

MEMORANDUM

To: R. Morgan
From: M. Hale
Date: January 7
Subject: Customer Satisfaction
          Account #76–49244; Route #30

Recently I received a letter from Georgia Electronics regarding a number of TOP PRIORITY shipments, which have been arriving over the holiday period. They have been more than pleased with the service that CPA has extended them during this busy season. They stated that none of the sensitive equipment they received was damaged, and that the driver was very courteous during all transactions (even when he had to wait a few minutes for one package).

In connection with our recognition of drivers, I believe this kind of effort cannot go unnoticed.

M. Hale

M. Hale

Participant Action

1. How important is this item?

_____

_____

_____

2. What should be done about this item?

_____

_____

_____

ITEM 5a

VACATION REQUESTS
JANUARY–FEBRUARY

Name	*Dates Requested*
Doris Moses	Jan. 14–18
George Dillon	Jan. 28–Feb. 1
Art Johnson	Jan. 28–Feb. 1
Brian Ryals	Feb. 4–8
Dan Wright	Feb. 4–8
Carl Fristoe	Feb. 11–15
Jeffrey Farnsworth	Feb. 18–22

Participant Action

1. How important is this item?

_____

_____

_____

2. What should be done about this item?

_____

_____

_____

ITEM 5b

MEMORANDUM

To: All Personnel

From: R. Morgan, Station Manager

Date: January 3

Subject: Official Holiday Notice

Lincoln's birthday, Tuesday, February 12th, will be observed as one of the drifting holidays.

R. Morgan

R. Morgan
Station Manager
Eastern Section

Participant Action

1. How important is this item?

_____

_____

_____

2. What should be done about this item?

_____

_____

_____

ITEM 6

MEMORANDUM

To: M. Richards, C. Barr, R. Lake, G. Allport
From: Patrick Bennett
Date: January 8
Subject: Mardi Gras Rush Season

As we approach the Mardi Gras seasonal rush, please be aware that it is imperative for us to plan and coordinate all activities toward the increased service required.

Be prepared to present your project plans, suggestions, or problems on January 18 at 9 A.M. in the Charter Room, Central Office Building. At that time we will discuss and review all plans on a citywide basis.

Patrick Bennett
Patrick Bennett

Participant Action

1. How important is this item?

_____

_____

_____

2. What should be done about this item?

_____

_____

_____

ITEM 7

CONTINENTAL PARCEL OF AMERICA
Eastern Station, Jacksonville, Florida

CONSIGNEE COMPLAINT REPORT LOG
Monthly Report: October

Acct. No.	Route No.	Date	Complaint	Action
76–82560	11	10/3	Damaged content goods	Filed: C/dama
75–29326	21	10/3	Broken carton; no content damages	
76–92501	12	10/3	Damaged carton; no content damages	
75–30256	3	10/4	Late pickup	
76–49244	25	10/5	Top priority item late; Ex 9/30	
74–92366	25	10/5	Late pickup	
74–90275	11	10/7	Damaged content goods	Filed: C/dama
76–50247	4	10/10	Damaged carton; slight content damage	
75–30256	3	10/11	Late delivery; Ex 10/7	
76–82560	11	10/11	Carton damaged	
76–49244	25	10/14	Top priority team late; Ex 10/11	
77–29260	8	10/17	Late pickup	
74–92856	10	10/19	Late delivery; Ex 10/17	
77–29260	3	10/21	Damaged content goods	Filed: C/dama
74–86027	3	10/21	Carton damaged	
76–07250	13	10/25	Late delivery; Ex 10/20	
76–08200	11	10/25	Damaged content goods	
74–92301	13	10/26	Late pickup	
74–96666	18	10/26	Late delivery; Ex 10/21	
74–82596	11	10/27	Damaged content goods	Filed: C/dama
75–92506	9	10/27	Late delivery; Ex 10/24	

Participant Action

1. How important is this item?

_____

_____

_____

2. What should be done about this item?

_____

_____

_____

ITEM 8

MEMORANDUM

To: All Station Managers

From: Patrick W. Bennett

Date: December 17

Subject: Compliance with Company Policy

The new company policy manual has been in effect for two (2) months. This manual contains many needed revisions to standard operating procedures in all phases of our operations. It is apparent from a review of our customer complaints and operating data that we are not complying with these new policies.

Therefore, it is imperative that each of you meet with your staff members by December 28, review these policies, and specify what corrective action is required. I also expect you to inform me as to what date these meetings took place, staff reaction, problems encountered, and what further action(s) you plan to undertake for the full and complete compliance with the new standards.

Patrick W. Bennett

Patrick W. Bennett

CC: Assistant Managers

Participant Action

1. How important is this item?

    _____

    _____

    _____

2. What should be done about this item?

    _____

    _____

    _____

ITEM 8a

MEMORANDUM

To: Jeffrey Farnsworth

From: Robert Morgan

Date: December 21

Subject: December 17 Memo from Patrick Bennett

In accordance with our previous agreement, i.e., that you will handle all matters dealing with company policy changes, please follow up on Patrick Bennett's requests. Keep me informed on what action is being taken and what progress is being made.

Participant Action

1. How important is this item?

    _____

    _____

    _____

2. What should be done about this item?

    _____

    _____

    _____

ITEM 9

MEMORANDUM

January 1

Dear Mr. Morgan:

I do not understand the policy for assigning overtime to the couriers. It seems to me it should be fairly and evenly distributed, but it obviously is not. I have talked to Wright several times but he continues to have other drivers work overtime delivering in areas that I am supposed to cover on my route. I think something should be done about this situation.

Sincerely,

C. Stover

C. Stover
Courier, Route #20

Participant Action

1. How important is this item?

_____

_____

_____

2. What should be done about this item?

_____

_____

_____

ITEM 10

MEMORANDUM

To: Chris Barr

From: J. Farnsworth

Date: January 9

When I recently assumed the position of assistant manager, I was told that I would be allowed to take a week off for vacation fairly soon. I put in my request and the dates were OK'd.

I have made plans for that week and I intend to take that time off. I believe I have a good grasp of the operating procedure and my taking this vacation will not interfere with my job responsibilities.

J. Farnsworth

J. Farnsworth

Participant Action

1. How important is this item?

_____

_____

_____

2. What should be done about this item?

_____

_____

_____

ITEM 11

MEMORANDUM

January 4

Mr. Morgan:

I'm very sorry about the recent late delivery from ABC Manufacturing to Georgia Electronics. I had assigned this particular delivery to one driver, but Mr. Farnsworth interceded and gave it to C. Stover, whose Route #20 was close to this delivery point. I hope this didn't cause any undue problems for those concerned.

Sincerely,

Dan Wright

Dan Wright

Participant Action

1.   How important is this item?

_____

_____

_____

2.   What should be done about this item?

_____

_____

_____

ITEM 12

Nevins Novelty Company
24 Revine Avenue
New Orleans, LA
January 8

Continental Parcel of America
Eastern Section
1476 Orange Street
New Orleans, LA

ATTENTION: Robert Morgan, City Station Manager

Gentlemen:

This is to inform you, per contract agreement, that we will need to increase daily shipping allotments beginning February 18th through the 25th. We anticipate, by present order requests, shipping more than 25 packages per day to different consignees. Packages should be no more than 45 pounds each. These will be TOP PRIORITY shipments, and we wish to avoid weekend overcharges if possible.

In view of this early request for increased service and being a long-term customer, we feel it appropriate that you grant us a special discount on this large consignment. Without a discount we may be forced to ship by rail. A decision by January 25th would be appreciated.

Sincerely,

B.S. Pully

B.S. Pully
Manager, Shipping Department
Account #75–95320

Participant Action

1. How important is this item?

_____

_____

_____

2. What should be done about this item?

_____

_____

_____

_____

ITEM 13

MEMORANDUM

To: Chris Barr, City Station Manager, Eastern Section
From: Ray Lake, City Station Manager, Southern Section
Date: January 8

Welcome to the New Orleans District! I wanted to alert you to a problem we share as soon as possible. For some time our two districts have overlapped in the southeast section. My route 20 overlaps with your route 18. Some shipments have been missed because we duplicate pickups for four (4) customers. I don't know where the problem really lies—with the dispatcher, couriers, or the routing. Morgan never got around to meeting with me to resolve this problem.

Bennett runs a tight district and does not like mixups. We really should take care of this, considering the fact that you and I have the most congested areas to cover, especially the upcoming Mardi Gras rush.

Could we meet, have lunch, and discuss our mutual problems on January 22?

Again—welcome aboard. Look forward to meeting you.

Ray Lake

Ray Lake

Participant Action

1. How important is this item?

_____

_____

_____

2. What should be done about this item?

_____

_____

_____

ITEM 14

MEMORANDUM

To: Chris Barr

From: J. Farnsworth

Date: January 8

We should meet as soon as possible to discuss the continuing policy of this station. Due to Mr. Morgan's untimely illness, a few items need to be cleared up.

At this time, I don't see any major problems as Mr. Morgan let me handle quite a number of the administrative and other details. Everything is running along smoothly. We'll be waiting for you to effect your transfer.

J. Farnsworth

J. Farnsworth

Participant Action

1. How important is this item?

_____

_____

_____

2. What should be done about this item?

_____

_____

_____

ITEM 15

December 10

Mr. Morgan:

I have a bit of a problem on my route. A customer of ours, whom we service almost every day, is the brother of my ex-wife. He tries his best to make life very hard for me every time I make a stop there. He is a manager at Jason's, LTD. I would like very much to stay at Continental, but if I am forced to continue servicing this route, I may have to look for another job. Hopefully, I can get another route or at least delete this customer from my present route. I talked to Mr. Wright and he said something might be worked out if I wrote you and explained the situation.

Thanks,

Charlie Bedsole

Charlie Bedsole
Route #15

Participant Action

1. How important is this item?

_____

_____

_____

2. What should be done about this item?

_____

_____

_____

ITEM 16

Ormond Antiques
3211 Broad St.
New Orleans, LA

November 29

Continental Parcel of America
Eastern Section
1476 Orange St.
New Orleans, LA

> REGARDING: Account #72–15460, Route #20
> ATTENTION: M. Hale, Customer Service

Gentlemen:

On November 27th, we received a valuable shipment of antiques from Rockefeller Center in New York. Several very valuable ceramic figures were damaged beyond repair, and the carton was visibly damaged. The driver left before the receipt of delivery was signed. We consider this flagrant disregard of company policy. Obviously, we cannot tolerate any further reoccurrence of this nature.

Sincerely,

George Hardwell

George Hardwell
Manager

Mr. Morgan
I talked to Mr. Farnsworth, and he said he'd take care of it. That was over a month ago, and nothing has been done. They did not file for damages. What should I do?

M. Hall

Participant Action

1. How important is this item?

_____

_____

_____

2.   What should be done about this item?

_____

_____

_____

ITEM 17

Bithlo Computers
119 Fountain Street
New Orleans, LA

January 3

Continental Parcel of America
1476 Orange Street
New Orleans, LA

ATTENTION: Manager, New Accounts

Gentlemen:

We have to ship 10 pieces of a computer to Saint Louis, Missouri, within the next 20 days. We usually ship by water, but because of the urgency of this delivery we require special handling and service. We normally send these in a box type 411, which is $43'' \times 75'' \times 24''$, 100 pounds.

We need to know the packing and shipping prices as soon possible.

Sincerely,

Marlene Dubois

Marlene Dubois
453–9238

This is a possible new customer, but the measurements exceed our limits. I've talked to them and they could change the size, but I prefer the box they have now. Should I accept their boxes for shipping?

M. Hall

Participant Action

1. How important is this item?

_____

_____

_____

2. What should be done about this item?

_____

_____

_____

ITEM 18

MEMORANDUM

To: R. Morgan
From: J. Farnsworth
Date: January 7
Subject: Covering of Courier Routes

I have a problem with Dan Wright. It seems that the dispatcher, Dan Wright, doesn't want to have each courier cover his own route. I've talked to him about it, but all he says is that some couriers can handle more than others. I don't understand his reasoning.

J. Farnsworth

J. Farnsworth

Participant Action

1. How important is this item?

_____

_____

_____

2.   What should be done about this item?

_____

_____

_____

ITEM 19

November 30

Mr. Morgan:

The change to the new radial tire has drastically cut down on the number of blow-outs that the courier trucks have received. However, the other change to a different type starter system has resulted in many operating difficulties and has negated any time savings that the tire change gave us.

We as a group have discussed this with Clyde Joiner, but he doesn't seem to realize the extra costs of maintenance and efficient customer service. It is making us have to hurry through our routes, not allowing us to serve the customers, and having to speed between points.

Sincerely,

Ron Rockey

Ron Rockey, Route #4

R. Sizemore

R. Sizemore, Route #1

Art J ohnson

Art Johnson, Route #7

Charlie Bedsole

Charlie Bedsole, Route #15

Steve Lucas

Steve Lucas, Route #24

Participant Action

1. How important is this item?

_____

_____

_____

2. What should be done about this item?

_____

_____

_____

ITEM 20

MEMORANDUM

To: R. Morgan
From: Dan Wright
Date: December 28
Subject: Continued Service for Overdue Account

I thought some clarification of policy should be made, so that some things can be cleared up.

Recently, Ms. Hale sent me a letter concerning Account #76–32095, an overdue account, requesting a termination of service until further notice. I did this as per company policy, but Mr. Farnsworth came in and said to keep servicing the account, that it would be taken care of. I then received another letter from Ms. Hale wanting to know why I was still giving service to this client. I again asked Mr. Farnsworth, and he said not to worry about it.

The client is asking for a parcel to be picked up in three days, a special package. Should I continue giving service to them or not?

Dan Wright

Dan Wright

Participant Action

1. How important is this item?

   _____

   _____

   _____

2. What should be done about this item?

   _____

   _____

   _____

ITEM 21

MEMORANDUM

To: R. Morgan

From: Clyde Joiner

Date: January 3

The recent maintenance changes for our trucks seem to be having a generally positive effect on truck performance. Since changing to NEWYEAR tires and using Ben's Repairs Shop we have cut down on vehicle problems.

Clyde Joiner

Clyde Joiner

Participant Action

1. How important is this item?

   _____

   _____

   _____

2. What should be done about this item?

_____

_____

_____

ITEM 22

December 27

Continental Parcel of America
Eastern Section
1476 Orange Street
New Orleans, LA

ATTENTION: Manager

A person whom I know, Clyde Joiner, works in your company and doesn't seem to represent the type of organization in which he works. He spends most of his time at the "Hole in the Wall" bar, day and night, and hangs out there with a rough crowd from Ben's Repairs Shop.

They are almost always causing problems in the neighborhood by instigating arguments and fights. I'm surprised a man like this is allowed to work for a company which uses the name of our country.

A Helpful Citizen

Participant Action

1. How important is this item?

_____

_____

_____

2. What should be done about this item?

_____

_____

_____

ITEM 23

MEMORANDUM

To: R. Morgan

From: J.J. Stewart

Date: December 31

We now have the new performance appraisal forms which, by new policy regulations, should be put to use immediately. Since we have not yet received your quarterly courier reports, I urge you to get the forms as soon as possible. They are more thorough than the ones formerly used, and will also make the reports much easier to complete.

As you are aware, we need these appraisals before we can compile any bonus and raise proposals. Please get to it as soon as possible.

J. J. Stewart

J. J. Stewart

Participant Action

1. How important is this item?

_____

_____

_____

2. What should be done about this item?

_____

_____

_____

ITEM 24

MEMORANDUM

To: R. Morgan, City Station Manager

From: J.J. Stewart, Administrative Department Manager

The following is a list of courier applicants who meet standard qualifications for hire on a regular or substitute basis. All will be available beginning January 3. Initial screening interviews have been conducted; it is up to you to interview and hire as station needs dictate after receiving the necessary operations department approval.

Jim C. Kilgallen
7283 West Real Street
423-9783

Edgar Redding
3954 5th Street
425-6203

Jody Llewyn
1578 Spring Terrace
425-1782

Alex Curry
SW 19th Street, Apt. 2
423-7860

Ray Leecher
85 King Street
623-7908

Ny Simmons
119 West Haven
423-1892

Pat Beecker
36 River Street, Apt. 29
623-8025

Robert Lee
3429 Juniper Lane
623-1785

Ramond Cortez
2209 39th Street, S.E.
Apt. 3225

Roberta Simon
69 Jules Avenue
623-9781

Jimon Waraz
2209 30th Street, S.E.
Apt. 3112
425-4098

Mr. Morgan
Operations has approved the hiring of one more courier as of January 3rd A few worked during the Christmas holidays. Robert Lee and Ny Simmons both worked well.

Doris

Participant Action

1. How important is this item?

_____

_____

_____

2. What should be done about this item?

_____

_____

_____

ITEM 25

MEMORANDUM

To: R. Morgan

From: Mark Clay, City Station Assistant Manager

        Western Section

Date: January 4

We have heard that your use of a new type and brand of tire has helped to reduce maintenance costs in that area, and increased customer service.

When you get a chance, please send the name and brand of tire you have switched to.

Mark Clay

Mark Clay

Participant Action

1. How important is this item?

_____

_____

_____

2. What should be done about this item?

_____

_____

_____

ITEM 26

MEMORANDUM

To: R. Morgan

From: Dan Wright

Date: January 3

Subject: Expected Increased Business

Just to remind you, with the Mardi Gras season beginning the day before Ash Wednesday, I've already started to receive inquiries concerning our ability to handle extra business during that period of time.

This period of time traditionally is one of excessive work loads, and the need for extra help will become imperative in the near future. I believe I can work out a schedule to help alleviate the burden, if we know what manpower will be available.

If I can be of any further assistance during this time, please feel free to call me.

Dan Wright

Dan Wright

Participant Action

1. How important is this item?

2. What should be done about this item?

ITEM 27

MEMORANDUM

To: R. Morgan
From: J. Farnsworth
Date: December 28

I have received several inquiries from the drivers as to when their reviews will be completed. They are pressing for raises and are curious to know how their performances have been rated.

If you sign the authorization I've typed up, I'll go ahead and complete the reviews and award merit raises.

I authorize the assistant manager, J. Farnsworth, to complete all reviews and take action as he sees fit.

Station Manager

Participant Action

1. How important is this item?

_____

_____

_____

2. What should be done about this item?

_____

_____

_____

ITEM 28

MEMORANDUM

To: R. Morgan, City Station Manager

From: J.J. Stewart, Administrative Department Manager

Date: January 2

Subject: Traffic Violation Report

Our office has received notification of a speeding and failure to yield right of way ticket to courier Jack Brown, while driving CPA vehicle 90 on December 7th, 2:36 P.M. To date the only confirmation we have received is from the New Orleans Police Department.

I'm sure I need not remind you of CPA regulations. Please handle this immediately or it may affect more than the driver's record.

J.J. Stewart

J. J. Stewart

Participant Action

1. How important is this item?

   _____

   _____

   _____

2. What should be done about this item?

   _____

   _____

   _____

Part 5

Appendixes

Appendix A

Glossary of Human Resource Management Terms

absentees Absentees are employees who are scheduled to be at work but are not present.

accident and sickness policies Accident and sickness policies usually provide a minimum-care stipend for several weeks up to six months to help employees defray the loss of income while they are sick or recovering from an accident.

accreditation Accreditation is a process of certifying the competence of a person in an area of capability. The Society for Human Resource Management operates an accreditation program for personnel professionals.

active listening Active listening requires the listener to stop talking, to remove distractions, to be patient, and to empathize with the talker.

adverse selection Adverse selection occurs when an insurance company has a disproportionately high percentage of insureds who will make claims in the future. Adverse selection often results when people are given a chance to buy insurance without prescreening, which often means that a higher than normal proportion have a condition that is likely to cause them to be frequent claimants.

affirmative action programs Affirmative action programs are detailed plans developed by employers to undo the results of past employment discrimination, or to ensure equal opportunity in the future.

Age Discrimination in Employment Act of 1967 (as amended) This act prohibits discrimination on employment because of age against those who are 40 and older.

American Federation of Labor and Congress of Industrial Organization (AFL-CIO) The AFL-CIO is a federation of most national unions. It exists to provide a unified focal point for the labor movement, to assist national unions, and to influence government policies that affect members and working people.

applied research Applied research is a study of practical problems, the solutions of which will lead to improved performance.

arbitration Arbitration is the submission of a dispute to a neutral third party.

assessment centers Assessment centers are a standardized form of employee appraisal that relies on multiple types of evaluation and multiple raters.

associate membership Associate membership in a labor organization allows people who are not employed under a union contract to affiliate with a union by paying fees and dues in return for union-supported benefits.

attitude surveys Attitude surveys are systematic methods of determining what employees think about their organization. The surveys are usually done through questionnaires. Attitude survey feedback results when the information collected is reported back to the participants. This process then is usually followed by action planning to identify and resolve specific areas of employee concern.

attrition Attrition is the loss of employees who leave the organization's employment.

audit report The audit report is a comprehensive description of personnel activities. It includes both commendation for effective practices and recommendations for improving practices that are ineffective.

audit team An audit team consists of those people who are responsible for evaluating the performance of the personnel department.

authorization cards Authorization cards are forms that prospective union members sign. The cards indicate their wish to have an election to determine whether a labor organization will represent the workers in their dealings with management.

autonomous work groups Autonomous work groups are teams of workers, without a formal company-appointed leader, who decide among themselves most decisions traditionally handled by supervisors.

autonomy Autonomy is having control over one's work.

bargaining book A bargaining book is a compilation of the negotiation team's plans for collective bargaining with labor or management. Increasingly, the bargaining book is being replaced by information stored in a company or union computer.

bargaining committee The union bargaining committee consists of union officials and stewards who negotiate with management's representatives to determine wages, hours, and working conditions to be embodied in the labor agreement.

behaviorally anchored rating scales (BARS) BARS rate employees on a scale that has specific behavioral examples on it to guide the rater.

behavioral modeling Behavioral modeling relies on the initiation or emulation of a desired behavior. A repetition of behavior modeling helps to develop appropriate responses in specified situations.

behavior modification Behavior modification states that behavior depends on its consequences.

blind ads Blind ads are want ads that do not identify the employer.

bona fide occupational qualifications (BFOQ) A BFOQ occurs when an employer has a justified business reason for discriminating against a member of a protected class. The burden of proving a BFOQ generally falls on the employer.

bottom-line test The bottom-line test is applied by the Equal Employment Opportunity Commission to determine if a firm's overall selection process is having an adverse impact on protected groups. Even though individual steps in the selection process might exhibit an adverse impact on a protected group, the firm will be considered in compliance if the overall process does not have an adverse effect.

Boulwarism Boulwarism is a negotiation strategy developed by General Electric. Using this approach the company made its "best" offer to the union at the beginning of negotiations. Then it remained firm unless the union could find where management had erred in the calculations used to arrive at the offer. This strategy has been ruled as an unfair labor practice by the National Labor Relations Board and by the federal courts.

brainstorming Brainstorming is a process by which participants provide their ideas on a stated problem during a freewheeling group session.

buddy system The "buddy system" of orientation exists when an experienced employee is asked to show a new worker around the job site, conduct introduction, and answer the newcomer's questions.

burnout Burnout is a condition of mental, emotional, and sometimes physical exhaustion that results from substantial prolonged stress.

business agent A business agent is a full-time employee of a local (usually craft) union. The business agent helps employees resolve their problems with management.

business unionism Business unionism describes unions that seek to improve the wages, hours, and working conditions of their members in a business-like manner. (See social unionism.)

buy-back Buy-backs occur when an employee who attempts to resign is convinced to stay in the employment of the organization. Normally the person is "bought back" with an offer of increased wages or salary.

cafeteria benefit programs Cafeteria benefit programs allow employees to select the fringe benefits and services that answer their individual needs.

career A career is all the jobs that are held during one's working life.

career counseling Career counseling assists employees in finding appropriate career goals and paths.

career development   Career development consists of those experiences and personal improvements that one undertakes to achieve a career plan.

career goals   Career goals are the future positions that one strives to reach. These goals serve as benchmarks along one's career path.

career path   A career path is the sequential pattern of jobs that form one's career.

career planning   Career planning is the process by which one selects career goals and paths to those goals.

career plateau   A career plateau occurs when an employee is in a position that he or she does well enough not to be demoted or fired but not well enough to be promoted.

change agents   Change agents are people who have the role of stimulating change within a group.

checkoff   A checkoff provision in a union-management labor agreement requires the employer to deduct union dues from employee paychecks and to remit those moneys to the union.

Civil Rights Act of 1964   This act was passed to make various forms of discrimination illegal.

closed shop   A closed shop is a workplace where all employees are required to be members of the union *before* they are hired. These arrangements are illegal under the National Labor Relations Act.

codetermination   Codetermination is a form of industrial democracy first popularized in West Germany. It gives workers the right to have representatives vote on management decisions.

coinsurance clause   A coinsurance clause is a provision in an insurance policy that requires the employee to pay a percentage of the insured's expenses.

communication   Communication is the transfer of information and understanding from one person to another.

comparable worth   Comparable worth is the idea that a job should be evaluated as to its value to the organization and then paid accordingly. Thus jobs of comparable worth would be paid equally. For example, two people with widely different jobs would both receive the same pay if the two jobs were of equal value to the employer.

comparative evaluation approaches   Comparative evaluation approaches are a collection of different methods that compare one person's performance with that of co-workers.

compensation   Compensation is what employees receive in exchange for their work.

Comprehensive Employment and Training Act of 1973 (CETA)   CETA was a broad-ranging act designed to provide job training, employment, and job-hunting assistance to less advantaged persons. It has since been replaced by the *Job Partnership Training Act*.

concentration in employment Concentration exists when an employer (or some subdivision such as a department) has a higher proportion of employees from a protected class than is found in the employer's labor market. (See *underutilization.*)

concessionary bargaining Concessionary bargaining occurs when labor-management negotiations result in fewer employer-paid fringe benefits or wage concessions, such as a freeze or wage cut.

conciliation agreement a conciliation agreement is a negotiated settlement agreeable to the EEOC and to all parties involved. Its acceptances closes the case.

Consolidated Omnibus Budget Reconciliation Act of 1985 (COBRA) This act was signed into law in 1986. COBRA requires employers that provide group benefits to employees through a group plan to also provide group benefits to qualified beneficiaries with the right to elect to continue their coverage for a certain period of time after their coverage would otherwise terminate, with a few exceptions.

constructs Constructs are substitutes for actual performance. For example, a score on a test is a construct for actual learning.

contract labor Contract labor consists of people who are hired (and often trained) by an independent agency that supplies companies with needed human resources for a fee.

contributory benefit plans Contributory benefit plans are fringe benefits that require both the employer and the employee to contribute to the cost of the insurance, retirement, or other employer benefit.

coordinated organizing Coordinated organizing occurs when two or more unions pool their resources to organize a targeted employer or group of employees.

corrective discipline Corrective discipline is an action that follows a rule infraction and seeks to discourage further infractions so that future acts are in compliance with standards.

counseling Counseling is the discussion of an employee problem with the general objective of helping the worker cope with it.

counseling functions Counseling functions are the activities performed by counselors. They include advice, reassurance, communication, release of emotional tension, clarified thinking, and reorientation.

craft unions Craft unions are labor organizations that seek to include all workers who have a common skill, such as carpenters or plumbers.

critical incident method The critical incident method requires the rater to report statements that describe extremely good or extremely bad employee behavior. These statements are called *critical incidents,* and they are used as examples of good or bad performance in rating the employee.

decision-making authority See *line authority.*

deductible clause   A deductible clause is a provision in an insurance policy that requires the insured to pay a specified amount of a claim before the insurer is obligated to pay.

deferral jurisdictions   Deferral jurisdictions are areas in the United States where the EEOC will refer a case to another (usually a state or local) agency; for example, Florida Human Relations Commission.

deferred stock incentive systems   These incentives award stock that becomes owned by the executive gradually over several years.

delegation   Delegation is the process of getting others to share a manager's work. It requires the manager to assign duties, grant authority, and create a sense of responsibility.

Delphi technique   The Delphi technique solicits predictions from a panel of experts about some specified future development(s). The collective estimates are then reported back to the panel so that the members may adjust their opinions. This process is repeated until a general agreement on future trends emerges.

demographics   Demographics is the study of population characteristics.

demotions   Demotions occur when an employee is moved from one job to another that is lower in pay, responsibility, and organizational level.

development   Development represents those activities that prepare an employee for future responsibilities.

Dictionary of Occupational Titles (DOT)   The *Dictionary of Occupational Titles* is a federal government publication that provides detailed job descriptions and job codes for most occupations in government and industry.

differential validity   Differential validity is used to demonstrate that tests or other selection criteria are valid for different subgroups or protected classes.

directive counseling   Directive counseling is the process of listening to an employee's emotional problems, deciding with the employee what should be done, and then telling and motivating the employee to do it. (See nondirective counseling.)

discipline   Discipline is management action to encourage compliance with the organization's standards.

dismissal   Dismissal is the ultimate disciplinary action because it separates the employee from the employer for a cause.

disparate impact   Disparate impact occurs when the results of an employer's actions have a different effect on one or more protected classes.

disparate treatment   Disparate treatment occurs when members of a protected class receive unequal treatment.

Drug-Free Workplace Act of 1988   This legislation requires that organizations applying for federal grants certify that they will make good-faith efforts to provide a drug-free workplace.

dual responsibility for personnel management Since both line and staff managers are responsible for employees, production, and quality of work life, a dual responsibility for personnel management exists.

due process Due process means that established rules and procedures for disciplinary action are followed and that employees have an opportunity to respond to the charges made against them.

early retirement Early retirement occurs when a worker retires from an employer before the "normal" retirement age.

Employee Assistance Programs (EAPs) EAPs are company-sponsored programs to help employees overcome their personal problems through direct company assistance, counseling, or outside referral.

employee handbook The employee handbook explains key benefits, policies, and general information about the employer.

The Employee Polygraph Protection Act The act prohibits the use of polygraphs in private industry by forbidding any employer engaged in commerce or in the production of goods for commerce from directly or indirectly requiring, requesting, or causing any employee or prospective employee to take or submit to a lie detector test. Restrictions also cover use of information regarding results of such a test and the taking of adverse employment action against any employee who refuses, declines, or fails to take a lie detector test.

Employee Retirement Income Security Act (ERISA) ERISA was passed by Congress to ensure that employer pension plans meet minimum participation, vesting, and funding requirements.

employment freeze An employment freeze occurs when the organization curtails future hiring.

employment function The employment function is that aspect of personnel responsible for recruiting, selecting, and hiring new workers. This function is usually handled by the employment section or employment manager of a large personnel department.

employment references Employment references are evaluations of an employee's work performance. They are provided by past employers.

employment tests Employment tests are devices that assess the probable match between the applicants and the job requirements.

Equal Employment Act of 1972 This act strengthened the role of the Equal Employment Opportunity Commission by amending the Civil Rights Act of 1964. The 1972 law empowered the EEOC to initiate court action against noncomplying organizations.

equal employment opportunity Equal employment opportunity means giving people a fair chance to succeed without discrimination based on factors unrelated to job performance—such as age, race, or national origin.

Equal Employment Opportunity Commission (EEOC) The EEOC is the federal agency responsible for enforcing Title VII of the Civil Rights Act, as amended and other laws such as the Age Discrimination in Employment Act.

equal employment opportunity laws   Equal employment opportunity laws are a family of federal and state acts that seek to ensure equal employment opportunities for members of protected groups.

Equal Pay Act of 1963   This act prohibits discrimination in pay because of a person's sex.

ergonomics   Ergonomics is the study of biotechnical relationships between the physical attributes of workers and the physical demands of the jobs. The object is to reduce physical and mental strain in order to increase productivity and quality of work life.

error of central tendency   The error of central tendency occurs when a rater evaluates employee performance as neither good nor poor, even when some employees perform exceptionally well or poorly. Instead, the rater rates everyone as average.

evaluation interviews   Evaluation interviews are performance review sessions that give employees feedback about their past performance or about their future potential.

executive order   Executive orders are presidential decrees that normally apply to government contractors or managers in the executive branches of the federal government.

exit interviews   Exit interviews are conversations with departing employees to learn their views of the organization.

expedited arbitration   Expedited arbitration is an attempt to speed up the arbitration process. It may include an arrangement with the arbitrator for him or her to be available on short notice (one or two days) and to render a quick decision at the conclusion of the hearings (sometimes an oral decision is used in these cases).

experience rating   Experience rating is a practice whereby state unemployment offices determine an employer's unemployment compensation tax rate based on the employer's previous experience in providing stable employment.

experiential learning   Experiential learning means that participants learn by experiencing in the training environment the kinds of problems they face on the job.

exposure   Exposure means becoming known by those who decide on promotions, transfers, and other career opportunities.

extrapolation   Extrapolation involves extending past rates of change into the future.

facilitator   A facilitator is someone who assists quality circles and the quality circle leader in identifying and solving workplace problems.

factor comparison method   The factor comparison method is a form of job evaluation that allocates a part of each job's wage to key factors of the job. The result is a relative evaluation of the organization's job.

fair employment practices   Fair employment practices are state and local laws that prohibit employer discrimination in employment against members of protected classes.

Fair Labor Standards Act of 1938 (FLSA)   FLSA is a comprehensive federal law affecting compensation management. It sets minimum wage, overtime pay, equal pay, child labor, and record-keeping requirements.

Federal Mediation and Conciliation Service (FMCS)   The FMCS was created by the Labor Management Relations Act of 1947 to help labor and management resolve negotiation impasses peacefully through mediation and conciliation without resort to a strike. The FMCS also is a course of qualified labor arbitrators.

feedback   Feedback is information that helps evaluate the success or failure of an action or system.

field experiment   A field experiment is research that allows the researchers to study employees under realistic conditions to learn how experimental and control subjects react to new programs and to other changes.

field review method   The field review method requires skilled representatives of the personnel department to go into the "field" and assist supervisors with their ratings. Often it is the personnel department's representative that actually fills out the evaluation form after interviewing the supervisor about employee performance.

flextime   Flextime is a scheduling innovation that abolishes rigid starting and ending times for each day's work. Instead, employees are allowed to begin and end the workday at their discretion, usually within a range of hours.

flexyear   Flexyear is an employee scheduling concept that allows workers to be off the job for part of the year. Employees usually work the normal work year in less than 12 months.

forced choice method   The forced choice method of employee performance evaluation requires the rater to choose the most descriptive statement in each pair of statements about the employee being rated.

forecasts   Forecasts predict the organization's future needs.

four-fifths rule   The four-fifths rule is a test used by the EEOC. When the election ratio of protected-class applicants is less than 80 percent (or four fifths) of the selection ratio for majority applicants, adverse impact is assumed.

fully insured workers   Fully insured workers are employees who have contributed 40 quarters (10 years) to social security.

functional authority   Functional authority allows staff experts to make decisions in specified circumstances that are usually reserved for line managers.

funded plan Funded plans require an employer to accumulate moneys in advance so that the organization's contribution plans plus interest will cover its obligation.

funded retirement plans A funded retirement plan is one in which the employer sets aside sufficient money to meet the future payout requirements.

gainsharing Gainsharing matches an improvement (gain) in company performance to some distribution (sharing) of the benefits with employees.

golden parachutes Golden parachutes are agreements by the company to compensate executives with bonuses and benefits if they should be displaced by a merger or acquisition.

grapevine communication Grapevine communication is an informal system that arises spontaneously from the social interaction of people in the organization.

grievance procedure A grievance procedure is a multistep process that the employer and union jointly use to resolve disputes that arise under the terms of the labor agreement.

Griggs* v. *Duke Power Company (1971) The U.S. Supreme Court case held that when an employment criterion disproportionately discriminates against a protected class, the employer is required to show how the criterion is job related.

guaranteed annual wage A guaranteed annual wage assures workers of receiving a minimum amount of work or pay during the course of a year.

halo effect The halo effect is a bias that occurs when a rater allows some information to disproportionately prejudice the final evaluation.

harassment Harassment occurs when a member of an organization treats an employee in a disparate manner because of the worker's sex, race, religion, age, or other protected classification.

health maintenance organizations (HMOs) HMOs are a form of health insurance whereby the insurer provides the professional staff and facilities needed to treat their insured policyholders for a predetermined monthly fee.

hot-stove rule The hot-stove rule states that disciplinary action should have the same characteristics as the penalty a person receives from touching a hot stove. That is, the discipline should be with warning, immediate, consistent, and impersonal.

house organs A house organ is any regularly published organizational magazine, newspaper, or bulletin directed to employees.

human resource forecasts Human resource forecasts predict the organization's future demand for employees.

human resource planning Human resource planning systematically forecasts an organization's future supply, and demand for, employees.

human resources Human resources are the people who are ready, willing, and able to contribute to organizational goals.

Immigration Reform and Control Act of 1986   Employers are required to screen out unauthorized aliens. The act requires an employment verification systems, a good faith effort, and specified record-keeping procedures.

imminent danger   An imminent danger is a situation that is likely to lead to death or serious injury if allowed to continue.

incentive systems   Incentive systems link compensation and performance by paying employees for actual results, not for seniority or hours worked.

indexation   Indexation is a method of estimating future employment needs by matching employment growth with some index, such as sales growth.

industrial democracy   Industrial democracy refers to giving employees a larger voice in making the work-related decisions that affect them.

industrial unions   Industrial unions are labor organizations that seek to include all of an employer's eligible workers regardless of whether they are skilled, semiskilled, or unskilled.

in-house complaint procedures   In-house complaint procedures are organizationally developed methods for employees to register their complaints about various aspects of the organization.

job analysis   Job analysis systematically collects, evaluates, and organizes information about jobs.

job analysis schedule   Job analysis schedules are checklists or questionnaires that seek to collect information about jobs in a uniform manner. (They are also called job analysis questionnaires.)

job banks   Job banks exist in state employment offices. They are used to match applicants with job openings.

job code   A job code uses numbers, letters, or both to provide a quick summary of the job and its content.

job description   A job description is a written statement that explains the duties, working conditions, and other aspects of a specified job.

job enlargement   Job enlargement means adding more tasks to a job in order to increase the job cycle.

job enrichment   Job enrichment means adding more responsibilities, autonomy, and control to a job.

job evaluations   Job evaluations are systematic procedures to determine the relative worth of jobs.

job families   Job families are groups of different jobs that require similar skills.

Job-Flo   Job-Flo is a monthly report of frequently listed openings from job banks throughout the country.

job grading   Job grading is a form of job evaluation that assigns jobs to predetermined classifications according to the job's relative worth to the organization. This technique is also called the job classification method.

jobholder reports Jobholder reports are reports to employees about the firm's economic performance.

Job Information Service The Job Information Service is a feature of state employment security agencies that enables job seekers to review job bank listings in their efforts to find employment.

job instruction training Job instruction training is training received directly on the job. It is also called on-the-job-training.

job performance standards Job performance standards are the work requirements that are expected from an employee on a particular job.

job posting Job posting informs employees of unfilled job openings and the qualifications for these jobs.

job progression ladder A job progression ladder is a particular career path where some jobs have prerequisites.

job ranking Job ranking is one form of job evaluation that subjectively ranks jobs according to their overall worth to the organization.

job rotation Job rotation is the process of moving employees from one job to another in order to allow them more variety on their jobs and the opportunity to learn new skills.

job satisfaction Job satisfaction is the favorableness or unfavorableness with which employees view their work.

job sharing Job sharing is a scheduling innovation that allows two or more workers to share the same job, usually by each working part-time.

job specifications A job specification describes what a job demands of employees who do it and the human skills that are required.

Job Training Partnership Act of 1983 This act provides federal funds to authorized training contractors, often city or state government agencies. These moneys are used to train people in new, employable skills. (It replaces the Comprehensive Education and Training Act of 1973.)

joint study committees Joint study committees include representatives from management and the union who meet away from the bargaining table to study some topic of mutual interest in the hope of finding a solution that is mutually satisfactory.

juniority Juniority provisions require that layoffs be first offered to senior workers who may accept or refuse them. If sufficient senior workers do not accept the layoffs, then management is free to lay off the least senior workers.

key jobs Key jobs are those that are common in the organization and in its labor market.

labor agreement A labor agreement, which is also called a labor contract, is a legal document that is negotiated between the union and the employer. It states the terms and conditions of employment.

laboratory training Laboratory training is a form of group training primarily used to enhance interpersonal skills.

Labor Management Relations Act of 1947 (LMRA) The LMRA, also know as the Taft-Hartley Act, amended the National Labor Relations Act of 1935 by designing specific union actions that were considered to be unfair labor practices. The act also created the Federal Mediation and Conciliation Service and enabled the president of the United States to call for injunctions in national emergency strikes.

Labor-Management Reporting and Disclosure Act of 1959 (LMRDA) The LMRDA, also called the Landrum-Griffin Act, amended the National Labor Relations Act. It created the union members' "bill of rights" by giving union members certain rights in dealing with their union. The law also established detailed reporting requirements for those who handle union funds.

labor market The labor market is the area in which the employer recruits.

labor market analysis Labor market analysis is the study of the employee's labor market to evaluate the present or future availability of workers.

Landrum-Griffin Act See Labor-Management Reporting and Disclosure Act of 1959.

law of effect (Thorndike's law) The law of effect states that people learn to repeat behaviors that have favorable consequences, and they learn to avoid behaviors that have unfavorable consequences.

layoffs Layoffs are the separation of employees from the organization for economic or business reasons.

learning curve A learning curve is a visual representation of the rate at which one learns given material through time.

learning principles Learning principles are guidelines to the ways in which people learn most effectively.

legal insurance Legal insurance is usually a group insurance plan provided by the employer that reimburses the insureds when they have specified legal expenses or provides the insureds with access to legal assistance at predetermined (and usually low) rates.

leniency bias A leniency bias occurs when employees are rated higher than their performance justifies.

leveraging Leveraging refers to resigning in order to further one's career with another employer.

line authority Line authority allows managers to direct others and to make decisions about the organization's operations.

local unions Local unions are the smallest organizational unit of a union. They are responsible for representing the members at the worksite.

long-term disability Long-term disability insurance provides a proportion of a disabled employee's wage or salary. These policies typically have long waiting periods and seldom allow the employee to attain the same income level that existed before the disability.

lost-time accidents   These are severe job-related accidents that cause the employee to lose time from his or her job.

maintenance factors   Maintenance factors are those elements in the work setting that lead to employee dissatisfaction when they are not adequately provided. These factors are also called hygiene factors or dissatisfiers. They include working conditions and fringe benefits.

"make-whole" remedies   When an individual is mistreated in violation of employment laws, the wrongdoer usually is required to make up the losses that were suffered by the employee because of the wrongdoing.

management by objectives (MBO)   MBO requires an employee and superior to jointly establish performance goals for the future. Employees are subsequently evaluated on how well they have obtained these agreed-upon objectives.

management inventories   Management inventories summarize the skills and abilities of management personnel. (See skills inventories, which are used for nonmanagement employees.)

management rights   Management rights are the rights and freedoms that an employer needs to manage the enterprise effectively. These areas of discretion usually are reserved by management in the labor agreement.

maturity curves   Maturity curves are used to compensate workers based on their seniority and performance. Normally, these compensation plans are limited to professional and technical workers.

mentor   A mentor is someone who offers informal career advice.

merit-based promotions   Merit-based promotions occur when an employee is promoted because of superior performance in the present job.

merit raises   Merit raises are pay increases given to individual workers according to an evaluation of their performance.

motivation   Motivation is a person's drive to take action because that person wants to do so.

National Institute of Occupational Safety and Health (NIOSH)   NIOSH was created by the Occupational Safety and Heath Act to conduct research and to develop additional safety and health standards.

National Labor Relations Act of 1935 (NLRA)   The NLRA, also known as the Wagner Act, was passed by Congress to ensure that covered employees could join (or refrain from joining) unions for the purpose of their own mutual aid and protection and for negotiating with employers. The act also created the National Labor Relations Board.

National Labor Relations Board (NLRB)   The NLRB was created by the National Labor Relations Act to prevent unfair labor practices and to conduct union representation elections.

national unions National unions are those parent bodies that help organize, charter, guide, and assist their affiliated local unions.

needs assessment Needs assessment diagnoses present problems and future challenges that can be met through training and development.

net benefit Net benefit means that there will be a surplus of benefits after all costs are included.

noncontributory benefit plans Noncontributory benefit plans are fringe benefits that are paid entirely by the employer. (See contributory benefit plans.)

nondeferral jurisdiction Nondeferral jurisdictions are areas where the EEOC finds no qualified agency to which it may defer cases.

nondirective counseling Nondirective, or client-centered, counseling is the process of skillfully listening to an employee and encouraging him or her to explain bothersome problems, to understand them, and to determine appropriate solutions.

nonverbal communication Nonverbal communication is action that communicates without spoken words.

obsolescence Obsolescence results when an employee no longer possesses the knowledge or ability to perform successfully.

Occupational Outlook Handbook The *Occupational Outlook Handbook* is published by the U.S. Department of Labor. It indicates the future need for certain jobs.

Occupational Safety and Health Act of 1970 (OSHA) OSHA is a broad-ranging law that requires employers to provide a work environment that is free of recognized safety and health hazards.

Occupational Safety and Health Administration The Occupational Safety and Health Administration is located in the U.S. Department of Labor and is responsible for enforcing the Occupational Safety and Health Act.

Occupational Safety and Health Review Commission The Occupational Safety and Health Review Commission is the federal agency that reviews on appeal the fines given to employers by the Occupational Safety and Health Administration for safety and health violations.

open communication Open communication exists when people feel free to communicate all relevant messages.

open-door policy An open-door policy encourages employees to go to their manager or even higher management with any problem that concerns them.

organizational climate Organizational climate is the favorableness or unfavorableness of the environment for people in the organization.

organizational development (OD) OD is an intervention strategy that uses group processes to focus on the whole organization in order to bring about planned change.

organizing committee   An organizing committee consists of employees who guide the efforts needed to organize their fellow workers into a labor organization.

orientation programs   Orientation programs familiarize primarily new employees with their roles, the organization, its policies, and other employees.

outplacement   Outplacement occurs when an organization assists its present employees in finding jobs with other employers.

Pareto analysis   Pareto analysis is a means of collecting data about the types or causes of production problems in descending order of frequency.

participation rates   Participation rates are the percentages of working-age men and women in the work force.

participative counseling   Participative counseling seeks to find a balance between directive and nondirective counseling techniques, with the counselor and the counselee participating in the discussion and solution of the problem.

part-time layoffs   Part-time layoffs occur when an employer lays off workers without pay for a part of each week, such as each Friday.

paternalism   Paternalisms exists when management assumes that it alone is the best judge of employee needs and therefore does not seek or act upon employee suggestions.

path-goal personnel strategy   The path-goal personnel strategy is used by the personnel department when it attempts to improve the path toward a goal (such as reducing red tape) and then tries to improve the outcomes at the end of the path (such as improving the amount of merit pay or other rewards).

pattern bargaining   Pattern bargaining occurs when the same or essentially the same contract is used for several firms, often in the same industry.

patterns and practices   When discrimination is found to exist against a large number of individuals who are in a protected class a *pattern and practice* case exists.

pay-for-knowledge compensation systems   These incentives provide employees higher pay as an incentive for each new skill or job they learn.

payout standards   Payout standards are the benchmarks or triggers that determine whether an incentive or gain–sharing award is earned.

performance appraisal   Performance appraisal is the process by which organizations evaluate employee performance.

performance measures   Performance measures are the ratings used to evaluate employee performance.

performance standards   Performance standards are the benchmarks against which performance is measured.

personal leave days   Personal leave days are normal workdays that an employee is entitled to take off. (In some firms personal leave days are used instead of sick days.)

personnel audit   A personnel audit evaluates the personnel activities used in an organization.

personnel barriers   Personnel barriers are communication interferences arising from human emotions, values, and limitations.

personnel management   Personnel management is the study of how employers obtain, develop, utilize, evaluate, maintain, and retain the right numbers and types of workers. Its purpose is to provide organizations with an effective work force.

Peter Principle   The Peter Principle states that, in a hierarchy, people tend to rise to their level of incompetence.

piecework   Piecework is a type of incentive system that compensates workers for each unit of output.

placement   Placement is the assignment of an employee to a new or different job.

point system   The point system is a form of job evaluation that assesses the relative importance of the job's key factors in order to arrive at the relative worth of jobs.

political grievances   Political grievances are filed or supported because of their political implications, not their merits.

portability clauses   Portability clauses allow workers to transfer accumulated pension rights to their subsequent employer when they change jobs.

Position Analysis Questionnaire (PAQ)   The PAQ is a standardized, preprinted form that collects specific information about jobs.

precedent   A precedent is a new standard that arises from past practices of either the company or the union.

preferential quota systems   Preferential quota systems exist when a proportion of the job openings, promotions, or other employment opportunities is reserved for members of a protected class who have been previously discriminated against.

Pregnancy Discrimination Act of 1978   This act prevents discrimination in employment against women who are pregnant and able to perform their jobs. The law amends the Civil Rights Act of 1964.

prevailing wage rates   Prevailing wage rates are the rates most commonly paid for a given job in a specific geographical area. They are determined by a wage and salary survey.

preventive discipline   Preventive discipline is action taken to encourage employees to follow standards and rules so that infractions are prevented.

private placement agencies   Private placement agencies are for-profit organizations that help job seekers find employment.

proactive management   Proactive management exists when decision makers anticipate problems and take affirmative action steps to minimize those problems rather than wait until after a problem occurs before taking action.

problem-solving interviews   These types of interviews rely on questions that are limited to hypothetical situations or problems. The applicant is evaluated on how well the problems are solved.

production bonuses   Production bonuses are a type of incentive system that provides employees with additional compensation when they surpass stated production goals.

productivity   Productivity is the ratio of a firm's output (goods and services) divided by its input (people, capital, materials, energy).

professional associations   Professional associations are groups of workers who voluntarily join together to further their profession and their professional development. When these associates undertake to negotiate for their members, they are also labor organizations.

profit sharing   Profit sharing exists when an organization shares a proportion of its profits with the workers, usually on an annual basis.

profit sharing plans   Profit sharing plans enable eligible employees to receive a proportion of the organization's profits.

progressive discipline   Progressive discipline requires strong penalties for repeated offenses.

promotion   A promotion occurs when an employee is moved from one job to another that is higher in pay, responsibility, and/or organizational level.

protected groups   Protected groups are classes of people who are protected from discrimination under one or more laws.

psychic costs   Psychic costs are the stresses, strains, and anxieties that affect a person's inner self during a period of change.

Pygmalion effect   The Pygmalion effect occurs when people live up to the highest expectations others hold of them.

qualifiable worker   A qualifiable worker is one who does not currently possess all of the requirements, knowledge, skills, or abilities to do the job, but who will become qualified through additional training and experience.

qualified handicapped   The qualified handicapped are those mentally or physically handicapped individuals who, with reasonable accommodations, perform successfully.

quality circles   Quality circles are small groups of employees who meet regularly with a common leader to identify and solve work-related problems.

quality of work life   Quality of work life means having good supervision, good working conditions, good pay and benefits, and an interesting, challenging, and rewarding job.

quality of work life efforts Quality of work life efforts are systematic attempts by an organization to give workers a greater opportunity to affect their jobs and their contributions to the organization's overall effectiveness.

rap sessions Rap sessions are meetings between managers and groups of employees to discuss complaints, suggestions, opinions, or questions.

rate ranges Rate ranges are pay ranges for each job class.

rating scale A rating scale requires the rater to provide a subjective evaluation of an individual's performance along a scale from low to high.

rational validity Rational validity exists when tests include reasonable samples of the skills needed to perform successfully or where there is an obvious relationship between performance and other characteristics that are assumed to be necessary for successful job performance.

reactive management Reactive management exists when decision makers respond to problems instead of anticipating problems before they occur. (See proactive management.)

realistic job preview (RJP) An RJP allows the job applicant to see the type of work, equipment, and working conditions involved in the job before the hiring decision is finalized.

recency effect The recency effect is a rater bias that occurs when a rater allows recent employee performance to sway the overall evaluation.

recruitment Recruitment is the process of find and attracting capable applicants for employment.

red-circle rates Red-circle rates are wages or salaries that are inappropriate for a given job according to the job evaluation plan.

refreezing Refreezing requires the integration of what has been learned into actual practice.

regulations Regulations are legally enforceable rules developed by government agencies to ensure compliance with laws that the agency interprets and administers.

Rehabilitation Act of 1973 This act prohibits discrimination against those who are handicapped but qualified to perform work. It applies to employees who receive federal moneys and to federal agencies.

reinforcement schedules Reinforcement schedules are the different ways that behavior reinforcement can be given.

relations by objectives Relations by objectives is a program created by the Federal Mediation and Conciliation Service to improve labor-management cooperation between participating parties.

reliability Reliability means that a selection device (usually a test) yields consistent results each time an individual takes it.

relocation programs Relocation programs are company-sponsored fringe benefits that assist employees who must move in connection with their jobs.

repetition   Repetition facilitates learning through repeated review of the material to be learned.

replacement charts   Replacement charts are visual presentations of who will replace whom in the organization when a job opening occurs.

resistance to change   Resistance to change arises from employee opposition to change.

résumé   A résumé is a brief listing of an applicant's work experience, education, personal data, and other information relevant to the applicant's employment qualifications.

reverse discrimination   Reverse discrimination occurs when an employer seeks to hire or to promote a member of a protected class over an equally (or better) qualified candidate who is not a member of a protected class.

sandwich model of discipline   The sandwich model suggests that a corrective comment would be sandwiched between two positive comments in order to make the corrective comments more acceptable.

Scanlon Plan   The Scanlon Plan is an incentive program that compensates eligible employees for improvements in labor costs that are better than the previously established company norms.

search firms   Search firms are private for-profit organizations that exist to help employers locate hard-to-find applicants.

Section 89, Internal Revenue Code   This controversial statute requires certain employee benefit plans to meet five qualification standards in order for benefits under the plans to be nontaxable to all covered employees. Almost all welfare benefit plans (i.e., group medical, group legal, group life, cafeteria, tuition reimbursement, fringe benefit plans) are subject to these rules.

selection interviews   Selection interviews are a step in the selection process whereby the applicant and the employer's representative have a face-to-face meeting.

selection process   The selection process is a series of specific steps used to decide which recruits should be hired.

selection ratio   The selection ratio of the number of applicants hired to the total number of applicants.

self-funding   Self-funding occurs when an organization agrees to meet its insurance obligations out of its own resources.

semantic barriers   Semantic barriers are limitations that arise from the words with which we communicate.

seniority   Seniority means the length of a worker's employment in relation to the other employees.

seniority-based promotions   Seniority-based promotions result when the most senior employee is promoted into a new position.

severance pay   Severance pay is a payment made to workers when they are dismissed from the company. Employees who are terminated because of their poor performance or behavior are usually not eligible.

shelf-sitters "Shelf-sitter" is a slang term for upwardly immobile managers who block promotion channels.

shorter workweeks Shorter workweeks are employee scheduling variations that allow full-time workers to complete their week's work in less than the traditional five days. One variation is 40 hours work in four days.

skills inventories Skills inventories are summaries of each employee's skills and abilities. (Skills inventories usually refer to nonmanagement workers. See management inventories.)

socialization Socialization is the ongoing process by which an employee adapts to an organization by understanding and accepting the values, norms, and belief held by others in the firm. Orientation programs—which familiarize primarily new employees with their role, the organization, its policies, and other employees—speed up the socialization process.

Social Security Act of 1935 This act established the social security program of the federal government, which taxes workers and employers in order to create a fund from which medicare, retirement, disability, and death payments are made to covered workers and their survivors.

social unionism Social unionism describes unions that seek to further their members' interests by influencing the social, economic, and legal policies of government at all levels—city, county, state, and federal. (See business unionism.)

Society for Human Resource Management SHRM is the major association for professional personnel specialists and administrators.

sociotechnical systems Sociotechnical systems are interventions in the work situation that restructure the work, the work groups, and the relationship between the workers and the technology they use to do their jobs.

specialization Specialization occurs when a very limited number of tasks are grouped into one job.

sponsor A sponsor is a person in an organization who can create career development opportunities for others.

staff authority Staff authority is the authority to advise, not direct, others.

staffing table A staffing table lists anticipated employment openings for each type of job.

state employment security agency A state employment security agency (or unemployment office) matches job seekers with employers who have job openings.

steering committee The steering committee is part of a quality circle or other employee involvement effort and usually includes the top manager of the work site (such as a plant manager) and his or her direct staff.

steward A union steward is elected by workers (or appointed by local union leaders) to help covered employees present their problems to management.

stock options Stock options are fringe benefits that give the holder the right to purchase the company's stock at a predetermined price.

strategic plan A strategic plan identifies a firm's long-range objectives and proposals for achieving those objectives.

stress Stress is a condition of strain that affects one's emotions, thought processes, and physical condition.

stress interviews Stress interviews rely on a series of harsh, rapid-fire questions that are intended to upset the applicant and show how the applicant handles stress.

stressors Stressors are conditions that tend to cause stress.

stress-performance model The stress-performance model shows the relationship between stress and job performance.

stress threshold A stress threshold is the level of stressors that a person can tolerate before feelings of distress begin.

strictness bias A strictness bias occurs when employees are rated lower than their performance justifies.

structural unemployment Structural unemployment occurs when people are ready, willing, and able to work, but their skills do not match the jobs available.

structured interviews Structured interviews use a predetermined checklist of questions that usually are asked of all applicants.

suggestion systems Suggestion systems are a formal method for generating, evaluating, and implementing useful employee ideas.

suitable employment Suitable employment means employment for which the person is suited as a result of education, training, or experience.

supplemental unemployment benefits (SUB) SUB is an employer-provided fringe benefit that supplements state unemployment insurance when an employee is laid off.

Taft-Hartley Act See Labor-Management Relations Act of 1947.

Taft-Hartley injunctions Taft-Hartley injunctions allow the president of the United States to seek a court order to delay a labor-management strike for 80 days. During this cooling off period, the government investigates the facts surrounding the dispute.

task identity Task identity means doing an identifiable piece of work, thus enabling the worker to have a sense of responsibility and pride.

task significance Task significance means knowing that the work one does is important to others in the organization and outside of it.

time studies Time studies are measurements of how long a job takes to perform.

Title VII Title VII refers to the part of the Civil Rights Act of 1964 that requires equal employment opportunities without regard to race, color, religion, sex, pregnancy, or national origin.

training Training represents activities that teach employees how to perform their present jobs.

transference Transference refers to how applicable the training is to actual job situations, as evaluated by how readily the trainee transfers the learning to his or her job.

transfers Transfers occur when an employee is moved from one job to another that is relatively equal in pay, responsibility, and organizational level.

turnover Turnover is the loss of employees by the organization. It represents those employees who depart for a variety of reasons.

two-tiered orientation program A two-tiered orientation program exists when both the personnel department and the immediate supervisor provide an orientation for new employees.

two-tier wage structure This pay structure occurs when one group of employees (usually new hires) receives a different wage rate than other employees. The employer achieves lower labor costs by paying new workers less while previously hired union members usually are able to retain their existing wage rates.

type A people Type A people are those who are aggressive and competitive, set high standards, and put themselves under constant time pressures.

type B people Type B people are more relaxed and easygoing. They tend to accept situations and work within them rather than fight them or put themselves under constant time pressures.

underutilization Underutilization occurs when a department or an entire organization has a smaller proportion of members of a protected class than is found in the firm's labor market. (See concentration in employment.)

unemployment compensation Unemployment compensation is payment to those who lose their jobs, are unemployed, are seeking new employment, and are willing and able to work.

unfair labor practices (ULPs) ULPs are violations of the National Labor Relations Act as amended. These unfair labor practices are specific activities that employers and labor organizations are prohibited from doing.

union-management agreement See labor agreement.

union members' bill of rights The union members' bill of rights refers to Title I of the Labor-Management Reporting and Disclosure Act of 1959, which established the specific rights of union members in dealing with their unions.

union organizers Union organizers are people who assist employees in forming a local union.

union shop A union shop is a workplace where all employees are required to join the local union as a condition of employment. New employees are usually given 30, 60, or 90 days in which to join.

unstructured interview An unstructured interview uses few, if any, planned questions to enable the interviewer to pursue, in depth, the applicant's responses.

upward communication Upward communication is communication that begins at some point in the organization and then proceeds up the hierarchy to inform or influence others.

validity Validity means that the selection device (usually a test) is related significantly to job performances or to some other relevant criterion.

vertical staff meetings Vertical staff meetings occur when managers meet with two or more levels of subordinates to learn of their concerns.

vestibule training Vestibule training occurs off the job on equipment or methods that are highly similar to those used on the job. This technique minimizes the disruption of operations caused by training activities.

vesting Vesting is a provision in retirement plans that gives workers rights to retirement benefits after a specified number of years of service, even if the employee quits before retirement.

Vietnam Era Veteran's Readjustment Act of 1974 This act prohibits certain government contractors from discriminating in employment against Vietnam era veterans.

wage and salary surveys Wage and salary surveys are studies made by an organization to discover what other employers in the same labor market are paying for specific key jobs.

wage compression Wage compression occurs when the difference between higher- and lower-paying jobs is reduced. This compression usually results from giving larger pay increases to lower-paying jobs.

Wagner Act See National Labor Relations Act of 1935.

walk-ins Walk-ins are job seekers who arrive at the personnel department in search of a job without any prior referrals and not in response to a specific ad or request.

want ads Want ads describe the job and its benefits, identify the employer, and tell those who are interested how to apply.

weighted checklist A weighted checklist requires the rater to select statements or words to describe an employee's performance or characteristics. After those selections are made, different responses are given different values or weights in order to determine a quantified total score.

weighted incentive systems These systems reward executives based on improvements in multiple areas of business performance. Depending on the weights used, part of the incentive bonus can be tied to improvements in market share, profit return on assets, cash flow, or other indexes.

welfare secretary The welfare secretary was a forerunner of the modern personnel specialist. Welfare secretaries existed to help workers meet their personal needs and to minimize any tendency of workers to join unions.

well pay Well pay is a fringe benefit, provided by some employers, that pays employees for unused sick leave.

wildcat strikes Wildcat strikes are spontaneous work stoppages that take place in violation of the labor contract and are officially against the wishes of the union leaders.

Worker Adjustment and Retraining Act Employers with 100 or more employees must provide employees 60 days advance written notice of plant closing or layoffs.

workers' compensation Workers' compensation is payment made to employees for work-related injuries or to their families in the event of the workers' job-caused death.

work flow Work flow is the sequence of jobs in an organization needed to produce the firm's goods or service.

work measurement techniques Work measurement techniques are methods for evaluating what a job's performance standards should be.

work practices Work practices are the set ways of performing work in an organization.

work sampling Work sampling means using a variety of observations on a particular job to measure the length of time devoted to certain aspects of the job.

work simplification Work simplification means simplifying jobs by eliminating unnecessary tasks or reducing the number of tasks by combining them.

write-ins Write-ins are those people who send in a written inquiry, often seeking a job application.

State and Federal Statutes Applicable to the Employment Relationship

CLAIMS BASED ON DISCRIMINATION

Title VII of the Civil Rights Act of 1964 [42 U.S.C. S2000e-2(a), et seq.]. It is an unlawful employment practice for an employer to refuse to hire or discharge any individual on the basis of race, color, religion, sex, or national origin. An employer is further prohibited from discriminating against an employee with respect to compensation, terms, conditions, or privileges of employment based on these factors.

The Florida Human Rights Act of 1977 (Chapter 760, Florida Statutes). An employer is prohibited from discriminating with respect to compensation, terms, conditions, or privileges of employment based on race, color, religion, sex, national origin, age, handicap, or marital status.

The Civil Rights Act (42 U.S.C. S1981 and S1983). Enacted following the Civil War, the Civil Rights Act attempted to ensure racial equality and provide the full benefit of all laws to the emancipated slaves. Section 1981 applies to private employers, whereas 1983 prohibits public employers from depriving any citizen of the rights, privileges, or immunities secured by the Constitution and other laws.

Age Discrimination in Employment Act of 1967 (29 U.S.C. S621, et seq.). An employer is prohibited from refusing to hire or to discharge any individual because of such individual's age. The act covers employees 40+ years of age. Any notice or advertisement relating to employment may not indicate a preference based on age unless certain narrow exceptions apply.

Discrimination Based on Religion   [42 U.S.C. S2000e-(j)]. An employer may not discriminate on the basis of religion unless the employer is unable to reasonably accommodate an employee's religious observances, practices, or beliefs without undue hardship on the conduct of the employer's business.

Sex Discrimination   [42 U.S.C. S2000e–2(a)]. It is an unlawful employment practice to classify a job as male or female unless sex is a bona fide occupational qualification for that particular job. Policies that restrict the employment of married women, without providing analogous limitations on married men, constitute discrimination based on sex.

The Pregnancy Discrimination Act of 1978   [42 U.S.C. S2000e(k)]. The prohibition against sex discrimination in Title VII includes discrimination on the basis of pregnancy, childbirth, or related medical conditions. Pregnancy-related disabilities should not be treated differently from other temporary disabilities.

Sexual Harassment   [42 U.S.C. S2000e–2(e)]. The prohibition against sex discrimination in Title VII includes unwelcomed sexual harassment in the form of sexual advances, requests for sexual favors, or other verbal or physical conduct of a sexual nature that has the effect of unreasonably interfering with work performance and creating an intimidating, hostile, or offensive work environment.

The Immigration Reform and Control Act of 1986   [8 U.S.C. S1324b(a)]. This act prohibits discrimination on account of national origin or citizenship status.

The Migrant and Seasonal Agricultural Worker Protection Act of 1983   (42 U.S.C. S8101, et seq.). Congress enacted this law to provide certain protections for migrant and seasonal agricultural workers with respect to wages, housing conditions, transportation, health standards, and other conditions of employment.

The Farm Labor Registration Law   (S450.27, et seq., Florida Statutes). This state statute provides comparable protections for migrant and seasonal workers as the federal scheme. A number of federal and state statutes regulate the employment of migrant workers.

The Rehabilitation Act of 1973   (29 U.S.C. S701, et seq.). The Rehabilitation Act of 1973 prohibits discrimination against handicapped individuals by employers who receive federal financial assistance or participate in contracts with the federal government in excess of $2,500. Affected employers must reasonably accommodate the needs of handicapped employees and take other affirmative action to advance such employees.

Discrimination Based on AIDS.   The definition of handicapped individual in both federal and state statutes includes any person with AIDS since this disease constitutes a physical or mental impairment which substantially limits one or more major life activities.

Discrimination Based on Sickle Cell   (S448.075–076, Florida Statutes). An employer may not refuse to hire or discharge any person solely because such applicant or employee has the sickle cell trait. No employer may require testing for the sickle cell trait as a condition for employment.

The Bankruptcy Code   (11 U.S.C. S525). No private or public employer may discharge or discriminate against an employee who has filed for bankruptcy.

The National Labor Relations Act   [29 U.S.C. S158(a)]. The National Labor Relations Act prohibits discharge or discrimination based upon union membership, union activity, or other protected concerted activity.

Award of Attorney's Fees   [42 U.S.C. S1988 and 42 U.S.C. S2000e–5(k)]. The court may exercise discretion in awarding attorney's fees to a prevailing party in certain discrimination actions.

EMPLOYEE COMPENSATION AND BENEFITS

Fair Labor Standards Act of 1938   (29 U.S.C. S201, et seq.). Employers must pay at least the minimum wage ($3.35 per hour) and in the event employees work more than 40 hours per week, the employee must be compensated at a rate not less than one-and-one-half times the regular wage rate.

State Law Regarding Minimum Wage and Hour Provisions   (S448.01, Florida Statutes). In Florida, 10 hours of labor is considered a legal day's work, and absent a written contract to the contrary, an employee is entitled to extra pay for work performed in excess of 10 hours per day.

The Equal Pay Act of 1963   [29 U.S.C. S206(d)]. The Equal Pay Act prohibits sex-based wage discrimination and mandates equal pay for equal work which is performed under similar working conditions and which requires equal skill, effort, and responsibility. Wage differentials are permitted when such payment is made pursuant to: (1) a seniority system, (2) a merit system, (3) a system which measures earnings by quantity or quality of production, or (4) a differential based on any reasonable factor other than sex.

Wage Rate Discrimination   (S448.07, Florida Statutes). Wage rate discrimination based on sex is prohibited unless one of the exceptions to the Equal Pay Act is applicable.

The Employee Retirement Income Security Act of 1974 (ERISA)   (29 U.S.C. S1001). ERISA provides a comprehensive federal scheme for the design and operation of employee pension benefit plans and employee welfare benefit plans. Financial and fiduciary standards of conduct are imposed on plan administrators to ensure that beneficiaries are not denied retirement benefits or otherwise discriminated against in pursuit of their rights under ERISA.

The Unemployment Compensation Law   (Chapter 443, Florida Statutes). This chapter is liberally construed to promote employment security by increasing opportunities for placement and mandating the compulsory setting aside of unemployment reserves. An employee discharged for misconduct connected with his work is disqualified from receiving benefits.

Workers' Compensation Law   (Chapter 440, Florida Statutes). This Florida statute provides for compensation to an employee if a disability or death results from injury arising out of and in the course of employment. No compensation shall be payable if the injury was occasioned primarily by the intoxication or drug use of the employee.

Attorney's Fees for Unpaid Wages   (S448.08, Florida Statutes). The court may exercise discretion in awarding a reasonable attorney's fee and court costs to a prevailing party in an action for unpaid wages.

THE HIRING PROCESS

The Immigration Reform and Control Act of 1986   (8 U.S.C. S1324a). Employers must verify that every job applicant is either a U.S. citizen or authorized to be employed in the United States by examining certain documents specified in the statute.

The Employee Polygraph Protection Act of 1988 (29 U.S.C. S2001, et seq.). This statute prohibits most private employers from discharging or disciplining an employee based on the results of a polygraph test. The act provides for certain exceptions from employers engaged in national defense or other security operations. The state of Florida regulates the credentials of those licensed to administer polygraph tests (S493.561, Florida Statutes).

Serologic Testing (S775.083, Florida Statutes). It is unlawful for an employer to require an applicant or employee to submit to a serologic exam as a condition of employment.

Manipulation of Drug Tests (S817.565, Florida Statutes). It is unlawful for any person to willfully defraud any lawfully administered urine test designed to detect the presence of chemical or controlled substances.

The Racketeer Influenced and Corrupt Organizations Act (RICO) (28 U.S.C. S1961, et seq.). Where an employer offers employment through the mails or via an interstate telephone call, an employee may have a cause of action for treble damages if the employer engaged in fraud or deliberate misrepresentation in the offer.

EVALUATION AND TERMINATION

Consolidated Omnibus Budget Reconciliation Act of 1985 (COBRA) (29 U.S.C. S1161, et seq.). Certain employers must make available continued health insurance coverage to discharged employees on a contributory basis for 18 months following termination. An employee terminated for gross misconduct is not entitled to the continuation of insurance coverage. The Florida legislature has enacted comparable provisions in S627.6675 of the Florida Statutes.

The Worker Adjustment and Retraining Act (WARN) (23 U.S.C. S2101, et seq.). Employers with 100 or more employees must provide employees 60 days' advance written notice of plant closings or layoffs that will result in the employment loss of 50 or more full-time employees.

SAFETY IN THE WORKPLACE

The Florida Clean Indoor Air Act (S386.201, et seq., Florida Statutes). The act expressly prohibits any person from smoking in a public place or a public meeting except in designated smoking areas. Although existing physical barriers and ventilation systems should be used to minimize smoke in adjacent nonsmoking areas, an employer is not required to physically modify an area. In a workplace that includes both smokers and nonsmokers, employers are required to develop, implement, and post a policy regarding designation of smoking and nonsmoking areas which takes into consideration the proportion of smokers and nonsmokers in the company.

Florida Right-to-Know Law   (Chapter 442, Florida Statutes). Employers who manufacture, process, use, or store toxic or hazardous substances in the workplace must provide employees information about these substances.

The Occupational Safety and Health Act   (OSHA). (29 U.S.C. S651, et seq.). OSHA regulates the safety and health of employees in the workplace and provides a comprehensive scheme of safety standards.

The Florida Occupational Health and Safety Act   (Chapter 442, Florida Statutes). Employers shall educate and train employees with respect to the nature and effects of toxic substances present in the workplace within 30 days of employment and at least annually thereafter. Every employer who manufactures, produces, uses, applies, or stores toxic substances in the workplace must post a notice regarding employee rights under this chapter.

The Hazardous Substances Release Act   (42 U.S.C. S9610). No employer shall discharge or discriminate against any employee who provides information to the government or agrees to testify in any proceeding regarding hazardous substance violations.

The Control of Sexually Transmissible Disease Act   (Chapter 384, Florida Statutes). Disclosure of confidential information relating to a sexually transmissible disease may be made only under the following circumstances: (1) with the consent of all persons to which the information applies; (2) for statistical purposes or epidemiological information which does not identify the names of the persons affected; (3) revelation to medical personnel, appropriate state agencies, or courts in medical emergencies; (4) disclosure pursuant to subpoena; and (5) in child or adult abuse investigations. Any person who maliciously disseminates any false information or report concerning the existence of any sexually transmissible disease is guilty of a misdemeanor of the second degree.

MISCELLANEOUS STATUTES AFFECTING THE WORKPLACE

The Consumer Credit Protection Act (15 U.S.C. S1601, et seq.). No employer may discharge any employee by reason of the fact that his earnings have been subject to garnishment.

The Protection of Jurors Employment Act (28 U.S.C. S1875). This act expressly prohibits the discharge or intimidation of any permanent employee for serving on a federal jury.

Jury Service Duty (S40.271, Florida Statutes). An employer may not discharge an employee for accepting jury duty in the state of Florida because of the nature or length of service.

Child Labor Law (S450.081, Florida Statutes). No minor 17 years of age or younger shall be employed in any gainful occupation for more than 6 consecutive days in any week or more than 10 hours per day. A minor may not be employed for more than 30 hours per week.

Election Code (S104.081, Florida Statutes). It is an unlawful employment practice for an employer to discharge or intimidate any employee for voting or failing to vote in any state, county, or municipal election.

Employment of Unauthorized Aliens (S448.09, Florida Statutes). It is an unlawful employment practice for any employer to knowingly employ, hire, or recruit for private or public employment an unauthorized alien.

Right to Work (S448.045, Florida Statutes). It is unlawful for two or more persons to conspire to discharge or intimidate any person from procuring work in a corporation.

Right to Strike (S447.13, Florida Statutes). An employer may not interfere or impede an employee's right to strike or right to work.

NOTICES REQUIRED BY LAW TO BE POSTED ON THE PREMISES

Certain state and federal laws and regulations require employers to post notices on the premises relating to employment matters. These notices may be obtained from the following offices:

1. U.S. Labor Department
   80 North Hughey Avenue
   Orlando, Florida 32801
   (407) 648-6471

    a. Polygraph Protection Act poster.

    b. Minimum wage poster.

2. Florida Commission on Human Relations
   2562 Executive Center Circle, East
   Tallahassee, Florida 32301
   1-800-342-8170

       a. General discrimination prohibition poster.

3. OSHA—Department of Labor
   Room 624
   700 Twiggs Street
   Tampa, Florida 33602
   (813) 228-2821

       a. Poster regarding Occupational Safety and Health Act of 1970

4. Equal Employment Opportunity Commission
   One Northeast First Street, 6th Floor
   Miami, Florida 33132
   (305) 536-4491

       a. EEOC poster regarding Title VII, ADEA, Equal Pay Act, Executive Order 11246, and the Rehabilitation Act.

	Title VII Civil Rights Act of 1964 42 U.S.C. S200e et seq.	Equal Pay Act 29 U.S.C. S206(d)	Age Discrimination in Employment (ADEA) 29 U.S.C. S621 (1976)	Handicap Discrim. Rehab. Act 1973 29 U.S.C. S701 et seq.	Civil Rights Act 1866 42 U.S.C. S1981
Jury trial	No	Yes	Yes		Yes
Application	Race, color, religion, sex, national origin.	Sex discrimination in wages for equal work requiring equal skill, effort, and responsibility in same establishment.	40+ years old, no cap.	Handicapped	Ethnic groups; race. All have right to make and enforce contracts like whites. Not apply to whites.
Attorney's fees	Yes, 42 USC S1988	Yes	Yes, but not for administrative hearing.	Yes	Yes
Injunction	Yes, order ER not to discriminate in future.		Yes	Yes	Yes
Punitive damages	No	No	No		Yes, if willful violation.
Front pay	Yes, if no reinstatement		Yes, where reinstatement ineffective.		
Back pay	Yes, reduced by interim earnings, if any, and only up to 2 years prior to filing of charges.	Yes, interest allowed if no liquidated damages. Recover difference between wages received and average wages paid to opposite sex employees performing equal work.	Yes	Yes, but not more than 2 years prior to filing charges and reduced by interim earnings.	Yes, difference between pay actually received and pay if no discrimination.

	Title VII Civil Rights Act of 1964 42 U.S.C. S2000e et seq.	*Equal Pay Act 29 U.S.C. S206(d)*	*Age Discrimination in Employment (ADEA) 29 U.S.C. S621 (1976)*	*Handicap Discrim. Rehab. Act 1973 29 U.S.C. S701 et seq.*	*Civil Rights Act 1866 42 U.S.C. S1981*
Compensatory		Not for physical and mental suffering.	Yes. "Court shall have jurisdiction to grant such legal and equitable relief as may be appropriate.		Yes; difference between actual earnings for period and amount would have earned absent discrimination.
Emotional distress	No	No	No		Yes; mental anguish, embarrassment, and humiliation
Employees covered	15+ employees in 20+ weeks in current or preceding calendar year.	2+ employees engaged in commerce.	20+ employees in 20+ weeks in current or preceding calendar year.	S503: Federal government contractors and subcontractors in excess of $2,500; S204: Recipients of federal financial assistance.	All.
Liquidated (double damages)		Yes, if willful violation	Yes, if willful violation		
Other	Disparate impact versus treatment. Exception: BFOQ is reasonably necessary to business operation (efficiency and safety).	Must *raise* wages of other employees; "equal pay for substantially equal work"; 4 affirmative defenses (p. 96)	Offset of earnings or amount earnable with reasonable diligence; applies to upper-class white males.	Does not include current drug and alcohol abusers; 1 out of 11 Americans is handicapped.	Findings of fact by jury re S1981 claim will be binding on court regarding Title VII claims in same action.

EEOC or private action	Both, but private action only after EEOC has failed to take action in 180 days. State or local agency, if any, must be given 60 days to take action.	Both	Both. After EEOC has case for 60 days, charging party can resort to court.	No private right of action under S503 but private claim under S504.	
Statute of limitations	Uniform federal requirements. Filing of charges by class representative tolls statute of limitations for all members. See 23(a), FRCP.	Two years if not willful; 3 years if willful		State law	
Procedural prerequisite to file suit	Must comply with administrative prerequisites prior to filing judicial action (e.g., EEOC)		File EEOC claim but EEOC issues no right to sue letter. File claim within 180 days of act, or 300 days if deferral agency.	Administrative process for Sections 503 and 504.	No administration prerequisites.
Cases on topic	*McDonnell–Douglas Corp. v. Green*, 411 U.S. 792 (1973); *Griggs v. Duke Power Co.*, 401 U.S. 424 (1972); *Albermarle Paper Co. v. Moody*, 422, U.S. 405 (1975).	*Garcia v. San Antonio Metropolitan Transit Authority*, 469 U.S. 528 (1985); *Corning Glass Works v. Brennan*, 417 U.S. 188 (1974).	*Western Airlines, Inc. v. Criswell*, 472 U.S. 400 (1985)	*School Board of Nassau County v. Arline*, 106 S.Ct. 1633 (1986); 41 CFR S60-741.2; 45 CFR X84.3(k) (1).	*Johnson v. Railway Express Agency, Inc.*, 421 U.S. 454 (1975); *Runyon v. McCrary*, 427 U.S. 160 (1976).

Index of Cases
and Exercises